MODERN ARABIC LITERATURE
1800–1970

Modern Arabic Literature 1800-1970

An introduction, with extracts in translation

JOHN A. HAYWOOD

Reader in Arabic, School of Oriental Studies
University of Durham

Lund Humphries, London

First edition 1971

Published by Lund Humphries Publishers Limited
12 Bedford Square, London WC1

SBN 85331 309 1

Also by the author:

ARABIC LEXICOGRAPHY – its history, and its place in the general history of lexicography.
E. J. Brill, Leiden, 1960: 2nd edition, 1965.

(with H. M. Nahmad)
A NEW ARABIC GRAMMAR OF THE WRITTEN LANGUAGE
Lund Humphries, London, 1962: 2nd edition, 1965.

Made and printed in Great Britain
by Lund Humphries, Bradford and London

TABLE OF CONTENTS

Preface vii

Introduction – Some explanatory notes ix

Chapter 1. THE CLASSICAL HERITAGE 1

Chapter 2. THE BEGINNINGS OF THE LITERARY RENAISSANCE 26
Introduction. The last years of the Age of Depression 26
Egypt 29
Syria and the Lebanon 36
Other countries – Iraq 65
EXTRACT I: A Description of Paris, by Rifāʿat al-Ṭaḥṭāwī 72

Chapter 3. THE FIRST FLOWERING OF THE LITERARY RENAISSANCE – the late Nineteenth and early Twentieth Centuries 78
Poetry
1. Egypt 78
2. Poetry in Iraq 105
3. Poetry elsewhere – Syria and the Lebanon 115
Prose
1. Polemics 115
2. The short story 126
3. The novel 131
4. The essay 137
EXTRACT II: Christianity and Islam and their followers, by Muḥammad ʿAbduh and Jamāl al-Dīn al-Afghānī 143
EXTRACT III: The Morrow, by Muṣṭafā Luṭfī al-Manfalūṭī 151
EXTRACT IV: The First Cup, by the same author 154
EXTRACT V: Baghdad, an ode by ʿAlī al-Jārim 158

Chapter 4. SOME MODERN WRITERS AND MODERN MOVEMENTS (1920 to 1970) 163

Introduction 163

Poetry
1. General 166
2. Poetry in Egypt 167
3. Arabic poetry in America (the *Mahjar*) 173
4. Poetry in the Lebanon and Syria 178
5. Iraqi poetry 184
6. Poetry elsewhere 186

Prose
1. Introduction 191
2. Egypt 193
3. Some Lebanese and Syrian prose 210
4. Prose in Iraq 213
5. Prose in other countries 215
ENVOI. Past achievements – future prospects 217

EXTRACT VI: The People of the Cave (Act I), by Taufīq al-Ḥakīm 219

EXTRACT VII: The Fare, by Maḥmūd Taimūr 235

EXTRACT VIII: Innocents in Cairo, by Ḥusain Mu'nis 241

EXTRACT IX: Arab Woman in the National Life, by Qusṭanṭīn Zuraiq 250

EXTRACT X: Abū Nuwās in America, by Ṣafā' Khulūṣī 256

EXTRACT XI: Pot-smoking, by Muḥammad al-'Arūsī al-Maṭwī 263

EXTRACT XII: A Stranger, by 'Abd al-Majīd Ben Jallūn 269

Notes 276

Glossary 289

Bibliography 294

Index 298

PREFACE

In the spring of 1968, Mr. John Taylor of Lund Humphries was kind enough to invite me to write a modest book on modern Arabic literature, to consist half of *long* extracts in translation, and half of a brief introduction to the subject. As the work progressed, however, its scope broadened. In my teaching at the University of Durham, where we have long had an Honours B.A. course in Modern Arabic Studies – the first wholly modern course of its kind in Britain – I had noted the lack of material in English on this increasingly important part of Arabic literature. In particular, while there was an excellent history of the classical Arabic literature by R. A. Nicholson, nothing comparable on the modern literature was to be found in European languages. I therefore decided to extend the historical account, while still retaining the long extracts, a dozen in number.

But in writing the book, I have tried to cater for two types of reader: the person who knows, or is learning, Arabic, and wants some guide to the modern literature; and the more general reader, of broad literary interests, who would like to gain some impression of Arabic writing of today, and compare it with other literatures he knows. Whether I have succeeded in this double aim is for the reader to judge. But I have been inspired by similar efforts by Sir Hamilton Gibb and the late Professor A. J. Arberry, who have demonstrated that works about Arabic literature can interest both the specialist and the tiro. If I can reach any standard remotely comparable to theirs, I will indeed be gratified. But, after all, they are 'giants'.

The task on which I entered so blissfully has proved very taxing. For example, I felt that an introductory chapter on the classical literature was essential for the non-specialist. In teaching at Durham, it has been abundantly clear that no introduction to the modern literature could have much meaning without at least a bird's-eye view of the classical literature. Again, something had to be said about the so-called 'Age of Depression', in which literature of value almost disappeared from Arabic for three centuries. We cannot speak of a reawakening unless we know something about the sleep which preceded it.

It is obvious that no one man can know all worthwhile modern Arabic literature, so that I must at times retail second-hand knowledge and judgements, and at others speak from first-hand knowledge. Error, too, can scarcely be avoided – even Arabic sources are sometimes incomplete or erroneous; quite apart from my own errors. The indulgence of readers is requested, and corrections and suggestions will be gratefully received.

The most difficult part of a preface is the list of acknowledgements. It would be impossible for me to mention by name all the individuals and institutions who have helped me so generously. I would especially thank Arab governments, embassies, and universities, who willingly responded to my requests for information when I started this survey. Arab scholars, too, assisted me, and I received copies of articles and books from some of the sources above-mentioned which greatly assisted my references to post-1939 literature, brief as these are.

I have also to thank the staff of the Oriental Section of Durham University Library, at the School of Oriental Studies, Elvet Hill, Durham, under Mr. C. J. Foster, Keeper of Oriental Books, for their unfailing kindness and courtesy in assisting me to find the many books I required. There is a good collection of modern Arabic literature in the Durham library.

A special word of appreciation is due to my two Arab colleagues in Durham — Dr. Husain Dabbagh and Mr. A. M. T. Farouki, both lecturers in Arabic – for little pieces of advice and illumination. Mr. Farouki helped me to elucidate some poetical extracts for translation purposes. But, of course, I myself must take full responsibility for the translations.

Finally, I must add that the aim of this book is to arouse interest in a great literature. If it does no more than that, I will be content.

John A. Haywood

27 April 1970

INTRODUCTION

Some explanatory notes

1. Translations from modern Arabic literature; selection

An important feature of this book is the inclusion of quotations from literary works. Twelve major extracts have been included, separate from the actual chapters of the book. It is hoped that readers will read these as they occur. They have been drawn from several Arab countries: seven from Egypt (I, III, IV, V, VI, VII and VIII); and one each from the Lebanon (IX), Iraq (X), Tunis (XI) and Morocco (XII). One (II) was published in Paris written by a Persian and/or an Egyptian. The preponderance of Egyptian writing may appear unfortunate, though it is not quite as unfair as it seems, having regard to the wealth of Egyptian literature, quantitatively and qualitatively. In any case, the balance is redressed to a considerable extent in the translations of poetry which, with one exception, occur in the body of the chapters. These come from almost every Arab land, and number about one hundred pieces, many of them whole poems. Again, there are a few prose extracts also in the chapters.

2. Translation techniques

Translation for a book such as this presents problems. There is something to be said for literal translation, which, though apt to be stilted, sometimes gives the flavour of the original. On the other hand, free translation can produce better literature and pleasanter reading. I have tried to steer a middle course between these two extremes, though aware of the risks involved.

I am quite convinced that poetry should not be translated as prose: this is a certain road to boring the reader. So verse has been translated in verse, almost invariably with rhyme. But no attempt has been made to imitate the precise metres or rhyme-patterns of the Arabic.

In translating rhymed prose (*saj'*), I have tried to reflect the rhymes in some measure – especially in the extract from Yāzijī, in Chapter II.* Similarly, I have tried to give some representation of rhetorical (*balāgha*) devices, where they are part of the flavour of the original.

The Arab habit of tautology or near-tautology has usually been imitated in English, giving pairs of words in sentences such as 'he was seized with *anger* and *wrath*'. In my view, this is so typical of Arabic means of expression and patterns of thought, that to omit it takes away something vital. Occasionally, I have been forced to write in this way where the Arabic does not have it, owing to metrical difficulties. Thus, in a poem by Shauqi,† the line:

'The teacher is almost an apostle, *an elect*'

includes the words 'an elect' which are not in the original, but they give the line its correct length and rhyme. In general, I have permitted myself much more freedom in translating poetry than prose. Yet I hope that the freedom has not been abused.

Arab writers use little colloquial language or slang either in description or dialogue in the works quoted in this book. But I have always believed in the judicious use of slang and colloquialisms in English, to give accurate meaning. Thus, my slang must on no account be taken to reflect similar idioms in the Arabic. For instance, in Extract XII, I make the infuriated André call Fatima a 'bitch',‡ a word which certainly does not indicate that used by the Arab author. But it seemed to me the sort of word André might have used in that particular situation had he been speaking English.

3. Transliteration

While the non-specialist – not to mention the poor printer! – may find dots under consonants and lines over vowels an irritant, I thought it best to use a recognizable and scientific system for printing Arabic names of authors, titles of books, and other words, in the Latin alphabet. Thus the reader who knows Arabic will be able to identify their spelling in the Arabic script. The system used is that found in *A New Arabic Grammar of the Written Language*,§ save that the letter *'ain*

* pp. 51-2.
† p. 89.
‡ p. 273.
§ See p. iv, *supra*.

is here represented by a comma thus ʻ, as opposed to the latter *hamza*, which is a comma thus ʼ. The initial *hamza* is rarely shown at all. Thus the more correct ʼ*Aḥmad* occurs as *Aḥmad.*

After an author or a book has been first mentioned, or a character in a story translation has been introduced, their spelling has usually been simplified in subsequent references to them, by omitting the extra dots and lines. So *Aḥmad S̲h̲auqī* becomes *Ahmad Shauqi.* Similarly, after the first mention of a name which includes the definite article, *al-*, the latter has been subsequently eliminated: *al-Manfalūṭī* becomes simply *Manfaluti.*

Incidentally, as Arab names have nothing approximating to fore-names and surnames, abbreviating them is difficult. Nevertheless, after first mention, it is too much to expect the non-specialist to go on reading such 'mouthfuls' as Nasif al-Yaziji or Jamal al-Din al-Afghani: so Yaziji and Afghani are used, however odd it may sound to Arabists.

In the case of one author, Ben Jallūn, the spelling is that normal in names from north-west Africa. There is no letter 'e' in correct transliteration, and the first part of the name would be 'ibn' in classical spelling.

Arabs do not normally transliterate their own names in the Latin alphabet according to any scientific system. In any case, their transliteration may vary in accordance with whether their European contacts have been French or English. So, in quoting books in English or French written by Arabs, the spelling on the title-pages has been followed.

4. Dates

All dates are given according to the Christian (A.D.) calendar, now used almost exclusively on Arabic title-pages. Older books, however, more particularly those printed in the nineteenth century, often merely have the Muslim (*Hijrī* or A.H.) date. In such instances, the Muslim date has been converted to a Christian one. However, as the Muslim year is a few days shorter, the correct Christian year can only be determined if the month and day are mentioned, and after consulting a conversion table.* There is, therefore, the possibility of an error of one year.

* Such as M. O. Jiménez, *Tablas de conversión de datas islámicas a cristianas y vice versa*, Madrid–Granada, 1946.

Unfortunately, I do not know whether certain modern authors are still alive or not. There is, therefore, a possibility that a few authors for whom birth dates alone are given may be no longer be living.

5. Glossary

In a work like this, dealing with a non-European cultural area, a large number of technical terms known only to the specialist must inevitably occur. These consist chiefly of three categories of Arabic words: literary, historical and religious. Little effort has been made to explain the third category, as this would involve embarking on an account of Islam. Readers curious to know what such terms as *sunnite, shiʿite, hadith* and the like really mean are advised to read through some primer of Islam, of which the following may prove useful:

H. A. R. Gibb, *Muhammedanism*, Home University Library, 1949, 2nd edn. 1953, new edition in Mentor Books, 1956.

Alfred Guillaume, *Islam*, Pelican Books, 2nd edn. 1953.

K. W. Morgan (ed.), *Islam, the Straight Path: Islam interpreted by Muslims*, New York, 1958.

Philip K. Hitti, *Islam, a way of life*, O.U.P., 1970.

For historical terms such as names of dynasties, C. R. Bosworth's *The Islamic Dynasties*, Edinburgh, 1967, can be consulted. Stanley Lane-Poole's *The Mohammadan Dynasties* (London, 1893) may still be encountered in libraries and second-hand bookshops.

Terms relating to literary forms and styles, and literary criticism, are explained as they occur in this book, the more important ones in Chapter 1. It was felt, however, that a short glossary of the more common terms might prove useful for quick reference; while largely literary, it does include a few historical and religious terms.

6. Index

It is hoped that this book will be used partly for reference. So a comprehensive index has been included. At the same time, some limits had to be imposed, especially for what might be called incidental information. The following guiding principles have been observed, though not absolutely rigidly.

First, Arabic terms basic to the whole work, such as *Nahḍa* (Arab literary renaissance) occur in the index, but with reference only to the page where they are first defined.

Second, names of Arab countries, and of other countries mentioned fairly frequently, such as Turkey, India, France and England, have no index entry. Any reader who wants to find all major references to any one Arab country should have little difficulty, by skimming through the pages with the aid of the Table of Contents.

Names of important cities in the Arab world, such as Cairo and Beirut and also Istanboul, are omitted from the index, because of their great frequency. It was felt that no useful purpose would be served by listing in the index every page on which Cairo was mentioned, for example.

Great care has been taken to include in the index every author mentioned, whether Arab or non-Arab.

Unfortunately there seems to be no simple rule to determine which part of an Arab name should determine its alphabetical position. Many purists would prefer to place Taufīq al-Ḥakīm under t; here, we place him in the index under h, as *Ḥakīm, Taufīq al-*. Readers should note that the definite article *al-*, which is usually joined to the following word by a hyphen, never determines the position of a name in the index. Thus, ʿAlī al-Jārim occurs as *Jārim, ʿAlī al-*; not *Al-Jārim, ʿAlī.* The Classical lexicographer al-K͟halīl ibn Aḥmad occurs as *K͟halīl ibn Aḥmad, al-*; not as *Ibn Aḥmad, al-K͟halīl.* This is because Arab writers since the ninth century have always referred to him, briefly, as al-K͟halīl.

In this confused situation, which is none of my making, the reader is warned that, in looking up an author's name in the index, he must be prepared to try two or more alternatives. Thus, if he does not find Jamāl-al-Dīn al-Afg͟hānī under j, he should try under a (for Afg͟hānī), or even under d (for Dīn). Only the specialist will know that the latter possibility is highly unlikely.

CHAPTER 1

The classical heritage

While several histories of classical Arabic literature have been written in European languages, besides studies of individual authors and translations of their writings, modern Arabic literature has been largely neglected until the last few years. Many distinguished Arabists in the West fail to realize the extent of its achievements and its ability to face comparison with other modern literatures, even those of the West. Perhaps they can hardly be blamed, since Arabs themselves sometimes belittle their modern literature – especially if they are lovers of or experts on their old classics. The aim of the present book is to redress the balance, and provide a conspectus of modern Arabic literature in such a form as may prove helpful not only to Arabists, but also to informed general readers.

First, however, a few definitions are required. In *one* sense, all Arabic literature, medieval or modern, is classical, if by that word we are translating the Arabic adjective *faṣīḥ* or *afṣaḥ*. But Arabs generally apply these, in the feminine *faṣīḥa* or *fuṣḥā*, to language (*lugha*) rather than literature (*adab*). The opposite is *ʿāmmī*, *dārij* or even *dārijī*,[1] that is, colloquial. Although the colloquial dialects differ widely among themselves, as well as from the classical or written language, the latter – the classical language – is to all intents and purposes one and undivided, save in some minor variations of idiom and vocabulary. Moreover, not only have there been few attempts to write literary works wholly or largely in the colloquial, but even the dialogue of modern novels and plays is sparing in its use of colloquialisms, for fear of restricting the readership.

In the present work, the expression modern Arabic literature is taken to mean the literature of the nineteenth and twentieth centuries. Arab literary historians usually reckon their modern literature to have begun with Napoleon's invasion of Egypt in 1798, thus acknowledging the role of the West in providing the initial impetus. They use various adjectives to distinguish this literature – *ḥadīth* (new, recent), *ʿaṣrī* (relative adjective from *ʿaṣr* = era, age), and *muʿāṣir* (from the same root

= contemporary) – though the last term might not be very apt for nineteenth-century works. The Arab Literary Renaissance or Revival since 1800 is usually known as the *Nahḍa*, from the verb *nahaḍa* (to rise from a sitting position – sometimes, to rise up against one's enemy). Another term used is *iḥyā'* (revitalizing, resuscitating). There is really no overall Arabic term for the classical literature. The European word *kalāsikī* is used only of European culture and arts, particularly Graeco-Roman, but no Arab would ever write it in reference to his own civilization. In fact, the classical literature is usually designated by political eras: pre-Islamic as *Jāhilī*; that of the 'Orthodox' Caliphs as *Rāshidī*; Ommeyad as *Umawī*; and ʿAbbasid as *ʿAbbāsī*. More specialized studies often deal with centuries, designated according to the Muslim rather than the Christian calendar. When it is required to differentiate classical from modern literature, the former is called 'the old literature' (*al-Adab al-Qadīm*).

The period between the end of the Middle Ages and 1800, when practically no Arabic literature of outstanding merit was written, is termed *ʿaṣr al-inḥiṭāṭ* (The Age of Depression). Some even write as if it began in about 1258, the year when the Mongol Hulagu, in capturing Baghdad, destroyed the remains of Islamic unity. This is too arbitrary, however, as it would exclude from the classical era one of the most brilliant of Arab minds, Ibn Khaldūn (1332–1406), whose Introduction to his History was unique in medieval literature in any language.

A proper understanding of modern Arabic literature requires some knowledge not only of the general background – political, religious, social and economic – but also of the classical literature. On the former, there are a number of useful books in English. On the literature, books certainly exist. But they tend to deal with the subject chronologically, much in the manner used by Arabs, era by era. The student of modern Arabic literature, however, really requires for his background an account dealing briefly with questions of form, style, and language over the whole medieval period. For example, a general conspectus of the development of the medieval poetry will assist in the understanding of the modern poetry. An account of medieval Arabic biographical, anecdotal and narrative literature will aid the understanding of modern fiction – and so on. It is proposed therefore to explain briefly the chief classical literary forms, mentioning some of the works which might have served as models in the Literary Renaissance. To the reader already familiar with the classical literature, much of what follows will be *vieux jeux*. Again, there is the danger inherent in generalization. Still, the effort is worth making for the sake of less informed readers.

We usually divide literature into poetry and prose (*shiʿr* and *nathr*). But in Arabic there is a third genre – or rather a subdivision of prose, *sajʿ* – rhymed prose. In practice a whole work is seldom described as being in *sajʿ*, that is, *masjūʿ*. Rather was *sajʿ* one important feature of 'art prose' – that is, prose in which sound mattered as much as sense, sometimes more. Again, it might occur in 'purple patches', as alliteration in English. Incidentally, the language of the Koran is generally placed in a separate category, as being quite inimitable – though a non-Muslim might be tempted to describe it as a mixture of ordinary and rhymed prose.

In the heyday of the classical literature, the view was widely held that poetry was, by its very nature, superior to prose, and that the finest poetry was composed in the *Jāhiliyya* – that is, the pre-Islamic period of the sixth and early seventh centuries.[2] The best examples were thought to be the Seven Odes, called the *Muʿallaqāt*, because legend maintained that they were hung at the pagan shrine of the Kaʿba in Mecca. The Arabic for 'ode' is *qaṣīda* (pl. *qaṣīd/qaṣāʾid*). Writing in the first half of the eleventh century, the North African Ibn Rashīd averred that in both poetry and prose there were three categories – good, indifferent, and bad. In comparing a poetical with a prose work, if they came into the same category, the poetry would take first place. This almost mystical reverence for poetry has largely disappeared today. True, poetry is still highly revered, and recited on even minor public occasions in a way rare in the West. But it carries no built-in superiority: and there are many Arabs who, once they leave school or college, read virtually no more poetry except verse of dubious merit printed in the daily papers, frequently on nationalist subjects. Yet they will read prose literature, especially novels and short stories.

The first point to stress about the classical poetry is its preoccupation with people, whether individuals or groups – that is, tribe, party, sect or race. This truism is rather less valid after the end of the Ommeyad era (A.D. 750). To the poet, the proper study of mankind was man. This was his principle because his livelihood depended on it. In pre-Islamic times, the poet was the spokesman of his tribe, extolling and encouraging its heroes and leaders. As a corollary, he had to denigrate and castigate hostile tribes and their leaders. Some poets praised the kings of the buffer states of Ghassan (bordering Palestine) and Hira (bordering Iraq), in which case motives might be mercenary – expectation of reward, rather than a noble feeling of loyalty to one's clan. It was easy, at a later stage, to adapt this sort of poetry to support a dynasty, political party, or religious sect: and copious modern Arabic poetry championing Arab freedom and unity, and urging resistance to Imperialism and Zionism, may be regarded as a modern extension of such poetry.

The themes of pre-Islamic poetry were largely eulogy (madḥ – madiḥ), elegy (*rithā' – marthiya*), satire (*hijā'*), and love or eroticism (*nasīb – tashbīb – ghazal*). There were other incidental, though still important, themes. Eulogy could be directed at one's family, sect or tribe. It could also be self-pride (*fakhr*) which to us often seems tantamount to boasting. Contrariwise, satire could be directed against an individual enemy, his family, sect or tribe. Tribal warfare loomed large in poetry, enabling the poet to stress desert-Arab virtues such as bravery, fidelity, and loyalty. Such poetry was sometimes called *ḥamāsa* (chivalry). Nature was described more especially for its association with people. The sight of the deserted encampment reminded the poet of a beloved. Animals would figure in connexion with riding – the horse or camel, and hunting – the gazelle and lion, for instance.

The qasida (ode) in its finest form, as exemplified in the *Muʿallaqat*, was an amalgam of themes in a recognized sequence, which can be set out, over-simplified, as follows: ruined encampment – remembrance of the beloved – the horse or camel, which might bear the poet to his beloved, or have other associations with her – finally, the elegy, eulogy or satire of the subject of the poem. This composite form, though seemingly disjointed and stereotyped, lent itself to endless variations, and, in the hands of a master, could flow naturally from one theme to another. A striking example of variety is in the hunting scene in Zuhair ibn Abī Salmā's eulogy of Ḥiḍn ibn Ḥudhaifa ibn Badr, which dominates the poem. There is a shorter reference to hunting in the Muʿallaqa of Labīd.[3]

It is not known how this composite qasida form first developed –

whether as a combination of shorter poems on the separate themes, intended or fortuitous; or as a whole, the shorter themes being taken from it. Certainly pre-Islamic poetry affords numerous examples of short poems on a single theme, especially in the *ḥamāsa* poetry. These developed into well-recognized separate forms in the Ommeyad and early ʿAbbasid eras: and some new forms won acceptance.

Before discussing these, however, something must be said about metre and rhyme. The qasida – indeed, pre-Islamic poetry in general – was based on the verse (*bait*) divided into two hemistiches (*maṣraʿ*), generally of equal length. A verse appears in print as a single line, unless space does not permit. There were about 15 different metres, based on quantity rather than quality – that is, on length of syllable, whether short or long, rather than stress. The hemistich was frequently long by English standards, containing as many as 14 or 15 syllables in the weightier metres, which were popular in pre-Islamic times. Rhyme was based on a final consonant, homogeneously vowelled (occasionally without a vowel). Poems were monorhyme – that is, the same rhyme persisted throughout the poem at each verse-end. In longer poems, the rhyme also came at the end of the first hemistich of the first verse – probably to attune the listener's ear to it at the start.

This early poetry had a characteristically rich diction, based on familiar imagery and a large vocabulary with a fair sprinkling of rare words, of forms not so common in later literature, especially prose.[4] Such words may have been culled from various dialects of Arabia.

It might be thought that the composite qasida as outlined above could play no part in the modern literature. By ʿAbbasid times adherence to the old sequence had become typical of the poet with antique tastes. Abū Nuwās (*c.*756–*c.*810) wrote:

> Say to the weeper, standing at obliterated ruins,
> What harm would there be, were he to sit down?

Again, referring to the absent loved-ones, for whom Lailā and Hind were favourite names:

> Weep not for Laila, neither for Hind should you pine:
> Drink the red wine from a maiden ruddy as wine!

The name qasida came to be applied to any weighty poem of

between 30 and 120 verses of monorhyme, especially when preliminary or subsidiary themes were included. At the same time, it is easy to see that nostalgic references to past Arab greatness could properly include description of desert life, encampments, camels, and horses. Such nostalgia could form a natural prelude to a call to Arabs to reassert themselves, and carve out for themselves a respected place in the modern world. The qasida form could be emulated by the inclusion of a long preamble on varied subject-matter – not necessarily the old traditional sequence – before coming to the main subject of the ode. Thus the Egyptian poet al-Bārūdī (1838–1904)[5] devotes 23 out of 43 verses of an elegy on Shaikh Ḥasan al-Marṣafī and ʿAbdallāh Pasha Fikrī[6] to lamenting the passing of youth, and longing for his native land, while in exile in Ceylon. The same poet wrote an ode in praise of the ancient Arab's preoccupation with war, seeking pasturage for his animals, riding, drinking and love-poetry.[7] But the influence of the old qasida in the modern poetry can also be seen in the conventional imagery and rich vocabulary, varying according to how old-fashioned or up-to-date the poet is. It is certainly apparent in some fairly recent writers such as ʿAlī al-Jārim (1881–1949).[8]

The advent of the Ommeyad dynasty based on Damascus led to a decline of Bedouin influence, and a widening of the range of poetic themes. For example, two distinct types of love poetry developed in the Hedjaz (the region of Arabia lying along the west coast. This was not only the region where Islam originated, but the main centre of mercantile and cultural activity in the peninsula). They were much less stereotyped than the pre-Islamic brand. The profligate type, represented by ʿUmar ibn Abī Rabīʿa, was that of the city roué: the chaste type, retaining Bedouin idealism, was represented by Jamīl ibn ʿAbdallāh, who loved only one girl, Bu<u>th</u>aina, and loved in vain. In the ʿAbbasid age, the first of these types was developed further, and Abū Nuwās directed it to the male.

Ghazal is no less varied in modern Arabic poetry than it was in the Middle Ages. Its earlier manifestations tended to be idealized and stylized, with antique turns of phrase. On the whole, it was chaste rather than profligate, in tune with the notions of reviving all that was good and great in the glorious past. Sometimes we find it mourning lost youth, with more than a hint that this is *kināya* (metonymy) for the youth of the Arab nation. Such nostalgia was, perhaps, an inevitable ingredient in poetical revival, but it dies hard. More recent events, such as the Arab-Israeli conflict, have served to revive this nostalgia. It can be seen, again, in Barudi, in his ghazal with the letter *ḍād* rhyme,[9] which begins:

> Where are our nights in Wadi al-Ghadā?
> Would that those days had never passed away!
> I was content in that Utopia.
> It passed, and joy for ever passed away.

As the poem progresses, the poet speaks of his fortitude, and ends:

> My words are my defenders: when I cry
> To them in need, they readily reply.
> Ask Glory freely – she will testify,
> For glory knows the blade that she holds high.

This poem, while apparently personal, seems to symbolize the Arab predicament at the time of its composition: there is lament for the passing of the good days of old; there are present handicaps, yet a sense of worthiness of a better position.

The Ommeyad age was one of political, sectarian, and tribal partisanship, and this, too, entered into the poetry. The pre-Islamic concept of the poet as the spokesman of his community was adapted to the new conditions. This notion partly illuminates the role of the poet in the modern literary renaissance. Thus much of the poetry of the late nineteenth and early twentieth centuries may fairly be described as 'occasional', relevant to a particular situation or event of general interest. The venom of the Ommeyad party poets, Farazdaq, Jarīr, and al-Akhṭal may be weaker in the Egyptians Aḥmad Shauqī (1882–1932) and Ḥāfiẓ Ibrāhīm (1871–1932). But they were spokesmen of their generation in a broadly similar way. The former was sometimes called the 'poet of the palace', the latter 'the poet of the people'. Shauqi was to produce poems in honour of the Bank of Egypt, the Red Cross Society, the Egyptian University. Equally well, he could lament the abolition of the Caliphate in Turkey by Mustafa Kemal, or eulogize Ḥusain Kamāl, Sultan of Turkey from 1914 to 1917. Hafiz was at home writing an elegy on Muḥammad ʿAbduh – or on Queen Victoria. He could crystallize Egyptian resentment of the

British occupation, as in a short poem of 1932, 'To the English',[10] which ends:

You were just for a while, then became unjust,
And you left, in the Nile, a régime of shame:
So we saw the oppressive disguised as the just,
And an offer of friendship distaste inflame.
Then beware of the hurricane's angry gust –
It ends, I have seen, but in bitter blame!

Under the ʿAbbasid rulers (750–1258), radical changes took place in Arabic poetry. There was a move towards shorter, less stylized poems, with increased use of the shorter metres. Like other aspects of life, the arts became less typically Arab, due to foreign – and especially to Persian – influences. Sophisticated court and city life, luxury and opulence, varied vices, contact with countries further east – Turkestan, the Indies, even China – whether through trade or conquest; all these were reflected in poetry. The qasida was still an important form, but it was rarely of the traditional composite type. Rather was it a weighty monorhyme poem of reasonable length, devoted to one of several recognized themes (in Arabic, *aghrāḍ* = purposes) – eulogy, elegy, satire. Some odes were written on less personal themes – description (*waṣf*), for example. But the qasida was still, in the main, a poem written to, about, or against an individual, or a group of individuals, alive or dead. A large proportion of the output of the 'Arab Shakespeare', al-Mutanabbī (905–65)[11] belongs to this category. The poet, dependent on patronage, was not a free agent. He had to please his patron by praising him, often with sickening exaggeration; or by praising someone near and dear to his patron; or by satirizing and abusing his patron's enemies. At the same time it was a highly competitive literary environment; the poet had to 'show his mettle' to retain his position as a court poet. It is to al-Mutanabbi's credit that he did not try to emulate the ornate, artificial style of some of his predecessors, such as Abū Tammām (807–46), who matched in verse the rhetoric of 'art prose'.[12] This may have been due to al-Mutanabbi's predilection for philosophizing in gnomic verse which could be quoted, by those who knew it, to suit the events of everyday life. The qasidas of the last 150 years probably owe more to al-Mutanabbi than to any other classical poet, though, in imitating him, whether unconsciously or deliberately, modern poets have usually eschewed the excessive personal pride of their model. This would certainly not have gone down well with modern listeners.

Another new poetical type of the ʿAbbasid era was wine poetry (*khamriyyāt*). Then there were other new or renewed types, such as *ʿitāb* (chiding – a convenient vehicle for complaining to a patron if he seemed cold or mean); *zuhd* (religious poetry – literally asceticism) and *ṭard* (hunting poetry). Some poets created special themes of their own. Thus Abū Firās (932–67), whose cousin Saif al-Daula, ruler of Aleppo, was al-Mutanabbi's patron, wrote many poems of exile, while a prisoner-of-war in Byzantine hands. So new was the note they struck, that they have become known as his *Rūmiyyāt*, from *Rūm*, Arabic for Asia Minor, or for the whole Byzantine Empire (*cf.* Rome).[13] Love and wine poetry was later turned to religious account in mystical (*Ṣūfī*) poetry, made famous in Arabic by Ibn al-Fāriḍ. But this genre made a much greater impact in Persian (for example, Ḥāfiẓ, and, possibly, ʿUmar-i-Khayyām) and in Indian literatures, such as Urdu, Pashto, Sindhi, Panjabi and Bengali.

The greatest need, technically, was to break away from the tyranny of the monorhyme, and this was not easy to achieve. The rhymed couplet – *mathnawī* – might have been the answer. It enjoyed a great and continued vogue in Persian, whence it probably came to Arabic. But its use in Arabic was practically confined to didactic verse, such as the versified grammatical treatise of Ibn Mālik known as the *Alfiyya* (a reference to the length of the poem, *alf* meaning 1000). In mathnawi, the two hemistiches of each verse rhyme together, and the rhyme is changed from verse to verse. Thus it resembles the rhymed couplets of Dryden and Pope. This verse-form has been revived by some modern Arabic poets, but not on a wide scale.

It was the introduction of the stanza late in the ʿAbbasid era which, though largely restricted to popular verse, provided the means of liberating Arabic poetry which twentieth-century poets have not been slow to seize. Such poetry is based on stanzas of 4, 5 and 6 – sometimes more – units, the unit being comparable to the old hemistich. Its old names were *zajal* or *muwashshaḥ*. Several varieties are designated according to the number of units per stanza or verse – *rubāʿī* (4 lines), *mukhhammas* (5), *musaddas* (6), and so on. Rubaʿi, though popular in Persian and various Indian literatures, did not find much favour in Arabic. But the collected verse of al-Ḥājirī (d. *c.*1235), the son of a Turkish soldier, includes both rubaʿi and mukhammas. Muwashshah is generally reckoned to have originated in Muslim Spain in the early tenth century, and to have spread eastwards from the twelfth century onwards. Its connexion with Provençal poetry is interesting, but does not concern us here. In any case, it is only fair to admit that the introduction of stanza poetry in modern Arabic literature probably owes as much to European models as to medieval Arabic popular poetry. This may account for the important role played by Lebanese – especially Lebanese-American – poets in developing it. The name of Īlīyā Abū Māḍī (?1890–1958) comes readily to mind in this connexion. Yet again, there is evidence that popular stanza poetry was particularly strong in the Lebanon. We shall later be noting that some poets of the early Nahḍa – Nāṣīf al-Yāzijī, for example – in the Lebanon are known to have composed muwashshahat.

But many poets avoided stanza poetry because they were traditionalists by inclination – ʿAli al-Jarim, for instance. Others, though thoroughly up-to-date in their themes and spirit, preferred classical forms. This would apply to Ahmad Shauqi, though his period of exile in Spain might have been expected to change his taste. His children's verse, however, contains quatrains entitled 'The Nile', 'Song of Egypt', and 'Scout Song'.[14]

It is convenient to refer here to blank verse (*shiʿr mursal*) and *vers libres* (*shiʿr ḥurr/shiʿr ṭalīq*), though they are no part of the classical heritage, and, indeed, typify Western influence. The pioneer of Arabic blank verse was probably the Iraqi Jamīl Ṣidqī al-Zahāwī (1863–1936),[15] unless we count a translation of a chapter of the Book of Job by the Lebanese Rizq Allāh Ḥassūn (1825–80)[16] in 1870. Yet blank verse seems to have little prospect of general acceptance. With *vers libres*, the case is different – perhaps because classical rhymed-prose made the idea seem familiar. S. Moreh tells us[17] that Amīn al-Riḥānī tried his hand at what he called *shiʿr manthūr* (prosified poetry) in 1905, in imitation of Walt Whitman. The true pioneer, however, was the Egyptian Aḥmad Zakī Abū Shādī, who was deeply interested in English literature, and an experimenter by nature. Free verse has gained so firm a foothold, that its validity as a form is hardly disputed now. As we shall see, the Lebanon made a great contribution to its development. But some of the essays of al-Manfalūṭī are really poems in prose.[18] Here one can see classical *maqāma* influence (see page 13).

In the medieval Arabic literature, poetry was in general more conservative than prose. It is thus not surprising that there should have been much in the classical prose literature that could be easily adapted to modern requirements. Three aspects are involved – language, form, and content. Perhaps the most crucial is language. To us there seems to be a problem of the simple and natural versus the studied and artificial, though it is doubtful whether any medieval Arabic writer really saw it in that light. To put it another way, the question was the relative importance of meaning and expression. The earliest examples of Arabic prose – in so far as they are authentic – are the sermons of the Prophet Muhammad and the early caliphs.[19] As might be expected, they are reminiscent of the Koran in their phraseology. They are characterized by rhetorical style (*balāgha*). Arab secondary schoolboys have, to this day, to study the various devices of balagha, often in an excellent text-book by ʿAli al-Jarim.[20] Of this more later. Yet these sermons seldom appear forced, and though uncommon words occur, it does not seem that a rich and recondite vocabulary was deliberately cultivated. And if there is studied effect, it does not offend Western ears: for we accept in oratory (such as Sir Winston Churchill's speeches) what we might deplore in literature intended for silent reading. Incidentally, the fact that medieval Arabic literature was intended largely for reading aloud may explain some apparent straining after effect, including the love for sajʿ (rhyme).

While poetry developed apace in the Ommeyad period (661–750), prose was slow to gain acceptance as literature. Towards the end of the period, however, a style which may be termed 'epistolary', or *risāla*-style, emerged, heavily charged with balagha devices. Modern Arab writers call it 'art prose' (*al-nathr al-fannī*), and this is as good a name as any. It probably arose as a medium for official letters, as written by court secretaries, who were usually Persians or other non-Arabs who had been thoroughly trained in Arabic. The word *risāla*, which means 'letter', was also applied to a monograph or essay. The first famous exponent of this genre was ʿAbd al-Ḥamīd known as al-Kātib (the Secretary) (d. 750), Persian in origin, and a familiar figure at the court of the last Ommeyad caliph, Marwān II. On the Caliph's behalf, he wrote a letter to the heir-apparent, ʿAbdallah, when the latter was setting out to fight the rebel Kharijites. It has become known as *Risāla fī naṣīha Walī al-ʿAhd* (Letter of Advice to the Heir-apparent), and is considered a model of epistolary style, or art prose. To the modern reader it is ornate and complex to the point of obscurity.

The characteristics of art prose, as described in any balagha text-book, are as follows:

(1) Much use of metaphor (*istiʿāra*) and simile (*tashbīh*), each of which is divided into several categories by the text-books.

(2) The balancing of sentence against sentence, phrase against phrase, and word against word. Again, there are recognized subdivisions, depending partly on whether similar or contrasting meanings are involved. Among the terms used are *izdiwāj* and *ṭibāq* (*muṭābaqa*).[21]

(3) The device called *jinās*. This was the use of two or more words from the same or similar roots, producing an effect akin to a combination of alliteration and assonance. Such pairs or trios of words would be highlighted by the positions in which they were placed – for example, at the ends of, or at comparable places within, the balanced phrases or sentences mentioned in (2) above. Again, there are subdivisions, dependent on the degree of identity of the two or three words involved. Perfect *jinās* consisted of the repetition of the same word, whether with identical or different meanings. Thus, if the word *ʿain* occurred twice, it could mean 'eye' in both cases, or 'eye' in one, and 'spring of water' or 'the same' in the other.

(4) Sajʿ (rhyme), often in association with izdiwaj and jinas.

(5) The use of rich vocabulary with rare words. Clearly the features already mentioned would encourage this, whether or not the writer set out deliberately to achieve it. But with the passage of time, the conclusion is inescapable that authors often made rich vocabulary an end in itself – perhaps a sort of linguistic 'keeping up with the Joneses'.

(6) Verbosity and repetitiveness inevitably resulted from all the above; for example, the use of two or three adjectives where one would have done, or emphasizing a statement by repeating it in nicely balanced sentences almost identical in meaning.

(7) Although the aim behind balagha was often said to be the clarification and enhancement of meaning – hence the use of the word *bayān* (= clear meaning) as a description of writing of this sort – the ultimate effect, at any rate to the Western ear, was to stress language at the expense of meaning. To put it more kindly, it suggests a poetical approach to prose.

Unfortunately the effect of Arabic art prose is hard to reproduce in English. But an example of jinas would be Christopher Fry's 'The *god*dess, in her *god*-like way, is *God* knows where!'. Some effort has been made, in the translations in this book, to reflect balagha,[22] with what success it is for the reader to judge.

The history of art prose can be followed through the Middle Ages. It can be seen in early masters such as Ibn al-Muqaffaʿ (724–74), author of the famous *Kalīla wa Dimna*; in al-Jāḥiẓ (775–89), noted for his *Kitāb al-Bukhalāʾ* (Book of Misers), and later in the works of the historian-geographer, al-Masʿūdī (d. 958). It reached its apogee in the *maqāmāt* (séances) of Badīʿ al-Zamān al-Hamadhānī (968–1007) and al-Ḥarīrī (1054–1122).[23] The maqama was well adapted to this sort of writing, being essentially a linguistic and stylistic *tour de force*. A number of them were grouped together under the umbrella of a 'frame' story or situation; and individual maqamat varied from the frankly pedagogic and didactic to the essay and anecdote. Risala style could not be entirely ignored even by writers of medieval 'scientific' or practical literature – philosophical, critical, biographical, historical, geographical, and so on, in which a more utilitarian style might seem more apt. This can be seen in descriptive passages in travel literature, such as works by Ibn Jubair (1145–1217) and Ibn Baṭūṭa (1304–77). Ibn Khaldūn also shows the influence of this style.

During the Age of Depression, preoccupation with the sound of language dominated prose, and the maqamat of al-Hamadhani and al-Hariri were the models followed. This accounts for the immense number of manuscripts of them that have survived – for printing had not yet reached the Islamic world.

Yet in the Middle Ages, alongside this art prose, a large number of prose works *were* being written in simple style. This could be called 'utilitarian': perhaps it could be termed 'scientific prose' (*al-nathr al-ʿilmī*) as opposed to 'art prose' (*al-nathr al-fannī*). Such prose could still be impressive: moreover it served its purpose by its very clarity, especially in narrative and scientific literature.

All this is very relevant to the question of language and style in modern Arabic prose. The maqama provided the obvious model for the writers of the nineteenth century. But there were snags. While the literary language had remained virtually static since the seventh century, the spoken language had changed considerably. Inflection had disappeared, and certain grammatical usages had gone by the board. Numerous idioms had become obsolete or obsolescent, and much vocabulary was now known only to specialist students of the language. The old system of patronage by rulers, officials, and rich men, was on the decline, since the ruling classes were Turkish. The language of government was Turkish – a language which, though then written in Arabic characters, belonged to a totally different language family. Thus it became less easy for an author to write for a small educated élite. True, some Turks were sensible of the beauties of Arabic; and the autonomous Khedives of Egypt, as well as Christian institutions in the Lebanon, were ready to support some Arabic literary activity. But the patron's place was taken by the nascent Arabic press, which offered the budding author a livelihood. This, together with the spread of education, largely at a low level, indicated to writers the advantage of simplifying their language, to appeal to a wider audience, for whom the spoken language took priority over the written.

Still, art prose, and the maqama which had highlighted it, died hard. Thus the Lebanese Nāṣīf al-Yāzijī (1800–71) wrote his collection of maqamat, *Majmaʿ al-Bahrain* (Beirut 1856), in unashamed imitation of al-Hariri. Another collection of maqamat, eighty in number, by Ibrāhīm al-Aḥdab (1826–97) was published, undated, in Beirut. At Kerbala in Iraq, five by S͟hihāb al-Dīn Maḥmūd al-Ālūsī appeared in 1856–7. Examples could be multiplied, to show how strongly the maqama and its ornate style influenced nineteenth-century prose writers. Yet, in the long run, the incongruity of this style, in an area of increasing Western influence and contacts, and technological advance, was bound to become apparent. Writers came to realize that a simpler style could have literary merits of its own. A modern Arab reading the works of Ṭaha Ḥusain and Najīb Maḥfūẓ recognizes the artistry of the language, though he may find it rather elusive to explain. The old guiding lights of rhetorical devices now rarely figure in literary criticism of contemporary writers: canons of criticism are very similar to those in the West. One result of the 'new' Arabic style has been to make works sound more natural in English (or French, or German) translation. Incidentally, this style is not essentially 'new'. One has only to read the 'Thousand and One Nights' – of which more later – to appreciate that medieval Arabic prose was not always ornate.

The *forms* of modern Arabic prose literature nearly all have some roots in the classical literature: the outstanding exception is drama. The chief modern forms are novel, short story, essay, and drama. In addition, mention should be made of less creative forms, such as biography, autobiography, history, literary criticism, and a large body of literature which, for want of a better term, may be called 'polemical'. Into the latter category go books on social reform; books calling on the Arabs to reform themselves and their institutions, to gain their proper place in the world, to revive their former glories. A good deal of such literature is, to our ears, vague and repetitive: but in so far as it aspires to recognition as creative literature by aiming at a high literary style, to make an emotional appeal to the reader, it is worthy of mention. In any case, the tremendous influence of some of the writers of this sort of literature makes it essential to refer to them, and even include some long extracts.

On the other hand, we are not concerned here with a large quantity of published material which makes no pretence to literary worth – text-books and scientific works. Scientific works are now being turned out in Arabic by the hundred; and there are scientific magazines, both popular and specialized. Yet it must be remarked that science has affected the more creative literature. Modern fiction owes a great deal to psychology imported from the West.

Though the novel as we know it did not exist in classical times, there was a large body of narrative and fictional literature: after all, the Arab has always been a good story-teller. Most fiction came under the headings of anecdote or short story: but some longer stories have survived, often allegorical or symbolical. It must be admitted that they hardly reached what we would consider full novel length, but fell midway between short story and novel. Perhaps the two best-known are the 'Epistle of Forgiveness' (*Risālat al-Ghufrān*)[24] by Abū al-'Alā' al-Maʿarrī (973–1057), and *Ḥayy ibn Yaqẓān*[25], by the Andalusian Ibn Tufail (d. 1185). The former – sometimes, rather exaggeratedly, considered the forerunner of Dante's *Inferno* – describes an imaginary visit to the Next World, to see dead poets. The great ones, having led evil lives, are in hell; while the inferior versifiers are in heaven. Dialogue and description of sorts occur, together with quotation from poetry, but no real incident. *Ḥayy ibn Yaqẓān* appears to foreshadow *Robinson Crusoe*, but is basically concerned with religion and philosophy. A child is nurtured by animals on a remote island. By contemplation and observation, he is led to a knowledge of God – to natural religion, there being no other humans on the island. At the age of 50 he is brought into contact with men from a neighbouring island, but finds them too attached to material things to listen to his precepts. Only one of them, ʿAsal, who had found him on the island, and taken him back with him to 'civilization', shows sympathy with him. At the end of the book, the two return to Hayy's desert island, to spend the rest of their days in the search for divine truth and the worship of God.

The nearest approach to the novel was in popular stories told orally. These were mostly short stories, as we shall see. A few, however, developed into long stories, by piecing together a series of stories about the same hero or characters. The piecemeal character of their compilation is confirmed by the variation between different texts when they came to be written down. The best-known is the 'Romance of ʿAntar',[26] concerning the dark-skinned son of an Arab chief by a captive negress. ʿAntar typified pre-Islamic Arab prowess in war and chivalry. His saga, sometimes attributed to an eighth- or ninth-century philologer, grew to large proportions as the centuries passed. As now available, it covers the hero's career from birth to death, and probably dates from the crusading era. Incidents from it still figure in Arab children's story books and in other popular literature.

Unlike some other oriental languages – Urdu for instance – the English word 'novel' has not been Arabicized to denote the European-style novel. Nor, like Persian *roman* (*rumān*), has the French word 'roman' been taken over – though the word *rūmān* is sometimes used by literary historians for modern English 'romance', to describe a popular love story. Generally, the classical words *qiṣṣa* (pl. *qiṣaṣ*), *riwāya* (pl. *riwāyāt*), and less commonly, *ḥikāya* (pl. *ḥikāyāt*), are used. The first of these is now the commonest. All three are derived from verbs meaning to recount, relate. The second is also used to mean a play, especially with a following adjective from *masraḥ* (= theatre: *riwāya masraḥiyya*).

But the medieval Arab story-teller was usually short-winded. The literature is full of delightful anecdotes, which were a stock method of bringing home a point or sketching a character. Biographical works, such as Ibn Khallikān's *Biographical Dictionary*[27] abound in them. Jahiz's *Book of Misers*[28] is an extremely witty collection of anecdotes. Historians like al-Ṭabarī (838–923) depended on them. Then there were fables, like *Kalila wa Dimna*[29] already mentioned. However, an anecdote is not a short story. It is in several collections of popular tales that we find the classical forerunner of the form. The chief collection is the 'Thousand and One Nights' (*alf laila wa-laila*),[30] known in English as the *Arabian Nights*. This work is familiar in Europe in several translations such as that by Sir Richard Burton. Some of the stories, like those of Aladdin and Sindbad the Sailor, have, perhaps chiefly due to the pantomime, almost become part of English folklore.

The 'Thousand and One Nights' is based on the widely used technique of the frame story, into which are placed short stories of various types and varying origins – Arab, Persian, Indian, Greek and Turkish, and so on. The book is thought to date, in part, from the eighth–ninth centuries. But the present texts must belong to the late Middle Ages. From these and stories in other popular collections the Arab writer of the last 150 years could learn many useful lessons: simple, direct style, devoid of padding; natural dialogue; incident and action proceeding at a pace which retains the reader's interest, with an element of mystery and surprise; and credible characterization sketched with the minimum of words. On the other hand, they lack the psychological insight, and detailed and developing characterization, which we expect of modern fiction.

We know from Taha Husain's *al-Ayyām*[31] that in Egypt, at the turn of the century, village story-tellers were still active, telling the tales of Abū Zaid, the Banī Hilāl, and 'Antar.[32]

A short story is usually called an *uqṣūṣa* (pl. *aqāṣīṣ*), a word derived from the same root as *qiṣṣa*. But *riwāya qaṣīra* is also used, *qaṣīra* meaning 'short'.

Early attempts at novel and short-story writing tended to be in rhymed prose, full of balagha devices. The poet Ahmad Shauqi wrote three stories in this vein, before his exile to Spain in 1913.[33] Even translations of French and English fiction were frequently written in ornate prose; for writers, with their traditional training in the Arabic language, found it difficult to envisage any other sort of prose in any literature which could claim to be considered as 'creative'. Ḥusain Ḥaykal's novel, *Zainab*, published in Cairo in 1914, at first passed almost unnoticed, probably because of its straightforward style. Yet within a few years of its publication, maqama influence had practically disappeared from Arabic fiction: and authors like Taha Husain, al-Māzinī, Maḥmūd Taimūr, and Taufīq al-Ḥakīm have found means of writing stylish, well-written, expressive, attractive, yet easily understood prose. Their means are hard to define: but they have depended partly on what, for want of a better description, may be termed the witty turn of phrase, and on succinctness, which are very much in tune with the genius of the Arabic language – qualities which had become hidden in the craze for rhetorical 'Jack Horner-ism', qualities which had been much in evidence in some medieval prose writers, such as Jahiz. The language lends itself to exact and detailed description by its very richness; and its wealth of forms derived, with fine shades of meaning, from a single verbal root. The modern author has, indeed, a full linguistic palette at his disposal, to depict his imagination and thought accurately and fully. He has no need to lay it on with a trowel, and strain after effect.

Forerunners of the modern essay are to be found in the shorter medieval risala, and, of course, the maqama. 'Abd al-Hamid al-Katib's 'Letter to Writers' (*Risāla ilā al-Kūttab*),[34] instructing them on their work, is about 1,000 words in length. In another risala,[35] he expresses, in strong language, the caliph's disapproval of those who are addicted to the game of chess, to the neglect of their civil and religious obligations. But this style would seem ludicrously incongruous in an essay on some subject of current interest, such as woman in family life, or the evils of drink. Fortunately essayists have been dependent on the press for their bread and butter. The modern Arabic for an essay is the same as that for a newspaper article – *maqāla* (pl. *maqālāt*). A 'leader' is *maqāla iftitāḥiyya* = opening article. For schoolboy essays, the word *inshā*' is used. The word *risāla* was still used by many writers in the nineteenth and early twentieth centuries.

The magazines and journals which began to appear in the second half of the nineteenth century were as important as the daily newspapers in changing the style of writing essays. Among the best known, with dates of foundation, were: *al-Muqtaṭaf* (Beirut 1878, Cairo from 1881 onwards); *al-Hilāl* (Cairo, 1892); *al-Mas͟hriq* (Beirut, 1898); and *al-Ḍiyāʿ* (Cairo, 1898).

The evolution of modern essay style can be seen by comparing the maqalat and maqamat of Ahmad Fāris al-S͟hidyāq (Lebanese, 1804?–87), one of the great architects of the Nahda, with those of Yaʿqūb Ṣarūf, a co-founder of *al-Muqtataf*, who went to Cairo when that magazine was transferred there. A series of 80 articles which he wrote for the magazine were published in book form after his death – *Chapters on animal and plant life* (Cairo 1931). This seemingly scientific title conceals delightful essays, which, by analogy, concern man as much as animals and plants. For example, in 'The Spider' (*al-ʿankabūt*), there is an imaginary conversation in which the spider describes his cruel and dangerous way of life to the author. It is all truly educational; but there is more than a hint that human society can be no less cruel. Saruf uses a style basically simple, yet charming. There are some uncommon expressions, but there is strict economy of words. The great master of the essay was al-Manfalūṭī (1876–1924), who in style falls somewhere between the old and the new. His numerous essays, first published in the newspaper *al-Muʾayyid*, were published in a three-volume collection as *al-Naẓarāt* (Cairo, 1925–6).[36]

No account of the classical roots of modern Arabic literature would be complete without at least a passing reference to the less strictly creative forms – biography and autobiography, literary criticism, history and polemical literature. It is a vast subject.

The classical literature includes many collected biographies, some general, others specialized. These are, in fact, biographical dictionaries, though the entries – generally a few pages each in length at the most – are sometimes entered under categories (*ṭabaqāt*) rather than alphabetically. Ibn Khallikan has already been mentioned. The present-day equivalent of such short biographies is the encyclopaedia article. Buṭrus al-Bustānī started publication of the first modern large-scale Arabic encyclopaedia (*Dāʾira al-Maʿārif*) in Beirut in 1876.

There are also medieval full-length biographies. Indeed, one of the very earliest Arabic prose works is the *Life of the Prophet* by Ibn Isḥāq (d. 768), which has survived as the basis of the later compilation by Ibn Hisẖām (d. 834). Several centuries later, biographies of Saladin were written. And Usāma ibn Munqidẖ (1095–1188) wrote an autobiography which also shed much light on Saladin and the Crusades.[37]

Another type of autobiographical book was travellers' reminiscences. The best-known example, the *Travels of Ibn Batuta* (1304–77), is available in several European translations.[38] Medieval Arabic autobiographical literature is characterized by accurate description, a sense of the dramatic, vividness, and a wealth of anecdotes (called *ḥikāya*). When not relying on personal experience, the authors attempted to verify their facts by consulting authorities – preferably by word of mouth rather than from books, where there might be copyists' errors, or even deliberate changes, omissions and interpolations. They were not above including incredible wonders, but were not so addicted to this as some European contemporaries such as Sir John Mandeville. At the same time, when writing for patrons, they often had an axe to grind, and they were subject to sectarian and political prejudice. Their style varied considerably, even within a single work. Sometimes it might be simple and unaffected: sometimes, especially in purple patches, where the subject-matter seemed to demand it, they had recourse to the rhetorical style of art prose. Still, few modern writers have equalled the classical best: though here, Taha Husain's *al-Ayyam* is a brilliant exception.

During the nineteenth century some biographers wrote simply, others rhetorically. Among the former was Butrus al-Bustani, who wrote a life of Napoleon, and another of a contemporary who died young, Asʿad al-Sẖidyāq. Reference has already been made to the latter's brother, Ahmad Faris al-Shidyaq. His account of his visit to Malta (*al-Wāsiṭa fi ahwāl Māl(i)ta* – Tunis, 1886) foreshadows its ornate style in the medieval-type rhyming jingle of its title. So also does another of his autobiographical works (*al-Sāq ʿalā al-Sāq* – 'Leg over Leg' – Paris 1855).

As time went on, biographers tended to concentrate more on matter than on manner. At the end of Chapter 2 will be found an extract from a description of Paris by Rifāʿat al-Ṭahṭāwī (1801–73), which contrasts sharply with al-Shidyaq. More recently, al-ʿAqqād's series of biographies of the early caliphs[39] and of the poet Ibn al-Rumi[40] show an enlightened attitude to Islamic heroes, without offending traditional religious views. The language is modern and syntactically straightforward, yet fairly rich, with a feeling for fine style. Taha Husain's biographical writing really comes under the category of literary criticism. Like all his work, it is clearly written in an identifiably personal manner, treating the reader as his confidant. What is notable and new is his deep psychological insight into the minds of the subjects of his study – for example, al-Mutanabbi, and Abu al-ʿAlaʾ al-Maʿarri.[41] Simpler still are some biographies now being written – as, for example, ʿUthmān Amīn's *Muḥammad ʿAbduh*.[42] Autobiography has even invaded the realm of fiction. For example, Taufiq al-Hakim has used his experiences as an Egyptian provincial legal officer to write, in diary form, his *Yaumiyyāt nāʾib fī al-aryāf* (Diary of a provincial legal officer).[43]

It is not proposed to deal with historical literature in the present work: but the question of medieval models may be stated simply. In general, the Arab historian wrote chronicles,[44] on a year-by-year, decade-by-decade, or dynasty-by-dynasty basis. The aim was to tabulate facts, which were verified by asking those who knew, where events within living memory were concerned, or by reference to reliable written sources. This by no means excluded partisanship and fabrication: but orientalists believe that on the whole medieval Arab historians were more scrupulous than their European counterparts. At the same time, it is hardly surprising that they should rarely have expressed broad views, or shown deep insight in interpretation. A notable exception was Ibn Khaldun, whose *Muqaddima* (Introduction) to his history[45] expounded a whole philosophy of history, to explain the rise and fall of empires, particularly the Islamic/Arab Empire. His style matches the importance of his subject. The modern Arab world has as yet produced no Arnold Toynbee of its own to repeat this feat. But it *has* produced historians of merit who write like their European fellows. There was much history-writing by Lebanese Christians in the nineteenth century. Yet the standard history of the Arabs by an Arab, Philip Hitti, was written in English,[46] the writer being a Lebanese American. An abridged version has since been translated into Arabic. The best historian to write in Arabic about his people was Aḥmad Amīn (1878–1954), who covered the history of the Caliphate in three major works.[47] However, at university – as opposed to school – level, Arab students still rely largely on works by non-Muslims, in English or French. It is not that Muslim historians are any less critical than their European counterparts – quite the contrary, when one considers the ignorance of anything but the most superficial manifestations of Islam shown in Christendom. But it is hard for the Muslim Arab to write dispassionately about Arab history: he is too emotionally involved. In contrast, Europeans have often written their own history as sceptics – witness Gibbon's *Decline and Fall.*

The effect of European models has been noticeable in literary criticism during the last 50 years. But old methods are by no means dead. Assessment of merit, in the classical period, was dominated by textual criticism (*sharḥ*) – sentence by sentence, even word by word, explanation and commentary. The critic was too often obsessed by language and mannerisms of style, supplemented by biographical and historical observations. This technique seldom penetrated into the writer's mind, and paid little attention to social background. To say this is not to belittle the Arabs' achievements in criticism: in fact, here also, comparisons with contemporary Europe only emphasize Arab greatness. There were, for example, compendia and anthologies which at least attempted to lay down canons of criticism, to show what was best, and why it was best. It is sufficient merely to mention a few of the best known: Ibn Qutaiba's *Kitāb al-Shiʿr wa-l-shuʿara'*[48] (Book of Poetry and Poets) and his *ʿUyūn al-Akhbār*;[49] Abū al-Faraj al-Iṣfahānī's *Kitāb al-Aghānī*[50] (Book of Songs); and the *Ḥamāsa* of Abū Tammān[51] and that of al-Buḥturī[52] – both collections of poetry of old chivalry.

In the nineteenth century, Beirut was the first centre for publishing classical texts with annotations and commentaries. The famous Bulaq centre in Cairo followed suit. At first, few Arabs were willing to consider old and respected literature with an open mind, let alone scepticism. It was like cutting the ground from under one's own feet, denying a cultural heritage which produced pride and self-respect. But the work of European orientalists made its mark,[53] not only in their printed books, but by personal contact. It was probably as a result of reading articles by Margoliouth[54] that Taha Husain was able to throw his bombshell into traditional literary criticism, his book *Fī al-shiʿr al-ʿArabī*, which will be mentioned in Chapter 4 of the present work. This was an epoch-making work, challenging the authenticity of the oldest and most revered secular literature, the pre-Islamic poetry. When the dust had cleared from the furore produced by this book, literary criticism could never be the same again, however much the author might have mollified his views. Old methods did not entirely die – in fact they still have some part to play; for the understanding of ancient texts demands a deep knowledge of obsolete language. But a new type of literary criticism arose, a type not content to take things at their face value, which searched for truth with the open mind of the European researcher. The critic had to become an interpreter as well as a commentator, trying to get at the heart and mind of the author, inculcating in his readers true appreciation and enjoyment, not merely the meaning of words and identification of stylistic mannerisms and rhetorical devices. Among leading exponents of this 'new' criticism have been al-Māzinī (1890–1949), al-ʿAqqād, and Amīn al-Rīḥānī (1876–1940). So widely has this criticism been accepted, that it has become standard reading for upper-form schoolboys and university students. For example, Taha Husain's study of al-Mutanabbi is now recognized as a perceptive study of the poet, and a useful aid to the understanding of his poetry.

Modern Arabic literature has developed during a period of violent political, social and intellectual upheaval in the Middle East. Hardly were the Arabs liberated from Turkish domination than they were subjected to Anglo-French control. Western technology was introduced; also, Western doubts and vices. The young educated Arab became sceptical of his own heritage. Yet, as al-Manfaluti realised,[55] his apparent Westernization was largely a veneer. He asked himself why, despite his glorious past, his people were backward and enslaved. He wondered whether his centuries-old social system – which Westerners suggested was holding him back – was really Islamic, and whether social reform could be reconciled with Islam. Whatever he proposed was bound to draw forth refutation from the old-fashioned – the 'ulamā' who claimed to know Islam backwards. Thus a large body of polemical literature appeared, especially in Egypt and the Lebanon, the countries which had closest contact with the West, and therefore with liberal ideas. Among the chief themes explored were: the Islamic social system, with special reference to the position of women; the relative merits and distinguishing qualities of East and West, Islam and Christianity; and the evils of foreign rule – imperialism and colonialism. Similar literature can be seen during the same period in other Western-dominated countries. For example, the writings of Sir Sayyid Ahmad Khan (1817–98) and Altaf Husain Hali (1837–1914) in India contain arguments which can be found in the works of Jamāl al-Dīn al-Afghānī (1838–98), Muhammad ʿAbduh, Ahmad Amin (in his *East and West*) and Qāsim Amīn (1865–1908). At first sight, such literature would appear to have little in common with the classical literature. Indeed, some misguided Europeans imagine that the Arabic language is not taut enough for dialectics, despite its rich and exact vocabulary. (They mention in this connexion the poverty of Semitic verb-tenses.) But they are wide of the mark. The classical literature abounds in examples of closely reasoned arguments, particularly theological and philosophical. Among the best models were al-Ghazzālī (1049–1111) and Avicenna (Ibn Sīnā, 980–1037). In fact some modern polemicists seem to the present writer to write too precisely – Qasim Amin like a lawyer and Qusṭanṭīn Zuraiq like a diplomat. Even the religious tolerance of some modern Arab polemicists had precedents in the medieval literature. They may take some of their arguments and evidence from Europe and America when it suits them: but they are following old traditions of argument and disputation.

The themes of modern Arabic prose literature are partly medieval, partly modern. But there is a dominant urge to write about the present rather than the past. The average Arab man-in-the-street cares as little about al-Mutanabbi and al-Ghazzali as the average Englishman cares about Shakespeare and Milton. Prose literature as inherited at the opening of the nineteenth century had become almost as conservative as poetry. Moreover, in the early Nahda, nostalgia for past glory, which we have seen in poetry, was bound to affect prose as well. It was the press, and the impact of current events, which induced authors to concentrate on actuality rather than the past. The spread of literacy and education – including the education of girls – induced the prose writer to write for a wide circle of predominantly middle-class readers, who were more concerned with the problems of daily life than with the distant past. Thus whereas stories of medieval heroes are found in historical novels and plays, writers have turned increasingly to the modern scene. An essayist like al-Manfaluti, despite certain antique elements in his style, deals with the problems he saw around him. Literary critics and historians, too, now consider the literature of the last 150 years worthy of their attention.

The previous pages have shown, it is hoped, that modern Arabic literature owes much to the past. Only drama was an absolutely new form imported directly from the West. In poetry, blank verse has not caught on; and *vers libres*, though inspired by Western models, has much in common with rhymed prose. Western ideas affected different authors to different extents, and at one time there was controversy between the 'modernists' and 'traditionalists'. But this is a thing of the past, and the literature has a well-integrated character and considerable homogeneity – though it would be surprising if a Moroccan were to write like an Iraqi, or a Sudanese like a Syrian. The surprising thing, however, is not the differences, but the similarities. Despite Western influence, Arabic literature is still essentially Arab in spirit and expression. There can be no greater mistake in approaching it than to consider it as a rather exotic extension of European literature. And it is probably true that no amount of speaking to Arabs in English and visiting their countries can bring real understanding of the Arabs, without some contact with the modern literature.

This chapter has foreshadowed what follows, even anticipating references to leading authors. In the remainder of the book, the subject is dealt with, somewhat arbitrarily, in chronological sequence in three periods, with subdivisions of each period by countries and by literary forms. Chapter 2 deals with the nineteenth century as far as about 1870, before the literature had emerged as truly 'modern'. Chapter 3 takes the story to the end of the First World War, by which time some great writers of what we may call the 'old generation' had emerged. Chapter 4 takes the story to 1970, and shows the impact of European modernist movements on Arabic literature. Here we meet the greatest prose writers, more especially novelists and short-story writers, as well as some very original poets.

This chronological division, however, is not rigidly based on dates. Many writers, of course, overlap two of these periods; but their placing has been determined only partly by date of birth, but partly also by the spirit of their major works.

CHAPTER 2

The beginnings of the Literary Renaissance

Introduction. The last years of the Age of Depression

In 1516–17, the Ottoman Turks, who already ruled the Balkans and Asia Minor (Anatolia) from their capital Istanboul, conquered Syria and Egypt. The Sherif of Mecca voluntarily surrendered control of the Arabian Holy places (Mecca and Medina) to the Sultan Selim I. The next sultan, Solomon the Magnificent, extended his empire to include North Africa and Iraq, and the whole Arab world was thus incorporated in the Ottoman Empire. An Egyptian literary historian[1] refers to 'three centuries of misrule' which followed, during which 'Egypt and the rest of the Arab world were merely a source of wealth to the conquerors. All culture decayed, and the Arabic language decayed in face of the official language, Turkish.' This is a slight exaggeration. In the Age of Depression, the decline in the literature was in quality rather than quantity. Brockelmann's *Geschichte der Arabischen Litteratur* takes about 600 pages merely to list the authors and their works from 1517 to 1798. But with the exception of a handful of titles, these would mean little to the majority of Arabs and Arabists. Paradoxically, while those peoples with literatures of their own whom the Arabs had conquered – Persians, Byzantines, and Indians – greatly influenced Arabic literature, revitalizing it, almost moulding it, the Turks, who conquered the Arabs, hardly influenced Arabic literature. In fact the influence was rather the other way, as the Ottoman Turks adopted not only vocabulary, but literary forms from the Arabs. They used Arabic as the language of religion, rather as Latin was so used in the Middle Ages.

It may well be that the vast literature of the Age of Depression would repay greater study. But it is hardly likely that any unsuspected masterpiece will be brought to light. Arabic creative literature was sharply declining long before the Ottoman conquest. The literature of the Age of Depression was artificial and imitative, lacking originality. In the prose, rhyme abounded. As for the poetry, much of which was eulogy, it was rhetorical in style and exaggerated in sentiment.

Some poets included acrostics and chronograms in their poems. An example is the poet ʿAbd al-Raḥmān Bahlūl[2] (d. 1749). He was so poor that he had to *walk* all the way to Mecca, earning his keep by working as a cameleer. When he at last found a patron, he stretched ingenuity to the limit in a panegyric. He tells his patron that the poem consists of 80 'starry' and 9 'pearly' verses. The initial letters of these verses can be arranged to form two further verses, ending with the patron's name. Taking the numerical value of the letters in these two verses, each verse contains four chronograms – dates 'like bright torches'. Every verse of the main poem also contains two chronograms. This poet was the most skilled of his age in composing chronograms. In the introduction to the poem, in ornate rhymed prose, he admits that he may not equal the poetical geniuses of the past: yet he claims that the poem is a faithful description of his patron. He likens its rhetorical language to a smiling mouth which reveals beautiful meanings like flashing teeth.

This may be an extreme case, but it is by no means unique. It is understandable that when writers took pride in their ability to manage language and prosody like this, thought should be of secondary importance, and was as cliché-ridden as the language in which it was clothed. Much can be learned of the literary background of this era – especially in Egypt – from the history entitled *ʿAjāʾib al-Athār* by ʿAbd al-Raḥmān al-Jabartī (1754–1825/6). This work is available in a French translation.[3] It includes short biographies of many writers with extracts from their works.

The Arabic author of the Age of Depression had to write for a limited audience, being dependent on the patronage of governors and nobles, like his medieval predecessors. Louis Cheikho tells us[4] that at the beginning of the nineteenth century, education in the Arab world was practically confined to a few primary schools, especially those attached to Christian monasteries. There were high schools only in big cities such as Damascus, Aleppo, Cairo and Alexandria – and their curricula were mostly restricted to Islamic religious sciences and Arabic language. Books, being as yet still hand-written, were rare and expensive, and thus only within reach of a well-off minority. Arabic printing presses were located only in Beirut (one press) and in Istanboul (where the emphasis was mainly on printing Ottoman Turkish books or religious texts).

It is arguable that, if writers had had anything original to say, they could have produced works of genius even within the patronage system. Yet when one reads of officials like the administrator (*Katkhudā*) Raḍwān al-Jalfī[5] (who died a fugitive in Upper Egypt in 1755), one wonders. Leaving the work to his colleague Ibrahim Katkhuda, he abandoned himself to the wildest excesses and built himself fine houses with gardens and pools. In his days, Jabarti tells us, Cairo became like 'gazelle-filled meadows or an abode of *houris* and *mignons*. It was as if the inhabitants of that city had been exempt from the final Reckoning, and quit of all accounting and calling to question.' In these luxurious surroundings, Radwan was ready to listen to the plaudits of poets and rhymed-prose writers, who competed for his favours. Jabarti quotes a poem in 55 stanzas by a certain Qāsim al-Tūnisī in praise of Radwan, which begins with a description of a garden, of which the following is typical:

> The eye of the narcissus wept rosy tears,
> Bringing laughter to the red-lipped mouth of the calomile.
> The rose, assuming its red attire,
> Opened its calix for all to see,
> And perfumed the garden by scattering its scent.

In praising his patron, he says:

> A prince unequalled in his time,
> Above perfection's perfect paragon.
> If his shining Yemenite sword approached
> Antar, amidst his thousand warriors,
> Antar would say, 'Let us defer our encounter
> till Judgment Day, my friend'.
> He is a sea of generosity, accustomed to plenty,
> Swift and far-ranging in liberality,
> The caliph of his age, become unique –
> Ever successful, ever wise,
> In every thought guided aright.

It cannot be denied that such hyperbole of praise was not new to Arabic poetry: al-Mutanabbi went as far as any in this respect, even praising the Negro eunuch ruler of Egypt, Kāfūr, whom he secretly despised. But he did have flashes of genius which make his hyperbole tolerable – even attractive. In the Age of Depression, there is a feeling of sterility, of unworthiness of the object. The similes and metaphors, the figures of speech, the turns of phrase, are nearly all old. A musical parallel would be a modern composer writing Baroque music.

Perhaps the most satisfactory – or least unsatisfactory – literature of this period was the poetry of asceticism (*zuhd*), preaching the rejection of worldly pleasures. Here the best classical model was Abū al-ʿAtāhiyya (748–828); and, like him, his imitators often used simple language. Here is an example from Sayyid Muḥammad al-Amīr al-Kabīr (1741–1818), born in Assiyut Province, Egypt:

Reject this world for there is no delight
   Complete and perfect in it, free from care.
   Be in it as a stranger, and prepare
That which the life eternal will requite.

This then was typical of the literary scene, on the eve of the 'Renaissance'. In fact, the most influential Arabic book written in the eighteenth century was the large-scale dictionary *Tāj al-ʿArūs* compiled by the Egyptian Murtaḍā al-Zabīdī.[6]

Egypt

In this situation, only contact with another culture could arouse Arabic literature from its torpor. That culture, by one of the accidents of history, was to be European – and at first, more particularly, French. The points of contact were Cairo, as a result of Napoleon's Egyptian Expedition of 1798; and Beirut, where the Maronite Church was in communion with the Roman Catholic Church.

We must first consider Egypt, where the Ottoman régime was anything but popular. In a work on literature, only a brief sketch can be given of the political background. The Ottoman Empire was divided into provinces, each governed by a *wālī*. Egypt was such a province. Under the wali were other officials of non-Arab origin – Turks, Albanians and the like. Only the junior officials were natives. In Egypt, the fertile land there was parcelled out among foreigners, who were called *mamelukes*. Arabic *mamlūk* (pl. *mamālīk*) means 'owned, possessed', and these men were descended from enfranchised slaves. The Egyptian population, though primarily Muslim, also included a Coptic Christian community, descended from the pre-Arab Hamitic population. Their numbers had declined gradually, through spasmodic persecution under the Fatimid and Mamluk régimes. The Copts were an educated minority who used the Coptic language in religion, but otherwise used Arabic. They have traditionally provided clerical and administrative staff in government and commerce. When Napoleon came to Egypt, he broke the power of the mamelukes, and could therefore present himself as a champion of the Arabs.

Napoleon took with him to Egypt not only an army, but two printing presses and a number of scholars. One of these presses belonged to a printer, Pierre Aurel. But it was later bought by the French military, and, like the other press, came under the direction of the orientalist, Jean-Joseph Marcel,[7] head of the Imprimerie Nationale in Egypt. The presses had as their primary function the printing of proclamations and other official matter. Though the chief language used was French, Arabic translations – at times, even Greek and Turkish also – were provided. For example, after Napoleon left Egypt to return to France (1799), General Kléber, whom he left in charge, was murdered (June, 1800). The official account of his assassin's trial was published in French, Arabic and Turkish.[8] The French gave the Egyptians their first experience of a newspaper in the *Courier de l'Egypte*, which appeared – nominally at least – every five days, from 29 August 1798 onwards. It was an official and military newspaper, but included some Cairo and provincial news, besides propaganda for French revolutionary principles. A scientific and literary magazine, *La Décade égyptienne*, was published from November 1798, every ten days for Volume I – the first nine issues, then subsequently on a monthly basis. Its aim was to record the writings of the Institut d'Egypte founded by the French. Its contents were therefore largely scientific, including articles on agriculture, medicine and archaeology, even one on the Cairo lunatic asylum. The contents were in French, but an Arabic ode in glorification of Napoleon's military might was included in one issue.

Neither the *Courier* nor the *Décade* survived the departure of the French. Baron Jacques François de Menou succeeded Kléber as general commander of the French expeditionary force. He was defeated by the British at Alexandria in March 1801, and his forces were repatriated under the terms of the Treaty of Amiens of 1802. Menou did plan to publish an Arabic newspaper, called *al-Tanbīh*, when he felt the need to strengthen the population's confidence in the French, but apparently this plan was never implemented. It may therefore be asked how the occupation can have been a factor working for the Literary Renaissance. Arab authors in particular have no doubts on that point. Salahiddine Boustany says:[9] 'Had it not been for the press of Bonaparte, Muhammad Ali would have been unable to start Boulaq Press, and consequently *Al Waqae' el-Mesriah*, as early as 1828.' The Renaissance is inconceivable without a press, and at least the French showed Egyptians its potential. Further, by opening Egyptians' eyes to French culture and European sciences, in however modest a way, the occupation made them aware of a civilization different from the Islamic civilization they shared with their Turkish masters, and made them receptive to foreign ideas. It was a first step towards ending that literary inbreeding which had long stultified Arab literary development.

The psychological effect of the invasion is obvious in the writings of those who witnessed it. Jabarti[10] says of the year when it occurred that it was 'the beginning of a period of great battles, terrible events, disastrous occurrences, ghastly calamities, ever-increasing misfortunes, successive trials and tribulations, persecutions, disorders, upsetting of the order of things, continual terrors, revolutions, administrative disorders, catastrophes and general devastation. In a word, it was the beginning of a whole series of misfortunes. "Thy Lord would not destroy cities unjustly." '[11]

So unexpected and radical an upheaval must have made the existing cultural scene seem irrelevant.

Yet clearly the mere presence of Europeans for a few years could not of itself lead to a literary revival. There had also to be a stimulus from within. This was encouraged by Muḥammad ʿAlī Pasha, Governor of Egypt for the Ottoman Sultan from 1805 to 1848, and his successors. Muhammad Ali was an Albanian soldier in the Turkish army, which came to Egypt to dislodge the French. But he stayed on as Governor. As will be seen later, his educational policy of sending 'missions' to Europe assisted Western influence on the literature.

One factor which made Cairo a suitable centre for the Renaissance was the presence of the Azhar. This was an institute of Islamic education founded by the Fatimids. Though preoccupied with the religious sciences, it was still the leading repository of knowledge of Arabic language and literature. And whatever stimulus might come from the West, any new Arabic literature would still need a solid foundation in the past. From this point of view, Cairo had a distinct advantage over Beirut as a centre of revival.

Muhammad Ali made Egypt autonomous *de facto*, though still *de jure* subject to Istanboul. He organized a strong army and navy, and made the country of his adoption a power to be reckoned with, by conquests and victories.[12] His senior officers were non-Arabs, like himself. But military successes must have given Egyptians a sense of pride they had not known for centuries. Muhammad Ali established military schools, and a medical school. Foreign officers were employed as instructors at first: but Egyptians, mostly of mameluke stock, were sent to Europe – to France, Italy and Britain – to study. The necessity to adapt Arabic to modern science led to the combing of old Arabic literature for technical terms: it also led to a somewhat less ready acceptance of high-flown literary style. Of the 44 officers who went to the west – mostly to France – the most distinguished was Rifāʿat al-Ṭahṭāwī. But they also included four princes of the blood, one of whom, Ismāʿīl, Muhammad Ali's grandson, was later to rule Egypt.

Tahtawi (1801–73)[13] was born in Upper Egypt of a family famed for religious learning which had come down in the world. From 1817 he studied at the Azhar, where he subsequently taught for a while. In 1824 he was appointed *imām* (chaplain) to an army battalion. Then he went as imam on a large educational mission to Paris. He remained there from 1826 to 1831, and learned enough French to be able to translate from it accurately. Among orientalists he met was the celebrated Sylvestre de Sacy.[14] He read a good deal of French literature, including the works of Racine, Voltaire, Montesquieu and Rousseau. He studied all sorts of arts and sciences, ranging from ancient history and Greek philosophy to geography and arithmetic. On his return to Cairo, he taught French in the Medical School, then worked in a military academy, translating mathematical and military works into Arabic. In 1836 he was appointed director of a new School of Languages, whose *raison d'être* was the preparation of students for the professional schools and the training of officials and translators. A Bureau of Translation was attached to the school. Tahtawi, apart from planning and supervising the translations of others, himself translated a number of works on geography, history, logic, engineering and metallurgy. Indeed, text-books – whether original or translated – form the greater part of his 27 published works.

He also became a schools inspector, and editor of the official newspaper, *al-Waqā'iʿ al-Miṣriyya*. The latter was founded by Muhammad Ali in 1828, in succession to the monthly *Journal al-Khedive* founded a year earlier. It appeared irregularly, first in Turkish, then in both Turkish and Arabic, finally in Arabic only. Tahtawi helped to change it from a dry official organ into a modern newspaper, publishing articles, discussions and translations, as well as official news. Thus Tahtawi is considered a pioneer not only of the Nahda in general, and of translation in particular, but also of Arabic journalism.[15]

Muhammad Ali died in 1848, and was succeeded by his grandson ʿAbbās I. The School of Languages was one of several casualties in the interests of economy. For some reason or other, Tahtawi incurred the displeasure of the new ruler: he was exiled to Khartoum,[16] on the pretext of opening a school there. He bemoaned his fate in verse as his old colleagues died off one by one, and also busied himself translating Fénélon's *Télémaque*, thus becoming a pioneer of the novel in Arabic.

He returned to favour under Saʿīd Pasha (1854–63) and Ismail (1863–79), and became director of a military college. In 1863, he became head of the Translation Department of the Ministry of Education. He was member of several government commissions, and supervised the translation of the *Code Napoléon*. He encouraged the government press at Būlāq, on the outskirts of Cairo, founded in 1822, to publish Arabic literary classics. He called for girls' education, and a year before his death, founded the first Egyptian girls' school.

Tahtawi was not a great writer, but rather a man of ideas and influence. Those who wish to understand his basic attitudes should read what Albert Hourani has to say about his book on Egyptian society *Manāhij al-albāb al-Miṣriyya fī mabāhij al-ādāb al-ʿaṣriyya* (The Paths of Egyptian Hearts in the Joys of Contemporary Arts) published in 1869.[17] While believing that Islam was as relevant to his generation as to those of the past, he implied that Islamic law should be reinterpreted. He believed in girls' education, but did not suggest abolition of the veil and the *harīm* (harem). He believed in modern education, and was convinced that revealed religion could not be hostile to scientific progress. He was a nationalist, aware of some sort of Arab solidarity, yet Egyptian rather than Arab in his loyalties.

He had seen French democracy in action. But he held the conventional Islamic view of the absolute ruler, who must, however, rule in accordance with the divine law.

We have, then, in him almost the text-book figure of the enlightened Arab of the early Nahda, taking the best from the West, to revive 'Arabism'. Thoroughly balanced and practical, he did not make the mistake of accepting all the West had to offer. Thus, his picture of Paris, from which an extract is given later in this book,[18] does not show excessive adulation. His Arabic style, while not merely functional or conversational, is straightforward. Despite his knowledge of French, with its clarity, Tahtawi's prose is Arabic in feeling as well as language.

His contribution to literature was greater than the list of his works might suggest. Gibb[18a] says that his students translated more than 2,000 books into Arabic. 'The effect on Arabic literature was not immediate, but bore fruit in the second wave of Occidentalism under Khedive Ismail.'

To return to Muhammad Ali: though not a great patron of literature himself,[19] he played a decisive, if indirect, part in getting the Literary Renaissance under way. He introduced modern (as opposed to traditional Islamic) education, albeit vocational rather than liberal; he encouraged translation from European languages; he sent officials to study in Europe; he established the Arabic press at Bulaq; he founded the first Arabic newspaper. But above all he created a new environment, following the French occupation. He gave Egyptians something to write about, to feel strongly about, to feel proud of, instead of the sterile themes of the Age of Depression. A sense of purpose replaced the old torpor and sloth.

Among other writers of the time was Shaikh[20] Ḥasan al-ʿAṭṭār (1766–1835), who taught French officers Arabic during the Napoleonic occupation. He travelled widely in the Arab world and subsequently became Principal of the Azhar. Tahtawi was one of his pupils. He continued writing prose and verse on a variety of subjects until his death. From the thirteenth to the sixteenth centuries, Arabic literature had many such prolific polygraphs; he was possibly the last of the species. He wrote on religion, grammar, rhetoric and logic. He was especially interested in astronomy, and an expert maker of sundials and star-dials. He seems to have been able to write poetry in simple style, though not very inspired or inspiring. The following is an extract from one of his elegies:[21]

> He strove to achieve God's blessing all his life,
> Nor would you see him in any other strife.
> The world with rosy picture could not lure him
> From learning, lest it prove spurious and allure him.
> He spent his days in study and holiness,
> Watchful – no evening passed him profitless.

Apart from Tahtawi, perhaps Attar's most distinguished pupil, though now, like his master, long forgotten, was Shaikh Ḥasan Quwaidir (1789–1846), who wrote grammatical and philological works. He also wrote a commentary on the grammar which Attar had written in verse. It may surprise the uninitiated to learn of grammatical treatises in verse. They were well known in Persian, Urdu and Sanskrit as well as Arabic. The most famous in Arabic is the *Alfiyya* of Ibn Mālik (1203–71), which has been mentioned in the previous chapter. This work is still studied in Arab universities as part of degree courses in Arabic, usually in conjunction with one of several famous commentaries on it, the best known being that by Ibn ʿAqīl.

Another contemporary, Sayyid ʿAlī al-Darwīsh[22] (d. 1853), wrote poetry and maqamat on the Hariri model, besides editing al-Mutanabbi's poetry.

No account of literary activity in Egypt during this period would be complete without paying tribute to Jabarti.[23] His large-scale history of Egypt from 1708 to his own days is also a set of collected biographies, since from time to time he includes a section called *Among those who died during these years*.[24] In dealing with authors, he quotes from their works, sometimes at length. The whole work is of absorbing interest. This type of combined historio-biographical work had medieval precedents, such as the History of Baghdad by al- Khaṭīb al-Baghdādī, and that of Damascus by Ibn ʿAsākir. Heyworth-Dunne[25] mentions two previous Egyptian historians, ʿAbdallāh al-Shubrāwī and ʿAbdallāh al-Sharqāwī, but neither appears to have produced anything of note.

From what has been said, it will be seen that in the first half of the nineteenth century – roughly to the end of the reign of Muhammad Ali – the Renaissance had only just begun in Egypt. It has often been pointed out that Muhammad Ali's revival of culture was largely confined to science. The books published were scientific, translations or travel; and text-books predominated rather than creative literature. On the other hand, in Syria and the Lebanon, the Renaissance was literary from the start. Here there was no Muhammad Ali trying to build a modern state, but only Turkish governors and officials – and, in the Lebanon, local protected princes or *amīrs*.

Syria and the Lebanon

In Syria and the Lebanon the Renaissance was, at first, largely due to the activities of non-Muslims. In the Lebanon there was the Maronite Church. The Roman Catholic Church also had its hierarchy in the Levant. In addition, Armenian Christians were interested in Arabic language and literature. Church leaders supported libraries containing valuable Arabic books: and, while it cannot be denied that their main interest was in the Arabic scriptures and the extensive Christian-Arabic literature, secular literature also was read, and copies of medieval classics were preserved. A genuine love for the classical language and its literature was widespread among Christians. In the mid-nineteenth century this led to the production of creative works of great brilliance – though both the language and themes were sometimes antiquarian.

Contact with Rome was maintained by visits, and Beirut was both a European gateway to the Arab world and an Arab gateway to Europe. In the eighteenth century the European merchant communities in the Levant dwindled, and local Christians and Jews of Aleppo and the coast towns took over from them. Hourani speaks[26] of a 'trading network . . . reaching to Alexandria, Livorno, Trieste and Marseilles'.

During the seventeenth and eighteenth centuries a few Arabic local histories were written. The Maronite Patriarch Istifānūs (1603–1704) wrote a *History of the times*, largely dealing with the Maronite Church.

A brief reference is necessary to the political situation in the Lebanon, which helped to make it a centre of the Nahda.[26a] The Lebanon became part of the Ottoman Empire in 1516. Under the provincial administration (*vilayet*), the northern part came under the

Governor of (Syrian) Tripoli: the central and southern parts were under the Governor of Damascus. Provincial boundaries were changed from time to time. The Lebanon was a mosaic of feudal fiefs – Druze and Maronite. The Ottomans left the amīrs of these fiefs autonomous, so long as taxes were collected. Mutual interest drew the different sects together – Shiʿite (Druze) and Sunnite Muslims; Catholic and Maronite; and Armenian, Syrian and Greek Orthodox Christians. Until the late seventeenth century the Druze Maʿanī amirs achieved a sort of hegemony over the whole area. They died out and were replaced by the (Sunnite) Shihābī family, who had intermarried with them. From time to time the princes of these dynasties would attempt to turn their autonomy into independence. They would deal with the Sultan in Istanboul direct, instead of through the local governor: they might even aim at real independence as sovereign states. Fakhr al-Dīn II (1585–1635), succeeding at the age of 12, asserted his supremacy over the other princes by agreement, marriage and military action. He bribed Ottoman officials, built up an efficient private army with the aid of foreign mercenaries, encouraged European trade with the Lebanon, and, as his trump card, formed an offensive-defensive alliance with the Grand Duke of Tuscany, chiefly to obtain naval help. He went too far, and was finally strangled on the Sultan's orders.

No other such amir appeared again until the Shihabi Bashīr II (ruled 1789–1840). He built a fine palace, Bait al-Dīn, near his mountain capital. He played a subtle power game with rival amirs, Turkish Governors, the Sultan, Napoleon Bonaparte, and European states. His religious views were subordinate to political needs, being himself Maronite, Druze or Sunnite as circumstances demanded. He had to submit to the Egyptian occupation of Ibrahim, Muhammad Ali's son, but found the consequences too difficult for him. The Egyptian policy of religious toleration, which incidentally encouraged the entry of American Protestants, set Druze against Maronite. A British naval force, aided by Austrian and Turkish vessels and a Turkish landing force, ended Egyptian rule, and deprived Bashir of his authority. He went into exile in Malta, and later Istanboul.

Bashir II encouraged education and outside contacts. He was also an important patron of writers, giving them administrative posts, as well as accepting their poetical eulogies. Thus of writers to be mentioned later, Nikūlā al-Turk, Buṭrus Karāma, Amīn al-Jundī, and Nāṣīf al-Yāzijī, all worked for him at one time or other.

A Maronite priest, Jabrīl ibn Farḥāt, known as Germanos (1670–1732), is generally regarded as the forerunner of the literary revival in Syria and the Lebanon.[27] Born in Aleppo, he studied Syriac and Arabic, and, later, Italian. He visited Rome, and became a monk at 23. In 1725 he was made Bishop of Aleppo, taking the name of Germanos. His Arabic Grammar (*Baḥth al-maṭālib*) was several times printed between 1836 and 1891, and was a much-used text-book. He left a diwan of poetry on 'sacred and edifying subjects'. The historians suggest that there gathered around him a literary circle which became famous in an era of general decay and decadence.[28] Wiet goes even further,[29] and supposes that this nucleus may have continued and survived to welcome the revival of interest in the Arab past.

One of the most interesting eighteenth-century Lebanese authors was Aḥmad al-Barbīr (1747–1811)[30] – a Muslim, indeed a qadi and expert on Islamic jurisprudence (*fiqh*). Born in Damietta, Egypt, of Lebanese stock, he made a thorough study of the religious sciences, and of Arabic language – the latter under the lexicographer Murtada al-Zabidi to whom reference has been made.[31] He then went to Beirut and Damascus to continue his studies. He was a judge in the Lebanon for several years. In 1788 he retired, and lived in Damascus until his death. He wrote maqamat, of which only one has been published, and poetry both secular and religious. His religious poetry is in simple language, as the following example shows:

Oh trader, ever full of hope to earn
  Profit, and by the fear of loss dismayed,
The worship of your God, at ev'ry turn,
  Is better than this world's delights – and trade.

The love for the maqama was an important factor in the Renaissance in Syria and the Lebanon no less than in Egypt.

Two further Lebanese Christian writers deserve mention among the precursors of the Nahda – and both lived on into the nineteenth century. They are Nikūlā (Nicholas) Yūsuf al-Turk (1763–1828) and Buṭrus Ibrāhīm Karāma (1774–1861). The former was born in the Lebanon of a Greek father who had come there to escape Turkish tyranny. Until Muhammad Ali made Egypt autonomous, the Lebanon was considered the only haven of liberty in the Ottoman Empire. Al-Turk visited Egypt from 1789 to 1793, and on his return became court poet, secretary and companion to the amir Bashir II. To this prince he addressed many eulogistic poems, which were published in 1949 in a *diwan* (collection) of over 900 pages.[32] These poems, antique in flavour, were hardly likely to contribute to the regeneration of Arabic poetry. His maqamat have long been forgotten – because of the same antique flavour, no doubt, and also because superior examples were produced by al-Yaziji and others. His essays in contemporary history are another matter, being free from artificiality. The most important is his long account of the Napoleonic occupation of Egypt.[33] He also wrote a History of Napoleon from the death of Louis XVI until Napoleon's death. Cheikho also attributes to him two anonymous historical works. The first is a history of Napoleon's Austrian Campaign of 1805 culminating in the Battle of Austerlitz: this was published in Paris in 1807. The second is a history of the Shihabi family.

Buṭrus Ibrahim Karāma followed al-Turk as poet and confidant to Bashir II, whose adviser on foreign affairs he became, because of his intelligence and command of Turkish. He later rose to be chief minister, and accompanied his master on his travels, even to Egypt. When Bashir fell foul of Istanboul, Karama accompanied him in 1840 to exile in Malta, and later, Istanboul. His merits were soon recognized there, and he was appointed chief interpreter at the Sultan's Palace. Karama had written panegyric poetry to local notables during his youth in Aleppo: he had continued this activity while working for Bashir in the Lebanon. In Istanboul he found plenty of ministers and notables ready to receive and reward his efforts. He died in Istanboul a few years after Bashir.

His literary remains are almost entirely poetry, most of which was published in a diwan in Beirut in 1898. Cheikho[34] considers him to have played an important role in the improvement of Arabic literature in the first half of the nineteenth century, while Dagher[35] refers to his great innovations in poetical spirit, style and shape. It must be admitted that it is difficult to see him in that light today. True, in his panegyrics, he did not confine himself to his employer, and his language is apter and more natural than some contemporaries. The fact remains that he was a eulogist by his literary (as opposed to his work-a-day) vocation, and does not give the impression of writing from the heart with the sincerity of later poets. His collection of muwashshahat has been published. Cheikho refers to his unpublished works – *musājalāt* (contentions, vying) exchanged with literary men of Istanboul presumably in verse, and other verse written in Istanboul. Not all the latter is eulogistic. There is an entertaining discussion between a clay-pipe and a nargileh (hubble-bubble) – which are personified as women, and a neat account of the virtues of the chase. A congratulatory poem to Bashir on the birth of a grandson in 1835 is at least simple, if conventional. But when we read an ode in which he makes the word *al-k͟hālu* with its various meanings[36] the rich rhyme; and of the admiration, even emulation, this *tour de force* evinced among the professionals, we realize that with his poetry we are not so far removed from the Age of Depression.

His poem on the virtues of the chase[37] is here freely translated:

The chase has the advantage of eight benefits:
  With ten more which confirm its popularity:
Relief from trouble, and an end to idleness,
  Eloquence, self expression, superiority,
Good thoughts, agreeableness and activity,
  Awareness and observation and energy,
Bodily exercise, and then good vision,
  Sweetness of temper, with knightly bravery,
Self preservation and a means of livelihood,
  Knowledge of tracks and paths, and then, authority.

Such categorization of virtues and vices, advantages and disadvantages, was an Arabic rhetorical stock-in-trade. The sermons of the early caliphs contain many examples, as does medieval poetry. They are sometimes described as *ḥikma* (pl. *ḥikam* – wise saws – gnomic utterances). Karama had doubtless read the neat – if bawdy – couplet of the 25th maqama of Hariri called the *K's of Winter*,[38] here translated as:

The C's of Winter

Winter is with us, and of its needs are mine
  Seven, should the falling rain make us our work foreswear:
A *c*ottage, a *c*ase of *c*ash, a *c*ooker, a *c*up of wine
  After a *c*utlet, a soft *c*——, and *c*lothes to wear.

It must be confessed that Hariri is superior to Karama, though less suitable for children.

The following is Karama's poem in honour of the birth of Bashir's grandson:

O Lord of justice and goodness, may your honour increase,
As God has increased his blessing and support.
You are blessed with a grandson, whose nativity
Is glory to the stars, from Heaven brought.
He shall ever remain blessed in his leadership,
The darling of his age, so long as he shall live:
And your days shall be ever smiling, and your life
Luxurious, with many good years still to give.

The poem on the rivalry between the nargileh (hubble-bubble) and (clay-)pipe (*ghaliyūn – māsūra*) was published by Cheikho in Vol. II of *al-Mashriq*.[39] Only part of it is given here.

Oh! for Ṭahmāz's* mistress, fair divine,
Refined by nature, yet a foreigner.
Though long I loved her, she would constantly
Reject me as she might a foreigner.
Then in the Pipe I would indulge myself,
Wandering in mind, without an evil thought.
I wandered with her, and she came with me;
Whither I went, she came as my escort.
And when I lacked tobacco, and my pouch
Gave of its all, leaving an empty bowl,
She moaned her hunger, craving to be filled,
Distant, beyond my powers to cajole.
I told her of my love, but she was wrath.
I chided her – she proudly turned from me.
Then came the other, sprightly as a fawn,
When my tobacco shortage she could see.
And she abused me, saying proudly: I
Am the young girl, bedecked, for pleasure sent;

* A corruption of Tahmasp, the name of two Persian kings. The nargileh here referred to is a Persian type of pipe.

I speak the language of all poetry,
  My voice is like the reed-pipe's soft lament.
My head is gilded, brim-full of the gold
  Of the tobacco, and the fire aglow.
My stem is slender, moist, as if it were
  Fashioned with dew which liberal hands bestow.
I am the eloquent Nargileh, I
  The boon companion of the clever man.
In Tahmaz's home I grew, as if I were
  A beautiful young maiden of Iran.
I do not moan for food, as this co-wife,
  Dumb and depressed, this very morn made moan.
Weeping for lack of sustenance she went,
  Skulking in corners, crying all alone.

A Muslim poet who differed from the general run was Shaikh Amīn al-Jundī,[40] whose life spanned the second half of the eighteenth and the first half of the nineteenth centuries. He was born of a distinguished Homs family, and died there. He also spent some time in Damascus. Though he wrote qasidas in the classical tradition, he was best known for his popular verse of the muwashshah type, much of it intended to be sung, and extremely popular. He was the Syrian 'pop' idol of his era. Collections of his verse have been published several times since 1870. The following song, entitled *The Quarrel between the Daffodil and the Rose* is worth quoting. It is a mukhammas.[41] Unfortunately the translation cannot reproduce the lightness of the original, which is in short half-verses of eight syllables each – very short by Arabic standards – ending in closed syllables, the final vowel being artificially omitted where necessary, as in the colloquial. The translation is rather free:

  The daffodil importuned me, and she said:
  'To fight the rose the flow'rs must all be led'.
  I said: 'Such words as these are full of dread:
  Turn back, oh daffodil, be not misled.
To you the prize cannot belong!

  'Return to ways of justice with all speed,
  And to my words of wise advice give heed.

Renew your homage to the rose, obedi-
-ently, and with th'assembled flowers plead
Your purposes misplaced and wrong.

'How ill you knew the rose in times gone by!
"Such beauty is a slight!" you us'd to cry.
But with your betters, why not tolerance try?
And do not, as a foe, the rose defy!
To her great priv'leges belong.

'You were secure, till you became too proud,
Lurking in meadows, hidd'n among the crowd.
But if to stir up trouble you have vow'd,
Though with a cutting sword you are endow'd,
The rose's thorn is sharp and strong!'

To the first half of the nineteenth century four important Lebanese writers belong – though three of them produced their best works during the third quarter of the century. All four were Christians, though one – Shidyaq – turned Muslim. Nāṣīf al-Yāzijī (1800–71) and Aḥmad Fāris al-S̲h̲idyāq (1805–87) are famed for books antique in form and style: but by their brilliant manipulation of the Arabic language, they pointed the way to future possibilities. Mārūn Naqqās̲h̲ (1817–55) was not a great writer, but he pioneered Arabic drama. Buṭrus al-Bustānī (1819–83) was the literary patriarch who, though not primarily a creative writer himself, perhaps did more for the Nahda than any other single man in the nineteenth century. With these writers we encounter a phenomenon peculiar, though not unique, to Lebanese literature: literary families each producing several writers of above-average attainment. At least half a dozen of the Yazijis achieved distinction, a dozen of the Bustanis and several Naqqash's, by the beginning of the present century. Other common family names involved are K̲h̲ūrī and Daḥdaḥ.

Nasif al-Yaziji was born in Kufr S̲h̲īmā on the coast near Beirut. The family originated in the Byzantine community of Homs, some of them coming to the Lebanon at the end of the seventeenth century. One of them worked as a writer or clerk in Turkish government offices, and took the name of *yāzijī* – Turkish for 'writer', and this became a recognized *laqab* (patronymic) passed on from father to son. This branch of the family was converted to Roman Catholicism towards the end of the eighteenth century, along with several other Lebanese families. Our author's father was some sort of doctor. Cheikho[42] says merely that he studied medicine under a monk, did well, and practised as a doctor.[43] Others describe him as a doctor of the Avicenna school.[44] All agree that he had literary tastes, which he passed on to his son, and even wrote some poetry. Nasif was educated in language and literature, and also medicine, by his father, and then by a Maronite monk. He continued his studies by reading avidly in monastery libraries, and displayed scholarly leanings and a love for Arabic. For example, he is said to have learned by heart not only the whole of the poetry of Mutanabbi and various other poets, but also the Koran – an unusual accomplishment for a Christian. He was quite precocious, and composed a good deal of *zajal* (popular poetry) in his youth, most of it as yet unpublished, the very idea of which seems to conflict with the image of his maturity. He worked for a time as clerk to the Maronite Patriarch. But he became known to poets at the court of Bashir II, such as al-Turk and Karama, and they in their turn recommended him to the prince. So in 1827, Bashir made him his confidential secretary, and he remained in his service till the prince's exile in 1840. Then Yaziji moved down to Beirut, to reside there for the rest of his life, dividing his time between writing and teaching.

He contacted American missionaries, and assisted them as proofreader with their publications, especially with the Arabic translation of the Bible. He taught successively in Butrus al-Bustani's National School, the 'Patriarchal School' founded by the Maronites, and lastly the Syrian English College, which later became the American University in Beirut (the 'AUB'). By the end of his life he had become famous. European orientalists corresponded with him; and he was a most distinguished member of the Syrian Academy, a learned body founded in Damascus in 1848, presumably on the model of the Académie Française. During the last two years of his life he suffered from paralysis of the right side. He bore this disability with fortitude, until his eldest son died suddenly in the prime of manhood. Not long afterwards he died of a stroke.

Yaziji's principal works come under three categories, apart from miscellaneous writings on such subjects as medicine, logic, and history: linguistic text-books, poetry, and art-prose.

He was noted for his works on grammar and rhetoric, which ran through several editions. His abridged grammar, *Faṣl al- Khiṭāb*, first published in Malta in 1836, is still studied in at least one Western university's[45] Arabic Department. In the East, al-Jārim's primers on grammar and rhetoric have now superseded Yaziji's. Unfortunately, the latter could not equal the abridged guides to the language by medieval writers. The *Mufaṣṣal* of al-Zamakhsharī[46] makes *Fasl al-Khitab* sound distinctly fuddy-duddy, and the present writer must admit that he finds Zamakhshari more clearly written. The fact remains that Yaziji's work filled a need, and must have seemed a welcome substitute for medieval masterpieces.

Some writers[47] see his poetry as an exercise in imitation of classical poetry in general and Mutanabbi in particular. (He did, in fact, write a commentary on the latter's diwan.[48]) It can be said of Yaziji in general that he appears to have set out to emulate the classical writers in those fields which interested him – on the basis, no doubt, that 'anything they could do I could do almost as well'. It is an over-simplification to suggest that his poetry is merely pseudo-Mutanabbi. But his main trouble was his devotion to learning. He did not show any other burning enthusiasm which could direct his poetry to new themes of current interest in the Arab world. A virtuoso in the language, he could only use his virtuosity on old themes with time-honoured ideas and imagery. One of his early zajals is reproduced by Munīr Alyās Wahība.[49] If typical, it does not suggest that Yaziji would have been any more original had he continued in this genre. For zajal, no less than classical poetry, had its clichés and conventional ideas, comparable to 'June and the moon' in Anglo-American popular music of the 1920's and 1930's. In the poem reproduced by Wahiba, the loved one is several times called the moon or full moon:

> You, dandy, are the moon and the full-moon.

The loved one is cold, and says:

> My eyes ever entice,
> Setting the heart on fire.
> I am as white as ice,
> But ice can set hearts on fire.

Yaziji's period as a court poet to Bashir II accustomed him to the old themes of eulogy and elegy, and he found himself displaying his virtuosity in the old qasida. Thus he sometimes begins by halting at old encampments or familiar evocative places. Imru' al-Qais had begun his muʿallaqa *qifā nabki* (stay, let us weep . . .), thus keeping commentators busy for centuries by putting the verb apparently in the dual. We are told that hundreds of other pre-Islamic poems began with these two words: how many began with *qifā* followed by some other word – or in the singular or plural (*qif*/*qifū*) heaven alone knows. Yaziji swelled the number. In an ode celebrating Saʿid's accession in Egypt in 1854[49a] he begins with the dual:

Stop twixt the craggy path and the oratory
On a mountain o'erhanging precipitously,
And if you espy a fire, then you should say
'Who may he be – the leader for whom they pray?'

An ode to the Ottoman Sultan ʿAdb al-ʿAzīz written in 1865–6 begins with the singular *qif*:[49b]

Stop by al-Maṭāya on D͟hū Salam's high plains;
Say 'salām' to him who in the pitched tents remains.

This ode is preceded by a couplet formed from the initial letters of the 81 verses of the ode, each line of which gives 4 chronograms of the year of composition. Each hemistich of the ode proper also gives a chronogram of that year. In fact, Yaziji had a passion for manipulating verses and hemistiches in various ways, including chronograms – a sure sign of his antique tastes. This, by the way, was not typical of the classical poetry at its best; it came in towards the end of the Middle Ages. It became popular in Turkish, Persian and Urdu poetry.

An elegy on Mārūn Naqqās͟h in 1855 shows Yaziji's limitations and strength.[49c] Surely here was a moving occasion, the death of a friend, a promising poet, in his prime. Here was a chance to praise Naqqash's pioneer work in Arabic drama. But all the poet can think of is the cruelty of fate and conventional ideas. The earlier verses on the transitory nature of this world and the impartiality of death to rich and poor alike are reminiscent of Abu al-ʿAtahiyya:

Which of you was a prince, who were the braves,
Oh ashes? Who the followers and slaves?

Who was the hero who defended lands?
Whose were the noble speeches and commands?

Who was the man who filled the world with fear,
Round whom the army gathered yester-year?

And think you, he who num'rous heroes beat,
Could he the ravages of worms defeat?

So the poem continues from one familiar phrase to another: the slave and freeman are equal in death . . . pen and sword alike lie hid . . . our happiness died with the death of the dear one . . . he had piety, purity, forbearance, determination, kindness and nobility. (What a catalogue of perfections!) . . . Oh Naqqash, rhymes, inkwells, pens, pages, thoughts and cares all mourn you . . . we hoped for mature fruits from you, but fate forestalled us, rushing upon you . . .

Part of his virtuosity lay in his command of balagha devices, of which his poems are full. This can be seen in comparatively simple passages like the following verse written on Queen Victoria's accession:[50]

1. Today a brilliant girl sat on the throne;
   Before her sat famed forebears on that throne:
2. Scion of roots established long ago,
   Her joy 'tis that on branches fruits should grow.
3. Her pure heart wears the ring of piety,
   Her hand the peerless ring of majesty.
4. God's worship and the world meet at her court,
   Like the collyrium to brown eyelids brought.

Thus in verse 1 occur *qāmat* and *qāma* (ascended, here translated as sat), forming jinas. In verse 4 there is imperfect jinas between *dīn* (religion, here translated worship) and *dunyā*, the world; also between *kuḥlu* (collyrium) and *kaḥalu* (the brown of the eyelid). In verse 3, the word 'ring' comes twice, forming perfect jinas. In verse 2 there is the contrast between 'roots' and 'branches'.

The following final example is taken from Yaziji's elegy on his son Ḥabīb.[51] This was his last poem, written only a month before his death. The personal involvement is obvious in the original. But, as befits a classicist, the emotion is restrained, and the phraseology is conventional, if unforced:

Habib is dead, so melt, my mourning heart,
For sorrow, and let tears my eyes engulf.

I trained him for the time when we must part:
It came by night, and snatched him like a wolf.

Oh mother! Bear your sorrow patiently,
For patience best can heal a heart forlorn.

Do not take off your black: be constantly
In mourning, as befits the one we mourn.

This is the slender bough struck down by fate,
Whose arrow killed him ere his prime was through.

He had few equals – he was separate:
I say that without shame, for it is true.

I stood beside his grave, my eyes afloat,
Wat'ring the moistened soil in which he lay.

And on its sides, these words of him I wrote,
And oh! the pain of what I had to say!

'Oh tomb! You hold my honour and my love,
Because Habib lies in you, whom I love!'

The third category of Yaziji's work is his art prose – rhymed prose, of which his collection of sixty maqamat known as *Majmaʿ al-Bahrain*[52] is the chief example. It is said that the encouragement of the French Consul in Beirut helped to stimulate him to write these maqamat, which were composed over several years, and published in 1855. Others think that the edition of Hariri's Maqamat by the great French orientalist de Sacy, about which he wrote a critical letter, may have helped to encourage Yaziji's interest in the maqama form. In any case, it was obvious that sajʿ suited his taste, and he was brilliantly successful in it. He proved that the language was as expressive as it had ever been.

Muslims must have been shamed to have to learn this lesson from a Christian. Some saw in it an illustration of the old Arabic saying, that 'the Arabic language could not be Christianised', since even when a Christian of genius wrote it, the language was the same as ever, unpolluted. None the less, Yaziji was antiquarian here, no less than in his poetry, and he displayed the same preoccupation with language rather than thought. In his short introduction, in medieval rhymed prose,[53] he describes himself as a Christian of Jebel Lebanon, who has poached on the preserves of Arab literary men by composing stories under the title of maqamat, because of their resemblance to that form.[54] He has called his hero Maimūn ibn K͟huzām, and the narrator, Suhail ibn ʿAbbād – both imaginary, and of no specific country. His aim is to provide profit and pleasure, with the strange and unusual, morals and maxims, stories coming trippingly from the tongue to charm the reader, stylistic beauties, and rare constructions and words found only after diligent search. None the less, he realizes that it may all be rather redundant, in view of the fame of former masters of the form (Hariri and Hamadhani). Yet he is trespassing in this field, with the ambition of producing the first light of the new day,[55] though it might be as worthless bric-à-brac. So he begs his readers to pardon him, as forbearance from blaming others is a mark of nobility.

'The first light of the new day!' Surely Yaziji was, consciously or unconsciously, summing up his whole position in the Arab Literary Renaissance. But, to return to the *Majmaʿ al-Bahrain*: anyone who has read Hariri will be familiar with the pattern of Yaziji's work. The latter's 'stories' are, on the whole, shorter, which is no bad thing. They contain some of his neatest poetry too. (The title of the work means 'the conjunction of the two seas'– a metaphorical reference to prose and poetry.) The hero Maimun is a man out to make money, a trickster, with something of the nature of Till Eulenspiegel. Unlike Till, he does not come to a sticky end, and repents in the final maqama. The Narrator meets him in a succession of improbable situations, usually surrounded by an attentive crowd, which he controls, to quote from the metaphor in the 10th maqama,[56] 'leading the restive horse with fine discourse' (*qāda l-shamūsa bi l-shumūs*). It is a succession of situations, rather than incidents, which we find. The maqama is not a short story, though it may include anecdote.

Like Hariri and Hamadhani before him, Yaziji gives many of his maqamat place-names as titles – Yemenite, Baghdadi, Upper Egyptian, Allepan, and so on. But they are particular neither to these places in any but a casual sense, nor to the time at which the author wrote. The overall theme is the hero's virtuosity (and therefore the author's too), sometimes in recondite knowledge, but fundamentally in the manipulation of language, in rhymed prose or verse. Rare words abound; hence there are abundant footnotes to explain them, as many as fifty for a single maqama. Every device of rhetoric is displayed; while the verse reaches a limit of ingenuity which makes mere chronograms seem like lower-form schoolboy exercises.

The first meeting between the Narrator and the Hero takes place in the desert. By a wily stratagem, the Hero effects the capture of some brigands, securing their booty for himself. He leaves the Narrator with nothing but his camel and a cheeky note thanking the Narrator for saving him from the brigands, and saying that, out of the kindness of his heart, he has left him his camel. The Narrator is so intrigued by Maimun's behaviour that he is sorry to lose him. Subsequently he sees him in many roles – as a bogus doctor; lecturing learnedly on grammar in Kufa, and on rhetoric in Basra, especially on jinas. He discusses the rare form of jinas in which two words have the same root letters in reverse order. He then quotes a 14-verse poem he had written when young, in which the second hemistich of every verse mirrors the first (*i.e.* the successive letters are the same, but in reverse order). Later, we find him showing his mettle as an astronomer-astrologer among desert Arabs, listing the signs of the zodiac in verse, telling fortunes, then going away loaded with money.

The final scene is at the Aqṣā mosque in Jerusalem. The congregation are reduced to tears as Maimun preaches a sermon. As they leave afterwards, they each offer him money to pray for them. But he says that he has renounced this world's goods, and will not accept a penny. He turns to the Narrator, and together they spend the night in prayer. At dawn, Maimun recites a religious poem. The Narrator stays with him a month, 'gathering flowers from his garden, and watching the bright stars on the horizon, until the destined day of departure, and his "crow cawed". He gave me a parting embrace, returning my farewell, and said: "We shall meet again in Paradise." And that was the last I saw of him.'

There follows an *envoi*, apologetic like the Introduction, but it is an anti-climax. For in that last maqama, Yaziji achieved greatness. We have gradually come to love the rogue Maimun, when the author's craving for linguistic legerdemain has allowed us. His passing – or rather fading out – is, in its way, comparable to the passing of Don Quixote or Falstaff. It is in imitation of Hariri, but much superior to Hariri's final maqama because of its tautness and pathos.

Some readers may feel that this work is a masterpiece manqué. If only Yaziji had simplified the language, they may say, he would have given us an outstanding work of genius. But in so doing, he would have destroyed the very essence of the work. And whatever its standing, it undeniably demonstrated the possibilities in a complete mastery of the Arabic language which might inspire others – though none was likely to match its antique splendour.

In view of what has been said of rhymed prose, it seems essential to illustrate it by an actual translation, however difficult that might be. So we follow with an English version of the first half of Yaziji's final maqama:

'Said Suhail ibn Abbas: I met Abu Laila (Maimun) in the Aqsa mosque in Jerusalem, in a crowd so great that none could number them. The people encompassed him like the two tribes of Ajrab and surrounded him like the two (Meccan) mountains of Akhshab. He preached to them with warnings dire, threatening the punishment of the Fire, and the requital the Next World will require. Their tears poured forth in spate, so that their vitals were ready to disintegrate. Then when Maimun saw me he fixed me with his eyes, and seemed ready to rise.

'So I pounced on him like a hawk, and dropped on him like a rock. He greeted me with friendliness, and proceeded with his pious address, saying: "Thanks be to God, who made his sanctuary as a refuge for his creatures and a house for his worshippers. It is he who created and corrected, decreed and directed; bringing man tears and laughter, death and life hereafter. I stand before you in place of a religious lawyer, and it is a bad exchange for you. For long did I succumb to the sins that hurt, and defile my flesh with dirt. I committed acts of criminality, and indulged in immorality. I went to the limit in slanderous attack on my fellow men, making white seem black. That has ever been my endeavour, from the days of my youthful agility, to the days of my shuffling senility. I am not fit to preach to anyone, nor that my sermon should reach anyone. For in my teaching, it is to myself I should be preaching. Now here I am, having returned from where I went, determined to repent. So I pray God to treat me with forbearance, and not to pass heavy sentence: to show me partiality, not strict impartiality." Then he began to speak heatedly, his voice alternating repeatedly between wailing and sobbing: till he brought tears to his congregation, whether nomads or of settled habitation. The people began to quieten his quaking and quivering, their preacher from his distress delivering, until his emotion was abated, and his tears dissipated.'

Despite the large number of maqamat written since Hariri's time, including many in the nineteenth century, only Yaziji's have been considered worthy to be mentioned in the same breath. Indeed, modern literary historians and university courses alike bracket Yaziji with Hamadhani and Hariri in the trio of outstanding maqama writers. University students in Syria and the Lebanon are expected to be able to compare the merits of *Majma' al-Bahrain* with those of the other two collections. At the same time, Yaziji is generally considered inferior to the other two, primarily because of his greater preoccupation with language and lack of variety.

Yaziji has been considered at some length because, however backward-looking and imitative, he was the first genius – or near-genius – of the Nahda. It is difficult to make a just assessment of his literary merits. It may be suspected that few Western orientalists have read his maqamat; while Arabs, at first adulatory, have begun to place him in the museum of literary history. The time will come when nobody save a few specialists will read him. Gabrieli[57] sees him, beyond his imitation of Mutanabbi, bringing purity and elegance to a barbarized culture. Wiet[58] speaks of him as purifying the language of neologisms borrowed from foreign languages. It would be interesting to know which neologisms were current in the Lebanon when Yaziji wrote. Wiet calls him also an *attardé volontaire*, retiring into the past, and refusing every contact with European literature. He is presumably referring here to his ignorance of foreign languages. Abd-el-Jalil[59] describes him as being interested, above all, in language. 'His poems imitate those of the great classical poets, especially al-Mutanabbi. He wrote maqamat which testify to his real mastery of the Arabic language.'

As far as poetry was concerned, Arabic needed a Shelley or a Byron: but first and foremost it needed a Wordsworth, who could say worthwhile things in simple language, classically acceptable, but near to the colloquial, and relevant to the contemporary scene. In prose, too, the need was similar. Yaziji was no Wordsworth. But he proved the language's flexibility, and showed that it was not divided by religion

– though anyone familiar with the poetry of Ibn al-Rūmī (ninth century) needed no reminding of this.

Aḥmad Fāris al-Shidyāq as a writer has many points of resemblance with Yaziji. He, too, was greatly interested in language, wrote linguistic books, and was addicted to rhymed prose and rhetoric. On the other hand, unlike Yaziji, he did visit foreign countries, including Malta, Britain, France and Tunis, and he knew foreign languages. He was also a pioneer of Arab journalism. Above all, he was a 'romantic' – not to say eccentric – figure, as his religious connexions illustrate. A Christian and Bible translator, he turned Muslim, and, perhaps, died a Christian. There is something picaresque about him – the name Faris even means 'knight'. It is perhaps uncharitable to say that his love of language was kept in check by an even greater love, that of Shidyaq. The subject of much of his writing is himself. But the subordinate themes are not antique, like Yaziji's, but modern. Again, he had a great sense of humour – humour often piercing and satirical. One may dislike the man and his work, but one could never ignore them. His very name Shidyaq is so un-Arabic as to be easily remembered: it is from the Greek, and means a sub-deacon or chorister.

He was born in a village north of Beirut, the fifth of five sons of a Maronite employed as a taxation officer.[60] All five had literary talent. The father unfortunately became involved in Druze politics, supporting a party attempting to oust a local amir. When the attempt failed, the leaders fled to Damascus. Ahmad Faris's father was one of them, and he died in Damascus in 1820. Ahmad Faris received his secondary education in the Maronite school of ʿAin Waraqa, learning Syriac, French and English. On leaving school he found difficulty in settling down – a problem which plagued him all his life. He tells us in his autobiographical *al-Sāq ʿalā al-Sāq* of several efforts to work as a copyist, interspersed with excursions into commerce. At one stage he bought a donkey and became a pedlar. He tried tutoring the children of the rich in their homes, but became involved in more than teaching with the daughter of an amir. His life was changed by the death of his brother Asʿad (1798–1830). The latter had been employed by American missionaries, teaching them Arabic, and had become a Protestant. He was imprisoned by the Maronite Patriarch, and died, according to Hourani,[61] 'done to death'. Shidyaq apparently contacted the Americans in Beirut, and, like his brother, became a

Protestant. He went to Egypt, to work, it is believed, as a translator for the Americans. While there, he contacted distinguished scholars, and improved his grasp of Arabic language and literature. He entered journalism, writing for *al-Waqa'i' al-Misriyya*, succeeding Tahtawi as editor. He married a Syrian woman, and two sons were born.

In 1834 the American missionaries sent him to Malta. He spent 14 years working in their press there, supervising Arabic publications, editing, translating, writing.[62] He wrote his book referred to in Chapter 1, *al-Wasita fi Ma'rifa Mal(i)ta*. In 1848 he was invited to England by the British and Foreign Bible Society, to assist Samuel Lee in translating the Bible into Arabic. He spent some time in Cambridge, Oxford and London, as well as Royston, where the lack of amusements drove him to extreme boredom. Though not entirely happy in England, he took out British nationality.

He next went to Paris, where he ingratiated himself with the visiting Bey of Tunis by writing in his honour a eulogistic ode known as his *lāmiyya*, because the rhyme was the letter *lām* (= l), on the lines of the 'Lamiyya' of Ka'b ibn Zubair, a contemporary of the Prophet Muhammad. The grateful Bey invited him to Tunis, where he made him editor of his official newspaper, *al-Rā'id al-Tūnisī*, the first newspaper to appear in Tunis. Shidyaq also became a Muslim. In 1857 the Sultan invited him to Istanboul, to work as translator and proof-reader in the state press. In 1862 he founded his weekly newspaper, *al-Jawā'ib*. It was the first Arabic newspaper to have a wide circulation throughout the Arab world. At first the Turkish State Press published it: then Shidyaq founded his own printing house, Maṭba' al-Jawā'ib, technically the most up-to-date in the Ottoman Empire. Not only did it publish this newspaper, but many literary works from the numerous manuscripts in Istanboul libraries. Contemporary works, too, were published from all parts of the Islamic world. For example, several compilations by Ṣiddīq Ḥasan K͟hān (1832–90), Nawab Consort of Bhopal in India, were printed there. Shidyaq was generously subsidized by the Sultan – doubtless for his support for the idea of the Sultan, as Caliph, being the head of the Islamic world. He was likewise subsidized by the Bey of Tunis and the Khedive of Egypt. With the tendency towards independence in Ottoman peripheral provinces, such joint patronage could easily lead to strains. In 1879 *al-Jawa'ib* was banned for six months, because the editor refused to publish an article attacking the Khedive Isma'il. Later, in 1882, Shidyaq was to support the Sultan during the reign of Khedive Taufiq by publishing the Turkish declaration condemning 'Arabi Pasha's revolt, which resulted in the British shelling of Alexandria.

In 1883 the paper was moved to Cairo under Shidyaq's son Salīm, and it ceased to exist in its previous form under its old name. Shidyaq remained in Istanboul, no longer popular with the authorities. He died in 1887, and in accordance with his wish his remains were taken to the Lebanon. He was buried at the junction of the roads to 'Alay and al-Ḥadath. He had been at school at the latter village. Some say that he became a Christian once again on his deathbed. According to one story, he sent for a priest of the Armenian Uniate (Catholic) Church, and made his confession of faith and repentance. He was mourned throughout the Islamic world and among those in the West with a knowledge of and an interest in the Middle East.

His poetry is of little account. He could deal with up-to-date themes. He wrote a poem on the Franco-Prussian War of 1870, for instance. The expression falls far short of Yaziji's despite similar indulgence in rhetoric. The wise saws and homespun philosophizings are there, but he lacked the sincerity to rise above the trite. His poem on the Franco-Prussian War, for example, begins:[63]

Both wealth and humankind afflicted France –
Woe to her, after glory and advance.

(Uṣībat Farānsā bi l-rijāli wa bi l-māli,
Fa-waiḥahā min ba'da 'izzin wa iqbāli.)

In each hemistich we have the twin words beloved in balagha – *rijāl* (men) – *māl* (wealth): *'izz* (glory) -*iqbāl* (advance). There is also an internal rhyme between *rijāl* and *māl* in the first hemistich. But despite the paradox of the idea – men and wealth should make for victory, yet France was humbled – the expression is pedestrian. So the poem continues till its equally pedestrian *hikma* (wise saw) in the last verse; apparently taken from the psalms:

He whom the Lord Almighty does not guide
Has naught to turn malicious talk aside.

His prose works may be divided into philological and (broadly) autobiographical, the latter taking in a good deal of travel talk. His philological works ranged from grammars of French and English for Arabs, to complex works on Arabic lexicography. These weighty works are important in the history of Arabic dictionary-writing.[64] Shidyaq was a pioneer of modern Arabic lexicography. He had a knowledge of the language both wide and deep, and some sound ideas mixed with eccentric ones. Thus his *Jāsūs ʿAlā al-Qāmūs*[65] (Spy on the Qamus) is a criticism of the best-known medieval dictionary; in it he called for dictionaries arranged in the modern alphabetical order, instead of the rhyme-order, based on final root letters, which had held sway for centuries. When he came to compile a dictionary himself, however, *Sirr al-Layāl*,[66] he introduced a novel alphabetical order of his own, beginning with the gutturals, to support the theory of the onomatopoeic origin of language. It is also based on a theory of the bilateral origin of Arabic roots, treating any two letters anagrammatically, thus b–d with d–b, r–d with d–r and so on. Here there is a strange mixture of medieval Arab and modern European ideas. The anagrammatical idea came from al-Khalīl ibn Aḥmad (eighth century); the notion of basic meanings inherent in letter combinations in different permutations goes back at least to Ibn Jinnī (ninth century); while the theory of the onomatopoeic origin of human speech is a creation of nineteenth-century European philologists.

Shidyaq's lexicographical interests are clear also in his autobiographical travel works, in his love for rare words, and for groups of two or three near-synonyms. His books, like Yaziji's, require copious footnotes and a readiness in the reader to use a dictionary as he reads. No wonder Arab admiration for him is largely theoretical!

His autobiographical travel books are the one on Malta already mentioned;[67] his *Kashf al-Mukhabba' ʿan Funūn Urūbā*[68] (A Revelation of the secrets of the arts of Europe); and, above all his brilliant, discursive and ill-shaped autobiography, *al-Sāq ʿalā al-Sāq fīmā huwa al-Fāriyāq* (Leg over leg concerning what Fariyaq is).[69] It is doubtful whether the first two are ever read today, and neither they nor his lexicographical works would have perpetuated his name. Practically all Shidyaq did was purposeful in its planning, disorganized in its execution. Hourani,[70] in referring to his descriptions of England and France, describes him as less perceptive than Tahtawi. This is true: but he is more personal and individual and gives us many interesting sidelights.

Al-Saq ʿala al-Saq is very much a travel book. While written in the third person, the hero Fariyaq – a rhyme with Shidyaq – is the author himself. At one stage,[71] when describing how, living outside Cambridge, he complained to an English fellow student about the absence of his wife, who had not yet joined him in England, he says:

> His friend said to him after some days: 'You let it out yesterday that you missed your wife, when you should have said, your children.' 'What is wrong with a man mentioning his wife, as he mentions his son?' said Fariyaq: 'Were it not for the wife, there would be no children. Indeed, were it not for the wife, there would be nothing in this world, not even religion.' His friend said: 'Steady on! That's not a nice thing to say.'

What an interesting sidelight on Victorian attitudes we have here!

Kashf al-Mukhabba' is a hotch-potch of personal reminiscences, economic statistics, potted history, original poetry, and quotations from classical Arabic poets. Yaziji had a facility for acquiring knowledge of every sort: one feels that he would have done well in a quiz programme. Jacques Berque[71a] calls him 'Unstable, rebel, pedant, at times licentious, ironical and sarcastic, but with admirable curiosity' – a just comment. In the *Kashf*, before describing Edinburgh and Glasgow, he gives the historical background of the Union, and refers to Schiller's play *Mary Stuart*, which he describes as 'eloquent'.[72] He refers to British superstition, such as the bad luck ascribed to walking under a ladder; and Christmas customs, such as the use of mistletoe in house decoration, which he says goes back to the Druids.[73] One of the things that made him unhappy in Cambridge was that[74] 'the townspeople, despite the many colleges and seats of learning, are hostile to the stranger, especially if he dresses differently from them. They used to make fun of Fariyaq's red hat, with the result that he often stayed in his room, only emerging at night.'

Many such touches evincing his observation of all that was curious could be quoted. But something ought to be said about his prose style. In reality it is difficult to specify a style, since he is as inconsistent in this as in everything else. We have mentioned his addiction to rhymed prose – but only the *Saq* is consistent in this respect. In other books, there seems to be a tug-of-war between the ornate and the simple. This may be explained, as Huart[75] explains it, by saying that he had 'the inner lining of a journalist', combined with 'ingenuity of mind quite devoid of any critical power'. He reminds the present author of those prolific composers who never revised the first drafts of their compositions. In style, he had the same tensions as he had in general. He was torn between the simplicity apt to journalism and the maqama style demanded in fine literature. In *al-Wasita* and the *Kashf* simplicity seems to win: while in the *Saq*, the ornate dominates. There are even maqamas included,[76] and in one instance a maqama is followed by a chapter twice as long to explain the difficult vocabulary in it. Elsewhere in the *Saq*, where saj' does not predominate, there are lists of rare words and, always, verbosity.

The work is an autobiography, beginning with the hero's birth, but, on the flimsiest of pretexts, digressions occur. A maqama is written because the hero cannot sleep one night, having saj' on his mind. There is a section on *tawriya* (ambilogy) and one on dreams. At the end are several poems by the author, including two side by side, one praising, the other attacking Paris. The eulogy becomes an attack by merely changing a few odd words.

The whole work is relieved by humour, without which reading it would be a laborious operation. Here is one of the best parts, in which, having summoned his wife to join him in England, Fariyaq tells her how to behave with the English.[77] (He calls her al-Fariyaqa – feminine of al-Fariyaq):

> Fariyaqa began to learn the language of the people. One day her husband said to her: 'I want to give you a bit of advice on how to learn this lovely language.' She said: 'All right, tell me: for, my goodness, this is the first bit of your advice to reach my ear!' He said: 'Yes, and from my heart as well!' She said: 'Have your say!' He said: 'Beginners learning a foreign language usually start by learning things belonging to the human body, such as veins, muscles and so on . . .' She said: 'I understand what you mean! But this is hardly advice!' He said: 'I said "Praise the Lord who made humanity from heifers"[78]. What I mean to tell you is that whoever wants to learn this language should first begin with the names of Him who is in the heavens above, not with those on the earth below. For these people make a show of piety and righteousness.'
>
> She said: 'Good heavens! If this sort of talk were advice, wisdom would be very cheap! In God's name, how old are you? How does

this question relate to what has been said before?' She went on to say: 'What season are we in?' I said: 'Autumn'. She said: 'Then the season is to blame.' I said: 'Are you suggesting that I have gone out of my autumnal mind?'[78a] She said: 'If not, then what are these words you have pontificated?' I said: 'Please yourself! I have warned the unwarnable and chided the unchidable.'

Later, Fariyaq advises his wife to show restraint in social dealings with the English. She replies:

'How can I stand any dealings with them? Like all orientals, I am open in my nature and my speech, unable to hide my feelings from those around me.'

I said: 'Beware of that. You must always be restrained and careful, and not laugh loudly. Here people laugh with restraint and control, holding back, and keeping it in check.[79] . . . Otherwise you be a tittering female!'

She said: 'How can you tell me to be a tyrannical[80] female? You are forever complaining of women in general, even the most fair-minded ones!'

'What I said was "tittering", that is, excessive laughter. There is a saying: "The professional girl[81] tittered".'

She interrupted, saying: 'Enough! Enough! Do not say anything about the professional girl – or the girl next door.'[82]

I said: 'Yes! The English eat quietly, slowly, restrainedly, unhurriedly, sparsely, in morsels.[79] And they drink savouring, sipping, slowly[79]. . . So whenever you speak, you must avert your eyes and lower your voice. You must show extreme dignity, staidness, restraint, caution, grace, shrewdness, elegance, and refinement.'

She said: 'Woe to you! Woe to you! Have you, perchance, brought me to this country to mould me, and make me into a different woman?'

Mārūn Naqqāsh (or al-Naqqāsh with the definite article, *al*)[83] merits mention because he it was who introduced the dramatic form to Arabic literature. He was a friend of Yaziji, and wrote some poetry, including an ode to Lamartine. He was essentially a dilettante. Born in Sidon in 1817, he went with his father to Beirut in 1825, and received his education largely at the hands of Christian missionaries. (He himself, as his name suggests, was a Maronite Christian.) He learned Turkish, Italian and French, and studied accountancy. He was employed as a customs officer, then became a merchant. In this capacity he visited Egypt, then Italy. He was a good singer himself, and was taken with Italian opera. On his return to Beirut, he produced, in 1848, his first play – indeed, the first play in Arabic – *al-Bakhīl* (The Mean Man), a rough adaptation of Molière's *L'avare*. Like his other two dramas, it was a musical comedy in verse. In the printed version,[84] the tunes are indicated by name, not in musical notation, in an appendix. This first Arabic theatrical production was performed in the author's house, and was attended by local notables and foreign consuls. In 1850, his second play was produced. It was called *Abū al-Ḥasan al-Mughaffal* (Abu al-Hasan the Fool), based on an amusing story in the 'Thousand and One Nights'. The Turkish governor was in the audience. Finally, he wrote a third play, *al-Ḥasūd* (The Envious Man), based on Molière's *Le Misanthrope*. For its production he built a special theatre, the first in the Arab world. After his early death in 1855, it was turned into a church under the terms of his will.

These plays are a mixture of prose and verse, the verse being sung to familiar tunes, on the lines of *The Beggar's Opera*. The language is mostly classical, but awkwardly written and twisted for metrical and rhyme purposes. There are crude puns and plays on words. At the same time there is some use of the colloquial. The plays are comedies – at times, farces, and the humour is vulgar, even indecent occasionally by Arab standards. For example, Abu al-Hasan's wife calls him 'you fart of Satan'. The new form caught on steadily, if not startlingly, especially in schools in Syria and the Lebanon.

In Damascus in 1866, Aḥmad Abū Khalīl al-Qabbānī started a theatre in his grandfather's house. He had no apparent connexion with Marun al-Naqqash, though we know that the latter's brother Nicola and others tried their hands at the art. Midhat Pasha, the Governor of Syria, encouraged the author out of municipal funds. But the conservatives complained to the Sultan ʿAbd al-Ḥamīd, who ordered the closing of theatres. In the Lebanon, a customs clerk, Adīb Ishāq made a free translation of Racine's *Andromaque* for the French consul, and it was successfully produced for charity. He then collaborated with Salīm Naqqash, Marun's nephew, adapting Corneille's *Horace*. Salim took a theatrical troupe to Cairo, and the Opera

House opened its doors for him. In 1884 Qabbani himself came to Egypt, expelled from Syria. For some time afterwards the development of Arabic drama was chiefly concentrated in Egypt.

Ultimately, poetical heroic drama was to become an important literary genre. In poetical drama a rather bizarre role was played by another Lebanese, who though now forgotten was once considered a major figure in the Nahda – Ibrāhīm al-Aḥdab (1826–91). His maqamas were mentioned in Chapter 1. He wrote about twenty plays, some original, some adapted from European plays. His original plays were chiefly on Islamic historical themes. Among them, however, is one – *al-Tuḥfa al-Rāshidiyya fi ʿulūm al-ʿArabiyya.* Frankly didactic, to teach Arabic – it might be called a 'teaching aid' – its chief scene depicts an inspector visiting a school. The handsomeness of the boys is discussed in a manner bordering on the homosexual. This play is best forgotten, save that it seems to have been the first play written wholly in Arabic classical verse.

Buṭrus al-Busṭānī has been described already as the 'patriarch' of the Nahda. He was also the founder of a distinguished family of scholars and writers still active in the Lebanon. He cannot be considered a major creative writer. But he was a major influence in his two contributions to literature; firstly the revival of a knowledge and love of the Arabic language; secondly in his belief that the Arab world could revive only through knowledge of the thought and the discoveries of modern Europe.[85]

Born in 1819 in the Lebanese village of al-Dabbiyya, he was educated, like Shidyaq, in the Maronite Seminary at ʿAin Waraqa. He learned Syriac, Latin and Italian as well as Arabic. In 1840 he went to Beirut and worked in the British and American consulates, which offered good posts to Lebanese with a command of languages. Then he taught for two years in the American Mission School at Abey, a few miles inland from Beirut, under Cornelius Van Dyck, and became a Protestant. He assisted the Americans in translating the Bible into Arabic, and to this end himself learned Hebrew and Greek.

In 1860 there was a Syrian rebellion against the Turks. The Lebanon was torn by conflict between Druzes and Maronites, many of whom were massacred. The Great Powers gave France a mandate to intervene, and a French expeditionary force restored law and order. The French left in 1861, and the Turks gave the Lebanon a special constitution guaranteeing its autonomy. The internecine strife led Bustani to found a two-page newspaper in 1860, preaching tolerance and co-operation between the communities. It was called *Nafīr Sūriyya*,[86] and lasted for only thirteen issues. Three years later he established his National School in Beirut, and henceforward devoted himself chiefly to journalism and writing. In 1870 he founded his bi-monthly *al-Janān*, with the motto 'Patriotism derives from faith'. Politics, science, literature and history were among its subjects, and many writers found it a means of becoming known, particularly in the field of fiction. His son Salīm co-operated in the venture. In the same year, father and son started the weekly (later bi-weekly) *al-Janna*. In 1871 they founded *al-Junaina*, devoted to politics and trade – the first Arabic trade journal.

In 1870 Bustani's large 2-volume dictionary *Muhīṭ al-Muhīṭ* appeared. It was the first Arabic dictionary of the modern type – modern in its arrangement. He also began publication of his great encyclopaedia, *Dā'ira al-Mā'arif*, the 'Encyclopaedia Britannica' of the Arab world. It included articles on Western subjects, including the sciences. Six volumes were ready during his lifetime; two more were edited by Salim. The remaining volumes were completed by three other Bustanis – Najīb, Amīn Buṭrus, and Sulaimān.[87]

There is no need to list his other scholarly works and his text-books. But mention may be made of his 435-page *Life of Napoleon* (1868), his Arabic version of *Robinson Crusoe*, his *Women's Education* (two lectures published in 1849), and a comparison between Arab and European social customs of 1869. Bustani was not a great writer. But he set a salutary example of strong yet simple style, unencumbered by rhetorical devices. If he uses rhyme, it is only in occasional phrases, similar to alliterative phrases like 'first and foremost' in English. Thus, in writing of women's education, he says:

'Again, how great are the advantages to children which are derived from women's education. For the woman bestows on her children such knowledge, culture and civilization as she herself has. The child receives his first impressions from his mother, because she is the first thing to impinge on his senses and perceptions. So from looking into the light of her face, he obtains *his first thoughts* . . .'

In ordinary Arabic, 'his first thoughts' would be *afkāruhu al-ūlā*:

Bustani says *abkār afkārihi* (literally, the first fruits or virgins of his thoughts), doubtless for the rhyme and imperfect jinas between *abkār* and *afkār*.

Bustani broadened the outlook and knowledge of his contemporaries. In championing girls' education, he was ahead of his time, and it was right that this call should come from the Lebanon, with its large Christian population. His scientific outlook contrasted with that of his literary fellows such as Shidyaq. Dozens – nay hundreds – of Arabic writers have benefited, whether directly or indirectly, from this Arab Protestant 'Patriarch of Learning'. Yet practically everything he wrote, compiled, or edited is now obsolete or obsolescent.[88]

So far, little has been said about Syria. The fact is that Beirut, rather than Damascus, was the centre of the literary revival in this region. Syria did not come into her own until late in the century. Nevertheless, brief reference will here be made to two Syrian writers who became prominent in the third quarter of the century. Both came from Aleppo (*Halab*); both were Christians. Rizqallāh Ḥassūn (1825–80) belonged to an Armenian family of Persian origin.[89] Though born in Aleppo, he was educated in a Uniate Armenian monastery in the Lebanon. Besides Arabic and Armenian, he mastered Turkish and French, and later studied Russian and English. He became a merchant, and moved to Istanboul. There he was appointed overseer of tobacco customs and excise. In 1854, he founded there *Mirā'a al-Aḥwāl* (the Mirror of Circumstances), the first Arabic paper to appear in Istanboul. He was later imprisoned, falling foul of the powers that be. On his release he fled to Russia – Turkey's arch enemy. He proceeded to Paris, then London. Here he re-established his paper, which contained much bitter criticism of Turkish oppression.

In 1879 he started in London an Arabic bi-monthly, *Ḥall al-Mas'alatain al-Sharqiyya wa l-Misriyya* (The Solution of the Eastern and Egyptian Questions), whose title explains its purposes. He was befriended by orientalists, and helped G. P. Badger to compile his English–Arabic Dictionary.[90] He died in London in 1880.

His importance cannot be gauged from a list of his published works alone. His *Ash'ar al-Shi'r*, published by the Americans in Beirut, consists of metrical translations of some of the more poetical books of the Old Testament, such as the Song of Solomon. His short life of Jesus (*al-Sīra al-Sayyidiyya*) appeared from the same press in the same year

– 1870. His *Kitāb al-Nafathāt*, published in London in 1861, consists of translations in verse from the fables of the Russian writer Krylov, together with some original poetry and chronograms.

Hassun was a strong champion of liberty and reform in the Ottoman Empire – hence his long stay in Britain. He was possibly more important as a journalist than as a writer of originality.[91] He also edited some classical texts such as al-Akhṭal, Dhū al-Rumma, Jarīr and Farazdaq.[92] As an original writer he was pre-eminently a poet. It is interesting to note that Arab critics ascribe technical weakness in his poetry to his anxiety to write naturally. The following gives some idea of his translations from Krylov:[93]

In burning heat the cloud pass'd o'er
Dry sand, parched by the blazing sun.
Fast to the sea he scurried on,
Upon the waves his rain to pour.

When to the hills he boasted all
His rain and dew, the hills replied:
Your wasted kindness we deride!
Should not the rain on brown earth fall?

A brilliant man who died young was Francis Fatḥullah Marrāsh (1836–73).[94] He developed an early taste for language and science. His eyesight was weak, which perhaps explains his choice of a medical career. He studied medicine privately under a British doctor, then went to Paris to specialize in legal medicine. He had made a previous visit to that city with his father to have his eyes treated. He wrote an account of his journey which was published. After qualifying in Paris, he returned home to devote himself to writing, despite his failing sight and increasing general debility. He only survived his return to Syria by a few years.

Marrash wrote on natural history, politics and current social problems. One work, *Ghāba al-Ḥaqq* (The Forest of Truth)[95] deals with human rights in story form. He had leanings to the abstruse and rare vocabulary. A book on current problems, *Mashhad al-Aḥwāl*,[96] is in maqama form. His best-known poems, which are sometimes technically imperfect, are cluttered with rare words. One of his odes, though actually dealing with recent events, takes the form of an allegorical dream. Such allegorical poetry is rare in Arabic, though common in Persian, Turkish and Urdu. Among his best poems are his zuhdiyyāt – poems of asceticism, of which the following is typical:[97]

> God's creatures all are surely of one kind,
> From mighty monarchs to the humble hind.
>
> Each has his sorrows, each has his delights,
> His share of feastings and of fun'ral rites.
>
> How many a prince reclines with troubled mind,
> While the bound prisoner leaves his cares behind.
>
> In faults, the smallest like the greatest is –
> Each has his own peculiar qualities.
>
> The bee's hive is more marvellous a thing
> Than pillar'd palaces of any king.

Other Countries – Iraq

There is little more to be said of Arabic literature in the first sixty or so years of the nineteenth century, having dealt with Egypt, Syria and the Lebanon. The probable reason is that no other Arab country had the requisite combination of political autonomy (backed by Western powers), relative freedom of expression, easy contacts with the West, and men of outstanding literary talent.

Not that there was a complete lack of literary activity elsewhere. For example, in Arabia itself, in the Hedjaz, Aḥmad Zainī Daḥlān (1826–86), Shafiʿite Mufti of Mecca, wrote not only religious works, but an Islamic History (*Ta'rīkh al-Duwal al-Islāmiyya*). But a perusal of the Cairo edition of 1887 does not suggest that it is any more than a text-book of the traditional pattern.

In one other country, however, Iraq – there were definite signs of the Nahda, despite circumstances only spasmodically favourable. One or two writers achieved lasting fame. But this was largely local, and certainly did not match that of figures like Tahtawi and Yaziji.[98]

Iraq had been disputed between the Ottoman Turks and the Persians, but in 1534 it was taken over by the Turks. The Persians temporarily regained it in 1638. But Sultan Murad II himself led an army to reconquer it. It remained part of the Ottoman Empire till 1918. As elsewhere, lands and wealth were largely concentrated in the hands of mamelukes. Corruption was rife, as officials from governors downwards effectively purchased their posts and had not only to recoup what they had paid and defray their living expenses, but had also to put by enough to buy their next – and better – post. Despite the police and army, the governor was rarely able to control the more rural or remote areas, and brigandage was common. Sometimes the governor would take advantage of the distance from Istanboul, and the apathy of some pleasure-loving sultan, to assert his autonomy. Such autonomy, especially when coupled with reforming zeal and a generally more enlightened attitude to the Arab population, encouraged literary activity. Unfortunately, however, attempts at autonomy did not last long, as, in contrast to the situation in Egypt and the Lebanon, European intervention was difficult geographically.

The first great reforming governor was Sulaimān Pasha, in power from 1808 to 1816. He eased taxation and forbade bribery. He restored order, built mosques and schools, and patronized learning. His reforms displeased the Sultan, who sent a new governor to Mosul. From there he led an attack on Baghdad and sent Sulaiman's head to the Sultan. Later, Dā'ūd Pasha made an even bolder bid for independence and reform. Sold into slavery as a boy, he was educated in the household of Sulaiman Pasha, and became Katkhuda (palace chamberlain) to Sulaiman's son Saʿīd, when the latter became governor. Saʿid was a poor governor, and Da'ud fled to Kirkuk, whence he wrote to the Sultan, persuading him to make him governor. He marched on Baghdad, executed Saʿid, and restored public order. To achieve independence from Istanboul, he recruited a large army, employing a French officer to train it. He set up cloth and arms factories. At the same time he ruled justly, and founded schools and colleges (*maʿhad*, pl. *maʿāhid*),[99] on a hitherto unknown scale, providing teachers' salaries out of government funds. He was a scholar himself, with a knowledge of Turkish, Persian and Arabic. During his term of office several distinguished writers emerged. The Sultan feared him, and finally plucked up courage to send an army against him under Riẓā ʿAlī. Da'ud might possibly have held his own and emerged as a sort of Iraqi Muhammad ʿAli, but there was a plague, followed by a flooding of the Tigris which put many Baghdad houses under water; so the people became disenchanted with Da'ud. Riza entered Baghdad, and sent Da'ud as an honoured captive to Istanboul.

The third famous reforming governor was Midḥat Pasha, governor from 1869 to 1873, who later became Grand Vizier in Istanboul and published his new liberal constitution for the whole Turkish Empire in 1876. He had already served as a brilliant governor of Bulgaria and had also served in Syria, where he had patronized the playright Marun al-Naqqash. Not only was he a reformer, but he encouraged economic and industrial development. He founded the first Iraqi newspaper, the official Turkish-Arabic *al-Zaura'*. Two leading poets successively edited the Arabic section. The Sultan ordered Midhat to put a stop to his reform projects, so he resigned, and had even to sell his personal effects to pay his fare back to Istanboul. The new governor abolished his reforms, and enlightened rule did not return until the country shook off the shackles of Turkish rule, with British aid, in the Second World War.

During the Age of Depression Iraqi literature, like that elsewhere in the Arab world, was more concerned with form and conventional language than with thought – with the exception of religious literature, including ascetic poetry. Other poetry followed medieval models, while prose was rich, rhymed, and rhetorical, the maqama being highly esteemed. Typical writers of this era were Shaikh ʿAbdallāh al-Suwaidī (1692–1761)[100] and his son Abū al-Maḥāmid ibn ʿAbdallāh al-Suwaidī (1740–95).[101] The former was a leading writer of his time and the founder of a literary family. Other sons, Muḥammad Saʿīd al-Fatḥ Ibrāhīm and ʿAbd al-Raḥmān, were well-known writers. Abdallāh's works typify the tastes of the time. They include commentaries on classical poetries and grammars, a book on metaphor, a set of maqamat – a veritable show-case of rhetoric –, travel books, and poems. The poems are chiefly eulogy or on historical events. Abu al-Mahamid wrote similar types of books, including a maqama. The latter was published in Istanboul in 1913 in a collection of little-known maqamat by ten authors.[102] It describes an enchanted garden, which the careworn author visits. He meets a beautiful maiden and makes love to her. The rich imagery of the description is very reminiscent of Persian love-allegories. This is hardly surprising. Colloquial Iraqi Arabic contains many Persian and mixed Arabic-Persian expressions, and Persian influence can be seen in Iraqi literature. To this day, Iraq is a strongly literary land, and small groups of Baghdadis meet together in informal clubs called *nadwa* to discuss literature and recite their own poems. Often such poems are ghazals describing beautiful women. Felicitous and frank phrases describing the female form are applauded with a disarming absence of priggish prudery. Abu al-Mahamid's maqama, for those who are able to read it without constant resort to the dictionary, is a *fin de siècle* masterpiece, embodying in its imagery the varied colours of the garden, the music of the nightingale, lute, dulcimer, fife and flute, and the perfumes of art and nature.

Iraqi authors of the first seventy years of the nineteenth century made little impact in other Arab countries. On the whole, poetry predominated. While much of it was related to the contemporary scene in theme, in form and style it was normally antique, though some poets were willing to use imported words like 'telegraph', instead of classical euphemisms. Here we shall mention five poets and one writer of art-prose. The latter was the great polygraph pioneer, Shihāb al-Dīn Maḥmūd al-Ālūsī (1802–54). The poets are Ṣāliḥ al-Tamīmī (d. 1845); ʿAbd al-Bāqī al-ʿUmarī (1790–1862); ʿAbd al-Ghaffār al-Akhras (1805–75); Ḥaidar al-Ḥillī (1831–87) and Ibrāhīm al-Ṭabṭabā'ī (1832–1901). Poets tended to eulogize the Sultan or the local governor in similar language, irrespective of whether he were good or bad. On the other hand, they also wrote about freedom and bemoaned the prevalent corruption. The Sultan was an Islamic figurehead, and poets did not – perhaps dared not – call for Iraqi independence. Religious poetry was sometimes Sufi. The ʿAbbasid themes of love and wine were common also.

Alusi[103] belonged to a celebrated literary family of Baghdad. He was educated first by his father, then in Damascus, Beirut, and Istanboul. He specialized in religious and linguistic sciences. He taught in various schools when Da'ud was governor: and Riza Pasha, though at first hostile to him, later supported him. He wrote little poetry save such as came incidentally in his prose works. The latter include three books describing his travels. His religious books include Koranic commentary, and his linguistic commentaries on classical grammars and poetry. His best-known work was his collection of five maqamat (*Maqāmāt al-Ālūsī*), published in Kerbala in 1856. It is a brilliant example of the old art. In theme these maqamat contain autobiographical material, comment on social life, and guidance on right conduct. They cannot hold a candle to Yaziji's. Yet Alusi played a major part in the Nahda in Iraq, and was influential as a teacher. He was much respected by later writers.

Tamimi was educated at Najaf, the Shiʿite centre noted for its learning. Da'ud Pasha adopted him as his court poet, and gave him official employment as a court secretary. He was similarly favoured by Riza Pasha, and wrote eulogies to both these governors. Dagher speaks of much of his work having been lost, and of a diwan surviving in manuscript.[104] But al-ʿAzzāwī mentions an edition, full of errors, published in Najaf in 1948.[105] The present writer has not seen this poetry, but it seems to be ornate, having earned the poet the nickname of the 'lesser Abu Tammam'.

Al-ʿUmari[106] – sometimes called al-Fārūqī – spent his life as an official of the Turkish government in Iraq. A loyal subject of the Sultan, he was appointed lieutenant-governor of Baghdad after the failure of Da'ud Pasha's bid for independence. He wrote a good deal of religious poetry in praise of the Prophet and the members of his house (*Ahl al-bait*). As might be expected, he eulogized the Sultan. Though in many ways a conventional poet, he had great powers of description, as in the following verses inspired by moonlight over the Tigris:[107]

> As if the full-moon's rays
> Upon the Tigris rising,
> Amidst the rippling waves,
> And as the swell is rising
> Were mercury afloat
> On golden pieces rising.

He was not too much of a purist to use a modern word. Thus in his chronogram of Sultan ʿAbd al-ʿAzīz's accession in 1862, he says:[108]

> The telegraph has its virtues, for it brought
> Good news concerning you in language short.

He refers to the telegraph elsewhere:[109]

> The telegraph line has its propositions,
> Brought from afar by science profound;
> Mouthless, it mouths its propositions,
> With sharpened tongue of steely sound.

'The Nineteenth-century Abu Nuwas' is a nickname given to Akhras.[110] Like Abu Nuwas, he wrote of 'wine, women and boys'. He was at times bitter-tongued, at times foul-mouthed. He learned grammar – but not his tastes – from Alusi. He joined the court of Da'ud, who kindly sent him to India to have his stammer cured. The doctor treating him told him: 'I can treat your tongue with a remedy which will either make you fluent, or send you to join your ancestors.' The poet did not like this, and replied: 'I will not sell the whole of me for the part of me', and returned home uncured. His poetry was collected after his death and published by the Jawa'ib Press in Istanboul. Apart from the love and wine verse, it contains much eulogy of sultans, governors, friends and contemporaries such as ʿUmari. Of Sultan Maḥmūd II he said after some victory or other:[111]

Support has to the Faith accrued –
Thanks be to God – under Mahmud.

Though born in the second quarter of the century, Tabtaba'i[112] survived into the present century. Thus chronologically he hardly fits into the present chapter. But he was active in the middle of the century; and with his penchant for rare words, rich imagery and elegant language, he belongs – in spirit – to the first half of the century. He was extremely prolific and fluent: it was said that he could improvise a hundred-verse ode at one go. Unparalleled in ghazal, he wrote also eulogy and elegy. ʿIzz al-Din quotes his eulogy of a not very good governor:[113]

To you Iraq the flag of fealty has unfurled,
Its freedom or bondage depends on your liking.
Striking proverbs were said about you in the world,
While you, with your sharpened sword, men's
necks were striking.

The jinas of the second verse is reflected in the translation 'striking'. A triple internal rhyme in the first verse is matched by the alliteration in 'f'. Some freedom in translation has been unavoidable.

Ḥaidar al-Ḥillī[114], so named from his birthplace, al-Ḥilla, was considered so outstanding a poet as to be called, by some contemporaries, the 'poet of Iraq'. He also wrote sajʿ. His diwan, first published in Bombay in 1894, includes ghazal, eulogy and fakhr, all beautifully embellished in antique style.

From all that has been said, it can be seen that Arabic literature through the first three-quarters of the nineteenth century was characterized more by promise than by achievement. In theme, it had to some extent been related to contemporary events and problems: but old forms predominated in both prose and poetry. Simplification of language and style was needed; and if this had been rarely attempted, let alone achieved, the press had appeared, and this was likely, in due course to make its influence felt in creative literature, toning down the worst excesses of rhetoric. Some important figures had emerged – men, who, if not great geniuses themselves, could nurture, train, and inspire future geniuses. A few writers had almost achieved greatness, notably Yaziji and Shidyaq. Under European influence at least one new form had appeared, imported from Europe – drama. It will not have escaped notice that many writers knew foreign languages and travelled, both within the Ottoman Empire and to European countries. Short-story and novel were beginning to appear, but we have deferred consideration of these till the following chapter, where we shall see the important role played in encouraging them by Bustani's magazine, *al-Janān*. And while full justice may not have been done to other Arab countries, the predominant part played by the Lebanon in this stage of the Nahda will have been made clear. The centre of gravity, however, was about to move to Egypt.

EXTRACT I

A Description of Paris by Rifāʿat al-Ṭahṭāwī (1801–73)

(from *Takhlīṣ al-ibrīz fī talkhīṣ Parīz* – 'The refinement of gold in the résumé of Paris'), Cairo, 1905, pp. 96–102*

Part III, Chapter 4: How the people of Paris are normally housed, and allied matters

It is acknowledged that a country or city is civilized to the extent of its knowledge and its remoteness from a state of crudeness and wildness. European countries abound in various sorts of knowledge and arts which, as no man can deny, induce sociability and adorn civilization. It is recognized that the French people are outstanding among the European nations in their great attachment to arts and sciences. They are the greatest in literature and civilization.

The commercial towns are usually superior architecturally to the villages and hamlets; the major cities are superior to the other towns; and the capital is superior to the other cities of the kingdom. So it is not surprising that it should be said that Paris, the seat of the kings of France, is among the greatest cities of Europe in its buildings and architecture. Though its buildings may not be outstanding in their materials, none the less they are outstanding in design and construction. Moreover it is sometimes said that their materials are excellent, apart from a deficiency in marble and certain other things. This is hardly surprising, since their walls are made of stone chips, as also are other walls outside the houses. The internal walls are usually made of superior wood. The pillars are generally of brass (copper?), rarely of marble. The floors are paved with stone flags, and occasionally with black marble, interspersed with flag stones. The roads are always paved with square stones, the courtyards similarly, and the halls with baked bricks, or wood, or black marble with worked paving stones. The quality of stone or wood varies according to a man's means. The

* The paragraphing is the translator's. There are few paragraphs in the original, as was often the case in Arabic books at this time.

walls and floors of the rooms are of wood, as already mentioned. The wood is coated with varnish, and the walls are covered with protective paper, cleanly embossed. This is better than the custom of white-washing walls. For compared with whitewash, not only does nothing come off the paper when one touches it, but it is easier to change and better to look at; in fact more suitable, especially in their rooms adorned with various types of furniture. The French try to lighten the floor by fitting coloured curtains – especially green ones. The floors of their rooms are paved with wood or a sort of red brick. They polish these floors every day with a yellow wax which they call 'floor-polish'. They have polishers on hire specially trained for the purpose. Under their beds, which are covered with eiderdowns and counter-panes, there are carpets on which they tread wearing slippers.

In every room is a fire-chimney. It is shaped like a row of earthen-ware jars, surrounded by fine marble, surmounted by an encased clock. On either side are vases of imitation white marble or crystal. In them are real or imitation flowers. On either side are European-style candelabra, whose effect can only be appreciated by one who has seen them lit.

In most of their rooms is a musical instrument called the 'piano'. If the room is a study, it has a table (desk) with writing materials and so on, such as paper knives of ivory and box-wood.

Most of the rooms are filled with pictures, especially portraits of relatives. In the study there may also be remarkable pictures and an assortment of antiques. On the desk you may find miscellaneous documents. In the rooms of people of note you may see great chandeliers lit by beeswax. At receptions you may well see in their rooms a table on which are all the latest books, papers, and the like, for the diversion of any guests who wish to occupy their eyes and entertain their minds by reading such things. This demonstrates the great devotion of the French to reading books. For books are their familiar friends. Among their *bon mots* are the following: 'A book is a jar full of knowledge, and a vessel full of wit. It is a garden given you indoors, and an orchard carried in the sleeve.' This has been well put by a poet:

> My note-book is my friend by day,
> My thoughts comprise my friend by night.
> Serving myself I wend my way,
> While dreams, like friends, attend my night.

My only sword is my sharp tongue,
My strength lies in my verses sung.
My inkwell brings my daily bread:
Its fruits lie on a table spread.

Also:

We have companions who never bore us in what they say,
Sound and firm, ever for us, whether near or far away.
They help us with their knowledge, the knowledge of times gone by;
Intelligence and polish, with sound judgement, they supply.
You would be telling no lie if you described them as dead:
If you said they were alive, you would be true in what you said.

As someone said: 'The book tells a fine tale.' And a wit has said: 'I have never seen a weeper smile better than the pen.'

All these treasures are best appreciated in the presence of the lady of the house, that is, the householder's wife; for she is the first to greet guests, followed immediately by her husband. And how do these rooms, with their delights, compare with ours? In ours we greet a man by giving him a *shubūq* (Turkish pipe) to smoke, by the hands of a servant, usually a Negro.

The ceilings are of fine wood. The house is usually constructed in four floors, excluding the ground floor, which does not count as a storey. There may be as many as seven storeys, plus cellars which are used as stables, kitchens, and stores – especially for wine and firewood. With them the house, as in Cairo, consists of several apartments. On every floor are several apartments, each consisting of connected rooms.

It is their custom to divide houses into three categories: first, ordinary houses; secondly, notables' houses; and thirdly, houses for the king and his relatives, council chambers and the like. The first type is called a house (*bait*), the second a residence (*dār*), and the third a palace (*qaṣr*) or mansion (*sarāya*). Houses may also be divided on a different basis into three grades: first, houses with a concierge (*ḥājib*), and a door big enough to take a carriage; secondly, a house with interior passages with a concierge, through whose door, however, a carriage cannot fit; and thirdly, houses with no living quarters for a concierge. If a resident wishes to stay out in the city after midnight, he must warn the concierge to wait up for him, and also make it worth his while. There are whole quarters without concierges or doors such as they have in Cairo (Egypt).

Moreover, properties are expensive to buy and rent. So much so, that a large house may cost as much as a million francs, that is, about three million Egyptian piastres. Then, Paris properties may be rented unfurnished, or fully furnished with fine soft furnishings, furniture and household equipment – which, with the French, means cooking utensils and tableware as a whole, in complete sets. These include silver and the like; also bedding, which is usually a number of mattresses, one of them of feather, a sheet which is changed monthly, and blankets. There are pieces of furniture for show, and for the reception of visitors, namely chairs upholstered with embroidered silk and so on; also covered sofas and ordinary chairs. Then there are show-pieces such as large clocks called by them *pendule*, large flower vases; and other things such as gilt coffee pots, hanging candelabra lit by groups of candles, and book-cases with glass doors, through which one can see the finely bound books they contain. Every man, whether rich or poor, has a book-case, as all the lower classes read and write.

Usually the man sleeps in a separate room from his wife, if they have been married some time.

Among the nice customs is that the palaces of the king and his relatives are open (to the public) when the king* and his relatives go away every year to stay in the country for a few months. The rest of the people go in and walk around these palaces, to see the furniture and other things of note. But no one can enter without a piece of paper (ticket) on which is printed an entry permit for one or two persons or more. Many people have these tickets; and if a man asks one of his acquaintances for one, he gives him it. Thus you will see in the palace a great crowd looking at everything in the apartments of the king[104] and his relatives. I myself have been in many times, and have seen wonders well worth looking at. There are statues indistinguishable from actual people, save that they cannot speak. There are also portraits of the kings of France and others, including all the members of the royal family, and pictures of every conceivable novelty. Most of the things in the royal apartments are of the very best quality, in everything, from their uniformly fine workmanship to their excellent materials. Thus all the furniture, such as chairs, beds

* 'Sultan' (*sic*) in the original!

– even royal thrones – have fine wickerwork, and are overlaid with gold. Yet you do not find many precious stones on them, as is the case in great princes' houses in our country. For all French affairs are based on elegance, not ornamentation, display of wealth, and ostentation.

All the rich Parisians live in the city during the winter. We have already remarked, in mentioning the nature of the Paris region, that every house has fireplaces, in which fires burn in the halls and rooms. But in the hot season men of means live in the country. For the country châteaux have a more salubrious atmosphere than the city. Some people go to various parts of France or neighbouring countries to smell the scent of a foreign country; to study it, and learn the customs of its people. This is particularly so in a part of the year which they call the leave season or the holiday season, that is the off-work period. Even the women go away, travelling either on their own or accompanied by a man with whom they agree on the itinerary and on how long he is to travel with them. For women are also very fond of knowledge, and learning, and seeking the secrets of mankind. After all, do not some of them come from Europe to Egypt, to see its wonders such as the Pyramids and the ruined temples. They are like men in all that they do. You may even find among them young women who have an affair with a stranger without being married. When they find themselves pregnant, and fear public disgrace, they go on a journey ostensibly simply as tourists, or on some other pretext, to have the child. Then they put it with a foster-mother on payment, and have it brought up in a strange country. However, this is not universal; for, as they say, not every sword shines bright. Thus, among the women of France there are honourable women and the reverse. The latter predominate, since in France the art of love has taken hold of the hearts of the people of both sexes. Their love is unsound, because they cannot believe that it has any other purpose. It may take place between a young man and a girl, in which case it ends in marriage.

There is one thing for which Frenchwomen must be commended, and that is the cleanliness of their houses, which are free from all kinds of dirt – though they cannot hold a candle to the Flemings' houses. The Flemings surpass all nations in external cleanliness, just as in ancient times the Egyptians surpassed all other nations in cleanliness. Their descendants, the Copts, have not imitated them in this. Paris, being clean, is free from poisonous things, even insects. You never hear of anyone being bitten by a scorpion. The care of the French for cleanliness in their homes and in their clothing is astounding. Their houses are always cheerful, because of the many windows placed in excellent architectural settings to admit light and air. The window panes are invariably of glass, so that when they are closed the light is not obscured. Over them, rich and poor alike have curtains. In addition, net curtains are the order of the day for all Parisians.

CHAPTER 3

The First Flowering of the Literary Renaissance– the late Nineteenth and early Twentieth Centuries

Poetry

1. *Egypt*

The importance of political events in creating an environment favourable to the literary revival has, it is hoped, been made clear. This explains the success of Egypt and the Lebanon to a considerable extent. The events of 1860 in Syria and the Lebanon were not favourable to artistic progress, and it was not until after the First World War that the situation was redressed. Only Egypt now provided the right milieu for the Nahda, and scores of Lebanese and Syrians went to work there. At the end of the century they began also to emigrate to the New World.

Yet Muhammad ʿAli's immediate successors did not carry on his work.[1] ʿAbbās I (1848–54) and Saʿīd (1854–63) curtailed cultural missions to Europe, and slowed educational expansion. Abbas was hostile to Western – especially French – influence, and was somewhat subservient to the Ottoman Sultan. Muhammad Saʿid was more enlightened. He accepted a loan from British bankers and granted a concession to de Lesseps to build the Suez Canal.

It was under Ismāʿīl (1863–79) that great changes took place, and literature flourished. Partly educated in France, and widely travelled in Europe, he set out thoroughly to modernize Egypt, to complete the work of his grandfather. (He was the son of Muhammad Ali's son Ibrahim.) He carried out great public works – railways, irrigation, education. Over 4,000 primary schools were opened during his reign, and this was, of itself, a fillip to literacy and, therefore, to literature. In 1869 he officially opened the Suez Canal in the presence of the Emperor Franz Josef and the Empress Eugénie. He was also an empire-builder, employing Europeans like Sir Samuel and Valentine Baker, and General Gordon, to open up East Africa. Egyptian penetration of the Sudan was extended to Darfur and the Upper Nile. The Red Sea coast was occupied from Suakin to Massawa and the Somali coast. Widespread prosperity, however, came to be threatened by over-ambition, resulting in near-bankruptcy. In 1875 Ismail sold his majority shareholding in the Suez Canal Company to the British Government. To ensure reduction of debts, one British and one French financial controller were appointed, and hatred of foreigners became a feature of nationalism. Under Western pressure Ismail was deposed by the Turkish Sultan in 1879 and lived in exile in Istanboul till his death in 1895. Two years before his deposition he had assumed the title of Khedive.[2]

Under the Khedive Taufīq Western control was tightened, and it was to end in British occupation. Egyptian nationalism was reflected in literature, and also in conspiracies and rebellion. Colonel ʿArābī Pasha became the man of the hour. He was the central figure in a new Nationalist Party (*al-ḥizb al-waṭanī*),[3] which won the sympathy and support of the unlikely alliance of Egyptian fellaheen and Turkish notables. In 1881, with the threat of military action, Taufiq was compelled to appoint the soldier-poet Maḥmūd Sāmī al-Bārūdī as Prime Minister, and ʿArabi became under-secretary for war. The subsequent events are too involved to report in detail. Barudi resigned. Riots in Alexandria resulted in the death of about fifty Europeans. A British fleet bombarded the city. British troops landed and defeated ʿArabi's forces at Tel-el-Kebir. The British occupied Cairo, and ʿArabi was banished to Ceylon.

From 1883 to 1907, amidst mounting Egyptian resentment, Sir Evelyn Baring (later Lord Cromer) controlled Egypt as Resident and Consul-General. He undoubtedly put the country on its feet financially and economically; but he did little for education, to develop self-government, or to train Egyptians for posts of the highest responsibility. British advisers were installed in the major government offices. The Sudan was reconquered after a period of independence dating from Gordon's death in Khartoum in 1885.

The Egyptian attitude to Cromer – indeed, to British influence in general – is revealed in the literature, especially in poetry. It was a love-hate, or at least admiration-hate, relationship. Great harm was done to those relations by the Dinshawai affair.[4] The death of a British officer while in a military party out pigeon-shooting in the village of that name, and the subsequent trial of the villagers, left an almost indelible mark on Egyptian minds. Savage sentences were passed, and four of the accused were publicly hanged.[5] It was a cruel blow to mutual tolerance and respect between the occupiers and the occupied.

Cromer was succeeded by Sir Eldon Gorst, whose policy was more lenient, yet failed to placate the nationalists. Three parties were directly involved – the British, the nationalists and the Khedive. The nationalists did not want to exchange British domination for that of the Khedive. When British policy was apparently tolerant, it was suspected of being aimed at strengthening the Khedive against the nationalists. There was, in addition, a fourth party – the Turkish Sultan in Istanboul. Kitchener, Resident from 1911 to 1914, combined firmness with liberal concessions, and seems to have had some understanding of nationalist aspirations.

After the outbreak of the 1914–18 war, Abbas II, who had succeeded his father Taufiq in 1892, was deposed by the British, because he was suspected of pro-Turkish anti-British intrigues. Egypt was declared a British protectorate, and Abbas' uncle, Ḥusain Kāmil, succeeded him. He was allowed to take the title of Sultan[6] – no doubt to show that, holding the same title as his former suzerain in Istanboul, he could no longer be subordinate to him. Fu'ād I, who ruled from 1917 to 1937, assumed the title of king in 1922.

It will be convenient now to discuss Egyptian poetry up to 1920. The general picture is of old forms and language, with old themes adapted to the contemporary scene and some new themes, especially nationalism. This nationalism was sometimes Arabism (pan-Arabism would be a better term), sometimes Islamic, showing loyalty to the Turkish Sultan. Frequently, however, it was more Egyptian, either specifically or by implication. Despite the limitations of a traditional approach, there were several outstanding poets – notably al-Bārūdī, Aḥmad Shauqī, Ḥāfiẓ Ibrāhīm, and Khalīl Maṭrān (a Lebanese 'exile'). Another distinguished poet, who was also a great pedagogue and a gifted – though not great – prose-writer, was ʿAlī al-Jārim: in poetry he was the epitome of brilliant craftsmanship of antique flavour.

Khedive Ismail's achievements before financial stresses and strains appeared, did not inspire original poetry during his reign; rather was their effect felt after his deposition. ʿAlī Abū al-Naṣr (1800–81)[7] praised Ismail and his wife in several odes. A wit, and boon companion of princes, he went twice to Istanboul – first on a mission sent by

Muhammad Ali, and later in 1872 with Ismail. Though considered a brilliant poet in his day, he showed no individuality, and was preoccupied with verbal virtuosity. His first visit to Istanboul led him to praise that city as follows:[8]

Cairo the Fortunate we thought a paradise,
  Supreme, to every other place superior;
But when the Caliph's Seat appeared before our eyes,
  We clearly saw 'twas Cairo was inferior.

Owing to a *double entendre*[9] in the last line, the poem might be translated differently:

Cairo the Fortunate we thought a paradise,
  Supreme above all other places earth can show:
But when the Caliph's Seat appeared before our eyes,
  We clearly saw in her the whole world here below.

though the first interpretation seems the better. However, a reproduction of the Arabic in Latin script may help to discuss it further:

Wa kunnā narā Miṣra l-saʿīdata jannatan,
  Wa naḥsibuhā dūna l-bilādi hiya l-ʿulyā:
Fa-lammā ra'at Dāra l-K̲h̲ilafāti ʿainunā,
  ʿAlimnā yaqīnan annahā la-hiya l-dunyā.

The main effect is made by the contrast between *ʿulyā* (highest) and *dunyā* (lowest – also meaning this world, a contrast with *jannatan* = a garden or paradise). The two contrasted words are the words at the end of the verses, which rhyme and thus attract attention. The pronouns in each second hemistich. . . . naḥsibu*hā*. . . . *hiya*, and anna*hā* la-*hiya* (the la being merely an emphatic particle), while ostensibly for stress, really leave an impression of metrical filling-in, and emasculate the poetry.

Abu al-Nasr was a prolific poet, but his copious diwan is little read today.

Another of Ismail's boon companions was Shaikh ʿAlī al-Lait̲h̲ (1830–98).[10] He too accompanied Ismail on his 1878 trip to Istanboul. He praised Sultan ʿAbd al-ʿAziz in an ode beginning:

Leave mention of Chosroes, curtail the praises you recite
Of Roman Caesar – for their deeds are now forgotten quite.
Proclaim the deeds of him, instead, who on his course is sped
Accompanied by noble beasts by noble leaders led.

His failure to publish a diwan is probably no great loss. But he did at least have the courage to write an ode, with an 'l' rhyme, in sympathy with the ʿArabi rebels.

Maḥmūd Ṣafwat al-Saʿātī (1825–80)[11] is sometimes considered the forerunner and pioneer of the whole Nahda poetical movement. It is thought by some that some individuality can be discerned amidst conventional utterances. There is some wishful thinking here. Unlike his fellow poets, he was not educated at the Azhar. But a period spent as court poet to the Amir of Mecca, and a further stay in Istanboul before he returned to Egypt to settle in Cairo was hardly conducive to forward-looking poetry. He is said to have been influenced by Mutanabbi: and like his model, he took a rather mercenary view of the poetic profession. The characteristic wit of the Cairene is found in his verse – which may account for his success as a court poet. He sought the security of a government post in Egypt once his roving days were over.

On the other hand, ʿAbdullah Fikrī (1834–90)[12] was born in Mecca, the son of one of Muhammad Ali's officers, but was educated in Cairo. He entered government service, giving up a potentially brilliant career as a lecturer at the Azhar, and accompanied Ismail on his 1861 journey to Istanboul. He fell into disfavour, through suspicion of being implicated in the ʿArabi rising. He was pardoned, partly because of a complaining ode addressed to Ismail. Such complaining poetry – termed *ʿAtb* – is reminiscent of ʿAbbasid days. Indeed, Fikri imitated tenth-century poets. Incidentally, he called the Khedive in his verse *mulaiki* (my little king) – an apt nickname for the Khedive – though the diminutive used here is also used affectionately, as in *bunayya* – my little son. Fikri also wrote prose; some in maqama style, some less ornate. He represented Egypt at the International Congress of Orientalists in Stockholm in 1888. However, he is chiefly remembered for his services to education. After serving as headmaster, he became Minister of Education, and devoted himself to improving syllabuses and text-books. Many of his literary works were collected and published by his son in 1898.

It is remarkable, if not unique, that the first great modern Arab poet – one of the finest Arab poets since al-Mutanabbi – should have been a soldier and statesman: in fact, prime minister of Egypt for a short spell. How many medieval poets must have turned in their graves with envy. So many of them had fancied themselves as men of affairs as well as poets. Mutanabbi himself had boasted that he was as familiar with the sword as the pen; and a well-known story suggests that it was his servant's reminder of this boast when they were attacked by Bedouins that led him to turn on his attackers, and thus meet his end.

Bārūdī[13] was born in Cairo of Mameluke (Circassian) stock in 1838, and studied at the Military Academy. He went to Istanboul, where he applied himself to Turkish and Persian language and literature. On his return he obtained an army commission, despite the fact that the love of poetry was already strong in him. He served in Crete and the Crimea, and reached the rank of brigadier. Then he became successively Governor of Cairo, Minister of Education and Awqāf,[14] and Minister of War. As we have seen, the ʿArabi movement made him Prime Minister, but he soon resigned. After ʿArabi's failure, he was exiled to Ceylon for 17 years, living in Colombo. He returned to Egypt only four years before his death in 1904.

Reference has been made in Chapter I to Barudi's adaptation of old themes and forms to the contemporary situation. A glance at his diwan[15] leaves us in no doubt that we are in the presence of a towering figure. He might be described as a dilettante of genius – perhaps held back by his application to poetry of that discipline he had learned in the army. There was idealism: he was proud of his virtues, and shunned pleasures and women. A man of taste, he chose his words carefully: yet we sense that he often felt what he wrote. Though he praised the Khedive Taufiq, he was not a poet of patronage, but of patriotism – therein lies his strength. He found the means of expressing this patriotism within the classical qasida form and in hamasa poetry. His personal pride and ambition are themselves classical. He has been likened to Mutanabbi – but the resemblance with hamasa poetry is clearer. Though a political poet, he also excels in description, whether of nature, antiquities, or modern inventions. At the same time he often uses antique clichés about clouds, lightning, camels and horses – the whole verbal armoury of the pre-Islamic and Ommeyad poet. It is not, therefore, surprising, that he has been accused of plagiarism, and of exaggerated and forced figures of speech. Thus, he writes:

> One thing alone there was, to cause
> The waters of the Nile to rise:
> 'Twas when I stood upon its shores,
> Mourning my friends, tears in my eyes.

With this hyperbole, he sometimes combined amateurism in language and prosody.

Egyptians like to mention his 34-verse poem on the pyramids of Gizeh.[16] Verse like the following, however, though ingenious, will hardly endear this poet to non-Arabs. He describes the two pyramids as:

> Like twin breasts, pouring forth milk from the Nile,
> Moistening dry soil where it flows for a while.
> Between them the Sphinx stands – a crouching beast,
> Its fore-paws outstretched, lying on its chest,
> Turning a tender glance towards the East,
> Awaiting the dawn with eager interest.

There was something new about Barudi's poetry, something vital and of his age. He represents the first stage of the literary renaissance in poetry – the stage in which subject-matter is modern, but forms and language traditional. The idea of Barudi as a ghazal-poet seems unlikely. Yet he wrote both love- and wine-poetry. It is as if he said to himself: a complete poet must write every type of poetry; hamasa, satire, fakhr, elegy, eulogy and satire are not enough. I must also write on love and wine. And he did so, credibly, if not convincingly.

A contemporary of Barudi was the first Arab woman writer to achieve distinction – ʿĀ'is͟ha al-Taimūriyya (1840–1902).[17] She was the daughter of a Cairene Kurd, and, despite her mother's opposition, persuaded her father to provide her with a good education. Early widowhood increased her devotion to writing, and she produced poetical diwans in Arabic, Persian and Turkish. She praised the Khedive, wrote elegies on relatives – particularly a brother and daughter who died young, and also ghazal of a sufistic character. Her prose includes some writing on social problems. Her poetical style was old-fashioned, while her prose shows maqama influence.

Ismā'īl Ṣabrī (1854–1927)[18] is a more important figure. While in his teens he wrote odes in praise of the Khedive Ismail, which were published in a magazine. The Khedive helped him, sending him to the university of Aix to study law. On his return he held a number of government posts in the legal department, then served as governor of Alexandria, and, finally, Solicitor-General in 1899. He retired from government service in 1907, and made his house a gathering place for poets and other writers.

His own diwan, published in 1938, was modest in bulk – probably less than 2,000 verse/lines, generously set out in 200-odd pages. His verse achieved fame rather beyond its intrinsic merit, though he was able enough.

Love, death and nationalism were his main themes, but he was also noted for his description and philosophizing. During his long period in government service he was only a part-time poet and his official position restricted his freedom of expression. Though secretly a strong nationalist, he kept quiet about it, despite his known friendship for Muṣṭafā Kāmil. Thus, in writing about events of political importance, he would concentrate on non-political aspects – humanitarian, for example. The fall of the Sultan 'Abd al-Hamid he sees as a warning to rulers, rather than as a blow to Islamic states. As a writer, he reminds one of Boito as a composer. A generous patron of others, he was in his own writing a perfectionist, and therefore a severe self-critic. He would write, rewrite and polish a poem until he felt it was fit to be recited in public. The reference to music, by the way, is not inapt: Sabri was a music-lover who knew the leading Egyptian singers and instrumentalists of his day.

Cheikho[19] quoted admiringly the following verses by Sabri on 'Keeping a friend':[20]

When some firm old friend betrays me –
In defiance disobeys me,
  Once I raise my arrow ready,
  And my hand to shoot is steady;
Then the ghost of our affection
Comes 'twixt me and my direction –
  Breaks my arrow – so, retiring,
  I forbear no arrow firing.[21]

In the original this poem is just two verses, and it is significant that much of Sabri's poetry is taken up with brief poems of between two and five verses. They are what is called in Arabic, Persian, Urdu and Turkish literature, *qiṭ'a* (pl. *qiṭa'* = literally, a piece). To the present writer Sabri appears elegant rather than great – a short-winded poet.

Egyptian poetry between 1890 and 1930 was dominated by two giants – Aḥmad Shauqī (1868–1932) and Ḥāfiẓ Ibrāhīm (1871–1932); three, when one includes Khalīl Maṭrān[22] (1872–1949), who, though Lebanese by birth, lived and wrote mostly in Egypt. Shauqi and Hafiz were the twin geniuses who were for long considered the spokesmen of Egypt, and to a lesser extent of the whole Arab world. At times also they were champions of the Turkish sultans, of the 'Caliphate' idea, of the whole world of Islam. No theme of current interest, economic, political, personal or social, was beyond their range. Whether their poetry is to one's taste or not, there is no denying their dignity and majesty: they have that indefinable quality we may call 'stature'. The history of Egypt during their lifetime may be followed in their verse.

A hundred books or more have been written about them, separately or jointly; while hundreds of articles have dealt with various aspects of their works.[23] Both left a substantial output: Shauqi a diwan of about 1,000 pages, Hafiz rather more than half that size. Hafiz, in addition, produced an Arabic version of Hugo's *Les Misérables*; while Shauqi was the greatest exponent of verse-drama, and wrote six tragedies and one comedy. It will be obvious, then, that justice can hardly be done to these writers in the limited space available here.

Born in Cairo, Shauqi studied law in Montpelier, and afterwards visited England and Algeria. Back in Cairo he became a member of the Khedive's household. (He is often described as the 'poet of the court', Hafiz as the 'poet of the people'. Like most similar generalizations, this is too glib. Shauqi also came to be known throughout the Arab world as the 'Prince of Poets'.) Shauqi attended an Orientalists' Congress in Geneva, and was able to visit Belgium and Istanboul. He married into a wealthy family, and all was well with him until the First World War. Then he paid the penalty of being a 'Khedive's man'. When Abbas II was exiled, he suffered the same fate. He lived in Barcelona, returning to Egypt in 1919 after four years of exile.

What is important about these two poets – particularly Shauqi – is that they were no mere clever word-spinners, but used language and poetical techniques as a means to an end, to express thought. This thought at once echoed and stimulated the thoughts of educated and informed Egyptians in general. Shauqi is the more musical, the less heavy, of the two. When he uses a rare word, it is to give the shade of meaning or the flavour he wants. Though not a great innovator in metre or style, he could use shorter metres effectively when the theme seemed to require them. But many of his famous poems are on political themes, and therefore long, heavy metres are used. Later in life he wrote some short narrative poems – rather like fables – and these are among his most charming pieces. In them, he does not confine himself to monorhyme, but uses mathnawi.[24] His plays, with metre changed as different characters speak, provide his most felicitous use of metre.

Shauqi wrote eulogy, elegy, love poetry, descriptive poetry, political and social comment, and occasional poetry to celebrate particular occasions of public interest. He occupied a place not unlike that of the British poet-laureate. It has already been suggested, in Chapter I, that this was a harking-back to the role of the pre-Islamic and Ommeyad poet as the spokesman of the community or group. Of course, political poetry by no means began with Shauqi and Hafiz, as we have seen from discussion of previous poets. But with these two poets it reached its apogee. Subsequent poets have written about contemporary political events, but rarely with the same assurance and authority combined with absolute mastery of the forms they used.

A superficial acquaintance with Shauqi's diwan gives an impression of sameness. This is deceptive, despite the traditional forms and language. A glance at the titles of the poems in his 4-volume diwan, *al-Shauqiyyāt*,[25] indicates a tremendous range of subjects, of which the following is a random selection: The Victory of the Turks in Peace and War (referring to Mustafa Kamal); Remembrance of the Mulid;[26] Goodbye to Lord Cromer; Welcome to the Geographical Conference; Return from Exile; Remembrance of Dinshawai; Knowledge, Teaching, and the Teacher's Duty; The Red Crescent (= Red Cross); The Bosphorus; Journey to Andalusia; elegies on the musician Sid Darwish, on the writers Yaʿqūb Ṣarūf, Hafiz Ibrahim, ʿAbd al-Muṭṭalib, Hugo and Tolstoy, on Saʿd Zaghlūl, Muṣṭafā Kāmil, and the poet's father; a number of ghazals; short narrative poems, mostly fables with morals; children's poems; and the poetry in his plays.

Shauqi tended to be cautious in what he wrote about and the tone he used. After his return from exile, he became more frank. Thus, Hafiz wrote about Dinshawai fifteen days after the sentences had been passed, using bitter language:

> I wish I knew, was that the inquisition
> Returned, or Nero's reign in repetition?

Shauqi waited a year, then wrote a 14-verse poem, largely concerned with the plight of the widows and the imprisoned. He then echoes Hafiz, especially in the reference to Nero:

> Had Nero known Lord Cromer's régime, without a doubt,
> He would have known how sentences should be carried out.

He was restrained, too, in his elegy on Mustafa Kamil in 1908, hardly treating him as the national hero he had been. But in 1924 he made up for this in a second poem in a different vein.

It is surprising that historians of modern Egypt have failed to use Shauqi's poems as the important historical documents they really are. His strength compared with Hafiz is due in part to his wider experience of the world. He was also a careful and perceptive observer, who must be accorded an eminent position among Arab descriptive poets of all eras.

We quote here from two of his poems: first, his fable *The Fox and the Cock*:[27]

> The fox appeared to public eyes
> One day, in pious preacher's guise.
>   He wandered posing as a guide:
>   The crafty – cursing – he decried,
> Saying 'To God all praise be given,
> Lord of the Worlds, of Earth and Heav'n.
>   Oh men of God, to Him return,
>   He shelters those that to him turn.
> Further, from flesh of fowl abstain,
> The true ascetic lives on grain!
>   And tell the Cock, 'tis his affair

To summon us to morning prayer!'
So to the Cock an envoy came,
In the ascetics' leader's name.
He to the Cock th'idea proposed,
Hoping he would be well disposed.
The Cock, in his excuse, did say:
'Oh guide most like to lead astray,
Inform the Fox from me, because
I learn'd, from sainted ancestors,
Who learn'd from other cocks, who e'en
Had in th'accursed stomach been,
That they had stated – and the word
Of those who know should be preferred –
Methinks that one is quite mistaken
Who thinks the Fox to Faith has taken!'

The following verses are from *Knowledge and Teaching and the Teacher's Task*:[28]

Rise to the teacher! Give him his due of high respect:
The teacher is almost an apostle, an elect!
Are there men nobler or more glorious you can find
Than those who make and mould the character and mind?
Glory to you, oh God, the best Teacher of men;
You taught the earliest ages how to use the pen.
This human mind you drew from out its darkness drear,
Guiding it on the road towards the brightness clear.
You forged it by the teacher's hand, at times uncouth
As rusty steel; at other times you left it polished smooth.
Moses you sent to guide – the Pentateuch he brought;
And spotless Mary's son, he who the Gospel taught.
Muhammad, as a spring of eloquence you cleav'd.
He poured forth the Tradition, the Koran received.
You educated Greece and Egypt, and you let
Them turn aside from every sun which fain would set:
Today both lands have reached a state of childishness
In knowledge, which they seek with childish eagerness.
From Eastern lands earth's brightest suns first came first to view;

Why should control of them to Western lands accrue?
Oh World! Since first the teacher, stranded, lost his way,
Amidst these suns in Eastern lands, and went astray,
Those who defended truth in knowledge, for it bore
Dire punishment with steadfastness, they are no more!
Socrates raised the cup, though with sure fate 'twas filled,
To loving lips, desiring only to be killed.
They offered him his life, life with stupidity,
But he, refusing, chose death with nobility.
Those who are brave of heart are of a common kind,
But rarely do you find men who are brave of mind!

The poet goes on to refer specifically to Egypt, and the unenviable position to which it has been wrought by defective education. He ends this section by condemning Dunlop's educational reforms:

Nor Dunlop, nor the education he brought in
Were worth, in times of dire distress, a date-stone's skin.

He later refers to woman's role:

And when the women grow up in illit'racy,
The men impose ignorance and obscurity.

A few verses later, reference is made to the opening of the first Egyptian parliament on Saturday, 15 March 1924:

Egypt, if she went back to times long passed away,
Would never find the likes of that great Saturday.
Tomorrow, Parliament will spread its canopy,
A shady shelter o'er the happy Nile 'twill be.
If education rouses its anxiety,
May parliament to this land be not niggardly.

After addressing youth, the poet ends:

How distant these objectives! Yet I see, indeed,
Your steadfastness in them is amply guaranteed.
Entrust success to God and persevere, for He
Is the best surety for you and the best trustee.

Like many long odes by Shauqi, this is a polemical poem. Poetical polemics are notoriously difficult to sustain for long. In English literature, Dryden and Pope were masters, Wordsworth passable; Byron succeeded by his satire and wit. To the present writer, the poem quoted above seems too long and ponderous. This and the fact that the circumstances inspiring it no longer exist have caused its appeal – and that of similar poems by Shauqi – to dwindle.

The beginnings of Arabic drama have already been sketched. Heroic verse drama (as opposed to the 'musical' of Naqqash) began with Khalīl al-Yāzijī, Nasif's son (1856–89). He wrote 'Magnanimity and Loyalty' (*al-marū'a wa al-wafā'*) in 1878.[29] The subject concerns the pre-Islamic Arab virtues of bravery and fidelity: the theme is the conversion of Nu'mān, King of Hira, to Christianity. The young author tried to observe the Greek dramatic unities; but the poetry is too immature to match the theme.

Later, Egyptian writers tried their hand at heroic drama. Some of their plays were original, others translated or adapted from the French classics or Shakespeare. But no masterpiece appeared. Shauqi turned to this form in the last three years of his life. Of his seven plays, three are on Egyptian historical subjects – *Cleopatra*, *Cambyses*, and *'Alī Bey al-Kabīr*. Three more are on ancient Arab themes – *Majnūn Laila* about an early poet, a 'martyr of love', *'Antara*, and *Amīra al-Andalus* (the Princess of Andalucia). The seventh was a verse comedy, *al-Sitt Hudā* (Madame Huda), which was not published in full till 1960.

Shauqi was too restrained, serious and self-conscious to produce strong characterization in his plays. Nor, on the whole, does he make us identify ourselves with his tragic heroes and heroines – though the relevance of his *Cleopatra* to his readers is obvious. But the poetry is fine, and, with change of metre and rhyme from speaker to speaker, extremely varied and flexible. He was an admirer of Shakespeare; but, so far as any analogy is valid, his *Fall of Cleopatra* (*Maṣra' Kulyūbāt-rā*) seems nearer to Dryden. Unlike either, his play is of his native country. He therefore paints his heroine as a great patriot. Her adviser, the priest Anubis, pious and patriotic, is possibly the poet's idealized self-portrait.

Madame Huda has not won many plaudits. Yet it is a fine – and unexpected – achievement. Who would have imagined the poet writing a comedy in his old age? And how surprising that he should have chosen the particular plot. Set in Cairo in 1890, it is the story of a wealthy woman, nine times married. She outwits the male species, which she has found so unsatisfactory, by leaving her goods to female neighbours and relations. The tone of the play is set in the first pages, when Huda gives a witty account of her successive husbands to her friend Zainab.

Shauqi's plays have been fairly frequently acted, and he occupies an important position in the history of Arabic drama. One or two subsequent writers have surpassed him in heroic drama as drama, but not as poetry. Yet it would be a strange quirk of fate if future generations of critics were to see in his comedy his chief claim to fame as a dramatist.

There are so many points of contact, so many similarities of subject and style, so similar a measure of talent, between Hafiz and Shauqi, that the latter's greater reputation seems, at first sight, unfair. In his heyday Hafiz represented the feelings of the Egyptian people more closely than Shauqi. But he was a poor provincial, not a man of the world, and he had much less experience of the outside world. Born in Upper Egypt, he was orphaned early and went to Cairo, to be brought up by an uncle. He went to the Military Academy and was commissioned in the army. He served in the Sudan, where he was acquitted of a charge of inciting the Egyptian troops to mutiny. Returning to Cairo he became a follower of Muḥammad ʿAbduh.[30] In 1901 he resigned from the army, to devote himself to literature. He became recognized as a national poet. From 1911 he held a government post as a departmental chief in the Egyptian National Library (*Dār al-kutub al-miṣriyya*) and this somewhat restricted his freedom of expression. He became pro-British in some of his poems; in fact, the extent of his nationalist feelings was only fully realized after his death, when previously unpublished poems were published.

Like Shauqi, he expressed admiration for the Turkish sultan, as Caliph of Islam. Under Muhammad Abduh's influence, however, his loyalties became more Egyptian. He recognized the need for education and for social reform, and, while he began to look to Britain to lead Egypt to better times, he was not afraid to criticize the British. After Abduh's death in 1905 the tone of Hafiz's poetry became more openly nationalistic.

By nature Hafiz was conservative and ponderous. The only literature he knew was Arabic, and he was interested in the language. He tended to be preoccupied with the means of expressing his ideas.

When he was emotionally involved in the theme of a poem his language heightened the effect. At other times it increased the dullness. He did not show the same sureness of touch and variety as Shauqi in handling prosody. But he did not hesitate to run a sentence over from one verse to another – a fault to the classical purist.

The bulk of Hafiz's diwan[31] is taken up with political and social poetry, eulogy and elegy. Often he and Shauqi wrote poems on the same subject. Ḥasan Kāmil al-Ṣairāfī[32] has compared a number of such parallel poems – on Cromer, Saʿd Zaghlul and Mustafa Kamil; on the liberal Turkish constitution of 1908 and the Dinshawai incident; and on earthquakes – Shauqi on that of Tokyo, Hafiz on that of Messina. It is in elegy that Hafiz is superior. His feelings rise to the tragedy of the deaths of those he mourns. His elegies on Muhammad Abduh and Mustafa Kamil (three on the latter) are masterpieces in their genre – perhaps the last great classical marthiyas. Unlike Shauqi, he had no need to conceal lack of emotion by words of wisdom. He sees his subjects not only as individuals, but as representatives – ʿAbduh of rejuvenated Islam, Kamil of re-awakened Egypt.

But he could be even more dull than Shauqi, as can be seen in a political poem of 1907, entitled 'Egypt's Complaint against the [British] Occupation' (*Shakwā Miṣr min al-iḥtilāl*). Directed at the British Prime Minister, though not explicitly, it attacks inflation as having made apparent prosperity valueless, and expresses preference for Ismail's days. It is good polemics, but poor poetry, despite poetic use of contrasted words. The following translation makes no attempt at metrical regularity:[32]

Oppression was rampant among us, till its outward expression
Was corrected, then it merely became organized oppression.
Today you may recall your favours, in that wealth has multiplied,
And that Egyptians have become free, with good things supplied.
I say: Bring back Ismail's days, with their flogging and forced labour.
I find worse wounds and pains inflicted on us by your favour.
Things you have striven to set right – on *us* insults to heap;
Land you have priced too high – blood you have made too cheap.
When the earth is fertile, but its folk are distressed,
It produces no plants, and with heaven's rain is not blessed.
We were glad of a pound, till the time when its master,

Taking it to the shops, found it worth a piastre.
Do not think that much money is a valuable commodity,
When it brings nor provisions nor protection from poverty.
When ease of life is widespread, great wealth will count for little,
When we can see high prices descend on us and settle.

No doubt there would be a similar end-product were a modern British poet to write about the balance of payments problem.

Hafiz's elegy on Mustafa Kamil is marred only by the exaggeration of the first verse, though Mutanabbi was guilty of even worse hyperbole. In translation each verse has become a stanza, thus making the poem seem rather lighter than it really is:

Oh grave! This guest you welcome
  Gave hopes to a whole nation.
So praise God, and receive him,
  Respectful, in prostration.

Our honour 'tis Mustafa
  To see within you shaded,
A martyr to high purpose,
  In manhood's flower fast faded.

If we had lost him only,
  Were he the sole departed,
Then could we find some solace
  From sorrow brokenhearted.

We lost not but him only;
  We lost all else beside him!
Oh would that fate could send him –
  A second life provide him!

Oh you who ask where honour
  And manliness appear now?
Where wisdom, and sound judgement?
  Alas! You see them here now.

How lucky for the English![33]
  No more let them be frightened
Of any shouter, now that
  The loudest shout is quietened!

Now he is dead – that man who
  Revived in men their feeling;
Leading them on to glory,
  Their shattered spirits healing.

I praised you in your life-time,
  How weak my eulogizing!
Now you are dead, how strongly
  I speak in elegizing!

For you we sorrow – therefore,
  In sorrow unifying,
For you we weep – or wherefore
  Is this whole nation crying?

Curer of human minds, he
  Himself could not recover
From human ills within him –
  No cure could he discover.

You were alive and watchful,
  While we were soundly sleeping:
You, when grief dulled our senses,
  Were still your vigil keeping.

Oh martyr of high purpose,
  That voice of yours is sounding
Unchanged, today just as it
  Was yesterday resounding.

It shouts out, saying 'This is
  A building I erected:
Consign not to destruction
  This same thing I erected.'

It cries 'Let not the people
  Feel I am gone for ever,
And that those who survive me
  Are quit of all endeavour.'

It orders us: 'In God's name,
  Be ye not disunited:
Behave like men, and make not
  Your enemies delighted.

My spirit, from this high place,
  Looks down on you, surveying
Your actions for me, though I
  Am here below decaying.

Sadden it not: my fear is,
  Through promises forsaken,
By manifold misfortunes
  You may be overtaken.'

Yes! You who for our welfare
  The path of good presented,
Our whole life long, we're ready;
  So you may sleep contented.

Your building still is standing,
  Your spirit still beside us;
Your voice we still are hearing,
  Though distance may divide us.

We never saw you weeping,
  You hated it when others
In neighbouring lands were weeping,
  Among our suffering brothers.

Allow us one day's weeping!
  Then you will find us ready,
At dawn, as you would have us,
  Like mountains, firm and steady.

Oh River Nile! If you should
  Not flow, after his going,
Blood-red, I swear you will not,
  Oh Nile, be truly flowing.

Egypt, if you his mem'ry
  Fail to keep fresh within you
Until the Day of Judgement,
  Your weakness will continue.

Egyptians, if you know not
  The man we are regretting,
Know that the Star of Fortune
  Has sunk unto its setting.

Thirty odd years your life-span,
Like thirty pearls all gleaming,
Strung on night's necklace, brightly
Across the heavens streaming.

Their story will report you
Were no mere stripling, lacking
Companions to support you,
But a whole host, attacking![34]

If Shauqi and Hafiz closed the era of classical revival in Arabic poetry, Matran sealed it,[35] and foreshadowed poetical modernism. Literary historians regard him as the third of the trio. Born in Baalbek in the Lebanon in 1872, he was surrounded in his youth by scenery such as would inspire the imagination of anyone with poetic instincts. He studied in the Maronite High School in Beirut, becoming familiar with French as well as Arabic culture, and later he taught there. At the age of twenty he wrote a seditious article, and had to flee the country. He went first to France, where he imbibed French civilization at its source. The 'subtle nuances' of his poetry have been ascribed to French influence. But France could not permanently hold someone of his non-conforming spirit, and he went to Egypt, the one Arab country where the atmosphere was somewhat liberal.

He became more cautious and conservative politically, yet was secretly a supporter of Islamic solidarity and Arab independence. Thus, he favoured reform in Turkey, but was pro-Turkish in the Tripoli War against the Italians.[36] He was careful not to show hostility to the British occupation of Egypt at first, but later became involved with Mustafa Kamil and the Nationalist Party. He wrote elegies on both Queen Victoria and Mustafa Kamil and other nationalist leaders and politicians. He worked also as a journalist on *al Ahrām*, the daily newspaper. In fact, he accompanied the Khedive Abbas II to Istanboul in his capacity as a correspondent for that paper. He was the friend of Shauqi and other leading writers.

In 1947 he was honoured by fellow writers and the Egyptian Government in a celebration held in the Cairo Opera House to celebrate his fifty years as an author. He received decorations from several Arab governments, and a special 'Golden Book'[37] was published. It contained tributes to him in Arabic verse and Arabic and French prose.

Apart from his great poetical output, he also translated several plays from English and French: Shakespeare's *Macbeth*, *Hamlet*, *Othello* and *The Merchant of Venice*; Corneille's *Le Cid*, *Cinna* and *Polyceute*; and Hugo's *Hernani*.

Arab literary historians have no doubts whatsoever on Khalil Matran's importance in the Nahda. They class him with Shauqi and Hafiz, not only as a great poet, but as a pioneer (*rāʾid*, pl. *ruwwād* = scout, forager, forerunner). Which of the three is given preference depends partly on whether one is Egyptian or Lebanese-Syrian, partly on whether one's tastes are antiquarian or modern. To the non-Arab he must stand out as the greatest of the trio. The other two are great in the Arab tradition; Matran is great by European criteria. With his experience of French literature, Matran is truly lyrical. Like the other two, he wrote nationalistic odes and elegies and eulogies of Arab leaders. At a quick glance, these might seem similar to Shauqi's. A closer study, however, reveals how much freer they are. His ode, *Yaqẓa al-ʿArab* (the Arabs' awakening) can be read in translation in Arberry's fine book *Modern Arabic Poetry*.[38] It begins:

O noble company of Arabs, ye
My pride and boast, o'er every company,
Long have I chid your carelessness and sloth,
Yet not as one that might despair or loathe,
But candidly, as if to wake a friend
Unconscious of vast perils that impend.

The difference between Matran and Hafiz can be seen in his elegy on Mustafa Kamil.[39] It is long, but varied. Of the seven sections, which run the gamut of reaction to the hero's death, showing his importance to all Arabs, even non-Muslims, the fourth and fifth are truly dithyrambic. In the fourth, seven of the eleven verses begin with the word 'Egypt'. The fifth section has only six verses, each of which begins a rhetorical question with *man kāna* (who was?), followed by a comparative adjective . . . Who was bolder than you . . . who was abler . . . who was purer . . . and so on. Such series of verses beginning alike were not new to Arabic poetry: there are odd examples even from pre-Islamic verse. But how refreshing they are in eulogy on a political figure.

Matran's weightier poems inspiring the Arabs, whether in the guise of a direct appeal or an elegy, made a great impression on his contemporaries. Future generations will probably be more appreciative of his shorter, lighter lyrical poems, just as Englishmen prefer Wordsworth's lyrical ballads to his *Prelude* or *The Excursion*. In this type of poem, he tried everything, even free verse (prosified poetry – *Shiʿr manthūr*).

Here we reproduce, in translation, two poems. The first – *A Tragic Joke* – is in the traditional monorhyme. It is one of his earliest published poems, dating from 1893, and is an anecdote, which he says is based on fact, with a moral. The second, *A Lover's Bouquet*, is a late poem, composed with consummate craftsmanship, in delicate sextains with rich rhyme.

A TRAGIC JOKE (Diwan, I, 16–17)

They were eight boon companions, as close
  As stars in Gemini in friendliness.
In privacy the youths had met, and closed
  Their doors on everything but happiness.

They talked – and such as they only in talk
  Of beauty and of beauties find delight!
Till, when the night became intensely black,
  Then split asunder with dawn's shafts of light,

Heavy in body, but in spirit light,
  Their heads by drinking crimson wine inflamed,
To one bold youth among them they gave ear –
  A stripling whose desires could not be tamed.

'My friends', he said, 'ladies I hear next door,
  Holding a party – I can hear them sing:
Let's play a trick on them and bring them here:
  Without them, social life's a useless thing.'

'What trick?' they asked. He said: 'I will lie down,
  Pretending I have died before my time.
You wail: they'll come: then I'll appear from out
  My shroud, and we shall have a fine old time!'

The wailing frightened them, and in they came,
Confused, to bid farewell to that dead boy.
They wept, until they learn'd about the trick;
Then once again their hearts were filled with joy:

As when, on winter days, the sun appears,
The light with doubled radiance is bright.
They gathered round his bed and harried him
At will, while he, as solid stone, lay quiet.

But when they raised his covering, he appeared
More like the dead than anyone alive.
They thought that he had fainted – yet there was
Nothing could make him from his faint revive.

His friends then called the doctor: they were scared
When he declared the lad gone, past reclaim.
Their happy cries to fun'ral wails were turned,
Their laughter in a moment, tears became.

This jest with death had left them in the throes
Of the most lamentable of this world's woes.
If their friend lived, he would be comatose,
Sleeping the soundest sleep that this world knows.
Thus deeds done jokingly – or seriously –
Cause death and degradation equally.

A LOVER'S BOUQUET (Diwan, IV, 342–3)[40]

If only what we wished to
Were in our power to do,
A rose-garden I'd send you –
No mere bouquet would do:
But this card, written for you
In rhymes of blood must do . . .

As greetings from a lover
Despised – for you know not
How once he glanced towards you,
But you encouraged not:
One day he loomed before you –
No help from you he got.

This passion is a secret
   Between my heart and I.
By chance, unasked, you caused it
   In me – unique am I,
Alas! I put my trust in
   My treach'rous heart and eye.

Oh wish, in which all wishes
   Within my soul now grow,
I see the men around me,
   And watch them come and go . . .
Is there one love-lorn, like me,
   Who wounds like mine can show?

You saw me, yet ignored me,
   As though you had been wronged!
Then coldness was't, or purpose,
   Which thus my pains prolonged?
Or fate? – and only what was
   Foretold, to me belonged?

My heart, and – dare I say it? –
   My goods, I gave away.
My hopes all came to nothing,
   I threw my gifts away.
I blame not you: 'tis my fault.
   Why should I love this way?

I scanned a star, and yet I
   Of blame could feel no stain.
And how could any star know
   That coldness causes pain?
Or that some gazing lover
   Might of some wound complain?

Oh! Will fate smile, and one day
   My verses glow for her?
Or must I spend my whole life
   Despairing so for her?
Saki! What is this potion –
   This love I show for her?

The new atmosphere in Matran's poetry is obvious to the reader in much of his output – particularly his later poems; and Arab critics have not hesitated to ascribe it to French influence. Adjān Jallād[41] attributes his success to his taking over of the '*nuances* and *finesse*' of French poetry. At the same time, it all came naturally to Matran. For there were two sides to him; on the one hand, there was the traditional Arab writer, ready to indulge in long odes; on the other hand, there was the lyrical poet with the gossamer-light touch, composing delicate stanzas. Such lightness was not entirely unknown in classical poetry – it can be seen in the poetry of Abu Firas al-Hamadhani, mentioned in Chapter I.

A whole host of talented Egyptian poets were contemporaries of the great trio just discussed. Four only will be mentioned briefly. Muhammad ʿAbd al-Muṭṭalib (1879–1931) won the nickname of 'Bedouin poet', because he thought and wrote like a medieval poet, using rare words culled from pre-Islamic and early Islamic poetry. When he wrote about Arabs, he could actually imagine himself to be in Arabia. He composed ghazal and zuhd poetry also, and some Egyptian nationalistic verse. He was an Azharite (i.e. a graduate of al Azhar) with antique tastes, and no first-hand experience of European literature. He did, however, co-operate in a series of historical plays. Three of them were about early poets.

Muṣṭafā Ṣādiq al-Rāfiʿī (1880–1937)[42] is noted for his verse describing Egyptian scenes, in which he could write quite straightforwardly. He also wrote much prose, including a history of Arabic literature. But he is best remembered for his delicate and personal books in prose on love and beauty – *Rasāʾil al-aḥzān* (Letters of Sorrow), *al-Ṣāḥib al-Aḥmar* (the Red Friend) and *Hadīth al-Qamar* (Moon talk). The first-named, dating from 1924, made a great impression. It is a series of imaginary letters to a friend about the woman he loved, written in beautiful yet simple language. It earned him the description of 'the first symbolist in Arabic'.

Of all the minor poets of the era, perhaps none came so near the front rank, or has been so unjustly neglected, as Walī al-Dīn Yakan (1873–1921).[43] Born in Istanboul, his father returned with him to Egypt when he was six. Shortly afterwards his father died, and he was brought up by an uncle, who was head of the Treasury. He went to the School for the Sons of Notables, and acquired a good knowledge of French, and later English. After marrying a Greek, he learned that language also. Had he lived longer, travelled less, and been less interested in journalism and politics, he might have devoted himself more wholeheartedly to poetry. As it was, he wrote little, his diwan amounting to little over 100 pages – enough to show what he might have achieved. It has been suggested that his neglect by his contemporaries was due to suspicion of being pro-British.

Yakan's life consisted of alternate periods in Cairo and Istanboul. He wrote in support of the Young Turks in their call for constitutional reform, with the result that ʿAbd al-Hamid exiled him to Sevastopol in 1902. He was allowed to return to Egypt, after the promulgation of the new Turkish constitution six years later.

His poetry contains much that is familiar to students of Shauqi and Hafiz.[44] There is a good deal of political verse, elegy and eulogy. But often he strikes a personal note, especially in a few melancholy poems about his exile. One of the best is *Fī manfā – zafara min zafarātī* (In Exile – One of my sighs), from which the following verses are taken:[45]

A heart by memories obsessed,
  An eye made moist by streaming tears,
  The heart of one still young in years,
A body by old age distressed:

Hopes that have gone, all unawares,
  Time that has vanished all in vain,
  Life whose most pleasant part is pain,
Old age whose brightest part is cares.

Oh night! Will morning never break
  For those who sleepless vigil keep?
  While others' eyelids close in sleep,
Mine remain open, wide-awake.

My friends bid me bear patiently:
  But who can in the fire remain
  Patient, while Truth's opponents gain,
If Truth's own men the losers be?

Our fatherland we now can see
  Through death's dark door about to go;
  The grievers may gain pardon – though

It is a rare commodity.
So soil, may you for sorrow burn,
And rain, your tears to downpour turn!

Our foes how can we castigate
For evils that we let them do?
When in their prime, their powers we knew!
Now they are old, can we forget?

We counselled them – no heed they paid;
We scared them – but they would not scare.
We saw their hardened hearts laid bare,
As if their hearts of stone were made.

Truth may lie vanquished many a day,
Yet truth's triumphal day must dawn.
When once the swords of God are drawn,
They shall let none their progress stay!

The poet associates the political and his personal situations in a manner not to English tastes: but the Arabic is really excellent.

The Egyptians with whom we have been dealing have shown a mixture of *taqlīd* (imitation = traditionalism) and *tajdīd* (renewal = modernism). Khalil Matran is more of a *mujaddid* (modernist) and less of a *muqallid* (traditionalist) than the others. Before passing on to poets elsewhere, we shall mention one of the last Egyptian traditionalists – though perhaps this is unfair, and he should be placed in the halfway house along with Shauqi and Hafiz. He was ʿAlī al-Jārim (1881–1949).[46] He spent three years (1909–12) in Britain, studying education, English literature, logic and psychology. Subsequently he worked in the Egyptian Ministry of Education as inspector, then as Chief Inspector of Language-teaching. He was a founder member of the Egyptian Academy (*al-Majmaʿ al-lughawī al-Miṣrī*). In Chapter I we referred to his test-book on rhetoric, still in use. He also wrote a grammatical text-book in three volumes (*al-Naḥw al-wāḍiḥ*), with a teachers' supplementary volume. He edited classical literary texts, a famous dictionary,[47] and a famous grammar.[48] He also wrote historical fiction, notably *Ghāda al-Rashīd* (The girl of Rashid) and *Maraḥ al-Walīd* (al-Walid's cheerfulness). Some of his finest prose is found in his translation of Stanley Lane-Poole's 'The

Moors in Spain' (*al-ʿArab fī Isbāniyā*). Arab writers have often warmed to the subject of Arab civilization in Spain in the Middle Ages, and Jarim's rich vocabulary and rhetorical virtuosity enabled him to match the theme with his language.

Excellent taste, fine style, and a feeling for classical form and ideas inform all he wrote; and these qualities shine in his poetry, which constitutes a diwan of 500 pages.[49] His model was the classical qasida. He confined himself to monorhyme and preferred the weightier metres. His idioms are classical, and he liked to fill his poems with classical names of places and persons – a sort of literary name-dropping!

Yet within these limitations set by his personal inclinations, he wrote fine poetry. He too wrote much occasional poetry on diverse subjects, ranging from the opening of a broadcasting station to the formation of a new government. He produced elegies and eulogies too, including a eulogy of the young King Farouk. His ode on Baghdad will be found as Extract V on page 158 of this book.[50]

2. Poetry in Iraq

Shauqi, Hafiz, and Matran became famous throughout the Arab world. The only non-Egyptian poet to achieve fame at all comparable outside his own country was the Iraqi Maʿrūf al-Ruṣāfī (1875–1945), whose name still dominates Iraqi poetic circles. In the previous chapter, the political situation in Iraq to the end of the 1914–18 war was discussed. After this war Turkish rule was removed, but was replaced by the British Mandate. The country was given a monarchy from the Hedjaz, and was admitted into the League of Nations as an independent country in 1932. But Britain had air bases, and trained the army. The development of oil-fields brought prosperity, but increased dependence on Britain. A parliamentary system of government was established, and freedom of speech encouraged literary activity.

It is understandable, therefore, that Iraqi poets of the early twentieth century should have expressed the people's wish for independence, first from the Turks, then from the British. But they could not criticize the Turks with impunity, whereas the British were more tolerant. As in Egypt, social and economic themes were important too – particularly the emancipation of women, education, poverty, and the rural problem arising from rich landlords and poor peasants.[51] The old personal themes of elegy and eulogy continued, and there was some good descriptive poetry as well. Some stanza poetry was composed by Rusafi and others, but Iraqi poetry was comparatively conservative until very recently. This explains why in the present section we might appear to have gone ahead of schedule, so to speak, chronologically.

Muḥammad Saʿīd al-Ḥabbūbī (d. 1916)[52] forms a link with Iraqi poets discussed in the previous chapter, especially Haidar al-Hilli. He was born somewhere around the middle of the nineteenth century in the Shiʿite city of Najaf. Some considered him greater than Hilli, some gave the palm to the latter. But while Hilli excelled in elegy, Habbubi was noted for ghazal. He also wrote many muwashshahat. The editor of his diwan[53] compares him with Abu al-ʿAla' al-Maʿarri. The two had this in common, that both were suspected of atheism in some of their verse. An apter comparison would be with al-S͟harīf al-Raḍī (970–1016).[54] Both were experts on religious sciences; both wrote ghazal with religious overtones.[55] Habbubi was a strong nationalist, and met his death resisting the British occupation. As a poet, however, he was not very forward-looking.

Jamīl Ṣidqī al-Zahāwī (1863–1936)[56] is much more important. His parents were both Kurds, and he was born in Baghdad. He learned Kurdish, Persian and Turkish as well as Arabic. He worked in education, publishing and journalism. In the latter he was on the staff of *al-Zaurā'*, the official paper founded by Midhat Pasha. He visited both the Yemen and Istanboul. Under the Turkish constitution of 1908 he sat in the Chamber of Deputies as representative of Baghdad. When this chamber was abolished he returned to Baghdad. Later, under the Mandate, he was chairman of the committee set up to arabize Ottoman laws.

His literary output consists almost exclusively of his diwans, six in number, which were published between 1909 and 1939 in Beirut, Cairo and Baghdad. In addition, he translated the quatrains of Omar Khayyam into Arabic.[57] He was one of the few who successfully adapted the quatrain to Arabic poetry. In his preface to the collection of quatrains published in Beirut in 1924 he stresses that each quatrain should be treated as a separate poem, as with Omar Khayyam. Altogether there are nearly 300 quatrains. It is not surprising that one of the few serious attempts to write Arabic quatrains should be made in Iraq, since it is a neighbour of Iran. The Kurds occupy an area taking in parts of Persia as well as Iraq, Turkey and the U.S.S.R. But while the Persian and Indian quatrain has a triple rhyme – of the first, second and fourth lines, Zahawi rhymes only the second and fourth, as if he were thinking in terms of two rhyming Arabic verses of two hemistiches each. The quatrain is a suitable vehicle for gnomic verse. But such a collection of snippets, however neat, could hardly bring fame to an Arab poet. Moreover the Persian language and Persian rich rhymes seem more suited to the quatrain than Arabic – though it is difficult to explain why. The following examples from Zahawi reflect his simplicity rather than his neatness, and a quadruple rhyme is used in the translation, with varied metre:

> At night when I am sad,
> I think the night is sad.
> I used to think it glad,
> Like me, when I was glad.[58]

> Nigh is the time when we must part,
> And 'tis not gladly I depart.
> Gone is the time of joyous heart,
> Now is the turn of broken heart.[59]

> Over her neck there hangs her yellow hair,
> Adornment on adornment, past compare –
> As if some native ore of gold were there,
> Melting and spilling o'er some silver there.[60]

Zahawi was, indeed, interested in prosody, and in introducing variety; for despite the writing of muwashshahat and other stanza poetry already mentioned, Arabic poetry was still largely in monorhyme. His experimentation in blank verse (*shiʿr mursal*) was noted in Chapter I. An example dated 1909 will be found on pages 149 to 152 of Volume I of his collected verse. It is a creditable attempt, starting as a poem on death. It is soon apparent that there is a second related theme – the metaphorical death of the East. In the present writer's view, *vers libres* – with varied rhyme but no regular metre, is more suited to the particular genius of the Arabic language than blank verse. This may be because Arabic is fundamentally a language of syllable length rather than stress. Without some sort of rhyme, the poet is left with his imagery as his chief armoury, and has to fall back on rhetorical devices. The balance between ideas and expression is upset. Translation cannot here well represent the effect of the Arabic, but the following verses from the afore-mentioned poem by Zahawi may be of some slight interest. Lines of twelve syllables had to be used.

Death for the youth is better than a life in which
He is a heavy burden to his fellow men.

None is more troubled than the wise man who can see
The ignoramus honoured, while he is despised.

One-tenth of all mankind live with contented minds,
While nine-tenths of mankind live lives of misery.

In the whole wide world is there no reforming man
To give some small relief from all the woes of life?

If Eastern men do not rise up in unity,
Surely it is their rights men are most like to lose.

When ruin overtakes that land upon whose soil
You grew up, and you sorrow not, you are a stone.

Is it correct that one man should his stomach fill,
And most men's stomachs all the while should want for food?

The Western peoples have advanced and freed themselves.
Then why should not the Eastern peoples free themselves?

Oh woman, asking me about God's plan, keep quiet!
To such a question I have no pow'r to reply!

If I speak truth, I fear my hearer's blame; but if
I speak it not, the blame of conscience 'tis I fear.

People – save those of high intelligence – I see
As enemies, opposing all things that are new.

Take hold of learning – only learning benefits,
And men of learning only to mankind belong.

Refusal and submission both are evil things,
Yet of two evils, one may be more bearable.

Oh man! Have pity on other men, and place your trust
In peace, for peace is surely better far than war.

A young man's happiest times are when he is asleep,
Provided that the sleep he sleeps is free from dreams.

This world *repels* me, as one likely soon to die;
Compels me as one never like to pass away.

They say that salt will heal a wound which is decay'd:
But what avail if salt itself contain decay?

The man who fears the words of those who hatred brood
Must fail – only the bold obtain the joys they seek.

Moreover, men are not the same from age to age:
And what one people may esteem, another hates.

Oh you who blame me, blame me not because I weep;
'Tis the severest ills have overtaken me.

I feel some signs of warmth within the body of justice,
I maintain some hope it may not yet be dead.

The most forbearing of all men the thinker is,
Who, when the ignorant insult him, greets them fair.

He who resorts to rulers from th' oppressors' ills,
Jumps straight into the fire to flee the noon-day heat!

Though in this world some enemy may do me harm,
Yet must I say my say, still must I say my say!

Zahawi ranges widely in his themes – philosophizing, elegizing, eulogizing, translating from Persian, and writing on education and current problems. He deserves special mention for his championship of women's rights in his poetry; even though he is usually vague rather than specific, as Izzedien says.[61] Some Western readers may prefer this vagueness, because we rarely conceive of poetry as a vehicle for arguing the case for social reform. On the other hand, we do like a poet to speak of woman's inspiration and encouragement. Zahawi was stricken with paralysis fairly early in life, and depended greatly on his wife in everyday life. He therefore sees woman as man's helpmeet, looking after her husband and bringing him happiness. Another feature of this poet is constant commiseration with himself, doubtless due in part at any rate to his physical disabilities. Izzedien[62] expatiates on this – somewhat hardly. After all, complaining poetry (*ʿatab*) was common in the classical literature, particularly when a patron proved fickle; and at least Zahawi writes with a personal note.

Another poet of this era was ʿAbd al-Muḥsin al-Kāẓimī (1870–1938).[63] He criticized the government in some odes, and had to leave Iraq, taking refuge first in India, then Egypt. There he became a friend of Muhammad Abduh. He wrote many qasidas, some of them over 100 verses long, and was nicknamed 'the poet of the Arabs' (*S͟hāʿir al-ʿArab*).

But pre-eminent among Iraqi poets was Rusafi,[64] whose fame is still undimmed, his name almost a household word in Iraq. In the literary clubs (*nadwas*) he is quoted, analysed and discussed *ad infinitum*, if not *ad nauseam*. He was of mixed Kurdish-Arab parents, but his reticence about his father led to rumours that he was illegitimate. Born and brought up in Baghdad, he was inclined to solitude and did not mix with other children. His only youthful attachment seems to have been for his mother. He learned the whole Koran at school, but did not get beyond the primary stage, at the end of which he failed the examination, and left school. He then met one of the Ālūsī family, under whose influence he not only became a sincere Muslim and a Sufi, but determined to devote himself to literature. So successful was he that, after teaching in a primary school, he taught Arabic in a Baghdad secondary school. During this period he composed much poetry, which was published in Syria and Egypt. After the revolt of the Young Turks in 1908, he was invited to Istanboul by a newspaper proprietor. He went there hoping to edit an Arabic paper favouring Arab-Turkish friendship and co-operation. This came to nothing, and he returned home by way of Salonika and Beirut. Again he was called to Istanboul, and this time he did edit an Arabic daily, *Sabīl al-Ras͟hād*. He also lectured on Arabic literature. From 1912, he represented a district in Southern Iraq in the Turkish Chamber of Deputies. After an unsuccessful marriage he left Turkey, and after a spell lecturing in Jerusalem was back in Baghdad in 1921. He became active in politics, then from 1924 to 1929 entered the government education service, as inspector then lecturer on Arabic literature. He became an M.P. in 1930. During this period he wrote an (unpublished) book on 'The Personality of Muhammad, or the Solution of the Sacred

Enigma', which some consider his prose *chef-d'œuvre*. He also wrote books on literary criticism (based on his lectures), translations from Turkish, and a study of Arabic words in Turkish.

His final years were unfortunate. He was given substantial subventions by friends, but squandered the money. He thus mixed periods of poverty and near starvation with periods of spendthrift affluence.

As a poet, his position in Iraq is somewhat like that of Shauqi in Egypt. Zahawi was a nationalist and political poet, especially after the Turkish Constitution of 1908. But his peculiar personality apparent in his poetry militated against its popularity. It was Rusafi who first fully represented Iraq's national feelings and political aspirations in verse. The first of his diwans was published in Beirut in 1910. The authoritative diwan published after his death, containing poems hitherto unpublished, was printed in Baghdad in 1949.[65]

In prosody, he was no innovator: in this repect he was less original than Shauqi, but less of a stick-in-the-mud than Hafiz. He did write a few stanza poems, but preferred monorhyme and long metres. His themes are varied, and relevant to the contemporary scene. His descriptive poems range from the Lebanon and the Bosphorus to the Baghdad Barrage. He had an early interest in mechanical things, and wrote poems about the train, the motor-car, and the watch. He even described a game of football, as we shall see. He liked to shock people, but his pornographic poems have been omitted in his diwan. He wrote political and social poems, including eight poems specifically about woman. He could philosophize too, on such themes as 'What follows the grave?', ' 'Twixt soul and body', and 'Whence and whither?' He was an early admirer of al-Maʿarri, and was suspected of irreligion. His diwan also includes a number of short poems, ranging from two to fifteen verses each. They include an Iraqi National Anthem.

He was a thorough master of his craft. But he increasingly avoided mere verbal brilliance, and hated artificiality and imitation, shunning rhetorical devices as much as possible. He wanted his message to be intelligible to the greatest number, and was not above slipping in an odd colloquialism. His accuracy of expression in choosing the *mot juste*, allied to clarity and unaffectedness, led some to compare him with al-Buḥturī (820–97). Unfortunately Arab writers will attempt to find a classical parallel for a modern poet they admire – as if this would set the seal of fame on their protégé. In any case, such a comparison would be more valid for Rusafi's early poetry. An early poem, 'The Divorced Woman' (*al-Muṭallaqa*) is rich and difficult in vocabulary, yet every word is just right for the meaning the poet wishes to convey. At the same time, it is a touching picture of a divorced Muslim woman, and highlights a familiar problem, that of easy divorce by the man, which is being increasingly tackled in the Islamic world.

Rusafi prided himself on his frankness, a quality patent in his social and political poetry. He could be spiteful and venomous, too. In the following poem, *Ḥaqīqatī al-Salabiyya*[66] he boasts his frankness. We see in it, also, echoes of the religious scepticism of al-Maʿarri. Rusafi, incidentally, wrote a book about the latter.[67]

The Negative Truth about Me

In word and deed I favour honesty,
And loathe to lean towards hypocrisy.

To no-one have I dealt a nasty deal,
Nor do I ever broth in froth conceal.[68]

I am not one of those who think it best
To hide the truth in secret and suppress'd.

I do not think religions first were giv'n
To prophets in a message sent from heav'n,

But were imposed – those who invented them
Were men of intellect and stratagem.

I am not one of those who think and say
The spirit will ascend to heav'n one day:

Because the earth is hovering in space,
And heaven, as we know it, is but space.

I am not one of those who find pride good
In people who are proud of shedding blood;

Nor those who with the past are so entwined
That they spend all their lives looking behind.

I see no rule for people but the law
Of rulers, who themselves set up the law.

I do not show men amiability,
And then, behind their backs, hostility.

To me, no man of noble ancestry
Is thus entitled to nobility.

I am not one of those who, struck by plague,
Stammer in prayer 'Lord, save me from my plague!'

Nor of the herd who ever fast and pray
To gain the promised great reward one day!

Nor those who think that God will answer prayer
With the reward of houris pure and fair.[69]

Nor those who think that all things must become
As nothing, like an empty vacuum –

For as they join and separate, we see
Them change to pictures of eternity.

There is no great advantage, to my mind,
Possessed by mankind over womankind:

But, as new generations have been born,
These have subjected *those* to scoffs and scorn!

His descriptive and philosophical poetry may well last longer than his political and social, as the environment which inspired the latter passes into history. We give below his description of a football match.[70] No doubt many poems have been written about football in many languages. But how many can claim real poetic merit? What makes it so hard to translate is that the language is entirely classical, devoid of sportsmen's clichés, whether Arabic or arabicized.

At a Game of Football

Among them is a ball – exercise is their aim;
They exercise their bodies as they play the game,

They stand expectantly for it, then when at last
'Tis thrown, their feet take turns with it as it is pass'd:

They chase it, racing after it across a ground
In the town centre – clash and collision abound.

Kicking it with their feet, they drive the ball along,
But for a play'r to touch it with the hand is wrong!

It may soar through the air aloft; then, at its fall,
They stand prepared, and with their heads they butt the ball.

You might imagine it a shell shot from a gun
Sometimes, when with a swishing sound it scurries on:

And should it fall, before it stands some hero, thick
His brawny forearms, at the ready, poised to kick.

You might imagine it and him some fallen prey,
With a fierce roaring lion standing in their way.

Not for one moment will it tarry in one spot –
As if it were a hope, by human fancies shot!

To the North end 'tis driven with a kick; then back
Southwards some dashing player speeds it on its track.

The ball is kicked over the face of earth, and leaps
As one might leap o'er desert sign-posts, piled in heaps.

It moves among the players – one man stands aside;
Another bold one, kicking, takes it in his stride.

With people all around, 'tis like a human heart,
On which assailing cares and sorrows seem to dart.

They train their bodies with it, having lately sought
Learning, whereby to train their minds they have been taught:

For each one is a scholar, studying in some school,
Each one is in youth's prime, with elbows powerful.

The mind needs its diversions: straining enervates
But, resting for a while, it soon recuperates.

So, when you exercise the mind, still must you play
Awhile, for you will rest the weary mind through play.

Thought brings exhaustion: when persisted in, at length,
Our minds are weakened, and our bodies lose their strength!

No wonder Iraqis say that Rusafi could write a poem on any subject, however seemingly unpromising! He spoke to his listeners and readers of familiar things, whether rooted in the past or in the twentieth century. Like Hafiz and Shauqi, he was a thoroughly professional poet in the classical tradition. But he introduced new themes to poetry, and, like them, spoke of his age to his age.

3. *Poetry Elsewhere. Syria and the Lebanon*

It is monstrously unfair: but the poetry of the Lebanon, Syria, and other Arab lands must be skated over, with the mere mention of a handful of names. The poetry of the American school of Arab writers might come here, but it will be dealt with in the next chapter, as it is more modern in form and tone than that already mentioned. Nor shall we otherwise be neglecting any great master of the art. Matran, the greatest Lebanese poet of the period, is really as much Egyptian as the composer Handel was British.

Iskandar al-ʿĀzār (1855–1916) and Ilyās Fayyaḍ (1872–1930) were dramatists as well as poets. Ilyās Ṣāliḥ (1870–95), but for his early death, might have achieved greatness.[71] With Prince Shakīb Arsalān (1870–1946)[72] quite different considerations denied him front rank. He was far too prolific in too many fields. A journalist in Arabic and French, he founded a French monthly, *La Nation arabe*, and he is said to have written several hundred articles every year. He wrote a polemical work entitled *Why are the Muslims backward while others have advanced?*[73] He was also a man of affairs, tireless in the cause of Arab freedom. Thus he fought against the Italians in the war of 1911 leading to the Italian annexation of Libya. Later, he opposed the French Mandate in Syria, and consequently spent over twenty years in Switzerland as an unofficial Arab representative at the League of Nations. Most of his poetry belongs to his early manhood. The collection called *al-Bākūra* (First-fruits) was published in Beirut in 1887. His diwan, incorporating the former work, appeared in Cairo in 1935.

A great name in Syrian literature in the late nineteenth and early twentieth centuries was Salīm Rūfāʾīl ʿAnḥūrī (1856–1933),[74] an indefatigable writer of articles on every subject. What concerns us here is that he was also a poet. He was modern in subject matter, excelling in the description of modern inventions in verse.

Prose

1. *Polemics*

As we have seen, the Arab poet of the period under review was often the spokesman of Islam – or of the Arabs – or of his own particular part of the Arab world, in its struggle to come to terms with modern civilization and achieve independence from and parity with the West. He wrote on political, social, and even economic questions, and regarded himself as *vox populi*, if not *vox dei*. Meanwhile, an immense quantity of prose literature was taking up the same themes. The quantity is daunting; and – let us be frank – the bulk of it is boring. It hardly deserves mention in the same breath as creative literature. Several volumes could be devoted to articles in the Arabic press, which, as we have seen, was developing rapidly. Then there were hundreds of books written to justify the Arabs, Islam, and the East, and prick the bubble of the reputation of the West. If the author appeared to challenge the traditional Islamic position he could be sure that books would be written by the 'conservatives' to refute his arguments. The best account of the leading exponents of this literature, which is called here 'polemical', is by Albert Hourani in his book *Arab Thought in the Liberal Age, 1798–1939*.[75] There is therefore no need to tell the story here. It may be mentioned, however, that, just as the Arabs have achieved full political independence since the Second World War, and some respite from the spate of this literature might have been expected, events in the Middle East have now led to a new flood of it. It is possible to fill a whole library with books on the twin themes of Zionism and Imperialism.[76] Anyone sympathetic to the Arab cause will understand the depth of Arab feeling and appreciate why all these words should be written – but ask to be excused from reading them. It is doubtful whether there has emerged a second ʿAbduh among these polemicists.

In this chapter, we shall discuss the writings of Jamāl al-Dīn al-Afghānī (1838–98)[77] and his collaborator Muḥammad ʿAbduh (1849–1905),[78] together with Qāsim Amīn (1865–1908).[79] Aḥmad Amīn (1878–1954)[80] is included in the next chapter, in view of the late date of his book on 'East and West'.

First, however, we will mention a precursor, who might have achieved equal fame had he been born nearer the hub of Arab affairs than Tunis and had he been less involved in government. This man was Khair al-Dīn al-Tūnisī (1810–79).[81] His early life is reminiscent of the *Arabian Nights*. Born in the Caucasus of Circassian parents, he was abducted as a child and taken to the slave market in Istanboul. There he was sold to someone, who in turn sold him to an agent of Aḥmad Pasha, Bey of Tunis. He was brought up in the Bey's palace and learned French. He joined the Bey's army and rose to the rank of brigadier. Then in 1852 he was sent to Paris on a financial mission. On his return four years later he became a minister, and supported reform which took shape in the constitution of 1860. He himself became president of the Supreme Council. In 1878 we find him Grand Vizier of the Turkish Empire in Istanboul. A year later he lost his post and lived in retirement for the remainder of his life.

In his political career, Khair al-Din's objective was the preservation of the Islamic world from European interference; and for him the Ottoman Sultanate was the obvious unifying institution strong enough to enable the Europeans to be resisted. But there were two prerequisites. First, there must be reform within the Islamic world, and this could be achieved through representative institutions; such institutions could only flourish, however, if there were a new spirit. Second, skilful diplomacy was required. Unfortunately, Khair al-Din was unsuccessful in his public career: neither the Bey of Tunis nor the Sultan wanted their position weakened and their powers drastically curtailed. Again, in international politics, he was no match for the experienced practitioners in the chanceries and embassies of the Great European Powers.

His sole literary remains, apart from personal memoirs published after his death, consists of one book, *Aqwam al-masālik fī maʿrifa aḥwāl al-mamālik*, a 500-page book published in Tunis in 1867. A French translation published in Paris is entitled *Réformes nécessaires aux États musulmans*. The original title, in which the reader will note the rhyme typical of late medieval and nineteenth-century book titles, means 'The straightest path to the knowledge of the conditions of kingdoms'.[82] The work is largely descriptive of European states – historical, administrative, political, and military. The introduction, however, which states the purpose of the work, stresses the propriety of Muslims adopting what is best in the West – liberty, education, libraries, transport, and commercial organization. He points out that these things are what have enabled Europe to forge ahead: nor are they due to Christianity, which, like Islam, stresses the world to come rather than the present world. In its political institutions the Islamic world should go back to its medieval notion of the government of the nation (*umma* = the Islamic community) – that the ruler should rule by advice (*s̲haurā*). The latter he likens to the European conception of ministries and parliaments. His aim is not precisely parliamentary democracy – which, it may be argued, does not suit Islamic peoples even today – but a sort of Islamic 'enlightened despotism'. The heart of the matter is the restraining rather than the replacing of the ruler. In some respects, Khair al-Din set the pattern for later Islamic apologists. For example, similar ideas can be found with Maudūdī, the modern Pakistani thinker. Particularly characteristic of later Arab polemicists is the way he ranges from medieval Arabs to modern Europeans in support of his arguments. Thiers and John Stuart Mill stand beside Ibn Khaldun, al-Ghazzali, Hadith and the Koran.

Jamal al-Din al-Afghani as a writer can only be discussed as a collaborator or *alter ego* of Muhammad ʿAbduh. True, he provided much of the impetus and many of the ideas. In fact Arabs regard him as the mainspring of the idea of Arab unity and independence. But the articles in *al-ʿUrwa al-Wuthqā*, the newspaper he founded and for which ʿAbduh wrote, are not signed, and it is difficult to decide what he actually wrote himself. Though he undoubtedly taught in Egypt in Arabic, his ability to write that language adequately for the polemics he indulged in is open to serious doubt. Such works as he wrote – and they were not many – were originally in Persian, and were published in Cairo in ʿAbduh's translation.[83] As to the articles in al-ʿUrwa, while some have claimed to identify the hand of Afghani in certain of them, this is from their thought rather than language. One suspects that ʿAbduh licked them into shape – a suspicion confirmed by the fairly strong homogeneity in their Arabic style. Moreover, ʿAbduh was not the only collaborator: we know the names of one or two others. On the other hand, ʿAbduh's stature as a writer is undisputed. He wrote substantial Koranic commentaries, a full commentary on the maqamat of al-Hamadhani, an edition of a book on rhetoric ascribed to the third caliph, ʿAli (entitled *Nahj al-balāgha*), a famous essay on *tauḥīd* (the Islamic conception of monotheism), and a book on 'Islam and Christianity together with Science and Civilization'.[84]

The interaction of these two widely differing men would be a psychological study in itself. ʿAbduh had much of the traditionalist about him. He was an idealist, frank and straightforward, a reformer by temperament and, at one stage of his life, a reluctant revolutionary. Afghani defies categorization[85] – a revolutionary of doubtful nationality and obscure birth, an eccentric, wanderer and freemason – he was almost certainly born a Shiʿite, but sometimes seemed Sunnite. His arguments seem to have been modified to suit his audience and environment. He was no ascetic, in fact, he seems to have been asked to leave his lodgings in Paris because of a woman: but then, asceticism is not a fundamental feature of Islam. He seemed to have had great personal magnetism, and won friends easily. While not exactly 'canonized' by his contemporary admirers, their admiration went far beyond mere respect. On the face of it, his friendship with ʿAbduh seems almost like that of a gypsy befriended by a J.P. Or perhaps each saw in the other something he lacked in himself. Afghani certainly magnetized ʿAbduh as he magnetized so many other men of high intelligence and noble purpose. And one thing united them – their conviction that Islam was relevant to their own, and to every, generation; and that the Islamic nations should be free and command the respect of the West.

Afghani's[86] name suggests that he was an Afghan, or born in Afghanistan. But he sometimes called himself Istanbouli, when it suited him. Pakdaman's recent book on him, based partly on the documents unearthed by Mahdawi, seems to prove conclusively that he was born in Asadabad, near Hamadan in Iran. He later used Afghan travel documents; but at times he was glad enough of any documents he could obtain. Even the sequence of his travels is variously given and defies elucidation here; again the reader is referred to Pakdaman. He wandered from country to country, spending years here, and months there. He usually ended by becoming *persona non grata* with the rulers, to whom he appealed for support, but very much *persona grata* with leading intellectuals. He seems to have acquired his early education in Asadabad and Najaf (the Iraqi Shiʿite centre). In 1855 he was in India, learning, we are told, European sciences and mathematics. He then went on the pilgrimage and spent a year in Mecca. Later we find him in Afghanistan on intimate terms with the ruling Amir, opposing the British domination of India. In the end, the Amir expelled him. In 1869 he was in Istanboul – again *persona grata* with the powers that be. In 1870 he lectured at the inauguration of the new university called *Dār al-funūn*. But Istanboul could not hold him either: his ideas were at times so radical as to draw on him the charge of irreligion. He was asked to leave, despite his championship of Pan-Islamism, and spent 1871 to 1879 in Egypt. He had made a brief stay there a few years earlier.

In Cairo he set himself up as a teacher, both inside and outside the Azhar, his subjects being the religious sciences, philosophy, logic, Sufism and Arabic literature. His 'pupils' included many who achieved fame as writers – al-Muwaiḥilī, Adīb Isḥāq, Salīm Naqqāsh, and ʿAbduh himself; and the great Egyptian nationalist Saʿd Zaghlūl. The Egyptian government exiled him at the time of the Khedive Ismail's abdication for meddling in politics and the succession question. He went to India again, then, in 1883, to Paris. There he founded his Arabic newspaper already mentioned, *al-ʿUrwa al-Wuthqā* ('The firmest handle.' *ʿurwa* may mean not only a handle, but a loop, or something which secures a load firmly. In the title of the paper, it refers to Islam). Muhammad ʿAbduh came from his exile in Beirut to collaborate in the production of this paper. Only 18 issues appeared, but it achieved fame throughout the Islamic – especially the Arab – world. Lists of nearly a hundred regular recipients of this paper have survived, which is remarkable, seeing that the distribution had often to be secret. Articles from it have since been several times collected and reprinted. During this period, Afghani showed signs of favouring Anglo-Arab friendship, with Russia as the chief enemy of Islam. However, in visits to London, after discussions with men of influence, including politicians and ministers, he became disillusioned. When his paper failed, he went to Persia, then Russia, then back to Persia, where he was for a time adviser to the Shah, Nāṣir al-Dīn. The two soon quarrelled, and he was deported in 1891.

At the invitation of the Sultan ʿAbd al-Hamid, he went back to Istanboul. But though apparently an honoured guest, he became virtually a prisoner. As usual, he antagonized the authorities. Moreover he was suspected of being the inspirer or instigator of the assassination of the Shah in 1896, if not an actual conspirator. He certainly came to be regarded by many Persians as the 'father' of their revolutionary movement. In any case, he tried his best to inspire revolutionary reform movements wherever he went – India, Persia, Egypt, Turkey –or by remote control from Europe. It is by no means outside the bounds of possibility that the Sultan deliberately invited him to Istanboul to keep an eye on him and so neutralize a trouble-maker. During his last years in Istanboul he did little else save hold forth to those who visited him. He only survived the Shah by a year, and there were rumours that he was killed by the Sultan's order in the course of a throat operation. This is extremely doubtful; he seems to have had cancer of the throat.

Much has been written about Afghani, partly because he was so influential a figure, partly because of the mystery surrounding him. But we must pass on to Muhammad ʿAbduh, bearing in mind that possibly the finest polemical essays in modern Arabic literature, though probably owing their printed form to ʿAbduh, owe their spirit and thought partly to Afghani.

Muhammad ʿAbduh occupies a position in Arabic literature not unlike that of Sir Sayyed Ahmad Khan in Urdu. Both tried to awaken the Muslims in their countries. Ahmad Khan was the more radical – in fact ʿAbduh strongly opposed many of his views on Islam: but both realized the importance of private morals and public spirit. It would be interesting for someone to compare Ahmad Khan's ideas, and those of his pupil the poet Hali, with the ideas developed in the articles in *al-ʿUrwa al-Wuthqa*, and those of ʿAbduh's 'pupils' such as Qasim Amin, Ahmad Amin and Manfaluti. There is now a good biography of ʿAbduh in English, a translation of the Arabic biography by ʿUthman Amin, published thanks to the enterprise of the Near Eastern Programme of the American Council of Learned Societies.[87] ʿAbduh was a village boy, the son of a peasant who had 'made good'. He learned the Koran by heart at home, then studied in mosque schools in nearby towns. He rebelled against old fashioned methods of teaching, which concentrated on word-by-word commentary, and taught the Arabic language in over-theoretical grammar. Nothing he learned seemed to have much to do with the life around him. He was tempted to give it all up, and married at the age of sixteen. But thanks partly to the influence of a great-uncle, Shaikh Darwīsh, who was a Sufi, he survived his crisis of conscience, and went to the Azhar to continue his education. There, he found the atmosphere more elevated, but no more enlightened, than that of provincial mosque schools which had aroused his dislike – interminable commentary and glosses, preoccupation with word-meanings. Manfaluti describes[88] how, if a professor found a student with a book of poetry in his pocket, he treated him like a criminal caught in the act. In religious studies, apart from preoccupation with language, precise details of observance were discussed in interminable detail – for example, the precise area constituting the face to be washed in the ritual ablutions before prayer. Apart from Islam and Arabic, little else was taught, and science was regarded with suspicion. So ʿAbduh studied other subjects such as mathematics in private reading.

Afghani's arrival in Cairo in 1871 proved a turning point in ʿAbduh's life. As we have seen, Afghani had a magnetic personality, and there is no doubt that he was a convincing talker and inspiring lecturer. Moreover, though he lectured like an expert on Koranic commentary and mysticism, he had a breadth of knowledge rare in Egypt, especially among masters of the religious sciences. He lectured also on classical Arabic literature, philosophy, history, politics, and sociology. He appeared to have an all-embracing philosophy which was exemplified as much in action as in talk and thought. This struck such a chord in ʿAbduh, that he became his most fervent follower – almost to the point of idolatry. The two spent months together, and Afghani saw in the young ʿAbduh his best pupil. The latter began to write newspaper articles reflecting a more liberal attitude to Islam.

This drew on him the dislike and suspicion of the professors of the Azhar. When he came to take his final (Diploma) examination in 1877, some of the examiners wanted to fail him, despite his outstanding intellect and sterling honesty. Fortunately, others were more just, and he was given a second-class pass, as a compromise.

Now he himself became a teacher at the Azhar, lecturing on theology, logic and ethics – in the last of which he was something of a pioneer: for there was, in his days, stress on belief and observance rather than behaviour. Like Sir Sayyid Ahmad Khan, he realized that reform must come first from within, if the Islamic world was to rise again. And he also saw the weakness of narrow and purely religious education. Perhaps it was his sense of the importance of ethics and his tolerance towards other 'people of the book', such as Christians, which attracted him to freemasonry. Or perhaps it was Afghani's urging.

At any rate, he was initiated in the Star in the East Lodge (number 1355 under the United Grand Lodge of England), whose membership included men of distinction in many fields. A copy of this Lodge's Book of Constitutions in Arabic is to be found in the Grand Lodge Library at Freemasons' Hall in London. During this period, the Khedevial family were patrons of freemasonry. Most Egyptian lodges came under the jurisdiction of the National Grand Lodge of Egypt, founded in 1876, which derived from the French Grand Orient, not from English freemasonry. Its influence went back to Napoleon's invasion of 1798.

When Afghani was exiled in 1879, ʿAbduh was dismissed from his posts, and ordered to retire to his village. But the Prime Minister brought him back to Cairo, as editor-in-chief of *al-Waqaʾiʿ al-Misriyya* – the official newspaper already mentioned. In this capacity he did much to raise the literary level of Egyptian journalism. He also kept an eye on, and exposed, abuses in government offices.

Though at first unsympathetic to ʿArabi Pasha, believing that independence could only succeed when education was more widespread, ʿAbduh did ultimately become committed to the movement. He helped to write the manifesto of the Nationalist Party, and composed the oath which the rebel officers took. He was arrested, imprisoned, and sentenced to three years' exile. He went first to Beirut, then, as we have seen, joined Afghani in Paris to cooperate with him on *al-ʿUrwa.*

When the paper failed, he returned to Beirut to teach theology. In 1888 he was allowed back into Egypt, and occupied a number of important official posts. He was a judge in the Native Tribunals, then in 1899 Grand Mufti of Egypt – the most important post for a 'doctor of religion', which required him to give religious rulings for the whole country. Among his other activities was his Muslim Benevolent Society, and membership of a Khedevial administrative council for the Azhar. Then he was also busy with his writings – especially Koranic commentary, and his *Risāla al-tauhīd* – still considered a classic on the Islamic conception of God.

Those wishing to explore ʿAbduh's ideas may consult the references already given,[89] and the bibliographies they contain. In a brief generalization, it may be said that for him Islam was dynamic: its essentials were immutable eternal truth, but unessential externals could evolve to suit the changing environment. Among the essentials was the ethical code. This should bring about internal reform, which, in its turn, should lead to public virtue. His belief in public spiritedness is illustrated in his interest in benevolent societies. There is no doubt that public spirit was not strong in Islamic countries in his time, though there were any amount of rich Muslims who would pay to build a fine mosque. His ideas on charity and public spirit were taken over by pupils such as Manfaluti.

At the end of this chapter will be found – as Extract II – a translation of *Christianity and Islam and their followers* from *al-ʿUrwa al-Wuthqa.* It illustrates his skill in dialectics, and his fine style – dignified, majestic, yet not elaborate.

Belief in the need for change in woman's position was widespread among thinking men in the Arab world during the late nineteenth and early twentieth centuries. We have seen how Bustani advocated girls' education. But it was Qāsim Amīn, one of ʿAbduh's disciples, who made women's emancipation a burning issue disputed for a number of years, presenting it as an essential prerequisite for Muslim revival. A lawyer trained in France, he worked as an attorney in the Mixed Courts, then as an appeals judge. He was interested in social problems, and his training and work placed him in a good position to compare Islamic and European social customs. Moreover, like ʿAbduh, he had high ideals, and set great store by social virtues, which he saw as beginning in the home – in that area of Islamic life which was, by tradition, not for prying eyes to see.

In 1899, his book 'Woman's Emancipation' (*Taḥrīr al-Marʾa*) was published in Cairo. It caused a storm, and drew forth replies in reviews, articles, and books. Two years later he followed it with a second book, 'The New Woman' (*al-Marʾa al-jadīda*). In this he replied to his critics, reiterating and amplifying his views, and in some measure toning them down. But he spread his net more widely for illustrative examples, going even as far afield as Wyoming. This book drew further replies and refutations from the conservatives.

Qasim Amin pleaded for better treatment of women not as a radical change in Islam, but as a return to fundamental Islam, regarding the veil and the ḥarīm (harem) as excrescences not prescribed by the Koran but imposed later. He saw woman as the champion of moral standards, and her influence in the home as crucial. Healthy public life had to begin with healthy family life. However, if women were to exert their proper influence in the home, husbands must treat them better, and no longer, by force and subterfuge, deprive them of their rights under the *sharīʿa* (religious law). Girls must receive some basic education, though he did not demand that it should be identical to boys'; in fact, he saw homecraft as an essential part of their syllabus.

Thirdly, veiling must no longer be imposed, as it put women at a disadvantage, and had no justification in Islam.

Abolition of the veil, and girls' education would also enable women to earn a living, should they wish. This would benefit widows, divorcees and spinsters; but it would also enable women to take jobs for which they were especially fitted – nursing and teaching chiefly.

Hourani[90] sees a radical difference between Qasim Amin's two works. In his second book he 'dissolved the relationship established by ʿAbduh between Islam and civilization, and created in its place a *de facto* division of spheres. While treating Islam with respect, he claims the right for civilization to develop its norms . . . This means also . . . that while Islam is the true religion, that does not necessarily mean that Islamic civilization is the highest civilization.'[91] This is a fair deduction from the arguments in *al-Marʾa al-Jadida*. But it may be doubted whether the author consciously drew these conclusions himself. A close study of the book suggests that Amin is falling over backwards to find support for his basic argument from whatever source is at hand, be it religious or secular, Islamic or non-Islamic, Eastern or Western.

It is a matter for regret that Amin's style leaves much to be desired. At times it is positively gauche, and, in lawyer fashion, he appears to mistake exactitude for clarity. Here he contrasts with ʿAbduh, whose Arabic sounds well and is clear. Qasim Amin's polemics are tremendously important historically, and spring from a noble mind. But they hardly deserve the title of literature, and no extract will be given.[92]

Women writers also joined in the 'paper battle' for their sex's rights. Zainab Fawwāz (1846–1914),[93] Lebanese by birth, knew the problem at first hand. After one unsuccessful marriage in her native Lebanon and a second in Syria, she married an Egyptian colonel and settled in Egypt for the rest of her life. She wrote newspaper articles and poems championing women's rights. Her views were embodied in a book, *al-Rasāʾil al-Zainabiyya* (Cairo, 1910). She also wrote fiction, and a play, *Love and Honour*. Other women authors spoke up for women's rights in fiction form – as, for example, Bint al-Shāṭiʾ,[94] who appears in the following chapter.

During this period, no polemical works written in other Arab countries gained widespread recognition.

2. *The Short Story*[95]

The pioneer of the Arabic short story seems to have been Salīm Buṭrus al-Bustānī, son of the great Butrus. He also wrote full-length novels and plays. Several magazines and newspapers of the late nineteenth century published short stories, though a few objected to them as being worthless and corrupting, especially if they were love-stories. Many early short stories were translations or adaptations from European literature, mostly French and English, though the sources were not always acknowledged. Butrus al-Bustani had founded the magazine *al-Janān* in 1870, and Salim was, from the first, a regular contributor of articles and short stories. The first, *Ramya min ghair rāmi*, nearly 1500 words in length, appeared in 1870. Other magazines which published short stories – and also serialized novels – were *al-Ḍiyā'* and *al-Mashriq*; but the latter, being prejudiced against fiction, usually confined its fiction to stories of moral or religious purpose.

The reader who has persevered through the foregoing pages will probably realize what changes were required for the transition from old-style anecdotal literature to the European-style short story. The fundamental change required was in language and style – simplification, and the curtailing of rhetorical devices and rare words, to ensure that incident, atmosphere and characterization took precedence. This was true of the novel – but even so more of the short story, which leaves no space for non-essentials. *Ramya min Ghair Rami*[96] embodies these changes. Its simple style, using non-classical nineteenth-century words where necessary, is totally different from the style of Yaziji and Shidyaq. The plot, too, is straightforward. A miserly husband blames his wife for spending too much. Before going on a business trip he gives her money to cover household expenses during his absence. However, putting his hand into the wrong pocket, he inadvertently gives her a very large sum, instead of the modest one which was in the other pocket. When he is gone, the wife spends it all not merely on routine expenses, but on long-needed repairs, furnishing, decoration, buying new clothes for the children and herself – even buying her husband a new suit. When he returns the husband is astonished, hardly recognizing the house. He asks his wife where she got the money, and she replies it is what he gave her. Feeling in his pockets he realizes his mistake; but his family's obvious happiness deters him from complaining too much. At the end of the story, while not pretending that such an incident could reform a miser, the author hints that it did start a steady improvement. For in future, whenever the wife wishes to 'get round' her husband she laughingly uses the expression 'you gave me from the wrong pocket'.

It is a neat little story, on which Abdel-Meguid is a little hard.[97] The moral purpose is apparent – it is a warning to husbands not to be niggardly to their wives, showing them that generosity will improve the home atmosphere.

Manfaluti (1876–1924) will be dealt with later as a novelist and essayist. But a good many of the essays in his collection known as the *Naẓarāt* are in story form, and not a few of them are adapted from Western sources. Nevertheless they can hardly be considered short stories. Incidents are few; characterization is two-dimensional, portraying types rather than individuals; and moral uplift is the prime aim. Indeed, it dominates all else save the polished form and beautiful – if rather old-fashioned – style.

His other collection, *al-ʿAbarāt* (Tears)[97a] does come into the short-story category, though in fact the longest of the stories runs to about 100 pages. Most of them range between 20 and 30. As was usual at the time, the stories, immediately after their titles, are variously designated as *mauḍūʿa* (lit. placed = original) or *mutarjama* (translated). The author is believed to have been ignorant of foreign languages, and the so-called translations would be better described as 'adapted from' or 'based on' foreign stories. Presumedly someone helped Manfaluti, unless he used existing Arabic translations as his guide. These stories are not to the taste of modern readers, with their melancholy and pessimism. Their language, too, is at times ornate, though perhaps less so than the *Nazarat*. An original story, *The Abyss*,[97b] tells the story of a friend who becomes an alcoholic, and describes his downward course till he ends up in a madhouse. One of the so-called translations, *The Victim*,[97c] is the pathetic tale of Margaret Gautier, who dies of a broken heart when her lover Armand deserts her. He returns in time to assist at her funeral together with her maid Prudence. In the latter part of the story, Manfaluti relies largely on his heroine's diary, in which she writes as if addressing her absent lover.

Thousands of short stories appeared in Egypt and the Lebanon between 1870 and 1914, mostly in magazines and newspapers. Other

Arab countries lagged behind. Syrian newspapers were not much interested, but some Syrians, who had often been educated alongside Lebanese story-writers-to-be, wrote short stories which were published in Lebanese magazines such as *al-Janan*. According to Shākir Muṣṭafā,[98] the first translated fiction by a Syrian author dates from 1871, and its author was an Armenian, Jurjī Jabrā'īl Balīṭ. Taken from a French newspaper, it is entitled *Rajul dhū imra'atain* (A man with two wives), and first appeared in *al-Janan*. This 7-page story tells how a famous lawyer is consulted by a wife whose husband has deserted her. From the evidence she produces, the lawyer is horrified to discover that the missing husband is none other than the man who has recently married his daughter, and the pair are just back from their honeymoon. The lawyer insists that the man return to his real wife. Three years later they all meet by chance in a remote village. But now the wife is incurably ill and at death's door. She dies, and the story ends with the lawyer's daughter and her bigamous 'husband' reunited, and going on a second honeymoon.

Interest in early short-story writing in other Arab countries is now increasing. Since 1967 a magazine called *Qaṣaṣ* (Fiction) has been appearing in Tunis. Already one or two pioneer short stories, dating from the few years prior to the First World War, have been republished in this magazine. They seem less modern in style and feeling than Lebanese efforts, though much later than the latter.

The first outstanding Arabic short story writer was, without doubt, Maḥmūd Taimūr (b. 1894), but his place is in the next chapter. However, mention must be made of Jibrān Khalīl Jibrān (1883–1931),[99] a wayward genius whose works have been translated into several languages. He was born in the Lebanon, but emigrated to the United States at an early age with his widowed mother, and settled in Boston. He later studied art in Paris, then returned to America. He lived in New York, till his premature death of cirrhosis of the liver and tuberculosis. Jibran imbibed Arabic, French, and Anglo-American culture. Indeed, he was tri-lingual. He was able to write whole books in English. His books on Muhammad and Christ were written in English, and translated into Arabic by other hands.

He was a rebel and an individualist. Many were the influences upon him, including, for a time, Nietzsche. To some critics, these various influences seem to coalesce into a thoroughly integrated personality.

For them he represents the liberated human spirit, and one of the first Arab symbolists. He is, indeed, a latter-day mystic. Orthodox belief meant little to him at the end of his life. He was brought up a Maronite, but rejected Catholicism on his death-bed. It is easy to see why Arabs find him unique. Here was their writer who had 'caught up' with European cultural development and broken out of the prison of tradition. It is to be doubted whether his religious and philosophical works will stand the test of time. But his prose poems may survive, and his short stories still seem fresh.

Two collections of his short stories were published, both in Arabic and English: *al-Arwāḥ al-mutamarrida* (Rebellious Spirits) and *ʿArāʾis al-murūj* (Nymphs of the Valley).[100] In his short stories he shows exactitude and conciseness of expression of which every perceptive student of classical Arabic knows the language is capable, but which had long ceased to be esteemed. He uses delicate similes and metaphors, and shows psychological insight in delineating character. He is also a realist. For like many another mystic and idealist, he felt a secret *nostalgie de la boue*. In fact, in both life and art, he represents the 'Romantic agony' through which Europe had passed during the nineteenth century. Both the contemplation and personal experience of suffering in some way uplifted him. Some would call it morbidity.

Thus his poignant story, *Martā al-Bāniyya* (Martha of the village of Ban),[101] tells of a Lebanese village girl, an orphan working as a cowherd and housemaid. She grows up to be beautiful, and as unspoiled as the nature around her. At sixteen, when she is sitting at a spring one day, a richly dressed man approaches on horse-back. He stops on the pretext of asking the way. Despite her initial shyness, we are led to understand that she goes away with the stranger; for we are told that the cow returned alone to its stall, and no more is seen or heard of the girl in her village. The second part of the story opens with the author sitting on the terrace of an hotel in Beirut. A five-year-old boy comes along selling flowers. The author takes pity on the poor, frail boy, and asks him his name and age, and whose son he is. He finds that the mother is that same Martha about whom he had heard so much – for her mysterious disappearance had been a regular topic of conversation locally. He goes with the boy to a hovel in a Beirut slum and meets Martha, who is dying. She tells the author her story: how the horseman told her he loved her, and kissed her. The poor girl was not used to kisses, and was deceived. The rider took her to Beirut, where he set her up in luxury as his mistress. Tiring of her later, he deserted her, and she was compelled to give her body to his friends to earn a livelihood. She finally ended up in utter degradation, with a son to bring up. She dies, muttering the Lord's Prayer – 'forgive us our trespasses'. The author and the small boy bury her in a field outside the city, as the priests refuse her a Christian burial in a proper cemetery.

Like several of Jibran's stories, it is in two parts. Part I paints a picture of purity and – within limits – happiness. Part II is clouded by misery and tragedy. Abdel-Meguid complains of 'flowery and abstract similes' and language 'inclined to be stylistic and full of affectation'.[102] There speaks the modern Arab. But this is not how Jibran's stories must have struck his contemporaries. The similes tend to suggest a oneness between nature and man in the countryside. Thus Martha looks at 'the movement of the yellowing leaves while the breeze plays with them, *like death plays with men's souls*'. Again, 'Martha reached the age of sixteen, and her soul had become like a polished mirror reflecting the beauties of the fields, and her heart like the wild spaces of the valley echoing every sound . . .'. Like many a Lebanese exile in America, Jibran never forgot his native land, for which he retained a sort of mystical love which accorded with his general mysticism.

In *Ṣarākh al-Qubūr* (The Shout of Graves)[103] the symbolism is clear. Part I shows an Amir trying criminals. He successively sentences to death a youth who has killed a soldier; a wife discovered by her husband in her lover's arms; and a miserable wretch who has stolen the altar-plate of a monastery. The first is sentenced to be beheaded, the second to be stoned (as in Islamic law), the third to be hanged. In Part II, the author goes into the fields outside the city. The nearest and dearest of each of the three takes the body to bury it, at the same time explaining the circumstances of each crime, in such a way as to justify it, or at least show mitigating circumstances. The author is exposing the evils of corrupt customs which lead to crime, and blind justice which punishes it. The whole story is a symbolical legend. But Jibran is more successful when his symbolism is more subtle. In fact, it may be argued that one of his troubles as a writer was that he imagined himself to be a thinker, whereas he was really dominated by emotion. He could discern the thoughts and feelings of others with a sure instinct and express them accurately.

At the same time his sense of social injustice in the wicked modern world is typical of much Arabic fiction and essays of his time – Manfaluti's essays, for example. Sin and sorrow are shown in a light quite different from the traditional Islamic attitude, as the fruits of social injustice, rather than human rebellion against God. Such an approach brings psychology to bear on the *sharīʿa*. (Jibran, though born a Christian, actually uses the term *sharīʿa* in the story just discussed.) And perhaps this attitude brings us back to what we have been saying about Qasim Amin, and his attitude to women.

3. *The Novel*

The novel began in the second half of the nineteenth century with translations from European languages – chiefly French and English, especially in Egypt and the Lebanon, with Egypt predominating. Later, original novels were written, especially in Syria and Egypt. Many novels appeared in serial form in magazines – in fact, in much the same way as in England and France. As with the short story, the major problem was shedding maqama style, and many of the early translations did not even attempt to do so. Another problem was the use of colloquial Arabic, especially in dialogue. Unfortunately, the spoken language diverges widely between one area and another. Thus a Baghdadi and a Cairene might find mutual intelligibility difficult, unless they resorted to a sort of halfway house between colloquial and classical Arabic – sometimes, in wishful thinking, called 'standard Arabic'. Even those authors who allowed themselves to use colloquialisms restricted them, and often mixed them with palpable classicisms such as are seldom heard spoken – for example, the particle *lam* with the imperfect jussive of the verb to deny the past.

To serious writers, prose was too often synonymous with *belles lettres*, and it was hard for them to consider plot and characterization as paramount, and language a mere tool. Much translation of fiction were therefore by second- and third-rate writers now forgotten.

The original, as opposed to translated, Arabic novel first flourished in Syria, though this fact has been little recognized in the Middle East or in Europe until recently, with the appearance of a book in Arabic on the subject.[104] Thirteen or more novelists were active between 1865 and 1914. Most were Christians, and had travelled abroad – whether to Britain, France, Russia, America, or Egypt. They knew foreign languages. Their stories had social, ethical or educational aims, and this was often indicated by the appropriate adjective with the word *qiṣṣa* (story) on the title page.[105] The first original novelist seems to have been Anṭūn al-Ṣaqqāl (1824–85), born in Aleppo, and educated first in Syria, then in Malta. He knew Arabic, Syriac, Turkish and English. Of his two novels, the better-known was 'Arrows of Fire' (*al-ashum al-nāriyya*).

Brief reference has been made to Francis Fatḥullah Marrāsh (1836–73) as a poet.[106] His novel, *Durr al-Ṣadaf fī Gharā'ib al-Ṣadaf*, written in 1870, was published in Beirut two years later. It takes the form of a number of stories within a frame story, somewhat in the manner of the Thousand and One Nights. The story starts with the writer feeling miserable at the news of France's reverses in the 1870 war with Prussia. He goes out for a walk in the city suburb, and meets a friend who tells him a story. And so the stories told to him continue – linked, however, by recurring characters such as the girl Su'dā.

Nu'mān ibn 'Abduh al-Qusāṭalī (1854–1920) wrote three novels which were published in serial form in *al-Janan* between 1880 and 1882.[107] 'The Faithful Girl and her Mother' illustrates how the course of true love may not run smooth for an Arab girl, when her mother is prepared to go to extreme lengths – even to the extent of binding her in chains – to prevent the match. The other two novels also are love-stories – 'Murshid and Fitna' and 'Anīs'.

Another writer of social serials – published in the magazine *al-Muqtabas* – was Shukrī ibn 'Alī al-'Asalī (1868–1916).[108] *Fajā'i' al-bā'isīn* (Misfortunes of the Miserable) (1907) is the life-story of Sa'īd, a poor boy who makes good. He marries his childhood sweetheart, Jamīla, after his first marriage, to Shahīra, has foundered owing to her spendthrift ways and her mother's machinations. The first wife dies of consumption, when she realizes the part played by her mother in the break-up of the marriage. Sa'id is set upon and murdered in the street by a man who says: 'Take that for your treatment of Shahira!' Thus, in the long novel, the evils of the traditional marriage set-up and the baneful influence of mothers-in-law are exemplified.

Another of ʿAsali's novels, *Natāʾij al-Ihmāl* (The Results of Neglect) of 1913, must surely be the first Arabic novel in which the story starts outside a cinema! The author describes the story as being based on fact, but so disguised as to prevent positive identification. Its aim is to show that social liberty can easily become licence. It was written shortly after the promulgation of the Ottoman constitution of 1908 (restoring that of 1876) which had given greater liberty. There had been a quarter of a century between Qusatali's novels and those of ʿAsali. This was the period of the oppression of ʿAbd al-Hamid, when little fiction was written in Syria.

Some Syrian novelists chose historical themes. ʿAbd al-Masīḥ Anṭakī wrote 'A Maiden of Israel' (1903), while ʿAbd al-Hamīd al-Zahāwī wrote 'Khadīja Mother of the Believers', the heroine being the Prophet Muhammad's first wife.

Thus the novel had made a start in Syria by the beginning of the 1914–18 war. These novels were often printed in Beirut, and serialized in various magazines. Christians played a major part in writing them. The shackles of high-flown classical language were being thrown off, and these novels were readable, but not of the first rank.

In the Lebanon, also, the novel was developing. Salīm the son of Butrus al-Bustani tried his hand at this too. He wrote a series of social novels serialized in *al-Janan*; notably *Salmā* (1878–9) and *Sāmiya* (1882–4). In the Lebanon, the historical novel appeared in Salim's *Zanūbiyā Malika Tadmur* (Zenobia Queen of Palmyra) – published in *al-Janan* in 1871. This subject has been one of the most popular with Arab novelists. The best novel on the subject is that by the living Egyptian writer, Muḥammad Farīd Abū Ḥadīd, entitled simply *Zanūbiyā*.

The historical novel was taken up with great vigour by Jurjī Zaidān (1861–1914),[108a] a Lebanese who, like Matran, spent most of his life in Egypt. He was born in Beirut, but only completed the primary stage of his education, having to leave school to work for his father. He learned English at night school, then did a year as a medical student at the American University. He left, and went to Egypt in 1882 to work as a journalist. Returning to Beirut in 1885, he studied Arabic and Syriac, and wrote the first of three philological works, *Arabic vocabulary and the science of Philology*. He visited England,

and then settled in Egypt. In 1892 he founded the famous literary monthly, *al-Hilāl*, which is still appearing.

Zaidan was an indefatigable and prolific writer in almost every field but drama. His 4-volume *History of Arabic Literature* (1911) and his 5-volume *History of Islamic Civilization* (1902–6) were unique at their time of publication; and they are but two of his several works on these subjects. His historical interests were diverse. He wrote histories of Greece and Rome, Modern Egypt, Britain and pre-Islamic Arabia – also a history of Freemasonry in Egypt. But above all, he wrote historical romances, forty in all.

In publishing these, Zaidan was able to use the services of the Hilal Press, set up to publish his magazine.

His historical romances were popular, and many have been frequently reprinted. Several have been translated into French, German, and into other oriental languages. Yet he cannot be deemed a great writer in the normal sense. He was above all an educator: and Gibb here,[108b] as so often, hits the mark in calling him 'Egypt's schoolmaster out of school'. He goes on to say: 'It is fully open to question whether his activity was not even more effectual than Muhammad Abduh's in leading contemporary Egyptian literature along the path which it has followed.'

Most of the historical novels deal with the glories of the medieval world of Islam. For example, *S͟hārl* (*Charles*) *wa ʿAbd al-Raḥmān* (1914) described the Muslims' advance into France, and their defeat at the hands of Charles Martel, King of France, at the Battle of Tours in 732. *al-ʿAbbāsa* tells the story of Hārūn al-Ras͟hīd's daughter of that name, and her secret marriage to his vizier, Jaʿfar the Barmecide. ʿAzīz Abāẓa's play on the same theme dates from 1947. Zaidan's novel is available in French translation.[108c] As we read this story, it is easy to appreciate its nostalgic appeal to Egyptian readers, when they read about characters they had heard of at school. In this novel, in addition to the chief characters, we meet the poets Abu Nuwas and Abu al-ʿAtahiyya – the latter an important character, for it is he who gives away the secret of the marriage to Harun al-Rashid.

We have said that Zaidan was not a great writer. But perhaps it is as well that he was not. Page after page of very readable Arabic keep the reader interested in the story from beginning to end. There is no great psychological insight, but the characters – already half-alive in the reader's mind – become real. By making great Arabs of the past seem no longer remote, and describing them in a modern literary form, Zaidan performed a double service – to his fellow-Arabs' self-respect, and to modern Arabic literature. The nearest European counterpart was Dumas, with his series of French historical novels.

Another Lebanese writer of historical novels was Faraḥ Anṭūn (1874–1922).[108d] His period in Egypt was broken by a stay in New York, where he did not achieve the success for which he had hoped. Like Zaidan, he was a polygraph, and he was also an active translator – for example, of Renan's Life of Christ, and works by Saint-Simon, Chateaubriand, St. Pierre (*Paul et Virginie*), Dumas, Sardou, and Sophocles. He wrote plays, too, many of the serious ones being translations – as were his 'musicals', including Carmen (Karmīnā). He is said to have been influenced by Rousseau, Marx, Tolstoy and George Bernard Shaw. His historical novels include a triology on the French Revolution, adapted and abridged from Dumas. His 'New Jerusalem' (*Ūrashalīm al-jadīda*),[108e] which tells of the Arabs' conquest of Palestine, enjoyed a considerable vogue at one time.

We have fortunately an account of the emergence of the novel in Egypt by Sir Hamilton Gibb. Called *The Egyptian Novel*, it forms Part IV of his *Studies in Contemporary Arabic Literature* which was published in 1933.[109] Gibb refers to the tardiness of the Egyptians in this field, compared with the Syrians. He speaks of the 'great variety and satisfaction to be enjoyed in classical Arabic literature', and of the fact that Egyptians with modern education could read French and English novels in the original. As the demand grew, instead of producing an 'indigenous novelistic literature', writers translated or adapted European novels. Perhaps another explanation is that Egyptian Christians – the Copts – were not as active in literature as their Syrian brethren. The use of rhymed prose and rhetorical devices characterized much Egyptian fiction, whether original or 'translated'. An outstanding example is 'Uthmān al-Jalāl's version of *Paul et Virginie*, published undated before 1892. Hafiz's adaptation of *Les Misérables* and Shauqi's early romances have already been mentioned.

Manfaluti[110] adapted several French Romantic novels – *Paul et Virginie*, Coppée's *Pour la couronne*, A. Karr's *Le Tilleul*, and Rostand's *Cyrano de Bergerac* among them.

Meanwhile, the maqama survived in Egypt at a time when it was dead or dying in Syria and the Lebanon. But the form was often used as a vehicle for social criticism, and there tended to be some toning-down of artificialities of language.

The first major original Egyptian novel was *Zainab: manāẓir wa akhlāq rīfiyya* (Zainab: Rural scenes and morals) published anonymously, as 'by an Egyptian peasant', in 1914. The second edition of 1929 showed that the author was Muḥammad Ḥusain Ḥaikal (1888–19—), a lawyer.[111] This novel portrays rural social life in Lower Egypt. It is the story of Zainab, a beautiful girl, who falls in love with Ibrahim, but is married to Hasan by her parents. She is a faithful wife: but when Ibrahim is conscripted into the army, she dies of consumption. Incidentally, Arab writers of fiction seemed very much addicted to their heroines dying of consumption or other dire diseases – and of broken hearts. One is reminded of French Romantic fiction of the nineteenth century. However, there was a classical literature of 'martyrs of love': and in the Arab environment, in the days before a fully modern health service existed, sorrow must often have brought out latent disease and led to death. At the same time, clearly the Syrians Qusatali and ʿAsali had already written this sort of thing in their novels, but with rather less success.

Haikal had studied in Paris between 1909 and 1913, and for him, writing this novel was a means of recalling his native land, especially its countryside. Descriptive passages therefore abound, and, but for them, the tale could have been told in half the space. As it is, the book is substantial – between 300 and 400 pages, according to the edition. The theme behind the story is the danger of outworn customs – in this case, the parentally arranged marriage, which was normal in those days. Various other rural abuses also come to light in the story. The language is free from artificiality, and the dialogue of peasants uses Egyptian colloquialisms.

The novel in Egypt was taken up by many authors, of whom ʿAbd al-Qādir al-Māzinī[112] is one of the best-known. He lived from 1890 to 1949, and wrote in every major genre except drama. He was a fine stylist with a deep knowledge of English literature. For example, he translated Galsworthy. Three major novels came from his pen: *Ibrāhīm al-Kātib* (1931); *Ibrāhīm al-Thānī* (1943); and *Thalātha rijāl wa imra'a* (Three men and a girl). Gibb,[113] in writing about the first-named of these three, refers to its 'defiant cynicism, subtle humour, and crisp and natural dialogue', though Mazini did not believe in using the colloquial. At the same time, Gibb says it is Western in feeling.

But we have gone rather ahead of our time-schedule: and further novelists will be considered in the next chapter.

4. *The Essay*

As has been said, the risala and maqama are the classical antecedents of the modern Arabic essay. The latter is, in a large measure, the product of the newspaper and magazine. It may owe something to the English essays of Bacon, Addison, Lamb, Hazlitt and De Quincey, especially with certain writers such as Mazini. But it is doubtful how widely Arab authors read such essays. They do not seem to talk about them much, whereas they frequently mention European novelists and dramatists. No-one appears, for instance, to have translated Lamb's *Essays of Elia* into Arabic.

The essay-form is difficult to define. It has been called 'a literary composition (usually prose and short) on any subject'.[113a] We are here only concerned with prose, save for the essayist's penchant for including poetical quotations to clinch his arguments, a habit as common with Arab as with European essayists. We certainly confine our attention to *short* essays, though no precise limit can be postulated. As to the subject, while there is, indeed, no limit, we are not concerned here with essays of a strongly polemical and dialectical character on such subjects as religion, politics, and economics. Thus the articles in *al-Urwa al-Wuthqa* may properly be described as essays: but we have treated them separately. By the essay, we mean a short piece of prose (ranging very roughly, perhaps, from one to thirty pages) devoted to a single subject. It must consciously aim at a good style – whatever that may mean – and an imaginative approach is almost mandatory. In fact, to use a term we have already over-used, it must be creative literature. While some sort of story may be apparent, as in some of Lamb's essays, the essay does not have the telling of a story as its principal aim: this is what distinguishes it from the normal type of short story. At the same time, the essayist often finds the relating of some incident a telling way of making his point. Such an incident may be fact or fiction, or a mixture of both. In telling a story, he is not expected to develop characters. These therefore tend to be types rather than individuals. Nor is realism required in dialogue or description.

The wide range and immense bulk of Arabic essays during the period under discussion preclude any attempt to present a conspectus. Fortunately there is now a comprehensive collection of over 400 pages in French translation,[114] from which the reader may judge the great variety in subject and treatment.

Chapter I mentions some essays by Lebanese Yaʿqūb Ṣarūf (1852–1927).[115] He was, by the way, yet another writer of historical novels, and an active journalist. A varied writer, who migrated from the Lebanon to America, and published works in both Arabic and English, was Amīn al-Rīḥānī (1876–1940),[116] to whom justice cannot be done in the present work. A sensitive writer, he wrote works on history, literary history and criticism, biography, travel, personal reminiscences, besides poetry. A number of his essays will be found in the 4-volume collection called *al-Rīḥāniyyāt*.[117]

However, at the risk of appearing prejudiced, we will conclude this account of the 'first flowering of the Arab literary renaissance' with an appreciation of an author who, more than any other author of the period, made the essay his own special form; a writer whose name long dominated accounts of modern Arabic literature in Arabic textbooks used in Arab schools; moreover one who, in his style and even his ideas, seems to typify the transition from the traditional to the 'modern'. This writer was Muṣṭafā Luṭfī al-Manfalūṭī (1876–1924).[118]

He was born in Manfalut in Assyut province, and was educated at the Azhar, where he spent ten years. In the introduction to the collected edition of *al-Naẓarāt*,[119] he speaks feelingly of the oppressive atmosphere there. He came under the influence of Muhammad ʿAbduh, whose reforming ideas are reflected in *al-Nazarat* – for example, in his support for benevolent societies. While at the Azhar, he read widely in classical Arabic poetry and prose, and acquired a rich and *recherché* vocabulary which he was able to use freely. He began writing, he tells us, at the age of thirteen. His poetical works did not make any mark. The turning point in his career was 1907, when he began writing his weekly articles for the paper *al-Mu'ayyid*. These were later collected and published as *al-Nazarat* (Views).

His life was not a happy one. Several of his children died in infancy, and a note of pessimism pervades much of his writing. The vices he saw around him added to his sorrow; for he believed, with Muhammad ʿAbduh, that internal reform and sound morals in the individual were the first requirement for Arab advancement. He addresses, however, Egyptians, rather than Arabs as a whole.

His translations of novels and his short stories have been briefly considered. But it was *al-Nazarat* which put him in the first flight of Arab authors. In fact they mark him as possibly the greatest of all Arab essayists. In subject they are varied, with a preference for ethical and social themes. He was a journalist of genius. In style he stands at the crossroads. He had a genuine desire to avoid artificiality, and to write simply and clearly for his age. In fact, in his introduction he gives the impression that he really has succeeded in writing simply, and states categorically that he is writing for the common man, not the intellectual. In practice he constantly lapses into a studied style which is anything but modern. His content seldom rises above what would be considered trite in the West – the evils of drink, poverty and riches, charity, the happy and unhappy marriage, tomorrow, and the like. Yet this very triteness struck a new note for his readers, being not only sincere, but relevant to everyday life as they saw it. He deals frequently with social evils, some of which show the effect of Western notions on traditional Islamic society. He was an idealist, but sometimes gives an impression of intolerance and a 'holier than thou' attitude.

In *Madīna al-saʿāda*[120] (The City of Happiness) he describes a Utopian city in which all are equal and have their needs supplied. In *al-Raḥma*[121] (Mercy) he preaches care for one's fellow men: 'Oh happy man! Be merciful . . . feed the starving . . . clothe the naked, comfort the sorrowful . . . pity the fallen woman, the widow . . . Pity your wife, pity your child and watch his physical and spiritual well-being . . . be kind to animals and birds . . . do not keep them in cages . . .' In *Iḥsān*[122] (kindness) he attacks misplaced charity, giving to *awqāf* (Muslim charitable foundations) and funds for building mosques, and, worst of all, giving to beggars. Provident societies, he says, are the answer.

These ideas are presented in language pervaded by classical rhetoric, toned down, however, to suit modern readers. In the collected edition, rare words have to be explained in footnotes: yet the language is plain compared with that of Yaziji and Shidyaq. He is a

Janus, looking forward and backward. Yet we must remember that the backward-looking elements appealed to his readers, who would hardly have respected the essays had they been written in everyday language. His balanced sentences and rhymed prose are still admired, though not as much as formerly.

His introduction is a good guide to his attitudes. Many people, he says, ask me about my style, so as to imitate it. This is undesirable, since style is a personal matter. His style, he says, is not consciously based on his reading, but on his love of beauty. All things interest him, whether good or evil, and he is able to enter into the spirit of them. He likes poetry, and likes tragic stories of unrequited love. But he does not write about what he does not feel, for he finds it hard to lie. He describes himself as a sensitive man, who has seen all sorts of misfortune and injustice, and feels the urge to protect people from them.

He goes on to state that mere imitation of Europeans is not enough. Arabic is a fine language, but few modern prose writers or poets really appreciate it. Language and literature should go hand in hand. It is taste which raises mere grammar to the status of literature. Tongue (*lisān*), brain (*ʿaql*) and heart (*qalb*) all play their part. He claims that he has tried to write as he would speak, and has never written truth without imagination, nor imagination without truth: for imagination is 'what makes the world go round'. He has not written for popularity, but to benefit people.

All this represents high ideals. It is, in fact, typical of that perfectionism which is sometimes almost a blemish. It is, moreover, naïve and oversimplified, and is more a statement of aims than of achievement. For by no stretch of imagination can his language be described as designed for ordinary readers, nor could he surely speak as he writes. He is, as it were, aiming to be a prose Shelley and Wordsworth rolled into one but cannot succeed in this. In fact, the merits of his style are quite different.

It is modern balagha at its best, full of rhyme, of balanced phrases and sentences, of simile and metaphor. It is also a veritable show-case of certain syntactical features of literary Arabic – for instance, complex groups of conditional sentences which dominate the short essay *Ayyuhā al-maḥzūn* (Oh sorrowful one);[123] doubly transitive verbs with twin pronominal objects attached to the verb; and involved circumstantial (*ḥāl*) clauses. These essays are as superb a display of classical Arabic prose-writing as will be found in the whole of the modern literature. At the same time, he could write simply – his essays often begin so. But as he warms to his subject, and his 'imagination' takes over, the complexities creep in – or rather burst in.

Yet if the style is rather antique, the themes and attitudes are up-to-date. Many classical writers had depicted men with vices – cruelty, immorality, meanness, neglect of children. But the medieval writer tended to be tolerant of eccentrics, so long as the eccentricity did not involve religion. Manfaluti looks at vice as a modern reformer, much concerned with personal ethics. His essay themes run the whole gamut of current ethical and social problems. Novelists and short-story writers were dealing with them: Manfaluti discusses them directly. He has essays on marital fidelity, polygamy, alcoholism, suicide, gambling, jealousy, pride, revenge, and conscience. At times he strikes an intensely personal note, as in *al-Dafīn al-Ṣaghīr* (the young buried one) in which he speaks of the burial of a young child of his who died in infancy.[124] He is satirical, even bitter, about whole classes of people – doctors, for example, who worship gold and silver, and fear the infection of poverty as much as the infection of disease.[125]

It is noteworthy that, when opposing vices, he rarely does so on strictly religious grounds, as a classical writer might have done. Rather are they an offence against the dignity and happiness of man. He speaks of God, of course, and expresses unquestioning faith shot through with fatalism. When describing misfortune, he constantly lays it at the door of *dahr* (= time, fate), which he depicts as ever ready to attack men; in fact, as giving man happiness for a short time merely in order to have the cruel satisfaction of taking it away. He is aften maudlin and sentimental to European ears, and inwardly perplexed by life. He too, then, was oppressed by a sort of 'Romantic agony'.

Special tribute must be paid to Manfaluti's exquisite sense of form in his essays. He often begins in a straightforward way, stating the problem under discussion, then gradually works up to a climax, and finally dies away to the end of the essay. The essay may be a cautionary tale, a reasoned argument, an impressionistic picture, or a poem in prose. In fact, he challenges comparison with essayists in many other languages, for the wide variety of his themes and their treatment, and his command of language and form. He pulls at the heart-strings, lapsing, as we have said, to the maudlin. In the West these days we do not like a writer to wear his heart on his sleeve. Arabs of Manfaluti's days – and even today – were (and are) not so inhibited.

One's final assessment of this author depends on one's taste. To the European with no feeling for classical Arabic literature, he seems Victorian, with the smugness and moral attitudes of a former generation. To those immersed in the classical literature, he must have seemed to represent the best that could be hoped for in modern literature. Gibb sums up his position accurately, in describing him as a 'transitional figure'.[126] Yet he calls *al-Nazarat* 'racy and sparkling'. 'Racy' surely implies 'brisk' – and this they certainly are not. In fact they are mostly sedate and dignified, proceeding inexorably to their appointed end. A few are impressionistic, and glide along. However, Gibb is correct in stressing that it was their content which won them special regard. Granted that his readers expected something identifiably fine in style, they were struck to find that this style could be so effectively used to discuss current everyday problems. With him, journalism had become art.

After this chapter will be found two essays from *al-Nazarat*: *Tomorrow* (Extract III) and *The First Cup* (Extract IV). An attempt has been made to reflect the Arabic style in the translations, but it has not been possible to transfer the rhymes to English.

Thus, by the end of the First World War and the early 1920's Arabic literature had progressed beyond the classical imitations of the mid-nineteenth century and was assuming a more modern character. Under Western influence new forms had appeared – notably the novel and short story. Religious changes, social reform, and political problems had all found expression in creative literature. A few writers of outstanding genius had appeared.

In the succeeding chapter, we shall see the literature reach full maturity, absorbing various European 'modernist' movements.

EXTRACT II

Christianity and Islam and their followers, by Muhammad ʿAbduh and Jamāl al-Dīn al-Afghānī

(from *al-ʿUrwa al-Wuthqā*, Beirut edition, 1909, pp. 72 ff.)

'In that there is a reminder for him who has a heart.
or who lends an ear, when he is a witness.'*

God created man endowed with knowledge and craftsmanship, and has made the way easy for him to work for himself, with the gift of originality and inventiveness. He ordained him to earn his own sustenance with the work of his own hands; indeed, he made this the foundation of his existence and the basis of his survival. Thus in all his circumstances, whether straitened or ample, rough or luxurious, primitive or civilized, his survival depends on his labours. His food is derived from land utilization, whether by agriculture or animal husbandry. His clothing and all that protects him from heat, or cold, or foot-sore are woven and sewn by his own handiwork. His shelter and housing are but manifestations of his foresight and thought. All the various causes of comfort and pleasure in which he exercises himself are reflections of his exertions and revelations of his thought. And were he, for one hour, to wash his hands of self-help, and stretch out his palms to nature to ask for a breath of life, nature would not merely be mean with it, but would even push him down into the abyss of non-existence. Yet man, in his making and inventing, needs a teacher to educate him, and a guide to direct him. For just as he works to multiply the requirements of his livelihood and the needs of his life, so also does he strive to learn how to work, and to enable himself to work. For his very workmanship also is of his own making. In all the affairs of his life, he is a conscious craftsman, as if he were separated from nature and remote from its influences: he needs nature

* Koran, L, 37.

as the worker needs his implement. This is man's position with regard to his food, drink, clothing and housing.

Let us leave him like this, then, and take a look at his spiritual and moral circumstances of cognition, ethics, faculties and spiritual reactions. You will find that in these also he is a conscious craftsman. You will find that his courage and cowardice, patience and impatience, generosity and avarice, vigour and vileness, cruelty and kindness, continence and greed, and similar perfections and imperfections – all these arise from the basic upbringing he happens to have, from what is implanted in his mind by the circumstances of those among whom he is brought up, from his ways of thought and his inclinations. It is parents, family, kinsfolk and acquaintances who instil in him his passions and desires, his longing for divine secrets, his penchant for investigating natural phenomena, his concern to discover the truth in everything, his acceptance of fundamental views of things, and all that is connected with intellectual movements.

As for the environmental factors of birth and upbringing, his type of brain and physique, and other natural external features, they have no influence on moral attitudes and spiritual qualities, save in preparedness and receptiveness, or weakness in that direction. For upbringing and the effect on the mind of the circumstances of acquaintances and the thoughts of tutors are dissipated as if they had not been deposited by nature. Yes! Thoughts can be revised, metaphysics develop, qualities be enhanced and improved, so that those possessing them become superior to their predecessors. So people think that this is the course of nature, not acquired characteristics. But the truth of the matter is that it is the fruit of something sown, and the result of what has been acquired. It is one product arising out of another. For man, in his intellect, character and spirit, is a conscious producer.

All this can be doubted by neither intellectuals nor simple men. Yet, despite this, have you considered that bodily exercise arises from spiritual endowments and determination, and that the spirit dominates the body? I think that you will not need reminding of this, because it is not hard to understand. However, before launching into my subject, I must state one fact about religion which I imagine no-one will contradict.

Religion is God-given, yet it is taught and proclaimed by men. The mind receives it from preachers and admonishers. This is how it is acquired by those not set aside by God for His revelation, and how it is passed on by them by declaration, study, teaching and instruction. In all peoples it is the first thing to involve the heart and become firmly implanted in it. The soul is stamped by its tenets and by the habits and customs which follow in its wake. The body is trained by the resultant activities, whether great or small. So religion has the major control over thoughts, and the resultant determinations and wishes. Religion is the ruler of the spirit, guiding it to what the body has planned. It is as if man, in his youth, were a *tabula rasa*, and religion the first writing on it. Then man is led to other activities by the call and the guidance of religion. And everything else affecting the soul is extremely rare and anomalous. So much so, that were a backslider to cast off his faith, he would not be able to cast off those qualities it has instilled in him. Indeed, its impress would remain in him, like the scar of a wound on his skin after it has been healed.

After this (preamble), the subject of our discussion now is the Christian and Islamic communities. It is a big subject, so we will deal with it in a general way which will lead you to further detail.

Christianity was based on reconciliation and forbearance in all things. It brought with it the removal of retaliation, the rejection of involvement in rule and authority, and the neglect of the world and its vanity. It preached submission to every authority ruling its devotees, 'rendering to Caesar that which is Caesar's', and the avoidance of personal, racial, and even religious quarrels. The Gospel says: 'He who strikes you on your right cheek, offer him your left.' Again: 'Kings rule over men's bodies which pass away. The true and lasting rule is over souls, and that belongs to God alone.'

Whoever is acquainted with the edifice this religon has constructed, bearing in mind what I have said about religion having the greatest power over thoughts – remembering that every idea has an influence over the will, which leads to a corresponding body movement – such a person will be absolutely astounded at the conduct of those adopting this peaceable religion and believing in its tenets. They vie with each other in pride and boasting of the adornments of this world, and in luxurious life. They know no bounds in the pursuit of all its pleasures. They rush to conquer kingdoms and overcome extensive domains. They are unequalled in the invention of murderous weapons of war, which they use one against the other, and to assault others. They pass all bounds in organizing armies, and planning their tactics on the battle-field. They tax their minds with the proper organization of these armies to such an extent that military science has become one of their most extensive and difficult sciences: all this despite the fact that their religion's principles (are supposed to) turn their minds away from concern to keep their possessions, let alone the inclination to acquire further possessions!

The Islamic religion (on the other hand) is based on the quest for victory, influence, conquest and power; and on the rejection of every law conflicting with its own legal code (*s̲harīʿa*); on the removal of every authority where the ruler is not committed to carrying out the laws of Islam. Anyone who looks at the bases of this religion, and reads a chapter of its revealed book, will come to the incontrovertible conclusion that those who believe in it should be the foremost military people in the world, superior to all others in the invention of murderous weapons of war, in mastering military sciences, in delving deeply into other sciences they demand, such as physics, chemistry, mechanics, geometry, and the like. Whoever reads the Koranic verse: 'And prepare for them such power as lies within your capacity', will confirm that those stamped with this religion are characterised by the love of conquest, the search for every means facilitating the way to it, and striving for it as far as is humanly possible – not to mention guarding themselves against being conquered by others with might and main. When one notices that Islamic law forbade gambling except in archery contests, one discovers the lawgiver's concern for the knowledge of, and practice in, military sciences. Despite all this, however, one must be surprised at the condition of the followers of this religion these days. One sees them neglectful of power, slothful in seeking its requirements. The Muslims have no interest or skill in military sciences, nor in the invention of weapons. So they have been overtaken by other nations in what should be their prime duty, and have been compelled to copy these other nations in their need for these sciences and weapons. Many have fallen under the sway of their aggression, humiliated by it, crushed under their laws. Anyone who compared the two religions would be confused in his mind as to how Krupp and Mitrailleuse guns could have been invented by Christians rather than Muslims, how Martin rifles could have been created in the countries of the former rather than the latter; how fortifications were perfected, warships armour-plated, and the oceans controlled by the people of peace and pacification, rather than the people of conquest and war.

Why should the wise man be confused, despite his learning? Why should the experienced and far-sighted fail to penetrate to the truth? Have past centuries and ages gone by been insufficient to implant the two religions firmly in the hearts of their devotees? Has each community rejected the tenets of its religion in its external manifestations for long generations? Have the Christians in their religion stopped short at the adoption of the Mosaic law, and the imitation of the life of Joshua the son of Jonah? Has the understanding of certain gospel verses become involved, consciously or unconsciously, in sermons and preachings from Muslim pulpits? Or has some part of them been instilled in the desires of their teachers, and the publishers of their laws, when they sat cross-legged as students in their classes? Has God's course been reversed in the two communities? Has the natural course of development been changed? Has the flesh tyrannized the spirit? Has the spirit found some other controller rather than thought and imagination? Has thought turned aside from the authority of religion? Or has the soul resisted being moulded by it, though it is (normally) the foremost ruler and strongest influence over it? Are the ills beyond its ken? Has the link between cause and effect been broken? What likelihood is there, indeed, of the mind's being guided to discovery of that which is veiled and obscured?

Can this be ascribed to racial differences, in view of the fact that many members of the two communities have common origins, and closely related descent? Can it be ascribed to difference of habitat, when many of the two categories live in lands of similar characteristics, and in adjacent areas? In the early days of their religion, did not the Muslims perform feats which dazzled the eyes and astonished the mind? Were there not among them Persians, Arabs, and Turks who subdued kingdoms, and sat on their thrones?

In the Crusades the Muslims had fire-weapons similar to artillery of which Christians were afraid, not knowing how they worked. The Englishman Sir John Malcolm mentions in his history of Persia that Maḥmūd al-Farzūnī used to fight the pagans of India (the Hindus) with artillery, and this was the reason for their defeat at his hands in the year 400 A.H.*

So what helping hand of fate was it which took the Christians and led them to what was not in the principles of their faith? And what blow of fate was it that struck the breasts of the Muslims, and made them backward in using the means to attain what was the prime duty imposed on them by their religion? Here are grounds for confusion and a situation for astonishment. It will be thought that there must surely be a reason for this paradox. There is one, indeed, and it would take a long time to go into it in detail. But we will confine ourselves to our previous premise – that Christianity's influence spread, and conversion to it became general, among Romans in European countries. These people had beliefs, culture, customs and habits inherited from their former faiths and their original learning and laws. Then Christianity came to them, pacifying their habits, actions, and minds. It gained access to them by way of persuasion and conviction, not by the hammer-blows of strength and force. Thus it was like embroidery on their garments: it did not deprive them of what they had inherited from their forebears. Yet the Gospel pages which call for peace and pacification were not, in former ages, accessible to all, but were jealously guarded by spiritual leaders. Then the Roman priesthood, when they set themselves up as lawgivers, called for the Crusades, making them a religious obligation, and causing its effects on the mind to become mingled with religious tenets. It became a fundamental of the religion, as a result of which Christian beliefs were shaken in Europe. The Christians split into sects, and adopted courses contrary to (the established) religion and its authority. Then a flash from those roots bequeathed them by their ancestors burst into flame. They widened the range of their thought, extending it into many arts (and sciences). Their skill in the art of war, and their invention of offensive and defensive weapons, became the driving force for their skill in other arts.

On the other hand, the Muslims, after their achievements in the early period of their religion, in which they acquired a share of every sort of military skill and obtained a quota of every warlike glory, indeed, after surpassing other peoples in the arts of strategy and the

* The original has *Mālkām Sarjam*. The reference is to Maḥmūd al-G͟haznawī. See C. E. Bosworth, *The Islamic Dynasties*, Edinburgh, 1967, 181 ff.

sciences of tactics and battle, then found among themselves people appearing under the guise of the true religion, but who were really innovators in it. They mixed alien elements with its fundamentals. The principles of human helplessness spread among them, and battered their minds till they entered them. They permeated their minds till they made them inactive. To this should be added what was introduced by the Manichaeans in the third and fourth centuries, and that which was occasioned by the Sophists, who denied external reality, which they considered as apparent things with no foundation of fact. Then again, there were the traditions produced by mendacious transmitters, which they attributed to the fountain-head of the divine law (the Prophet Muhammad), confirming them in books. Such traditions contained poison fatal to zeal. Indeed, whatever of them adheres to the mind necessarily weakens aspirations and enervates determination. The investigations of men of truth into all this, and their undertaking of the explanation of what was correct and what was false, could not dispel its effect on ordinary people, especially after the decline of education standards, and the failure to teach the masses the true bases and firm structures of their faith as called for by the Prophet and his Companions. For the study of religion in its correct manner is restricted to particular circles, to a small minority. Indeed, this is perhaps the defect of the Muslims' position and cause of their discomfiture. That is what we suffer from today, from which we ask God to save us.

Yet though these obstacles which have come upon religion and turned the Muslims' hearts from care for it constitute a dense screen, nevertheless, between them and true beliefs which they have not altogether abandoned is constant and ceaseless struggle and contention. The strife between truth and vanity is like the resistance of a strong constitution to illness. And seeing that religion is the first imprint placed by God on men's souls, and its lightning still flashes, shining in men's hearts amidst the intervening clouds, its light must surely one day spread and disperse the dark clouds. So long as the Koran is recited among Muslims – it being their revealed book and their true leader, superintending them, ordering them to protect their heritage and defend their dominion, to contend with their aggressors, to seek security by every means, without specifying any manner or singling out any way for it – we do not doubt that the Muslims will become once more as they were in their prime. They will then rise up and demand of time what it has deprived them of, outstripping others in the arts of solidarity, soldiering and assaulting their foes, to preserve their rights, tenaciously guarding themselves against degradation, and their people against dereliction. And to God everything must return.*

* A pious formula.

EXTRACT III

The Morrow, by Muṣṭafā Luṭfī al-Manfalūṭī

(from *al-Naẓarāt*, Vol. I, pp. 39 ff.)

I know that last night I was thinking about what I should write today. And I know that at this moment I am holding my pen between my fingers, and that in front of me is a white sheet of paper which is gradually becoming black as I move the pen over it. But I do not know whether the pen will reach its limit, or fall short of its objective: whether I shall be able to complete this essay of mine, or whether some obstacle of time will obstruct its course. For I know nothing of the morrow's matters, and the future is in God's hands.

I know that I put my clothes on this morning, and that I am still wearing them at this moment. Yet I do not know whether I shall take them off (later) with my own hands, or whether they will be taken off by the hand of him who washes the bodies of the dead.

The morrow is a confused spectre which looms into view from afar. It may be a merciful angel, or it may be a foul fiend. Indeed, it may be a black cloud, which, when a cool breeze blows on it, breaks up, scattering its particles; so that it becomes like a non-existence which has never known existence.

The morrow is a vast rolling sea, with swelling billows amid roaring waves. It does not tell you whether it hides in its depths pearl and jewel, or death violent and cruel.

The morrow is hidden from man's eyes, its form too abstruse to comprehend. So much so, that were a man to raise his foot to step outside his palace, he would not know whether he was stepping on to the threshhold of that palace (room)* or on to the margin of the tomb.

The morrow is a breast replete with secrets, round which men's minds hover, and which their intellects only gradually discover. It

* The word 'room' is inserted to rhyme with 'tomb'.

comes but slowly into view, and would never give away a single secret unless the solid rock were to pour forth cool water.*

It is almost as if I am with the morrow, yet it is hidden in its den, crouching in its lair, enfolded in a vast veil. It looks at our hopes and aspirations, with looks of scoffing and mockery. It smiles smiles of disparagement and contempt, saying to itself: If only this gatherer knew that he was gathering for his heir, this builder that he was building but for destruction, and this begetter that he was begetting for death; then the gatherer would not gather, nor the builder build, nor the begetter beget!

Man has surmounted every difficulty in this world. He has burrowed under the ground, and climbed a ladder to the skies. He has linked East and West with strings of steel and threads of brass. Then his mind has moved to the upper world. There, he has lived among its stars, and learned their depths and heights, their plains and vales, their fertile and their waste, their damp and their dry. He has invented instruments for measuring the distances of stars, the lengths of their rays. He has devised scales for weighing the globe of the earth as a whole and in part. He has dived into the seas and plumbed their depths. He has examined the sea-beds and disturbed the denizens of the deep. He has despoiled their buried secrets and stolen their treasures. He has plundered their pearls and gems. He has penetrated through rocks and mounds to past generations, seeing the people and their modes of life, their habitations, food, and drink. Then he has gained access to the inner senses by way of the external ones. He has learned about the soul and its nature, the mind and its methods, and the senses and their situations. Indeed, he can almost hear the discourse of the soul, and the creeping course of fate. With his intelligence he has torn down every veil and opened every door . . . Except that he has recoiled before the door of the morrow, powerless, repulsed, not daring to open it, or even to knock on it. For it is God's door, and 'God does not inform anyone of his hidden things'.**

Oh spectre enwrapped in the veil of secrecy, can you remove this veil just a little from your face, so that we can see one side of it? But no! Come a little nearer to us – maybe we can descry your shape through this veil which is drawn down before us. For we have lost our

* A Koranic echo referring to Moses striking the rock.

** An echo of the Koran.

hearts longing for you, and our minds have melted through passion for you.

Oh Morrow! We have our hopes, great and small, and our desires, good and bad. So tell us about our hopes, and how they stand with you; and inform us of our desires, and what you have done with them. Have you set them at naught and despised them, or have you been kind to them?

No . . . no! Keep your secret, and keep your veil over your face. Do not tell us a single thing about our hopes and desires, lest you terrify our spirits and souls. For we live by hopes, though they be vain, and are happy through our desires, though they be deceivers.

The life of man is made of hopes alone:
When they are lost, then life itself is gone.

EXTRACT IV

The First Cup, by Manfaluti

(from *al-Naẓarāt*, Vol. I, pp. 42 ff.)

Translator's note: This is the tale of the downfall of an alcoholic, who is described as a friend of the author. The same theme is dealt with at greater length in an original story in *al-ʿAbarāt* entitled *al-Hāwiya* (The Abyss).* In the latter, the story is still of a friend who takes to drink. The ending, however, is more gruesome. The alcoholic's wife bears a child, and immediately afterwards is stricken with puerperal fever. As she dies, for want of medical attention, he comes in, and is horror-struck to find his wife dead. As he steps back from the bed, he treads on the new-born child, killing it. He is so affected that he goes mad, and ends up in a lunatic asylum.

I once had a friend whom I loved. I loved him for the tranquillity of his mind, the purity of his heart, his honesty and fidelity, whether near or far, angry or forbearing, displeased or contented. Then circumstances separated us, in a separation of life, not of death. Yet today I weep for him, while he still lives, more than I would weep for him were he dead. Indeed, I only weep for his being alive, and only wish him to die . . . Have you ever heard of a quality more remarkable than this in the minds of men?

We were closely linked for a considerable period, during which I knew him and he knew me. Then he went his way – a way different from mine, and I denied him and he denied me. So in due course the thought of me ceased to pass through his mind. For that cup to which he had become attached left no room in his mind save for it and its adherents. It may well be that he pushed me out of his mind if I intruded into it; for when he remembered me, he remembered also those bitter words I used to him, at the beginning of his new life. And while he roamed aimlessly in the vacuum of his happiness – as he

* I, 116 ff.

imagined it – he could not trouble his pleasant thoughts with this sort of reminiscence.

From then onwards I completely lost touch with him. For the life of addicts is repetitive and unchanging, with no variation between morning and evening, yesterday and tomorrow. It consists merely of going to the taverns, drinking, hangover, sleeping, then going to the taverns. It is like a centreless circumference, whose extremities are unknown; or like an unchanging scene which neither draws the attention nor occupies the mind. It is as if someone were to sleep at the sound of the revolving mill-wheel, and only awaken when it stops – whereas one might expect its revolving to keep him awake.

Consequently this unfortunate man did not trouble my mind till *his* motions ceased and his movements quietened. No longer did I see him brawling in taverns, stretched out on pavements, or under police arrest. I asked the police about him, and was told he was ill. I was not surprised at something I had foreseen, counting the days and years to it, as the astronomer counts the hours and minutes to an eclipse of the sun or the conjunction of stars.

I went to visit him, and found no doctor, nor any other visitor with him, because he was poor; and doctors feign sympathy for the poor, but harbour love of silver and gold. And friends fear the contagion of poverty no less than the contagion of disease.

I entered his house, but I really found neither that house nor its master. For I did not find there that elevated spirit whose wings had fluttered in its rooms and halls. I did not see the kitchen smoke; I did not hear the hubbub of servants, the cries of children, the ringing of bells. It was as if I had entered a mausoleum to visit the dead, not a house to visit the living.

I approached the bed, and through its tattered net curtain I descried a spectre of which all that remained was skin clinging to frail bones. I said: 'Oh spectre gazing upwards to the sky! There used to be within this skin a beloved friend. Can you show me where he has gone?' After some effort, he managed to move his lips, and said: 'Is that So-and-so's voice I hear?' I said: 'Yes! What is your complaint?' He said: 'It is the first cup I am complaining of.' I said: 'What cup do you mean?' He said: 'I mean the cup to which I gave my mind, my health, my honour: now here I am giving it my life!' I said: 'Well, I *did* advise and admonish you, warning you of the very outcome you have reached; but all to no avail.' He said: 'When you advised me, you knew no more than I of the evils of this unprofitable life. But I had already drunk the first cup, and the matter was no longer in my hands.

'Every single cup I have drunk since has been brought on me by that first cup. As for the first cup, it was brought on me by my own weakness, and the inability of my mind to realize the deception of friends and boon companions.

'The appetite for drink is not instinctive like man's other appetites – for were that so, he could be excused for succumbing to it just as he succumbs to other natural appetites. It has no power over him till he takes the first cup. And why *does* he take it? He takes it because treacherous, lying friends and associates make him untrue to his own self concerning it; so that, by making him one of them, they can complete their pleasure, which can never be perfect except with the clinking of glasses and the clamour of a crowd. And if only you knew how they did deceive him, and painted an alluring picture of this abandonment of his true nature and familiar habits, and what means they adopted to that end; then you would verify that he was stupid to the very limit of stupidity, and weak to the point beyond which there could be no greater weakness.

'I am that stupid, weak man. Let me tell you how my friends deceived me, and painted for me a glowing picture such as Satan paints for man.

'They said: Your life is one of cares and woes, and there is no cure for these ills but drink. They said: Drink increases the well-being of the body, making it lively. It loosens the tongue, and teaches man eloquence. It encourages the coward, arousing boldness and bravery in the heart. This is what I heard. I believed it, and was deceived by it.

'I believed that in drink were four merits – happiness, health, eloquence and courage – but I found in it four demerits – poverty, disease, ruin and madness. They mistook for health that redness which drink leaves in its wake in the limbs, insinuating itself into the vital organs. They mistook for eloquence babbling, loquacity, obscene talk, and a filthy tongue. They mistook for courage that brawling which is only quietened in the prison cell. By happiness they meant those few moments when the drinker's mind is clouded, and he is too blind to see things around him as they really are. Thus reality is so reversed in his view, that he mistakes abuse for wit, and a slap on the face for a slap on the back. In such things he is roused to laughter by what should make only children and imbeciles laugh.

'What joy is there in a house where the mouths of those who live there are never graced with a smile? What joy is there for one whose family sees him off with sighs every morning, and welcomes him back in the evening with even deeper sighs? What happiness is there for one who goes on his way constantly staggering, dragging himself along, slinking into corners and lanes, hiding beside walls and fences, to avoid the looks of the butcher, the taunts of the druggist, and the shouts of the publican?

'I used to see these miserable men at the start of my life of misfortune. And there passed through my mind the same thought that passes through the minds of others like me. I said to myself that these were the victims of addiction, not of drink. I determined, in so far as lay in my power, that I would not go to their lengths or sink to their level. Then when I drank, I reckoned wrongly and lost count; my plan misfired, my resolve went awry. I was overcome as everyone deceived as I is overcome. But were it not for that first cup, I would not have come to grief, and would not now be bemoaning my fate. Were it not for that cup, my friends would not be avoiding me, nor my family shunning me. So will you be my friend for better or worse?'

I promised him that, and left him in a state which:

Brings deafness to the ear,
And blindness to the eye,
And makes us say, 'Oh, there,
But for God's grace go I!'*

* This verse – which is very freely translated – would seem to be by Manfaluti himself.

EXTRACT V

Baghdad – an ode by ʻAlī al-Jārim delivered at the Arab Medical Congress in Baghdad, on 9 February 1938

(text in *Dīwān al-Jārim*, 3 vv., Cairo, 1939, Vol. II, pp. 139 ff.)

City of Haroun al-Rashīd,
  Baghdad, with ancient glories bright,
Oh smile, still there, for all to heed,
  On Hist'ry's mouth – a rare delight:

Object of love for whom all pine,
  Subject of proverbs infinite,
Of Arabic a glorious line
  Upon creation's tablet writ:

Flag of Islam, the faith which did
  Once with such flutt'ring flags abound;
Sunset of hopes long ages hid,
  Sunrise of hopes reborn, new-found:

Daughter of Tigris, I have longed
  On your cool mouth my lips to feast:
That joy which to the world belonged,
  Oh desert flower, bring back, increas'd.

Oh garden of Islam, in which
  Our race has lain asleep so long,
The centre of an empire rich,
  Dominion's fortress, firm and strong;
Make this a fruitful visit which
  Revives hopes lain in limbo long.

Baghdad, oh home of brilliant thought
  And art, and poetry's fairest flow'rs,

Such verses grew – most beauteous wrought –
Upon your banks, midst roseate bow'rs.

They stole 'Inān's* charm in fair words,
And Waḥīd's voice's fair repute;
They sang as if the vocal chords
Were stretched upon the singing lute.

Baghdad, O where is Buḥturī,
And where, O where, Ibn al-Walīd?
The poets assembled happily
By Ibn Yaḥya and Rashid?

And where the laughing singing girls,
In proud embroider'd silk bedecked?
Th'enticing and the clinging girls,
Slender, wide-eye'd and supple-necked?

They stayed awake neath starry light,
All thoughts of sleep with scorn effaced,
With shapely necks all gleaming white,
Soft-bodied, slim of hips and waist.

The branches, as they walk and sway,
Admire their soft and supple frames,
And when their faces they display,
The sun their rosy cheeks acclaims.

They played with time – but time plays too,
As heedless as a babe in arms,
While beauty round their necklets threw
A treasure-trove of hidden charms.

How many knights your army thronged,
Archers, and princes nobly-born;
And victory to your flags belonged,
Through sharp swords from their scabbards drawn.

Imagination scarce can take
In your wide empire, overall;
The exploits of your conqu'rors make
Exploits of other men seem small.

* 'Inān and Waḥīd were famous singers.

Envoy on envoy thronged your court,
From Scythian steppes and Caspian Sea;
Dazzled by shining steel, they sought
Your 'Palace of Eternity';

Stumbling and shuffling, struck with awe,
Like pris'ners in their fetters tied,
Aloft, the shining swords they saw,
Below, the hordes of troops they spied:
Their knees, long after, bruises bore,
Which to long kneeling testified.

Baghdad, philosophies you knew,
When science was in its infancy:
The West, in darkness, saw in you
The slayer of obscurity.

How many a refugee you housed,
How many a student you received:
Jāḥiẓ, by joy and gaiety roused,
Who unique pearls of style achieved.

Baghdad, the writer's favoured niche,
The tree whence poetry used to flow;
You have brought back those dreams from which
I had awakened long ago.

Back flew my fancy, restless, fast,
Nothing could stay it in its course,
Across the centuries that had pass'd,
To learn the secrets at their source.

The mind was sad, when it recalled,
With longing, ages long ago:
Ghosts from the past the mind enthralled,
Excited by the dazzling show
Of Arab glory, firm installed
To guard its wide realm from the foe.

Make haste, Oh Arab nation, give
Full rein to bold and fearless flight.

Lead forth! For strength and will, which live
  On hopes, make leadership your right.

This is the time that calls for speed,
  Not sluggishness, in your advance!
A leap to glory is your need –
  A leap without a sideways glance.

Soar high into the starry skies –
  No rival and no like in view –
And when creation's anthems rise
  In praise, their praise shall be of you!

Make no mistake: the heights are there –
  They stretch beyond where eye can see:
And those who bounding tigers dare
  To hunt, mere cheetahs leave scot-free.

These are the first signs of rebirth,
  Scatt'ring all trace of idleness:
Baghdad's bright star above the earth
  Has ris'n, an omen of success.

She has won back her ancient pride,
  Following a high-road, broad and straight,
With brilliant leaders there to guide,
  The lion's claws to subjugate.

We, Egypt's delegates, at length,
  In love and longing's sure pursuit,
Have come to you, Baghdad, in strength,
  The arts and sciences to salute.

To see you is a festival
  On a real festival achieved;
We are one race remarkable,
  Our forebears in one womb conceived.

Our mutual love is great indeed,
  Like that of those by passion caught;
My people's palm-trees in Rashid*
  For love of yours are near-distraught.

* The name of 'Ali al-Jarim's birth-place in Egypt.

Distance our homes may disunite,
 But hearts require no rendezvous:
Euphrates and Tigris unite,
 Oh happy Nile, in love for you.

The shadow of the Arch* embraced
 That of the lofty Pyramid,
When we, coming to see you, raced,
 O'er valleys and o'er deserts sped.

So long the desert we went through,
 It seemed infinity to me;
For when we reached one distant view,
 Once more the same view we could see!

(As when some fair maid, to be quit
 Of one vow, will new vows profess) –
A shoreless sea – the whole of it
 Was high plateaux and wilderness.

My 'desert ship', the 'Narn',† in heat
 With my heart's heat kept company.
King Ghazi‡ came we here to greet,
 Arab of noble ancestry.

Amidst his gifts, we feel, with pride,
 The kindness of his generous hand.
Our hopes he has revivified,
 By high endeavour, wisely planned.

Now Arab loyalty can look
 To him for sweet encouragement;
The rise of Ghazi and Farouk ||
 Provides ample replenishment.

Long live Farouk, our hopes' well-spring,
With Ghazi, strong support to bring!
 Long live the East, in dignity,
 And life lived in prosperity!

* The Arch referred to is the famous ruin at Ctesiphon.
† The name of the company operating road services across the desert to Baghdad.
‡ King of Iraq.
|| King Farouk of Egypt.

CHAPTER 4

Some Modern Writers and Modern Movements (1920 to 1970)

Introduction

This final chapter aims to give a broad picture of Arabic literary activity during the period between the two world wars, continuing the story to the present time in some respects. It is more particularly concerned with living writers, or such as have died since 1950. Many writers active during this period have been mentioned in the previous chapter: but these were either active before 1920, or, by the character of their works, belong more properly to the previous chapter.

The task of selection is almost impossible, and the aim has been chiefly to include the names of leading writers. But the omission of any name known to the reader must not be taken as any reflection on such a writer's stature. It is merely that one man's knowledge of the subject is limited, and that selection is a matter of personal taste and the accidents of reading. For convenience only, poetry has been separated from prose, and in each, writers have been grouped under different countries. In addition, some notice has been taken of 'modern' literary movements as they have affected the Arab world. Monteil[1] lists these movements as: I Symbolism; II Lyrical Analysis; III Regionalism; IV Realism; V 'Committed' Literature (la littérature engagée) and VI Existentialism. Such an analysis, while useful as a guide, should not be taken to imply that one author may be committed to one to the exclusion of all the others. Arab authors tend to be eclectic in their attitude to foreign influence. Moreover the list is not complete. It excludes, for example, Expressionism – and one could include such influences as Dadaism.

The Arabs' speed in absorbing all these 'isms' has been remarkable. A hundred years ago they were translating and adapting Shakespeare, Racine and Corneille: fifty years ago Bernadin de St. Pierre was a popular idol, and Hugo, Chateaubriand and Rostand were in favour. During the last fifteen years, James Joyce has been translated in

Morocco and T. S. Eliot, W. B. Yeats, Rimbaud and Dylan Thomas in the Lebanon.

As in the nineteenth century, the Lebanon has been an important gateway for new ideas. Another point of contact was through the Arab writers of North America, many of whom came from the Lebanon or Syria, and visited or revisited their country of origin. Egypt has produced the greatest volume of literature, with the Lebanon coming a good second. There has also been increased activity in Syria and Iraq. Other Arab countries, such as Palestine, the Sudan, Morocco and Algiers, have much leeway to make up; but they already boast writers of considerable talent. Even the Arabian peninsula itself – the very centre of traditionalism – has forward-looking authors.

The politico-economic background again influenced literature. As we have seen, the provinces of the Ottoman Empire, after the First World War, went out of the Turkish frying-pan into the Anglo-French fire. On the whole there was greater freedom of expression under the new foreign régimes; and contacts with Western culture were widened. Thousands of Arabs studied in British and French universities. Not only did this affect literature, but the Arab social pattern began to change, with increased girls' education, and the slow modification and in some cases abandonment of the harem system. The liberation of literature – especially poetry – from classical shackles progressed apace.

However, Western domination naturally impelled many writers to use their weight against 'imperialism' in favour of national independence. This can be seen in all forms of literature. Polemical literature continued to be written. Much of it attempted to go back to first principles, and continue where 'Abduh had left off. In general, religion – or, at least, Islam – was little stressed. Rather did writers take pride in their country as the cradle of the three Semitic revealed religions. From this start, they were able to postulate the inherent spirituality of the East and the inherent materialism of the West. Again, the rise of Nazism and Communism were fitted glibly into the pattern of thought.

Western domination was naturally disliked, but with it came material prosperity, and higher standards of living, particularly with the exploitation of oil. Moreover, it was only a temporary phase. Iraq became an independent kingdom in 1921. The British Protectorate of Egypt was terminated in 1922, and a new constitution was proclaimed in 1923. In both countries, parliamentary government was introduced on the British model. Nevertheless, British armed forces remained and intervention in internal affairs was possible whenever the situation required it. Consequently national frustration remained. In Palestine, Britain made a number of mistakes. By admitting Jewish immigrants – especially after the rise of Hitler – and later, by failing to deal effectively with Jewish and Arab terrorists, she paved the way for an independent Israeli state after the Second World War. This has given the Arabs a sense of injustice greater even than their hatred of imperialism.

The French, too, had their troubles in their mandated territories. In 1925 there was a Druze rebellion. In 1926 the French declared the Lebanon (Grand Liban) a republic. A constituent assembly was convened by the French to work out a new constitution for Syria. But the constitution it produced did not recognize the French mandate. So the French imposed a constitution of their own in 1930. In 1933 a treaty with France fixed an interim period of 25 years, during which France was to retain control over foreign relations, defence and finance. The system was not unlike that in Egypt, with a parliament. But the French authorities had to suspend the constitution from 1934 to 1937. Meanwhile Syria became a centre for Arab insurgency in Palestine.

Since the Second World War all Arab countries have gained their independence, and various revolutionary governments have won power in practically all of them. Algeria, Morocco and Tunis have freed themselves from French domination. Libya was liberated from Italian rule during the Second World War, and has more recently ensured the removal of Anglo-American military bases.

In recent years, certain Arab countries have increased contacts with Russia. Arab students now study in Russia and other 'iron curtain' countries. As yet, however, this does not seem to have affected literature very much.

Finally, the expansion of education, resulting in the virtual disappearance of illiteracy except among the old, has vastly expanded the market for literature – especially the press and fiction. The quality of printing and publishing has improved. Arab scholarship, too, has made great strides. The time has now long passed when, to obtain a reliable text of a classical literary work, it was necessary to find a European edition, edited by some distinguished orientalist. The study of these texts in Arab schools and colleges has become more enlightened, and modern biographies of ancient authors are recognized reading. The study of modern Arabic texts, from Yaziji to Shauqi and Manfaluti – and even to Taha Husain and Taufiq al-Hakim, is now considered of value. An author writing on the techniques of poetry, for example, will feel impelled to take at least some of his illustrative examples from present-day poets.

Poetry

1. *General*

For the period 1920–45, the late A. J. Arberry's *Modern Arabic Poetry*[2] contains a good selection of poems from all parts of the Arabic-speaking world, with translations. (Arberry excelled as a translator of Arabic and Persian literature.) Consequently, there will be rather less translation of verse in this chapter than in previous chapters.

During the period under discussion, monorhyme qasidas continued to be written, but in ever-decreasing quantity. The younger writers found them no longer to their taste. So we find a preference for stanza poetry, and a leaning towards lighter metres with fewer syllables to the hemistich or line. In fact, lines get shorter and shorter, till, after the Second World War, we find them as short as two or three syllables at times. Free verse became popular, especially in the Lebanon, with lines of varying length, and rhyme often following no particular pattern.

Alongside this freer technique, the spirit of poetry has also changed. The attitude to life is often anything but Islamic, and expresses doubt and uncertainty – even black pessimism. Instead of the definite statements and clearly-defined pictures of Shauqi and Hafiz, we find vague and shifting impressions. The poet is no longer stating a creed or striking a familiar posture. He is like a lyre on which the breeze blows producing music: or he may be likened to rippling or flowing water, mirroring the world around imperfectly and vaguely. The poet searches his own soul, and finds it hard to understand himself, let alone the outside world. He draws on the psychological ideas of Freud and Jung to help him.

The neo-classical rebellion of previous poets is replaced by malaise – sometimes Romantic and vague, sometimes positive and bitter. During the last few years this bitter malaise has arisen from the struggle against Israel. The poet does not *argue* against Zionism as former poets argued about imperialism: but he writes bitterly about it with dark, macabre, symbolical pictures of suffering and death.

Such is the confused picture of Arabic poetry during the last fifty years. Needless to say, this picture only represents tendencies. Here and there, straightforward, even old-fashioned, poets are found, but seldom among those born since 1930.

2. *Poetry in Egypt*

In his account of contemporary poetry in Egypt,[3] M. H. Fahmi writes: 'If al-Barudi is considered the pioneer of conservative poets, and Shauqi the pioneer of the moderates, then Matran is the pioneer of the modernist poets'. Fahmi then goes on to explain what he means by 'modernist'. (The Arabic word *'aṣrī* means 'modern' rather than 'modernistic'.) He quotes al-'Aqqād, who said that the poetry after Matran was oriental in feeling, but regarded the world with the imagination of the westerner.[4] The poets of the generation after Matran tended towards political poetry and eulogy, but they expressed their personal feelings about life. They were thus Romantics, often unhappy; for, unlike their predecessors, they could not make any pretence of having all the answers. The poets who came into prominence at about the time of the First World War were Aḥmad Zakī Abū S͟hādī (1892–1955), al-Māzinī, al-'Aqqād, and 'Abd al-Raḥmān S͟hukrī.

There is much about Abu Shadi to interest the Englishman. He spent much time in Britain, married an Englishwoman, and finally settled in America. He was a doctor and bacteriologist, an expert on bee-keeping, and a freemason. We are lucky to have a study of him in English, even though it was written twenty years before his death.[5] The son of literary parents, he showed promise as a poet by the time he was twelve. He studied medicine in Cairo, and continued his studies in Britain from 1912, not leaving till 1922. His health had not been good, but it improved in Britain, and he not only pursued his medical studies, but studied agriculture as well. He developed a keen interest in English literature – especially Keats, Shelley, Wordsworth,

Dickens, Arnold Bennett, and G. B. Shaw. On his return to Egypt, he started a magazine on bee-keeping in both Arabic and English. He also founded a poetry review, *Apollo*, which became so associated with what were then considered *avante-garde* poets, that these were known as the 'Apollo' poets. Later, he started the magazine *Adabī* devoted to his own works and those of his friends. Neither lasted very long. He worked as a government bacteriologist in Suez, Port Said, and Alexandria, then as Professor of Bacteriology in the Faculty of Medicine at Alexandria University. It seems that he did not find the Egyptian atmosphere congenial, despite his love of his country. The reactionaries were suspicious of him, and in 1946 he settled in the United States. He worked in New York for the 'Voice of America', then in Washington, where he died. Some of the poetry of his American period has not yet been published.

He was a very prolific writer. Dagher lists eight magazines founded by him – either literary, or 'scientific', that is, to do with apiculture, agriculture or domestic fowl. He also wrote books on these subjects, plus a hefty work on practical medicine. He translated Shakespeare's *The Tempest* and Omar Khayyam into Arabic. His prose works include books on literary history, religion, history and freemasonry. While he is not thought of as an important dramatist, he composed a number of verse dramas – some of them 'musicals' or 'operas' (Arabic, *aubarā*). But it is as a poet that he is best remembered. Here again he was prolific, publishing no less than twenty books of verse, one of which is over 1,000 pages long. He is sometimes spoken of as a symbolist (*ramzī*) poet, and as an idealist. In reality, his poetry is wide-ranging in both style and subject. At one end of the scale is the *vers libres* of which he was a pioneer, as mentioned in Chapter I; at the other end are monorhyme odes. Then, apart from his dramatic verse, he wrote poetry on nature and love, as well as narrative and philosophical poetry.

Much of his love poetry dates from his youth, after which it tends to become poetry about feminine beauty which he almost deifies in a manner that is quite unclassical. Read, for example, Arberry's translation of the *Maid of Bekhten*:[6]

Great is the pomp of beauty; the glory of mortal power
Swift fades; beauty's pomp is a deathless flower;
Many the symbols of lesser gods in the world we view:
Beauty mirrors the One, the Everlasting, the True.

Again, in *Union Eternal*:[7]

And though dust in dust I lie,
Yet I shall not wholly die;
Dust that holds thy memory
Doth transcend mortality.

He is a scientific humanist, whose religous views often verge on the agnostic or pantheistic: yet he still talks of 'God'. With his wide knowledge of various cultures, religions and philosophies, he is equally at home with Islam, Christiantity, or the Greek pantheon. He wrote a drama about Akhnaton, another about Zenobia Queen of Palmyra, and was one of the most 'universal' writers produced by the Arab world. He feels at one with the Infinite – but modern science is, for him, a vital part of that Infinite. With his humanism is mingled a kind of mysticism: it is scientific mysticism too, which would have made him feel at home among present-day scientists. Personal immortality does not matter to him, for he sees the individual as a microcosm of the macrocosmic universe. In *al-Khulūd* (Eternity), he writes:[8]

I die, then live, each day revivified:
Where, then, my staying? Where, then, is my guide?

From Time's dawn have I come, like threads, perforce,
Beginning there, and stretching on their course.

My body like the growth of years has grown,
Eternal symbolism in it shown.

Millions of bees have lived on the same plane
As I, and dying, have not died in vain!

My body and my soul have changed – in me
Creations future, present, past you see.

Note the following, also, from 'Oh Universe' (*Yā kaun*):[9]

Oh Universe, you are like me,
And in your life, my life I see,

Is not my soul mirror'd in you,
And am I not your mirror too?

You are both whole and part of me,
And in your life my life I see.

Abu Shadi's nature poetry is influenced by European Romanticism. Some of it describes English scenes and is almost Wordsworthian. One poem is entitled 'The Land of Fog' (Waṭan al-Ḍabāb) and begins:[10]

> You have been called the land of fogs,
> But my delight is in your fogs.

This particular poem is not really descriptive, but about liberty: he writes about it as Wordsworth might have done. Edham[11] quotes a poem 'Autumn Leaves', a mathnawi. Like the true Romantic, he does not see nature as an end in itself: it is emotive, and leads to reflection on the world of men.

That Abu Shadi did not achieve a higher reputation as a poet may be because he wrote too much, and because he was too much like a 'sponge' in absorbing varied Western influences – scientific, artistic and intellectual, which could not coalesce to form a coherent whole, nor be assimilated by his contemporaries. So he throws off interesting ideas, and brilliant pearls of language by the hundred, which do not add up to a positive personal picture. Of the Arab poets between the two world wars, few merit further study more than he. As a bee-keeper poet, in any case, he is of interest. But he has not the stature of Matran.

A glance at his prose works shows why he felt he had to retreat to America. His ideas were enough to scare all but the most tolerant and bold of Islamic thinkers. What were people to make of statements such as the following?[12]

> Traditional religion simply implies selfishness and cowardice. People have to be good for fear of punishment or for hope of material reward ... We must not expect comparative eternity except for our species, for which we have to work and sacrifice in the same way as the *Apis Mellifica* behaves towards her colony, whether consciously or unconsciously ... The latest type of organized religion is Communism. It is far superior to traditional religions which are full of superstitions and ignorance. But nevertheless it has its defects in class hatred and prejudices ... Freud likens religion to a neurosis through which man passes in the course of his evolution ...

His final views on Islam are embodied in a series of essays published in Beirut after his death, in 1961, entitled *The Revolution of Islam*.[13] They constitute a virtuoso performance, quoting, among others, Thomas Carlyle, John Dewey, James Joyce and Billy Graham. He sees Islam as a religion of freedom and individuality, and is concerned with its civilization and its spirit, rather than details of dogma and practice. He might be compared, in his free-thinking within the framework of Islam, with John Robinson, former Bishop of Woolwich, in his interpretation of Christianity: not because their views are similar but because they are equally radical. No student of modern trends in Islam should fail to read *The Revolution of Islam*.

Abu Shadi was a scientific optimist. His fellow poets were pessimistic. ʿAqqad wrote:[14]

> Hope is barren in the end,
> Life is such an ancient ill,
> And defeats the highest skill.

For such poets, love and pain are seldom separated. The pain may be cured by love – or it may be an inevitable part of love.

Some poets indulged in a form of escapism, including poets of the Apollo Group – Nājī ʿAlī Maḥmūd Ṭaha and al-Ṣairāfī. These poets followed Abu Shadi in publishing their poems lavishly illustrated. Colour illustrations had as their leading motif the female form thinly veiled, while in the line drawings it was naked. Ṭaha's 'Spirits and Spectres' (*al-arwāḥ wa al-ashbāḥ*)[15] consists of a profusely illustrated 50 pages of poetry, with an introduction explaining the names of the main protagonists. For the work is in quasi-dramatic form, and the speakers include Sappho, Hermes and Thais. This work had been preceded by The Wandering Sailor (*al-Mallāḥ al-tāʾih*, 1934); Nights of the Wandering Sailor (*Layāli al-Mallāḥ al-tāʾih*, 1940); and Runaway Spectres (*al-Arwāḥ al-shārida*, 1941).

The symbolist movement in Egyptian poetry is represented well by Bishr Fāris, some of whose symbolist poems appeared in *al-Maqtataf*. The symbolist may escape from reality and describe unreality in such a way that the poet's unreal world must be taken on trust, however vague and incomprehensible it may be. Faris's poem 'To a visitor' (*Ilā Zāʾira*) seems to illustrate this:[16]

> If your forehead were as white as snow,
> Would that your visit at an end might be.

Can beauty lie where words clear meaning show?
Man is inspired by language-sorcery.
(Expressions that inspire are sorcery.)

Realism also has invaded Egyptian poetry. Thus, ʿAbd al-Raḥmān Sharqāwī wrote, in free verse, 'An open letter from an Egyptian to President Truman' depicting the misery of the poor in undeveloped countries.[17] Fauzī al-ʿAntīl has a poem called 'A Woman in the Night' (*Imraʾa fī al-lail*),[18] whose jerky lines, varying in length from three syllables upwards, seem to add point to the brief story of a miserable woman:

In the journey of life, adolescence and youth passed her by;
She gave to them what, as a price, gold would not be too high.

To Him who withholds, if He wishes, the breeze,
Or who makes, if he wishes, the things that can please,

When He passes, the hillocks with verdure shine;
In the evening he squeezes the juice of the vine,

All things, while people are sleeping,
Are in His keeping.

He weaves the woes upon the luckless sent,
The affliction of the innocent . . .

And each night strange is she,
Grievously:

Each night a victim, she,
Of misery.

Her days have been arranged in secrecy
By hands she cannot see.

These loving hands of mine her pains withstood,
And her blood

Is on my clothes,
And on mankind's clothes.

The reader can judge for himself how far Egyptian poetry has moved by comparing the above poem with Matran – let alone Hafiz and Shauqi. But to assess the merit of such a poem is almost impossible for the non-Arab.

3. *Arabic poetry in America* (*The Mahjar*)

After the insurrections of 1860, a steady stream of Arabs from the Lebanon and Syria emigrated to America – most to the U.S.A., but some to South American countries such as Brazil. These emigrés founded their own newspapers and magazines in their new countries, and they prospered in commerce. They did not forget their homeland, which they visited when they could, and they maintained their own culture and language. At the same time, they imbibed the culture of their new environment. Those in the U.S.A., for example, read Longfellow, Walt Whitman and Edgar Alan Poe. The result was a new kind of Arabic literature, known by the Arabs as 'Emigrant literature' (*adab al-mahjar*). Jibran has already been mentioned in connexion with prose. But the most significant contribution of the 'mahjar' writers was in poetry.

A few of these poets achieved real eminence. Their works were first published in America – often piecemeal in the Arabic press which was established in the U.S.A. But the definitive editions are largely Lebanese or Egyptian. This poetry was the mainspring of 'modernism' in Arabic poetry – though the word 'romanticism' would be apter.

A great deal has been written in Arabic about this poetry. One of the most useful studies is by I. ʿAbbās and N. Y. Najma.[19]

The best known poet was Īlīyā Abū Māḍī (1889–?). Other outstanding figures were Mīkhā'īl Naʿīma (b. 1889), Nasīb ʿArīḍa (1887–1946), Naḍra Ḥaddād (1881–1950) and Rashīd Ayyūb (1881–1941). One mahjar poet, Ilyās Abū Shabaka (1903–1947), was actually born in the U.S.A., but returned with his father to the Lebanon while still a child. He is best known for his translations of French literature, from Molière to Lamartine.

Abu Madi is the best-known Arab poet since Shauqi and Matran. Yet there is little that is indentifiably Arab about his poetry, save the language – and it has little to identify it as Islamic. His poetry reached the Arab world from the 'land of liberty' as something new, with a liberated spirit. The mahjar poets did not have the drawback of an environment with a strong Islamic conservative element, and thus did not have to fight a rearguard action to achieve recognition. It was probably this liberal atmosphere in which they lived and worked which enabled them to succeed where men like Abu Shadi failed.

When he left the Lebanon in 1900, Abu Madi went first to Egypt.

There his first diwan, *Tadhkār al-māḍī* (The Memorial of the Past) was published in 1911. That same year he went to the U.S.A. and settled in Cincinatti as a merchant. In 1916 he moved to New York and joined the Arab Writers' Union, which was founded there in 1920. His second diwan was published in 1919, with an introduction by Jibran. Henceforward he earned his living as a journalist in the American-Arabic press. His two best-known books of verse are *al-Jadāwil* (Brooks), which appeared in 1925, with an introduction by Naʿima; and *al-Khamāʾil* (Thickets), in 1940. It is said that a good deal of the poetry which he wrote for newspapers has not yet been reprinted.

He is a poet of the imagination rather than of the intellect. To him man is the measure of all, and he, the poet, lives in a continual state of divine discontent and indecision. His poems are either in short-verse monorhyme or in stanzas. His most famous poem, which typifies his doubts about life, is 'I do not know' (*Lastu adrī*);[20] of which the following are some of the early verses:

I came, I know not whence, yet came this way;
I saw a path – along it made my way;
I must go on – or say I yea or nay!
How have I come? How did I find the way?
    I do not know.

Am I new here, or have I been before?
Completely free, or a bound servitor?
My own soul's master, or inferior?
Oh! would that I were bless'd with knowledge, for . . .
    I do not know.

They tell me monks can this world's secrets find:
To me they seem pedestrian in mind:
Their tatter'd hearts have left all hope behind.
I am not blind – then are all others blind?
    I do not know.

I asked th'ascetics in the monast'ry –
They were like me in their uncertainty,
Submitting to despair despondently.
And on the door, these words were plain to see:
    I do not know.

Shall we rise from the tomb, after we die,
To life eternal – or extinguished lie?
Do men speak true, or do they falsify?
Is't true that some true knowledge can supply?
I do not know!

Abu Madi would seem even more of an agnostic than Abu Shadi: he is also unimpeded by deep philosophical ideas. It is true that in the above-quoted poem, in verse two, he alludes to the Indian idea of transmigration – 'have I been here before': but he does not develop it. He is vague and impressionistic, loving life and beauty, but unable to grasp their meaning. His beautiful Arabic style is greatly admired by Arabs. But Khemiri and Kampffmeyer are surely straining things when they say:[21] '. . . his style is purer and more Arabic in texture than the rest of the Syrian Americans. This may, perhaps, be attributed to the fact of his having lived so long in Egypt.'[22]

The mahjar poet who had the most varied life would seem to be Naʿima.[23] He was born of Christian parents in Biskenta in the Lebanon, and was educated in Russian (orthodox) schools in Biskenta and Nazareth (Palestine) – the latter being a teacher-training college. From 1906 to 1911 he studied in a seminary in Poltava in the Ukraine, and gained a considerable knowledge of Russian literature. He returned to the Lebanon, but emigrated to the U.S.A. in 1912. He studied law in Washington University. From 1917 to 1919 he served in the American army on the Western Front. Returning to America, he helped other Arabs to form the Arab Writers' Union (*al-Rābiṭa al-Qalamiyya*) in 1920. He returned to the Lebanon in 1932, and the present writer believes he was still living there in 1970 at the age of 83.

Like other mahjar writers, he was influenced by Jibran, of whom, as we have noted, he wrote a biography. He has achieved fame in the Arab world, and written with distinction in all branches of literature – fiction, drama, literary criticism, as well as poetry. His diwan, *Hamas al-jufūn* (The faint sound of eyelids) was published in the Lebanon in 1946.

Though he does write qasidas, he shows a preference for short metres: and he also writes free verse. His verse runs smoothly, with light rhythm untrammelled by too meticulous a care for long and short syllables, as demanded by strict classical Arabic canons of prosody. His verse has been described as influenced by Lebanese folk poetry. The 1914–18 war affected him deeply, and his period of greatest poetical activity was immediately following that war. His religious beliefs seem not unlike those of Abu Shadi. Like the latter, he seems to say 'amor vincit omnia'. But he is a mystic, and mystics in Islamic poetry have a good deal of latitude. If they appear to be writing like agnostics, some subtle meaning can be assumed. Certainly heaven and hell do not, with him, appear to have their orthodox meaning. Death seems to be a place of welcome relief and calm. In the following he speaks about death. The original monorhyme has been translated in stanzas:[24]

> Tomorrow I shall entrust
> The remaining dust to dust:
> My spirit I shall set free
> From the prison of 'maybe'.
>
> Death shall I leave to the dead,
> And those who have children bred:
> To the world and religion, ev-
> il and goodness I shall leave.
>
> My weakness I shall protect
> With a breastplate that can deflect
> The blows of th'angelic hand,
> And the demons' touch withstand.
>
> I cannot feel any fright
> Of the fires of Hell alight:
> Those houris will not entice,
> Assembled in Paradise.
>
> Tomorrow I pioneer
> Beyond range of eye and ear,
> That beginning I shall find,
> As yet hidden in my mind.
>
> For no stars my course can stay;
> Through them all I shall find a way.
> And no earth is there anywhere
> But my feet can travel there.

A spirit of calm optimism is found in some of his poems. He takes one of Longfellow's thoughts thus:[25]

If any time your sky
  By dark clouds is concealed
If you but close your eye,
  The stars will be revealed.

If on the ground should lie
  A covering of snow,
You will see, with closed eye,
  The grass that lies below.

Should you afflicted be,
  And there is no known cure,
Then close your eye, and see
  The ill is its own cure.

The emigrant writers repeated in the United States that publishing activity for which Beirut had long been famed. Nasīb ʿArīḍa[26] was the founder of the Atlantic Press in New York in 1912, and the magazine *al-Funūn* (The Arts) in 1913. The latter, for which Jibran and Naʿima wrote, disseminated interest in the 'new literature'. ʿArida was also on the editorial staff of several newspapers – *al-Hudā* (Guidance) and *Mirāʾa al-Nisāʾ* (The Women's Mirror) included. He hailed from Homs in Syria, and like Naʿima had been educated first in the local Russian school, then at the Russian School in Nazareth, where the two were contemporaries. Unlike Naʿima, he did not go to Russia for further study, but emigrated to the U.S.A. in 1905, and at first worked in commerce. But he preferred literature to wealth and hoped to find some stability for his writing career in journalism. He was not entirely happy, and seemed to be beset by difficulties. The First World War caused his magazine *Funūn* to fail for a time; and though it revived, it soon died again.

The leading mahjar poets all suffered, in varying degrees, from understandable malaise in the midst of their new environment. This malaise was both material and spiritual. ʿArida is no exception: but like Naʿima, there is a sort of Sufism beneath the surface in some of his poems. Apart from his two stories, his whole output is found in his diwan, 'Perplexed spirits' (*al-Arwāḥ al-ḥāʾira*). His scorn for wealth is expressed in the following poem:[27]

Come with me (lit. Go with me)

Oh friend of my imagination,
And pard'ner of my deviation,

Wand'ring with me around the curtain
Of th'impossible and uncertain;

Come with me, searching for a thought
Which yet no other mind has caught.

Leave other men enamoured by
Wealth, and loved-ones for whom they cry!

4. *Poetry in the Lebanon and Syria*

It is, perhaps, unkind to suggest that the good Lebanese-Syrian poetry written between the wars was written in America. True, there are other names. Wadīʿ al-Bustānī (1886–1954), for instance, translated Omar Khayyam into Arabic.[28] This was published in Cairo, where he settled in 1912. A few years later he wrote original 'War Quatrains' (*Rubāʿiyyat al-Ḥarb*), which appeared in Beirut in 1952. Late in life he tackled the translation of the great Sanskrit epic, the *Maharabatha*, printed at Beirut in 1952. But neither this nor previous attempts at poetical epics in Arabic seem likely to start a trend. The history of Islam offers marvellous material for epics: but it fell to the Urdu poet Ḥālī to use it with success in his celebrated *Musaddas*. One could conceive of Arabic 'Idylls of the King', but none has emerged. The truth is that Arabic narrative poetry is almost entirely small-scale fable or anecdote.

The 'Rustic Bard', Ras͟hīd al-K͟hūrī (*al-S͟hāʿir al-qarawī*), shared with Shauqi the honour of being the only poets included in a popular selection of modern Arabic literature published in Beirut a few years ago.[29] In one of the three poems quoted, *Taḥiyya al-Andalus* (Greetings to Andalusia), the poet neatly, in seven-line verses, contrasts the degraded position of the Lebanon and Syria with the glories of the Arab past seen in Spain, such as the Alhambra. But neatness is not enough.

In Bis͟hāra ʿAbdallāh al-Khūrī, who writes under the pseudonym of the Lesser Ak͟hṭal,[30] we have a poet of some stature. He writes some rhymeless poetry, some stanza poetry, and some free verse in very short lines. He is well known as a love-poet; but this is by no means his only theme, as can be seen by a perusal of his diwan, beautifully printed in Beirut in 1961 on fine paper with excellent – if rather romantic – full-page black-and-white drawings. Thus a poem of 1914, *al-Fuqarā'* (The Poor),[31] draws the attention of the rich to the plight of the poor, and incites the latter to rebel.

Oh rich men, the riches that you possess
Have been set up by the arms of the poor.

The palaces in which you now reside
Who is it built them for you, but the poor?

The food which, with such relish, you consume,
Who made it for you, then, if not the poor?

Sweet-smelling plants which in your gardens grow,
Who planted them for you, if not the poor?

The milk with which your children have been fed,
From whose breasts has it come? – mostly the poor!

Oh locusts, all your stores are scattered wide;
Then in your swarms upon the green grass pour!

Descend upon the field, burn what you see.
Spread death, for such is your just due, for sure!

Spread death as widely as lies in your power;
As we must die, let death the rich devour!

Against us, they helped war and locusts too . . .
Heav'ns miracles alone our lives ensure.

Say not: What use the weak plaints of the poor,
When great calamities knock at the door?

Poverty has its wealth, if you but knew,
Else would men flounder in their tears' downpour!

The following is an example of free verse, with very short lines, and occasional and irregular rhyme:[32]

Oh Glory! Oh Madness!
Oh Glory!
Oh Art!
Oh Madness!
Naught remains to me
Of the nights,

Except
Imagination's flights.

Neither bees
My honey sip,
Nor butterflies.
Yet on my neck
And on my cheek
They took their ease.

What though
My breast
Quenched what seemed endless
Thirsts?
I am now
Friendless.

Oh Glory!
Oh Art!
Oh Madness!
Where is desire
And the allurement
Of the band who admire?

Since the Second World War there have been wide-ranging and diverse developments in Lebanese poetry, of which the beginnings can be seen in poets like the Lesser Akhtal. As we might expect, French influence has been great. This can be seen in translations of Rimbaud and Lautréamont. French is, indeed, the language of the well-to-do and the educated in Beirut: in fact, when they speak Arabic they fill it with French words. Some Lebanese poets have written in French in preference to Arabic. Hector Klat is the best-known of these. He believes French to be a more precise language. Some parallels with Mallarmé and Valéry have been discerned in his poetry. Other poets have published their Arabic poems with their own translations in French verse, or *vice versa*. Examples are Ṣāliḥ Abū Hānī[33] and Laure Goraieb (Laur Gh̲urayyib).[34]

But the influence of modern English poetry has been great also. Dylan Thomas and Yeats have been important in this respect: but the most important has been T. S. Eliot. The present writer has heard Arab poets from several countries state that Eliot's *The Waste Land* has had a greater impact on Arab poetry of the last twenty years than any other single foreign-language poem.

The organ and propaganda-instrument of the 'new' poets has been the quarterly Shi'r (Poetry), founded in 1956. It consisted of original Arabic poems, translations from French and English poetry, and articles about modern poets. This magazine seems now to have ceased publication – though the present writer is not absolutely certain on this point. Some Lebanese poets have remained faithful to regular prosody, though not usually monorhyme. Most of the poets of *vers libres* who have come to the fore since *Shi'r* started have at some time or other written for that magazine. The same press published, in 1958, the first of a projected series of translations from Western poetry, and it was devoted to T. S. Eliot. It contains the whole of 'Murder in the Cathedral', 'The love song of J. Alfred Prufrock', 'Ash Wednesday', 'The hollow men', and 'The waste land'.

Among the best-known of the poets publishing in *Shi'r* is Shauqī Abī Shaqrā, four of whose short poems were published in the eleventh issue.[35] Here is one of them:

> Shall I, then, her attain,
> My city, woman,
> With her wild castle
> And her ivory walls?
> Shall I, then, her attain,
> And to her entrance gain?

According to Jamil Jabre,[36] Abi Shaqra 'seeks the freshness of the primitive world, or the universe of childhood, and so to be turned into a pure being, worthy to reflect the cares of others, and to communicate without intermediary and without circumlocution with the environment which he represents through force of circumstance'.

The free-verse poets are dominated by doubt, disbelief and depression. Feeling as strangers in the real world, they seek integration in another 'reality', through their own imaginings. They are misfits – even drop-outs. Read, for example, 'the Dead Man' (*al-rajul al-mayyit*) by Muḥammad Māghūṭ, which begins as follows:[37]

> Oh broken bridges in my soul,
> Oh slime clear as children's eyes,
> We were three.

We crossed the city like a canker,
Sitting in fields, coughing in front of ships.
No country had we, and no warning bell,
No cultivation, no controlling whip.
We searched for crime and woman neath the starlight,
Our feet ambling over the sand,
Opening up channels of blood.
We are the fallen youth,
The broken lances alien to the homeland.
Who will give us a woman with red cotton clothes?
Who will give us a lad, to strike his neck as cattle are struck?

The poem ends:

Oh my treachery-wounded heart,
We have but bread, and poetry and night,
And you, oh wounded Asia!
Oh withered rose within my heart,
Bread only will suffice,
The wandering golden wheat,
Filling your breasts with bullets and with wine!

A different note is struck by Adonis – the pen-name of ʿAlī Aḥmad Saʿīd, co-founder (with Yūsuf al-Khāl) of *Shiʿr.* It bespeaks the visionary, almost the prophet of the new age. His mission is to re-create the world in his own image. 'Every poem becomes a conscious or unconscious projection of the super-ego', the poet being a 'God in posse'.[38]

Such *avant-garde* verse would merit further study for the benefit of Western readers: but this would require the collaboration of a Western poet and a skilled Arabist.

Less revolutionary, and increasingly popular throughout the Arab world, even among women readers, is Nizār Qabbānī's love poetry.[39] Émile al-Khūrī, no mean writer himself, has described him as the 'greatest writer of his generation', admittedly in a publisher's 'blurb'. His collections of verse have run into several editions since they first appeared in 1944. Here is an example:[40]

To a dead one (*ilā mayyita* = a dead love)
Our coffee is finished,
Our story is finished.

The love is ended which I called powerful,
When I was a pityful
Fool . . .
My life each day
Was the stage for a trifling play,
When in your love I threw my brightest years away.
Our coffee has cooled,
Our room has cooled;
So let us express our thoughts
Frankly, let us express our thoughts.
I am no longer interested in your affairs,
You are no longer interested in my affairs.
What has brought this change in me?
In your eyes, no longer light I see.
What is it that has set me free
From your tales antique,
And your deeds so sick . . .
After you had been a princess,
After in you my imagination had seen a princess,
After millions of stars had been shining
Over your eyes all glittering,
Like sparrows twittering?
What moved me?
How did I tear the shroud's threads free,
And rebel against passion's slavery?
Against the night . . . the perfume . . . the silk tugging me?
Whereas my future, formerly,
I could, at times, but in a small poem see,
At other times 'twould in that little mouth but be.
What was't awakened me?
Returned my faith to me,
My distances and my spaces to me?
How did I destroy my God with my own hands,
When love had almost rusted me?
What led me?
To me now nothing in your common beauty lies,
I can see nothing in you or your eyes;
Yet once you were a peak, for me,

O'ertopping Time's claim, in your majesty,
In the days of my stupidity.

5. *Iraqi Poetry*

The poetic scene in Iraq between the two world wars was dominated by Rusafi; and even since 1945 his shadow still lies heavy over it, though free verse has 'arrived'. In Baghdad, Najaf, and other cities it seems as if most educated men are poets. Traditional types of poetry are still well entrenched; indeed, a collection of 1956 runs to a dozen volumes.[41] A recent book on *Poetry and Poets in Iraq*[42] divides the poetry into Traditional, Romantic and Realist, while admitting that some poets overlap these categories. Naturally the first category includes poets we have dealt with in the previous chapter – Rusafi, Zahawi and Kazimi. It must not be imagined that Traditional poets excluded stanza poetry with varied rhymes and short lines. This can be seen by studying three of the leading poets – ʿAlī al-S̲h̲arqī, Mahdī al-Jawāhirī, and Aḥmad al-Ṣāfī al-Najafī. They are traditional as much in their themes as in their form. Politics and social reform still loom large in the themes. Among the younger Traditionalists is Muṣṭafā Jamāl al-Dīn, born in Najaf in 1927.[43] He writes amatory, religious, descriptive and narrative poetry, and seems to prefer the monorhyme qasida.

The leading Romantic poets are Baland Ḥaidarī (b. 1926)[44] and the poetess Nāzik al-Malā'ika (b. 1923).[45] With them we have the dark tones we expect of the Romantic. Haidari was influenced by Lebanese poetry: indeed his earlier poems were published in Lebanese magazines such as *al-Adīb*. He was also influenced by Existentialism and Surrealism. His poetry is his private world, a world of vague pictures rather than precise facts. It is evocative of time, more than of place – as with the regular appearance of the postman in the poem called *Sāʿī al-barīd* (The Postman),[46] from which the following is taken:

Postman,
What is your plan?
From this world I'm remote, far out.
You're wrong! There is no news, without a doubt,
That earth can bring to this dejected man!

Mala'ika is well known throughout the Arab world. Some of her poems and a novel, *Yāsmīn*, have been published in Beirut. The

Romantic agony of her 'Five songs for pain' can be appreciated in Monteil's translations.[47] The very French titles set the tone: 'La douleur en chemin', 'Bonsoir tristesse', 'La douleur est une rose'. Sensitive and sad, hers is the poetry of an oriental woman who finds life frustrating and disappointing. She is preoccupied with pain, the tomb, and death the saviour. She writes some stanza verse, but excels in free verse. She has also written patriotic verse about Iraq, and about Arabs martyred in Palestine. Whatever she writes about, the sensitivity and sadness are still there. In 'Salute to the Iraqi Republic' she writes:[48]

> The orphans rejoice, by parental love embraced,
> Like a thirsty man, overjoyed by water's taste.
> Our republic is our rose – we shall not part with it.
> Until we savoured its sweetness, we had no part of it.
> Shall we now to the thief surrender it?

Among the so-called realists are Badr Shākir al-Sayyāb (b. 1926), Kāẓim Jawwād (b. 1929) and ʿAbd al-Rāziq ʿAbd al-Wāḥid. Sayyab's poetry[49] shows various stages of development, passing from one 'school' to another – Romantic, Symbolist and Realist. An example of his symbolism is his very effective poem from his collection 'Legends' (*Asāṭīr*), entitled 'An ancient song'.[50]

> In the crowded distant coffee-house one night,
> When my tired eyes had in sight
> Faces, and hands, and legs, and light,
> While the clock scoffed at the shouts of the strong,
> And struck . . . I heard the shadow of a song,
> The ghost of a song.

It is a song of love, reminding the poet of an old love he has left, but cannot forget. The ending is without hope:

> Specks of dust,
> Shaking and dancing in disgust,
> In the air with melody overladen.
> Specks of dust.
> The lover, no less than the maiden,
> Is specks of dust.

6. *Poetry elsewhere*

The free-verse movement we have seen in the Lebanon after the Second World War established itself elsewhere. But only brief mention can be made of these countries.

The Sudan is a case in point. Cultured Sudanese freely admit that until recently they had no creative writers to speak of. In the past they have read Egyptian literature and – because a number of Sudanese graduated at the American University of Beirut before they had universities of their own – Lebanese and Syrian. For the classical literature they had unbounded enthusiasm, as is to be expected in a peripheral region of any major culture area. At times the Northern Sudanese has seemed 'more Arab than the Arabs'. Yet the Sudanese Arab, with his lively sense of humour, could not long remain a mere imitator of the classical.

Aḥmad Abū Saʿd[51] mentions several poets of the Traditional school born as far back as the 1890's. Their names are familiar to the present writer – but not as poets. In fact, very little Sudanese poetry was published before 1945. The best living representative of the Traditionalists is Professor ʿAbdallāh al-Ṭayyib (b. 1921), the distinguished head of the Arabic department in the University of Khartoum. His knowledge of the classical poetry is phenomenal, and his two-volume book on the techniques of Arabic poetry is second to none.[52] It won the distinction of a preface by Taha Husain. The first of his three volumes of poetry so far published – 'Echoes of the Nile' (*Aṣdāʾ al-Nīl*) – dates from 1957.[53] His poetry is very varied in subject-matter, in many cases requiring footnotes to explain places and things familiar only to the few. Nor is he afraid to use modern words. Thus, in the poem *Ba<u>kh</u>t al-Riḍā* (Bakhter Ruda),[54] he mentions the *laurī* (lorry) which used to take teachers to the neighbouring town of Ed Dueim on the White Nile, on Thursdays. Tayyib obviously relishes the long qasidas he writes, with their classical echoes, but the reader needs the explanatory footnotes. His skill is undisputed, and his influence on Sudanese poetry has been great.

The first Sudanese poet to break away from the Classical tradition seems to have been al-Tījānī Yūsuf Ba<u>sh</u>īr, born in Omdurman in 1912. Unfortunately he died of tuberculosis in 1937. His poetry was modern not so much in its form and language as in its themes and attitude. He mirrors his environment, with its ugliness and beauty, expressing his own feeling about it. His descriptive poetry seems likely to last longest. Typical titles are 'Khartoum', 'Dawn in the desert' and 'Tutti Island at dawn'.[55]

Later poets have shown skill with free verse, but no-one yet seems to have emerged with a strong personal note. Tāj al-Sirr Ḥasan (b.1930) shows promise. Educated at the Azhar, his command of language is undisputed. He writes typical *vers libres*, and also poems in unwieldy stanzas of varying lengths. His more recent work is unknown to the present writer, and it may be that during the last ten years he has reached maturity as a poet.

Libya too has its poets. A book of 250 pages about them has been written by Muḥammad Ṣādiq ʿAfīfī[56] with samples from about 40 poets. The country does not yet appear to have caught up with the recent movements already described. Thus al-Hādī Maḥmūd Andaisha[57] (b. 1908) apparently approves of blank verse, at least theoretically. A gifted younger poet, ʿAlī Muḥammad al-Raqīʿī, writes like a mahjar poet.[58]

In the Maghrib – Tunis, Algeria, Morocco – there is an upsurge of literature, including poetry. Arberry gives a Moroccan example by Ben Jallūn,[59] in 5-line stanzas, entitled 'Who art thou'. He also gives two poems by the Tunisian Abū al-Qāsim al-Shābbī.[60] One of them, 'I weep for love', is charming, with the Romantic sadness of the mahjar poets.

A good deal of free verse has been written in various Arab countries on the subject of Arab liberation from Imperialism and Zionism. Such poems are readily printed in the daily and weekly press, especially in countries directly involved, such as Egypt, Jordan, Syria and Iraq. They are often realistic and violent, but rarely of great merit – though front-rank poets like Mala'ika have also joined in. That this movement reached countries far from the present battle-field can be seen from a collection by the Tunisian writer, Muḥammad al-ʿArūsī al-Maṭwī, published in 1963.[61] This little collection is addressed to the poet's daughter, and spans the period 1939–58. The tone can be seen from the following example:[62]

The call of the soil: 1952

(Author's introduction: . . . and the peaks of the Atlas mountains breathed from their furthest North-west to their furthest South-east

. . . they breathed forth their eternal call. So all parts of the Arab Maghrib were shaken and answered the call . . .)

> My soil am I:
> Into this world I came from it of yore;
> On its riches did the flowers of my noble forebears fructify.
> Is it not for me to restore
> It to its former glory once more?
> I belong to it,
> Though the ravishers' wrong claim be strong on it,
> And their stay long on it.
> I belong to it.

But we must remember that the Maghrib had its own 'resistance' to the French, and it is about this that its poets usually write.

Mention of this type of poetry leads us naturally to Palestinian and Jordanian poetry.[63] Before Israel was created, Palestine was a highly cultured Arab land. Before and during the Mandate, education was at a high level, partly owing to the presence of the holy places and the various Christian sects, with their schools, seminars and teacher training colleges. This had ameliorated Ottoman oppression. But this mixed environment had not produced a local literature of any consequence, though Christian Arabs from other countries were educated there, as we saw in the case of Naʿima and ʿArida.

The copious poetry about the Arab-Israeli conflict is termed Resistance Poetry (*S͟hiʿr al-muqāwama*). In present circumstances it is bound to predominate, but it is by no means the whole poetical product. Already by the end of the nineteenth century capable poets had appeared who praised Ottoman sultans and their officials. Among them were Yūsuf al-Nabahānī (b. 1850, d. ?) and Salīm ibn al-S͟haik͟h Ḥasan al-Yaʿqūbī (1880–1946). A new note was struck by Isʿāf al-Nas͟hās͟hībī (1882–1948).[64] He was the spokesman of Arab freedom. He wrote a celebrated ode about a Macedonian maiden in which he compares his own country with Macedonia. With Ibrāhīm Ṭūqān (1905–41),[65] who worked mostly outside Palestine, we reach the stage of free verse. His poem *Mautanī* (My Country), written in short lines varying from three to eight syllables, has become famous.

But traditional poetry was still being written. In fact the man who is considered Jordan's greatest poet so far, Muṣṭafā Wahabī al-Till

(1897–1949), preferred the monorhyme ode. He was a lawyer who alternated between private and government service. At one time he was secretary to King Abdullah, himself a poet.

One of the earliest 'Resistance Poets' was 'Abd al-Raḥīm Maḥmūd, who died on the field of battle near Nazareth in 1948 at the age of 35. Twelve years earlier, while in the hills with a gun in his hands, he wrote *The Martyr*, which is still read in Jordanian schools:[66]

In my hand I hold my soul,
Ready to throw it down into the abyss of death.
A man should live with honour and dignity;
If not, he should gloriously die.
A noble soul has but two aims –
Either to die or to attain glory.

Romantic realism and sorrow are shown in his poetry, and that of others like him. In *Elegy for a porter* who was found dead in a Haifa street, with a rope and basket by him, he writes:[67]

You lived a stranger among the people,
And as a stranger have you died.
By nature men are ever cruel,
Among them a wretched man
Can never find a place.

You have never done violence to anyone,
But violence has always been done to you:
And you were ever
Deprived of everything.
And now you are dead,
And no-one weeps,
And no-one feels sorry for you.

The number of able Jordanian women poets is remarkable, considering the size of the country. Al-Ānisa Danānīr, Salmā Jayūsī, and Fadwā Ṭūqān have all become well known; especially the last-named, who is a poetess of sorrow, pain, and loneliness, of the individual, and of her country. Her first book of verse was entitled 'Alone with the days'.

Free verse has proved the ideal medium for the erratic emotional outbursts of Resistance Poetry. A few years ago, a typical selection was published, undated, in Amman, edited by Taufīq Abū Sharīf and ʿĀdil Zawwātī.[68] About half the contents are by Maḥmūd Darwīsh – perhaps the finest resistance poet. Apart from a few poems by Taufīq Ziyād, the remainder are by Samīḥ al-Qāsim. Darwish is at his neatest in his short poem 'Wishes':[69]

Do not tell me: Would I were in Algiers selling bread:
No-one is by a rebel fed.
Do not tell me: Would that I were in Yemen, shepherding the sheep:
The fretting time no recompense can reap.
Do not tell me: Would that a waiter in some Havana café I could be:
There is no merit in a sorrowing victory.
Do not tell me: Would that I were a humble labourer in Aswan:
For rocks avail not any man.
Oh my friend: The Nile can never into the Volga go;
Congo and Jordan never to Euphrates flow.
Each river has its life – its source – its course.
Oh my friend: Our land is not barren and bare;
Every land must start somewhere;
Every new dawn new passion is born.

When Israel was established, many educated Palestinians quit their native land for other Arab countries – especially the Lebanon, Egypt and Jordan. The luckier ones are to be found as Arabic lecturers in British, American and European universities. Others teach in schools in the Arab world. True, some remained on the west bank of the Jordan which became part of Jordan. But there has been an exodus of these too, since the 1967 Arab-Israeli War. However, some Arabs did remain in their homes, to be ruled by Israel – usually occupying inferior positions. They did not provide an adequate nucleus for Arabic literary development in Israel. What is not always realized, however, is that there has been an influx of Arabic-speaking Jews from other Arab countries such as Iraq. Such immigrants have old and distinguished Arabic names, in some cases going back to pre-Islamic Arabian tribal names. It is therefore not always apparent from their names that they are Jews. Understandably, the poets from these families have tended to write about Arab-Jewish friendship. Among them is Salīm Shamshū', a lawyer, and president of the Arab Pen Club in Israel. Some non-Jewish poets have taken up the same theme. Others, bolder, write about the plight of the Arab refugees and the glories of the Arab past. One poet, Rāshid Ḥusain, deplored his fellow poets' preoccupation with political and occasional poetry.

An index of literature in Arabic produced in Israel between 1948 and 1964 has been prepared by S. Moreh, an Arabist at the Hebrew University, Jerusalem.[70] It mentions about twenty volumes of poetry.

Unfortunately, recent events have made it even less likely that any substantial worthwhile Arabic literature can develop in Israel. Reverses have led to much soul-searching among Arabs: pictures of a glorious but remote past are no panacea for present pains. It may be that this situation will give rise to a new Arabic poetry.

The resistance poetry, however, is likely to prove to be a dead end. It is too full of violent clichés, cant phrases and slogans. Too often the rhetoric is ranting, and the melancholy melodramatic. Nevertheless, and as is the way with poetry of patriotic appeal at a time when a community finds itself in a warlike posture, it finds a great response.

Prose

1. *Introduction*

The last fifty years have seen a rich harvest of Arabic prose literature – particularly in the case of the novel and short story, and, to a lesser extent, in prose drama. It has been swelled by a burst of literary activity since the Second World War in countries which had hitherto lagged behind, such as the countries of North-west Africa and the Sudan. The best prose writing is not that of men trying to reconcile Middle Eastern and Western cultures and not quite succeeding: the two elements have now become integrated into a literature that is technically assured, yet undeniably Arab. It challenges comparison with the best in other countries. Political events have kept polemical literature alive in the ʿAbduh tradition, but with a greater awareness of the spirit of the West.

Style has changed considerably. The process of escaping from the rhetorical straitjacket has been completed. In fact, the only balagha devices regularly and generally used are simile and metaphor – and these have become more related to modern life. Taufīq al-Ḥakīm[71] can talk of someone getting aboard a truck in dignified fashion 'as if he were getting into a Rolls Royce'. In fact, authors tend to address themselves to the widest possible readership, including those with fairly modest schooling, and so simplicity and clarity are preferred except among *avant-garde* writers. Literary Arabic has come a little nearer the colloquial, but without the regional idiosyncrasies of vocabulary and syntax, and without offending against classical grammatical rules except in dialogue.

Tribute must be paid here to popular series of cheap books, whether reprints of modern works, or studies in classical literature and civilization. The first Arabic equivalent comparable to the British Penguin and Pelican books was the Egyptian *Silsila iqra'* (The 'Read!' Series), which helped to put literature of all types within the range of the lower middle-class pocket.

The sheer quantity of published material would surprise all but those specialists who see the guides to current literature now being published annually in some Arab countries. There is, of course, much ephemeral popular literature – translated detective novels and thrillers, popular novels mildly erotic in character, and the like. Egypt, the Lebanon and the Sudan have produced modern school text-books, with pictures, maps and diagrams aiming at – and often reaching – European standards. One of the important legacies of Britain to the Sudan was the series of text-books and teachers' handbooks written at the Institute of Education, Bakhter Ruda, under the direction of V. L. Griffiths between 1940 and 1955.

Much children's literature is being written, too, especially Arabic readers. The most successful writer in this field has been the Egyptian Kāmil Kīlānī, whose products include a series of Shakespeare stories for children. The Maʿārif Press in Cairo has been active in publishing children's books by this author and others, as well as school text-books and reprints of classical texts.

Technical and scientific books are also being published in quantity. The requirements of the armed forces have been a stimulus.

The growth of journalism has been phenomenal. The best-known Arabic newspapers include *al-Ahrām* (possibly to be considered as *The Times* of the Arab world) and *al-Jumhūriyya* in Egypt; and *al-Ḥayāt* and *al-Jarīda* in Beirut. New linotype machines have been introduced into the Lebanon, and are being introduced elsewhere. They make use of a rather angular type fount, but it is clearer on poor paper than the older cursive fount.

From the great mass of literature of this period, a few leading authors – and one or two not so prominent – will be singled out for discussion. Happily, translations of modern Arabic prose literature are becoming available for certain leading writers, particularly in French and English. It is hoped that this is merely a start. There is a useful collection of short stories translated by Denys Johnson-Davies.[72] The plays of Maḥmūd Taimūr and Taufīq al-Ḥakīm can be read in French, and individual works by Ḥakīm and Ṭaha Ḥusain are available in English translation. Such translations will be mentioned as their authors are dealt with in the following pages.

2. *Egypt*

Ṭaha Ḥusain (b. 1889), who was known as the 'leader of the modernists' in the 1920's and 1930's, is the 'grand old man' of Arabic literature, and the most celebrated Arabic author of the last forty years. Fortunately, there is a full study of him in English.[73] To do justice to him within a small compass is hard. Born in a village of Upper Egypt to parents of modest means, within sight of an irrigation canal, he became blind at the age of two – probably through trachoma. He tells us of the drops his mother used to put in his eyes to try to cure his eye trouble. Despite his blindness, he went to the old-fashioned village school or *kuttāb*, where the aim was to teach pupils to learn the whole Koran by heart. At the age of thirteen he had shown such promise that he was sent to the Azhar in Cairo, and gained a mastery of the Arabic language. He also heard Muhammad ʿAbduh. Perhaps this, and his sense of detachment and rebellion due to his physical disability, helped to mould his qualities as a writer.

He remained ten years studying at the Azhar – *in* it, but hardly *of* it. Then he moved to the new Egyptian University. There, in addition to Egyptians, European orientalists such as Nallino and Littmann were lecturing on Arabic literature. He wrote a thesis on Abū al-ʿAlā' al-Maʿarrī,[74] the blind poet of strange ideas, with whom Taha Husain felt some sort of bond, as he tells us in *al-Ayyām*. From 1915 to 1919 he studied at the Sorbonne, and wrote a doctoral thesis on Ibn Khaldun.[75] He learned Latin and Greek, to further his research. On his return to Egypt he was appointed to a new chair of Ancient History (Graeco-Roman) in the Egyptian University, and later, to the chair of Ancient Arabic Literature.

By this time, he was already causing eyebrows to be raised among the conservative elements. He translated Greek and French classical drama into Arabic, and began to apply Western canons of criticism to Classical Arabic literature. At the same time, he wrote in an intimate and urbane – even at times almost casual – manner, making classical literature seem real and relevant to modern times. This manner contrasted sharply with that of the 'old guard', who adhered to medieval routines confined largely to textual criticism and the retailing of medieval literary criticism, which too often they accepted uncritically. His first work in this new vein was *Ḥadī<u>th</u> al-Arbaʿā'* (Wednesday Chats)[76] on Ommeyad and ʿAbbasid poetry. Later came *Maʿ al-Mutanabbī* (With Mutanabbi).[77] He embodied his ideas on education and literary criticism in *Mustaqbal al-<u>th</u>aqāfa fī Miṣr* (The future of culture in Egypt),[78] which Hourani discusses at some length.

But it was in the mid-twenties that his bombshell burst on Arabic literary circles, in the shape of his book 'About Pre-Islamic Poetry' (1926), reprinted in the following year with modifications and an additional chapter on prose literature, under the new title of 'About Pre-Islamic Literature'.[79] In this book he proposed, and attempted to prove, that the great bulk of pre-Islamic literature as we know it is largely later forgeries. The book caused an immediate outcry, and a crop of bitter replies. The idea was not new – only the extreme way in which it was put was new. Even medieval writers had been aware of some forgery; and there were variant readings, with textual variations and differing orders of the verses in many of the well-known poems. This was, no doubt, partly due to the fact that this poetry was not written down at the time of composition, but transmitted orally. The written versions date, in some instances, from 200 years after the presumed date of composition. The names of two forgers were well known – <u>Kh</u>alaf al-Aḥmar and Ḥammād al-Rāwiya. In the second half of the nineteenth century Nöldeke and Ahlwardt expressed doubts about their authenticity; but it was Margoliouth, Laudian Professor of Arabic at Oxford, who was most outspoken. In 1925[80] he postulated forgery on a grand scale, pointing out the lack of dialectical differences and the scanty references to Christianity or other religions in the poems. Taha Husain was aware of these suspicions entertained by certain Europeans: but in his book he argues the matter for himself, independently, and tries to show how tribal, political, and religious animosities led to forgery.

For Arabs, these arguments, coming from a fellow-Arab, were folly and treachery. Not only was pre-Islamic poetry their most highly revered literature, but they had been brought up to believe that it could be drawn on as confirmatory evidence in elucidating difficult language in the Koran. Taha Husain declared that the reverse was the truth; that, if anything, it was the language of the Koran which provided a yardstick for judging the authenticity of the language of the poetry. His conclusion was that 'the circumstances of Pre-Islamic literature are completely contrary to the unanimous view of professors and teachers', and that 'we look at it as an historian sees pre-history'. Nevertheless, all is not on the debit side, since in the Koran is the best view of Pre-Islamic Arabia. And Arabic literature begins with the Koran.

Even today, after the dust of controversy has settled, many educated Arabs regret that this book was ever written – and it is suspected that Taha Husain himself regrets that he ever wrote it. The old-fashioned Azharites regarded it as an implied attack on religious traditions, since it cast doubt on the accepted view of the environment in which Muhammad received his revelation. If was therefore tantamount to heresy. This is unjust to Taha Husain, who, despite his attachment to Maʿarri, could not be called irreligious. But he did regard religion as a personal matter, which was not affected by Western science and scientific methods. Today, the common view among Arabs and Arabists is that Pre-Islamic poetry, while not authentic in every detail, and while subjected to changes and interpolations since the time it was composed, none the less constitutes an authentic picture of certain aspects of life in Arabia before the rise of Islam. More than that, it is a genuine literary heritage as a whole, if not in all its parts.

During the 1930's and 1940's, religion played a considerable part in Taha Husain's writings. He applied the unassuming techniques of his literary criticism to the life of the Prophet in *ʿAlā Hāmish al-Sīra* (1937–43); to the tribulations of the early Muslims in *al-Waʿd al-Ḥaqq* (1950); to the Orthodox Caliphs in *al-Fiṭna al-Kubrā* (1947).

Meanwhile, his position in the world of education had passed from strength to strength. In 1936 he was appointed Rector of the University of Alexandria, and in 1950 Minister of Education. He lost this position when Nahas Pasha's government fell. His literary activity continued unabated, covering almost every genre except original drama. He tried his hand at fiction, in works such as *Du'ā' al-Qairawān* (The call of Qairawan), and *Adīb* (a Man of Letters, with the sub-title, 'a Western Adventure'). These are written in the familiar personal style, and with that psychological insight which pervades all his work. They are not novels with a lot of dialogue. And they have been compared with Gide's work. Taha Husain certainly knew Gide, both as man and as writer.

There is no denying his command of Arabic style: but his mastery is difficult to explain to non-Arabs, unless they know the language well. His idiosyncrasies are such that only a few lines are required to identify his authorship of any work. It has been said that 'his style combines the elaborateness of the Classical Arabic with the simplicity of the modern, and has a characteristic repetition which fascinates some and irritates others'. Again, he has been accused of 'pedantry, . . . as though he chewed his words'.[81] The term 'pedantry' is grossly unfair, though he is often 'clipped' and precise.

His autobiography, *al-Ayyām* (The Days), is the most celebrated book in modern Arabic literature. Part I appeared in 1927, Part II in 1939. Part I describes his village childhood, especially his education at the village school; Part II his life at the Azhar. As a social document it is absorbing; as a character study, it is vivid and moving. Moreover, it is perhaps the best introduction to good modern Arabic writing for the student. It is usually called an autobiography – and so it is. To the present writer it is not strictly an accurate life-story, but rather an imaginative one. It is an autobiography much as James Joyce's *Portrait of the Artist as a Young Man* is an autobiography. It is Taha Husain's *A la Recherche du temps perdu*, if you like, pervaded in parts with an air of innocence and unsophistication, by that art which conceals art. In fact, by avoiding the first person the author seems to stress that he does not want his work to be judged purely as an autobiography. He refers to himself always in the third person, as 'our Friend' (*ṣāhibunā*) – never as 'I'. In the first few pages he casts his mind back to the first memories of his early childhood, presenting impressions that have a strange vagueness. We soon realize that this vagueness is not due solely to the remoteness of the time, but to the child's virtual blindness. His awkwardness due to his blindness, his retiring within himself, and the enhanced appreciation of sounds, all these are revealed with sensitivity and understanding born, in a large measure, of his experience of Western literary methods. From the time he goes to the village school, a note of satire creeps in. He depicts for us the village schoolmaster, whose main aim is to teach pupils to recite the Koran by heart, but whose main motive is to please the boys' parents and obtain a reward. The schoolmaster is fundamentally lazy, but quick to benefit from success, or wriggle out of failure.

In Part II we see him at the Azhar, working hard to make good, yet always something of a fish out of water. In both parts the environment is faithfully recorded. But most of all, a clever and handicapped child and adolescent is depicted; and, as Wordsworth says, 'the child is father of the man'. It would be possible to pick out sentences and passages which say so much in so little – but good French and English translations are available.[82] Indeed, it is the most-translated modern Arabic book, having been translated also into Persian, Hebrew, Malay, and Chinese.

His name will live, if only for *al-Ayyām*. But his contribution to Arabic literature cannot be measured merely in terms of his own works. He is a 'father figure', greatly revered by his fellow writers. His ideas on literature and life have influenced Arabs. He typifies the new liberal spirit in Arab thought. He showed the way to a new Arabic style, as different from classical prose as Galsworthy is from Sir Thomas Browne.

Yet future generations may well give pride of place, as the greatest Arabic writer of the first half of the twentieth century, to Taufīq al-Ḥakīm. The year of his birth has been variously given as 1898, 1902 and 1903. He was born in Alexandria, and decided on a legal career. He continued his studies in Paris, where he seems to have imbibed French literary ideas, and frequented the theatre. On his return to Egypt he worked as a provincial government legal officer, but he later gave up this career to devote himself to literature. He has written successful novels, short stories, and essays, but his main contribution has been to drama. In fact, he may be said to have introduced a new type of drama to Arabic. As we have seen, Arabic drama began with musical comedy, and developed prose comedy and even farce. Indeed, music-hall playlets and plays could be seen in several Cairo music-halls and cabarets. Heroic verse-drama appeared, and the Cairo Opera House – built by the Khedive Ismail to celebrate the opening of the Suez Canal – became, and has remained, the only permanent theatre in the Arab world. Foreign plays and operas were produced there, but it also staged Arabic drama. Shauqi raised this serious poetical drama to its highest level. Then Taufiq al-Hakim introduced Arabic 'intellectual drama' – drama as a medium for discussing ideas. He may be likened to Shaw or to Priestley. But the influences on him were those of French and Greek drama.

He began writing one-act playlets in French. One of these, *Devant son guichet*, later appeared among his published plays translated by another hand.[83] It consists of a dialogue involving a young man apparently wanting to buy a ticket at the Paris Odéon. But it soon transpires that what he really wants is a place in the heart of the box-office girl, not one in the theatre. He is convinced that neither she, nor any other girl like her, really has a vacant place in her heart. We seem here to have a foresight of the author's one weakness in characterization – in depicting women. But this silly playlet certainly foreshadows Hakim's expertise in writing dialogue, if nothing else. It also foreshadows the fact that in his plays inner meaning is not always obvious.

Hakim's writings contain two main types of drama – first, intellectual drama, the drama of ideas or drama of fantasy; second, contemporary social drama, much of it in one-act plays, but including also several full-length plays. In the latter, he uses Egyptian colloquialisms, as in his fiction, though not continually, or in extreme form. Those interested in the problem of colloquial dialogue should read what P. Cachia has to say about it.[84] Hakim was content that actors should take some liberties with the text, using regional dialect where necessary; though he advocated a simplified correct Arabic which would be understood everywhere. In 1956 he did write an experimental play, *al-Ṣafqa*, which may be read in either classical or colloquial Arabic. But this involved 'straining classical syntax almost to the breaking point'.

Even in the social dramas some important idea is seldom lacking beneath the surface. He is, for instance, preoccupied with the position of the artist. In *al-ʿIs͟h al-Hādī* ('The Quiet Nest' – a sarcastic title) the chief protagonists are a (female) film star and a writer attempting to write the script for a film. Hakim often writes about the role of woman in the artist's life, as helpmate and partner.

Hakim has been successful in both the traditions of drama he has worked in. He has a fine sense of theatre, and is able to use dialogue with a sure touch to develop character and discuss ideas. However, it is surely his drama of ideas which will survive longest.

His first major play did not fit into any known category. Entitled *Muḥammad*,[85] it depicts the life of the Prophet in epic drama somewhat on the scale of Hardy's *The Dynasts*. Like the latter, it is not intended to be acted; for no Muslim could tolerate seeing the Prophet on the stage. But the mere fact of writing it, showed the author's boldness. The publication of his *Ahl al-Kahf* (The People of the Cave) in 1933 was hailed by Taha Husain as 'an event in the history of Arabic literature'. Like subsequent intellectual dramas by Hakim, it has not often been acted – which is a shame, as, in the present author's view, it is as suitable for the theatre as anything by Shaw. It has run into several editions in Arabic, and has been translated into several languages.[86] By any standards, it is a very great play. For his intellectual drama Hakim took his plots from legend, whether Greek or Islamic. In this case it was the Koranic[87] story of the 'People of the Cave', which is a variant of the Christian legend of the Seven Sleepers of Ephesus. The dramatist makes them three in number, as suggested in the Koran, with the fourth of them, the dog Qiṭmīr, 'stretching his forelegs at the entrance'. But while in the Koran they are just 'believers', to Hakim they are definitely Christians, believing, as they so often say, 'in God and Christ'.

In the first act, they wake up under the impression that they have been in the cave a night or two – not, as in reality, for three hundred years. They are Mis̲h̲līniyya, who has been in love with Pariskā (Prisca), the daughter of the local ruler, Decianus, and still hopes to see her again; Marnūs̲h̲, who has a wife and child he hopes to see; and Yamlīk̲h̲ā. The latter is a simple shepherd who wants to return to his flock. But he has an intuitive insight into truth, worldly and eternal. All have been shut up as a result of Decianus' persecutions of Christians. We see that, under stress, only the simple shepherd has real faith. The shepherd, having discovered that the cave entrance is no longer closed, goes out to buy food. His strange clothes and antique money arouse people's suspicions. He hastens back to the cave to tell the other two. Then, at the end of the act, a crowd bursts in with torches, and the sleepers emerge to a new world.

This is a wonderful first act – starting in a world of darkness and shadows, ending in a burst of light. A translation of it constitutes Extract VI in this book.

When the sleepers emerge – apparently to reality as they know it – all seems well at first. By a coincidence there is a governor of the city (which is Tarsus, not Ephesus, to Hakim), who has a daughter called Pariska; her tutor has always told her that she resembles the Pariska of three hundred years earlier. The next two acts show the three men gradually awakening to the truth that they have slept for hundreds of years. The new world is not really theirs, for they are 'the dreams of Time' and the 'property of History'. The shepherd is the first to realize this. Marnush no longer has a wife and child to see. Only Mishliniyya will not accept that the passage of the years matters – for the new Pariska is as the old one, and they love each other. The sleepers gradually feel their bodies beginning to decay, and they return to the grave to die properly. But Pariska accompanies her Mishliniyya to die with him. Thus 'love conquers all'. Is it, one wonders, a coincidence that the first work intended for performance at the Cairo Opera House, and actually performed there in 1871, should have been Verdi's *Aida*, in which, at the end, Aida chooses to be immured with Radames in a subterranean chamber, and die with him?

The dramatist shows great skill in adapting the legend for the theatre. He uses dialogue brilliantly, and makes the most of the minimal movement and action to develop the plot and his theme. There are dozens of telling touches. For example, we hear how the dog Qitmir has been shunned by other dogs, because they instinctively realize that he is 'otherworldly'. The theme is time, but not only time: religion and love are also involved, for they are the only things that transcend time. It may be argued that the characters are types rather than individuals – two- rather than three-dimensional. Yet a closer reading of the play would belie this assertion.

Other intellectual plays followed: *Shaharazād* (1938), *Solomon the Wise* (1943) – both on traditional Islamic themes; *Praxa* (1939), *Pigmalion* (1942) and *Oedipus Rex* (1949) on European classical subjects. Despite their real merits – and the present writer finds

Solomon the Wise the best of them – none has attained the near-perfection of *Ahl al-Kahf*.

Taufiq al-Hakim returned to the time theme later in a play with the totally different setting of science fiction and space travel. 'Journey into Tomorrow' (*al-Riḥla ilā al-g͟had*), published in about 1955, tells the story of two condemned murderers – one a brilliant doctor, who has murdered the apparent bounder of a husband of a woman patient, to save her from him; and has fallen in love with her and married her. He discovers that it was all a plot on her part to get rid of her husband and be united with her real lover. She leaves him to face the trial alone, and the court sentences him to death, accepting that she was not implicated. The other condemned man is an electronics engineer, who marries and murders several rich wives, to obtain money for his research. In the end he murders one wife too many, and is sentenced to death. Their death sentences are commuted on condition that they go as sole crew of a rocket to a star. The rocket goes astray, and they land on a star at the very edge of the universe. They are now the sole inhabitants of a desolate Utopia, where there is neither past, present nor future; no evil; no physical functions, not even breathing or circulation of the blood.

But they are bored, and decide that as they have no work they must invent some sort of diversion. Not only have they powers of telepathy, but they can materialize in the air any visions of the past they wish. The doctor materializes his faithless wife; the engineer is only interested in his work, and has no past he wishes to conjure up. In the end he repairs the rocket, and they return to earth.

It is a new earth; three hundred years have elapsed, as in 'The People of the Cave'. It is a world of science, where robots do all the work, and human beings are idle. It is also a George Orwell world, with 'big brother' spying on everyone through television devices and issuing orders by television-telephone. The two men are each given a female guide to look after them, as they write their important reports on their experiences across time and space. They change partners, so that the doctor has a companion who belongs to a party which is dissatisfied with idleness and a soulless life of science. They want work, purpose, ideals and art. The engineer has as his mate a girl of the ruling party – without moral scruples, and with scientific progress as its creed.

'Big brother' hears the seditious talk of the doctor and his companion, and sentences her to be taken to a place of isolation for such offenders. (The only other punishment permitted would have been a brain operation to prevent further seditious ideas being harboured.) The doctor begs to be taken in her place, and his sacrifice is accepted. As the engineer says, he has a second time sacrificed himself for a woman.

This play is obviously not meant for acting, for on their distant star the two men find themselves naked – hardly possible on the Arab stage.

Here time is again the theme, as we have seen. But there are several subsidiary themes – art and science, freedom and authority, the importance of meaningful work to humanity, idealism and practicality, woman in man's life. It is really surprising that an Arab should have written such a play when he did – indeed, it is almost prophetic. But it cannot really be put on the same plane as 'The People of the Cave'. There is too much general discussion of principles, too much philosophizing.

Of his full-length social dramas, *Sirr al-Muntaḥira* (The suicide-girl's secret) and *Raṣāṣa fi al-qalb* (A bullet in the heart) are excellent. The second was made into a film. In the first, produced in 1937, a married doctor, Maḥmūd, has been having an affair with a girl, ʿAzīza, who has committed suicide. This is a *cause célèbre*, and the thought that a beautiful young woman should die for love of him inflates the doctor's ego. But the dead girl's parents happen to have a chauffeur who is also called Mahmud. The doctor's wife deflates him by convincing him that it was the chauffeur, not he, for whom the girl died.

'A bullet in the heart' tells of an educated Cairene who is smitten by love for an unknown girl, whom he subsequently discovers is his best friend's betrothed. When he realizes the truth, he nobly withdraws from the competition for her hand, giving his friend the only thing of value he possesses – a ring. It is a tender and idealistic play.

Since the Second World War, Hakim has written many plays describing the post-war scene. He depicts injustice and the abuse of privilege by public men.

Hakim's dramatic output equals in quantity that of Shakespeare, Shaw or Galsworthy.[88] Among his other works, mention may be made of *Taḥt s͟hams al-fikr* ('Neath the sun of thought) (1938, several times reprinted). This is a series of essays, mostly reissued from newspaper articles. The subjects are religion, art, culture, politics, society and woman. The group about woman is interesting. Hakim shows himself full of misgivings about women's emancipation and the effect of Western institutions. Thus, in 'Woman in the home',[89] he describes the cinema and the university as the main bugbears which might prevent women from exercising their domestic virtues and duties. Like many an oriental – and occidental – man, he wants to have his cake and eat it: he wants the advantages of women's emancipation, without any of the disadvantages. In *ʿUṣfūr min al-Gharb* (A sparrow from the West) he takes up the theme of East and West in narrative form. It is the tale of Muḥsin, an Arab in Paris. At the opening he is sitting outside a café near the Comédie Française, by the statue of Alfred de Musset. As the rain patters down, he imagines he hears the statue whisper: 'Only a great pain can make us great'. The remainder of the book shows how this works out. He falls in love with a French girl, Suzi. They meet in cafés, and Hakim skilfully depicts the shyness with women typical of young Arabs brought up at the beginning of the present century. They quarrel, and Muhsin becomes the firm friend of a Russian, Ivanovitch. The latter has never visited the East, and they promise each other to do so together. At the end of the book the Russian dies, with Muhsin at his bedside. Only at the very end does the Russian realize that he will never see the East. His dying words end the book: 'You go my friend . . . go there . . . to the source . . . and take only my memory with you . . . farewell'. Here the East is called the 'source', recalling their conversations. For the book consists largely of conversations – first between Muhsin and Suzi, then between him and Ivanovitch. These conversations deal with art and life, East and West. Marxism and Fascism are compared.

To fiction Hakim brought the skill in dialogue he showed in his plays, together with an ability to write vivid description in straightforward, yet witty and occasionally poetical, prose. Johnson-Davies[90] translates a short story, *Miracles for Sale*. It is a satire on miraclemongering. But his novel in diary form, *Yaumiyyāt nāʾib fī al-aryāf* (The diary of a provincial legal officer), uses satirical and witty language to describe rural officialdom of the time. It recounts the investigation of a murder by the legal officer and police. (Egyptian procedure in criminal justice is based on the French system.) It is a 'Who-done-it' in which the criminal is never discovered, despite the advantages of *cherchez la femme*, with the strange and elusive country beauty of the girl Rīm. There is also the benefit of the ubiquitous presence of the 'village idiot', Shaikh ʿUṣfūr (Shaikh Sparrow), who can be relied on to put in an appearance whenever anything is afoot. The work is most entertaining, full of satire embodied in witty language, and masterly characterization of rural types – especially officialdom. The English translation by A. Eban[91] should be read by all who want to see a brilliant Egyptian writer in action.

We are introduced to the local officials' broken-down club, where the local commissioner (*ma'mūr*) wins the other officials' monthly salaries at cards, and then keeps them going till the end of the month on loans. We witness a slanging-match between the wives of two officials carried on from the roofs of their houses. The creation of Shaikh ʿUṣfūr is a master-stroke. He carries his stick as if it were a sceptre, and has a dignity which is mistaken for wisdom. The similes and metaphors throughout are amusing and apt. The local omdah's coffee tastes like chloroform. When he entertains a senior official he specifically asks his servant to bring coffee made with coffee-beans; but the author remarks that though the word *bunn* (coffee) enters into the construction of the omdah's sentence, it does not enter into the construction of the coffee. The tea made by the office boy at District Headquarters tastes like Fernet Branca. This satirical novel, unfolded in semi-autobiographical (diary) form, holds the attention throughout. Only the dénouement disappoints.

Hakim is still writing. A recent play, 'The tree-climber', has been translated into English.[92]

If Hakim perfected Arabic drama, Maḥmūd Taimūr (b. 1894) did the same for the short story. His historical prose dramas, though not so interesting to Western readers, for some time formed part of the stock repertoire of the Egyptian National Theatre Company, and were performed at the Cairo Opera House. His father Aḥmad, a Turk by descent, was a well-known man of letters;[93] and his brother Muḥammad[94] was a playwright. Mahmud wrote travel books, plays and short stories, and edited a magazine devoted to the short story.

He started serious play-writing in the 1940's. A promising play, *Qanābil* (Bombs), shows the same skill in exposing human foibles and failings as he shows in his short stories. It shows how, during the war, a wealthy Cairo family go to live on their country estate, ostensibly to improve the lot of the fellaheen, but really to escape the air raids. His historical plays are *al-Hawwā' al-khālid* (The Immortal Lover – about the pre-Islamic hero ʿAntar); *al-Yaum khamr* (Wine today – about the poet Imru' al-Qais); and *Ibn Jalā'*, about al-Hajjāj, the notorious governor of Basra. These plays have excellent dialogue, good characterization, and atmosphere. But they suggest he was not a master of large forms. They are long, sprawling plays – *Ibn Jalā'*, for example has eight acts.

In the short story he gave of his best. He writes of the Cairo scene, inventing characters which have become famous. Among his collections of short stories – named in each case after the title and leading character of one story – are *al-Ḥajj Shalabī*, *al-Shaikh al-Sayyid al-Abīṭ*, and *al-Shaikh Jumʿa*.

Many of the characters are taken from the poorer classes, or the least respectable – even the sleazy and disreputable. There is the decayed, morphine-addicted prostitute, for example, in *al-Ujra* (The fare)[95] a translation of which appears as Extract VII. Taimur appears to be apologetic about depicting the seamy side of life: but he considers it his duty as a story-writer to depict society in all its aspects. In fact, however, he obviously relishes depicting vice. There is something of de Maupassant about him – or Georges Courteline. One of his short stories, *Summer Journey*, will be found in Johnson-Davies's collection.[96] Several of his books of short stories have been translated into French.[97]

Taimur's contemporary and counterpart in verse drama on old Arab themes is ʿAzīz Abāẓa. He has aimed at great tragedy, but achieved chiefly pathos clothed in fine poetry. His *Qais was Lubnā* (1944) tells the well-known story of the Ommeyad poet Qais ibn Dharīḥ's love for Lubnā. He was one of the 'martyrs of love'. *Al-ʿAbbāsa* (1947) is about the daughter of Harun al-Rashid and her secret marriage to Jaʿfar the Barmecide, a story we have already encountered with Zaidan. These and other verse-dramas set the seal on the type of drama in which Shauqi excelled. They surpass Shauqi's as drama and action, and, with Taimur's plays, have formed the mainstay of the repertoire of the Egyptian National Theatre Company.

Among distinguished Egyptian women writers is one who writes under the pseudonym of 'The Riverside Girl' (Bint al-Shāti'). She has devoted her pen to the feminine cause, including studies of women famous in Islamic history – the mother, wives and daughters of the

Prophet, and the poetess Khansā'. She has also written sociological and economic studies on the Egyptian peasant. In *Qaḍīya al-Fallāḥ* (The Peasant Problem) she drew attention to the injustice of the distribution of land in Egypt which left the greater part of it in the hands of a few great landowners, while the great majority had small-holdings so tiny as to be inadequate to support them and their families. This situation was corrected by President Nasser's redistribution of land. She has also written novels and short stories about the lot of women. Thus her short novel of 1944, *Sayyid al-ʿIzba*, has the revealing subtitle of 'The story of a fallen woman'. *Ṣuwar min ḥayātihinna* (Pictures from their lives) consists of 24 short stories illustrating the problems faced by emancipated Arab woman. For example, 'The Fasting Woman' (*al-Ṣā'ima*)[98] describes the trials of a career-woman who has risen to a senior position in a government office, but finds marriage impossible. She would like to marry, but cannot find anyone good enough for her who will even look at her. In her forties she sees the advertisement of a student, in his early twenties, in a weekly magazine offering himself to any wealthy woman who will pay his college fees. She is at her wit's end, so answers the advertisement. The youth overcomes his revulsion, in the interests of his education and the career it will guarantee him, and they are married. The result is disastrous for the woman. She tries to look youthful by clothes and make-up. In the end the youth disappears, having met a girl he knew at college. The authoress, who remembers this woman decked out in her finery, drinking cooling drinks in her office during the fasting month of Ramadan, next sees her in the holy places of Mecca, dressed as befits her age. She invites her to join her for a meal, but the woman declines . . . and it is not even Ramadan.

The leading novelist today is undoubtedly the Egyptian Najīb Maḥfūẓ (b. 1911).[99] He graduated from Cairo University in philosophy. Between 1939 and 1944 he wrote three historical novels, then turned to novels of contemporary life. He also wrote short stories for the press, one of which can be found in Johnson-Davies's collection.[100] A collection of his short stories – *Hamas al-Junūn* – was published as long ago as 1937.

His reputation is based on his triology (*Bain al-Qaṣrain* – 1956; *Qaṣr al-Shauq* – 1957; and *al-Sukkariyya* – 1957). In this trilogy he traces the history of an Egyptian middle-class Muslim family between

1917 and 1944. The second volume won a state prize worth £1000. In these novels the family history is given against a background of politics and politicians, with much discussion of political as well as family matters in the coffee houses which loom so large in city social life in the Arab world. Among the most delightful sections is the account of the love-affair between Ahmad and Suzi in Part III, during the Second World War.[101] Without being too far-fetched, one might compare Mahfuz with Galsworthy, with whom he shares ideas of socialism and a sympathy for the under-dog. Indeed, this trilogy is a sort of Egyptian 'Forsyte Saga'. Mahfuz is Director of the official Cinema Association; and if this work were filmed as a television series, its success in Egypt and perhaps the whole Arab world would surely approach that of the television version of *The Forsyte Saga* in Britain and Europe.

Mahfuz describes the Egyptian scene with brilliant attention to detail: he gives us the 'portrait of an era'. He is skilful in his use of language, adapting classical syntax fairly freely to suit the modern printed language, with its absence of vowelling. His dialogue is realistic, without using many colloquialisms. According to Johnson-Davies,[102] 'his more recent novels are shorter, often allegorical in tone, and show an increasing preoccupation with technique'.

Another living novelist is ʿAbd al-Raḥmān al-Sharqāwī, who writes of peasant life and rural customs. His best-known novel is called 'The Earth' (*al-Arḍ*) and was published in 1954.[103]

So many outstanding Egyptian prose-writers have been active during the last fifty years, that even some well-known names must inevitably be omitted. Aḥmad Amīn (1878–1954),[104] the historian, at the end of his life made a major contribution to the polemics of East versus West, Muslim versus Christian, which ʿAbduh had pioneered. His 'East and West' (*al-Sharq wa al-gharb*), published in 1955, compares the inherent spirituality of the East with the inherent materialism of the West. If only the East will adopt all that is good and beneficial in the West it will influence the West with its own spirituality, as it did centuries ago when it gave the West its religions. Zakī Mubārak (1895–1952), who studied at the Sorbonne and taught in Baghdad, wrote perceptively on classical literature in such works as 'Art Prose in the 4th Century' (*i.e.* the tenth–eleventh centuries of the Christian Era), published in 1934.[105] Salāma Mūsā (1888–1958)[106] was a Copt, and a journalist. He translated Dostoievsky's *Crime and Punishment* into Arabic. He studied in Paris, and also in Britain, where he met Bernard Shaw. The subjects of his articles reflect his manifold interests and experiences – evolution, socialism, Utopia, the sub-conscious mind, heroes and heroines of history. After his death, a collection of his unpublished articles was printed in Beirut (1959) as 'Forbidden articles' (*Maqālāt mannūʿa*). Some were refused by editors, some had been censored. He stands as an Egyptian rather than Arab nationalist, a supporter of the maximum advantages the Arabs can derive from Western techniques and achievements, and an advocate of bringing the Arabic language up-to-date. Musa's works are being reprinted in Cairo, Beirut and Tunis, and his son has established a press especially for this purpose. Perhaps his position in modern Arabic literature is due for a reappraisal. Al-Māzinī (1890–1949)[107] has already received brief mention as poet and as novelist. Here we will refer to him as an essayist and literary critic. His 'Gleanings' (*Ḥisād al-Hashīm*) of 1925 – often reprinted and read in schools – puts him in the forefront of essayists on literary and general cultural subjects. Among the subjects in this collection are Omar Khayyam, Shakespeare, Mutanabbi, and 'imitation of old writers'.

However, we shall end this section on Egyptian prose with mention of a minor masterpiece, the novel *Ahlan wa Sahlan* (Welcome!) (1958) by Ḥusain Mu'nis. This amusing work combines the ruralism of Hakim's *Yaumiyyāt* with the Cairo scenes of Taimur. The choice of this book is appropriate, for much of Egyptian literature is characterized by a sense of humour and skill in satire. It is in Egypt that the best humorous magazines with funny cartoons are published, more especially *Rauz Yūsuf* (Rose Yousuf). It seems to the present author that there is much in common between the Cairene and the Cockney. Mu'nis depicts what happens to Kufr Suhail, an imaginary small town in Upper Egypt, when news is received that the King is going to honour it with a visit during his impending progress through Upper Egypt.

When the incredulous telephonist in the Omdah's office hears the news from the District Office, he 'transfers the receiver from his right hand to his left, in order to give it his due measure of pleasurable scratching. For the fleas are just in distributing their bites over his whole body; so he too was just in distributing his scratches . . . '.

When the Omdah hears the news, he calls his three brothers to discuss how best they can honour the King during his visit, to ensure that he, in return, will shower favours on them. In the end, they decide that the only way to find out is for the Omdah to visit Cairo and ingratiate himself with the Royal political party. However, he must creep stealthily out of the village, for, we are told, 'the people in these parts are quick to observe, but slow to understand. They will notice the Omdah's absence on Sunday, but will begin to think only after he has returned' a few days later.

A large part of the book is taken up with the adventures of the 'country cousins' in Cairo. They meet all sorts, from corrupt politicians and journalists to dancing girls.

The editor of the Royalist Party's newspaper strikes the Omdah as being very ugly: 'He had previously seen examples of ugliness and repulsiveness in men. After all, he lived in an area where most of the inhabitants looked like monkeys in a cage at the zoo. But the ugliness to which he was accustomed in the country was a stupid ugliness which repelled without terrifying.' After giving £200 to the party fund, he is advised to bring a few chickens as a present for the Secretary-general of the party. He turns to his factotum and says: 'Where are we, ʿAbd al-Jalīl? Where have we thrown ourselves? . . . We find ourselves in a shoreless sea, a sea full of whales and crocodiles, not knowing which of them will be the first to swallow us.'

The Omdah is introduced to alcoholic drinks. Trying a night club, he finds himself standing the chief dancing girl a drink. As she fails to drink it, and he has to pay for it, he says: 'If I'm paying for it, at least I'll drink it.' He does, only to find it is cold tea, meant to look like whisky. At a cocktail party, he is assured that whisky is non-alcoholic, and drinks freely.

He is greeted by a fellow-guest thus:

'Is this the first time you've entered the "world"?'

'Entered the world? What do you mean?' he replies: 'I have two wives and nine children!'

'Two wives? Then you've already entered the next world, not this one!'

The author is writing of the days of King Farouk, and satirizing pre-Nasser politicians, particularly those who were 'King's men'. When the politicians discuss with the Omdah how he can quieten the Wafdists during the royal visit, they say: 'Use everything but bullets!'

The corruption of the Omdah and his minions is pictured as an inevitable, and comparatively innocuous, part of the rural set-up. In Cairo he meets his match, as the corruption there is ten times worse.

As might be expected, the King does not visit Kufr Suhail at all in the end: his train merely goes through the station without stopping.

This minor masterpiece of wit and humour has something of the spirit of *Clochemerle*, and other stories by Gabriel Chevallier.

Mu'nis has worked in Spain at the Egyptian Institute of Islamic Studies in Madrid: his name is spelled 'Mones' there. He has written in Arabic and French on Andalusian history and culture during the Arab occupation in the Middle Ages. He has translated Spanish works on this subject into Arabic, and a book on Byzantine history and a novel by John Steinbeck. However, it is to be hoped that he will follow up *Ahlan wa Sahlan* with other novels, as he has an obvious flair for comedy.

3. *Some Lebanese and Syrian Prose*

It was in Beirut in 1939 that there appeared one of the most important of recent books on Arab nationalism. Its success may owe much to its clear, if repetitive argument, and the fact that the author is a Christian. The book in question is *al-Waʿy al-qaumī* (National awareness/consciousness) by Quṣṭanṭīn Zuraiq,[108] an Orthodox Christian from Damascus, and Professor of Medieval History at the American University, Beirut. The work has been several times reprinted. The author has been Lebanese representative at the United Nations 'National awareness' is a series of essays on the following topics: the meaning of national awareness; Arab woman and national life; Nationalism and race; National work and social projects; Arab nationalism and religion; the Arab cultural heritage – its preservation and revival; the paucity of our scientific culture; motivated literature and our need for it; true culture and its elements; how we can protect our culture; the cultural crisis; and the major struggle. The present writer confesses that he finds the book too generalized; yet there is no doubt that it gets to the heart of the Arabs' problem. Arabs, he says, need conviction, a sense of collective responsibility, an awareness of nationalism. They must realize the value of their culture which, though founded by Muhammad, is common also to Christian Arabs. A translation of the chapter on 'Arab woman and national life' appears as Extract IX. In 1948 Zuraiq wrote another book on Arabism, 'The meaning of the disaster' (*Maʿnā al-nakba*), which in a sense reinforced, in more urgent terms, the previous work. Now, he said, Zionism is the Arabs' main danger. The lack of national awareness was a fundamental cause of this disaster. The Arabs must unite, develop, and modernize: for the 'progressive, dynamic' mentality of the Jews will never be stopped by the 'primitive, static' mentality of the Arabs.[109]

The novel and short story have thrived in the Lebanon. Among leading novelists is Jamīl Jabr, author of biographical studies of ancient and modern authors, and of psychological novels. An extract from 'After the Storm' (*Baʿd al-ʿĀṣifa*) will be found in Monteil.[110] His biographical studies have included works on Tagore, Rihani, and May Ziyāda. The latter, by the way, was a well-known woman writer born at Nazareth in 1886. She moved with her family to Cairo at an early age, and died there in 1941. She knew Latin, Greek, and European languages. She published a collection of French poems under the pen-name of Isis Copia. She translated novels and other books from English and German, and wrote many essays on social and literary subjects. She is held in high respect as a woman writer, but she was not, in fact, very original.[111]

Karam Mulḥim Karam has written over a dozen novels – many of them on historical subjects, such as *Cleopatra*, and *Abū Jaʿfar al-Manṣūr* (the ʿAbbasid caliph). One of his best novels, however, is *al-Maṣdūr* (the Consumptive).[112] This is the tender story of a poor girl, Lulu, who loves a male singer, S͟hāfiʿ. The latter is the consumptive, and he dies in a sanatorium.

Anis Freyha (more properly, *Furaiḥa*)[113] is well known in America and Britain for an ably written Arabic grammar. He is a professor at the American University, and has written on Lebanese place-names and proverbs. He has won acclaim for his *Ismaʿ, yā Riḍā* (Listen, Rida). The Rida of the title is his son, to whom he describes various features of Lebanese life in the previous generation. This is a book of sociology and folklore charmingly written.

The two ʿAwwād brothers, Taufīq Yūsuf and Émile Yūsuf, have distinguished themselves in fiction. The elder, Taufiq, wrote a novel, *al-Gharīf* (The loaf) in 1939, which was hailed by some as a harbinger of the modern novel in Arabic. Émile has written short stories, of which 'The red rose' (*al-warda al-ḥamrā'*) is a recent collection. His smooth and straightforward style has much to recommend it.

Lastly, the name of Khalīl Rāmiz Sarkīs must be mentioned. He is a Christian from a most distinguished literary family. He is the author of a collection of essays, *Min lā shai'* (from nothing).[114]

Turning to Syria, 'Abd al-Salām al-'Ujailī (b. 1918) is the best-known recent short-story writer, despite the fact that he is a spare-time writer: for he has worked in government service, and has been a politician, too, as Minister of Culture. Fu'ād al-Shā'ib is another well-known short-story writer.[115]

Considerable interest has been aroused by the novels of Ma'rūf Aḥmad al-Arnā'ūṭ (1892–1948),[116] the giant of modern Syrian literature. Novel and drama were his chosen fields. In both he wrote original works, and translations from English and French, often without naming the source. As a young man, he both wrote and acted for the theatre. He was actually born in Beirut of an Albanian father, and served in the Turkish army in the First World War, visiting Istanboul. He afterwards settled in Damascus, making a living as a journalist, and founding his own newspapers and magazines. His identifiable translations include *La Dame aux Camélias* and works by Gautier and de Musset. The unidentified ones include *The Japanese Spy* and *The Dumb Murderer*.

In his major novels he followed the Zaidan tradition, but on a much grander scale. In fact some consider him the founder of the Arabic prose epic. His 'Lord of the Quraish' (*Sayyid Quraish*) about the Prophet Muhammad was published in Damascus in three volumes in 1931. 'The Maiden Fatima' (*Fāṭima al-Batūl*) of 1942 is about the Prophet's daughter, wife of the caliph 'Ali. *Ṭāriq ibn Ziyād* tells the story of the hero of the title, the Arab conqueror of Spain. Gibraltar (*Jabaltariq*) is named after him. In 1936 appeared the first two of the projected four volumes of *'Umar ibn al-Khaṭṭāb*, about the second caliph. The other two volumes were announced, but never appeared.

These epics brought Arna'ut great fame in his own country, but were not much read elsewhere. In real life he was quite different from the picture of him which might be assumed from his writings. Far from being heroic, or like an ancient Arab, he was short and fat, with a big round head. He drank and smoked heavily. It is said that when some admirers from another Arab country came to see him, he felt constrained to hire an old shaikh with a big white turban, an elegant beard, and gold spectacles to impersonate him and receive them, so that the sight of him should not disillusion them! It seems as if his preoccupation with the glorious Arabs of old was escapism. Mustafa[117] sees his literary leanings as based on his foreign reading and translations, which concentrated on Romantic writers; and on his love for history, culled not only from Arab sources, but from the works of orientalists such as Guidi and Nöldeke. A further element was his sense of drama, which his stage experience had emphasized. In addition, he was extremely ambitious, and wished to create a new form in Arabic literature – the historical prose epic. He even studied Byzantine history to further his ambition, so that he could see 'the other side's point of view'.

Analyses of these epics can be found in Shākir Muṣṭafā's book.[118] Arna'ut succeeded in recreating the past, using historical facts freely and mixing legends with them. He thrives on rich description and also has a sense of humour.

It is arguable that some Arab *had* to write such books. But such works went out in English after Scott, and in French after Dumas Père. After the Second World War they did not suit the taste or the mood of Arabs. The advent of Arab television is not conducive to the reading of long narratives. And in these depressing days, immersion in the glorious past is no remedy for the problems of the Arab-Israeli conflict.

4. *Prose in Iraq*

'Abd al-Malik Nūrī (b. 1921)[119] is the best-known living prose-writer in Iraq. He was born in a ship passing through the Suez Canal, and was educated at the American University, Beirut. He was a magistrate for some time, but lost his post because of his subversive ideas. He has published at least three volumes of short stories, and one play. His masterpiece is the novel 'Song of the earth' (*Nashīd al-Arḍ*). It is the story of a journalist from a village who becomes disillusioned with Baghdad. One evening, in despair, he sits on the bank of the Tigris and sees a vision of human beings clothed in white in a green countryside. It is highly personal, and the author is apparently an admirer of Dostoievsky and Chekhov. He also admires James Joyce.

Dhū al-Nūn Ayyūb (b. 1908) is another leading novelist and short-story writer.[120] Fu'ād Takarlī (b. 1927) – a lawyer like Nuri – has published a promising collection of short stories.[121]

However, we shall represent modern Iraqi prose, in Extract X, by an author who cannot be placed in the first flight by any manner of means. He is Professor Ṣafā' Khulūṣī, of the University of Baghdad. He has lectured at the School of Oriental and African Studies of the University of London, and at Yale. He is associated in the minds of the educated in Baghdad with the theory that Shakespeare was an Arab. How little we know in England of the two dozen or more 'Shakespeare claimants', including those from Germany and other foreign countries. The idea that the Bard of Avon may have been an Arab is not new. Indeed, it was facetiously bandied about staff-rooms in Sudan schools in the present author's hearing. The name Shakespeare was described as a corruption of (*al-*) *Shaikh* (*al-*) *Zubair*, Zubair being a common Arab name. How seriously Khulusi takes this theory, one does not know. The Baghdad daily press has certainly ridiculed it, while Khulusi *has* written about Shakespeare's knowledge of Arab place-names. But what concerns us here is the fact that he has published short stories,[122] and, more particularly, a semi-autobiographical novel, *Abu Nuwas in America* (1955). The latter book is reminiscent of the amusing fantasies of the late Thorn-Smith. Khulusi's book is a strange mixture of fact and fiction, and is illustrated by amusing line-drawings and actual photographs of women the author met in America.

The story begins with the author in his hotel room in New York, having just arrived in America. Suddenly the 'Abbasid poet Abu Nuwas materializes . . . Abu Nuwas, the poet noted for his addiction to wine, woman and boys. He insists on accompanying the author in his progress across the U.S.A., during which he combines success with the ladies with bright conversation embodying quotations from his own poetry.

Khulusi is to be congratulated on introducing a new conception to Arabic literature. He uses the book also to shed light on Abu Nuwas and on the classical literary tradition. It is, moreover, a post-war

Arab's comment on America. Unfortunately Khulusi is too busy with scholarly and pedagogic writing to develop his talent for fiction.

5. *Prose in other countries*

Non-Arabs know little about recent prose literature in other Arab countries. The output in them is comparatively slight, but it is still a matter for regret that justice cannot be done to it here.

In Jordan, the Palestine issue has made its mark on fiction. Khalīl Baidās is a prominent novelist, and Jabrā Ibrāhīm Jabrā a well-known short-story writer.

In the Sudan, Ṭayyib Ṣāliḥ (b. 1929)[123] is the author of short stories and a short novel. After studying at Khartoum University he went to Exeter, and subsequently worked for the drama section of the B.B.C. Arabic Service.

Some of the essays of the late Dr. Aḥmad al-Ṭayyib, whose thesis on Arabic drama has been referred to earlier, are shortly to be published. If they adequately reflect his original mind they should be interesting.

A remarkable autobiography, that of Shaikh Bābikar Badrī, was published posthumously in three volumes between 1959 and 1961, entitled 'My life' (*Ḥayātī*). Badri founded the first girls' school in the Sudan; and the Aḥfād complex of schools, to which a university is shortly to be added, stands in Omdurman as a memorial to him. The interest of the book is not, however, purely educational. The author lived into his eighties, and had actually witnessed the battle of Omdurman (*Kararī*) of 1898, when Kitchener, by defeating the army of the Mahdi's successor or *khalīfa*, established the Anglo-Egyptian Condominium in the Sudan. So this book, while not always felicitously written and occasionally marred by over-frankness in personal matters, is a document on the socio-political history of the Sudan over a period of sixty years.

Among the Maghrabi countries, Tunis seems destined to develop a worthy literature of its own. There is a quarterly devoted to fiction, *Qaṣaṣ*, of which every number includes several original short stories, extremely varied in their technique. Some are frankly realist, others Romantic or symbolist. Some of them are translations from Henry James and others. What are we to make of the three-page story by Taufīq al-Jibālī, 'When shall we dig the graves' (*Mattā naḥfir al-*

qubūr)?[124] It depicts a village burial-party waiting for the wind to drop before digging the grave. 'When shall we dig the grave? When the wind is quiet. When will the wind be quiet? When we dig the grave.' It breaks out into *vers libres*:

We will strike the earth on which there are rocks,
We will dig the graves.
We will bury serpents, winds and vultures,
For we are made of bones
That know not fatigue,
And create stubbornness from the remains of the impossible.
We cast forth thorns, and dreams, and the emaciated body.
We destroy life, and plant the dead in all the soil.
We will strike the earth on which are rocks,
We will dig the graves,
And dig the graves.
Let us dig the graves!
We have dug them, the graves.

The writer goes on to say that the bodies have not been buried because of the strong wind, which tears their clothes as it reaches its peak. The wind is described as a rebellion (*thaura*) and the members of the burial party as rebels (*thā'irīn*).

They weep and pray, yet the dead one is not buried. He moves, and flings his shroud over them. They want to shout, but stifle their shout, 'not wishing to prevent the dead man from reaching the abyss'. He seems to want to moan, but cannot . . . because no-one has dug a grave for him.

Then 'they rose like a cortège of overlaiden ants, their steps taking away the last remains of their sins, praying the wind to cease'.

It is hardly surprising that this symbolist 'story' should have been written by its author in Paris. But what strikes one is the skill with which the author has used evocative language and created the impression he desires. And a glance at the other stories in *Qaṣaṣ* shows that there is no lack of talent in this part of the Arab world.

Monteil[125] introduces us to a Tunisian playwright, Maḥmūd al-Mas'adī, whose eight-scene play, 'The Dam' (*al-sudd*) was written in 1940 and published in Tunis in 1955. It symbolizes the eternal human conflict, the struggle between reality and dreams, the anguish of faith and the strength of doubts. It has been likened to Ibsen, though such diverse elements as Islamic mysticism and Greek mythology can be seen behind it.

The city of Tunis has instituted a literary award, which in 1963 was won by Muḥammad al-ʿArūsī al-Maṭwī, who has been mentioned as a poet. His prize-winning novel was 'The bitter mulberry' (*al-tūt al-murr*). It is a story of village life, in which the smoking of *takrūrī* (*hashīsh* – 'pot') is a dangerous vice among adolescents. The 'heroine' is ʿĀ'isha, a cripple girl. One chapter is reproduced in translation as Extract XI.

In Morocco, the poet Ben Jallūn (b. 1915)[126] is the author of a book of recollections of his childhood (*Ṭufūla*), and a highly esteemed book of short stories, *Wādī al-Dimāʿ* (The Vale of Blood). These stories deal with the relations between the French and the Moroccans before independence. The tone is bitter and monotonous, and the melodrama is sometimes overdone. Yet there is no denying their power. One of them, *The Stranger*, figures as Extract XII at the end of this book.

ENVOI. Past achievements – future prospects

Looking back over the pages of the present book, the reader will surely have felt a sense of the magnitude of modern Arabic literature – its great strides, and its solid achievements. Indeed, considering the long period of torpor in the Age of Depression, it has made a miraculous recovery. The empty formalism of the eighteenth century, when literature was a minor diversion of the idle rich, on a par with modern crossword puzzles and acrostics, has given way to a stimulating literature written for, and in language understood by, the great mass of Arabs of many different countries and varying circumstances. Risala and maqama have been superseded by drama, short story, novel and essay. Poetry has shaken off the straitjacket of monorhyme and the limiting preoccupation with ingenuity. The modern writer has as rich a palette at his disposal as his Western confrère. Above all, Arabic literature is one of ideas and feeling, with many writers of originality and individuality.

But this is only the beginning. Social problems are gradually being solved; and if the political problems afflicting the Arabs and draining their life-blood can be solved also, there should be greater heights ahead. The future may see the predominance of Egypt and the Lebanon being challenged, and literature greater in quantity and quality being produced in other Arab countries. We look to the countries of the Maghrib to play a bigger part in literary production, and the Sudan to bring its special individuality into fiction. Saudi Arabia, too, with the prosperity brought by oil, the expansion of education, and the sending of numerous graduates to the west to take research degrees, may soon become known for its modern literature.

Meanwhile, we already have with us the masterpieces of Husain, Hakim, Mahfuz, Abu Madi, Rusafi . . . and dozens of others, to whet our appetites.

April 1970.

EXTRACT VI

The People of the Cave, by Taufīq al-Ḥakīm

(Act I of the play of that name – *Ahl al-Kahf*, first published Cairo, 1933.)

Dramatis personae in Act I:

Mis͟hlīniyyā (the lover) Marnūs͟h (the married man) Yamlīk͟hā (the simple shepherd)	} The people of the cave.

Crowd

(*The Cave at Raqīm.* Darkness, in which nothing is visible except spectres: those of two men squatting on the ground, and a dog stretching its fore-paws by the entrance.*)

MISHLINIYYA (one of the two): Marnush!

MARNUSH: So you're awake! What do you want?

MISH.: Where are you? I can hear your disquieted voice, but I can't see you! Oh! My back aches!

MARN.: Don't bother me! I too am in pain. My ribs hurt as though I had been lying on them for years!

MISH.: Where is the Shepherd? Where is the third one of us, the Shepherd?

MARN.: I can just make out the shadow of his dog here, stretching its paws.

MISH.: Don't you think the Shepherd is avoiding us? Where is he?

MARN.: Perhaps he is at the mouth of the cave, watching the dawn, as shepherds will.

MISH. (*stretching himself*): Oh, my back aches! How long have we been here, Marnush?

MARN.: Good heavens! You do annoy me with your questions!

MISH.: Me too . . . if only someone as dim-witted as you could realize it. Marnush, how long have we been here?

MARN.: A day, or part of one.

* The word *Raqīm* in the Koran is interpreted by many Muslim commentators as being the name of the cave.

MISH.: How do you know?

MARN.: Can one sleep longer than that?

MISH.: You're right. (*All is quiet . . . suddenly he says, in a fit of impatience*) I want to get out of here!

MARN.: Don't be silly! Where to?

MISH.: Do you want me to spend another night here?

MARN.: Another two or three nights, till our lives are safe from Decianus.

MISH. (*shouting in protest*): I can't! I can't!

MARN.: Then how is it I can . . . and I have a wife and child whom I love and adore!

MISH.: You are only living for them.

MARN.: And you? Don't you want to keep alive for the sake of . . . ?

MISH.: Yes, Marnush. But you see that I can't bear being parted from her a single day!

MARN.: Mishliniyya, have a care for yourself and for us! The slaughter is still on in the city. I won't tolerate your rashness another day!

(*A shape appears, groping in the darkness.*)

MISH.: Who's there?

YAMLIKHA: I'm the Shepherd, master!

MISH.: We had just noticed your absence.

YAM.: I went to search for the way out, without success.

MISH.: Come and sit with us. Since you led us to this cave, you have been silent, as if you didn't want to know us.

MARN.: What's your name, Shepherd?

YAM.: My name is Yamlikha, master.

MISH.: Why do you always call us master?

YAM.: And how should I address the King's two closest friends?

MARN.: Remarkable! Who told you we are friends of the King?

YAM.: Are the two ministers unknown then?

MISH.: Had you seen us before?

YAM.: Often.

MARN.: Where?

YAM.: In the city of Tarsus†– in the lions' arena. You were on either side of the King in his box. All eyes were on you, and the crowd were

† Hakim places the Sleepers in Tarsus, not Ephesus as in the Christian story of the Seven Sleepers, with which the Koranic story corresponds.

whispering: 'There's the King, and those two are Mishliniyya and Marnush.'

MISH.: And did you recognize us when we came running to you, asking for a refuge and hiding-place?

YAM.: I didn't recognize you at first. But I heard one of you say to the other: 'They are at our heels, Marnush, so let's hurry!' So he gave me the name at once. Then I left my sheep, and brought you to the Cave of Raqim.

MISH. (*after a pause*): Haven't we made you neglect your sheep?

YAM.: It doesn't matter! They are grazing safely, and nobody knows they belong to a Christian.

MARN.: So you too were concealing your faith?

YAM.: Yes, master.

MISH.: Yamlikha, the word 'master' offends my ears. We are brothers and Christians here – so there are no masters and slaves.

MARN.: Have you any family, Yamlikha?

YAM.: I've only Qitmir.

MISH.: And who is Qitmir?

YAM. (*pointing to the dog*): This dog of mine.

MARN.: Then you are better off than either of us.

(*Pause*)

YAM. (*hesitantly*): If I may make so bold as to ask . . . ?

MISH.: Ask what you like, Yamlikha, and have no fear.

YAM.: From the time I saw you running away from the slaughter, I conjectured and wondered. But the question of your escape put everything else out of my mind. Then we came to the cave, and I kept my own counsel, thinking about you, till I fell into a deep sleep . . . from which I have only just awakened, feeling as if my ribs were broken.

MISH.: What was it about us that confused you?

YAM.: That Decianus, the Christians' enemy, should not realize that his two ministers were Christians.

MARN. (*deliberately pressing the discussion forward*): . . . and that he should also be unaware that his own daughter was a Christian . . . this man who ordered the slaughter of Christians?

YAM. (*astonished*): His own daughter? The Princess Prisca?

MISH. (*in a shout of reproach and blame*): Marnush!!

MARN.: And what's the harm in telling Yamlikha about this . . . except that I may have brought back memories to you, Mishliniyya?

YAM.: I beg your pardon, master. There's only one thing I would like to know: how did the King discover your secret? Was it trickery, or tale-telling?

MARN.: It was you who told him, Mishliniyya.

MISH.: I want to get out of here!

MARN.: Again? What a nuisance you are to me!

MISH.: I tell you, I can't stay here a day longer!

MARN.: You feckless man! Isn't it enough that you have brought us to the present pass.

MISH.: You are jealous of me, that's what it is!

MARN.: On the contrary, I thank God that your ill-fated letter contained only two names. (*Mish. makes no reply.*) Yes, it was my misfortune, the first letter . . . and the last.

MISH.: Your misfortune indeed!

MARN.: I was for ever warning you against writing to Prisca.

MISH.: Enough of that!

MARN.: But this time, you threw all caution to the wind . . . So you wrote the letter, and handed it to a jealous maid who harboured malice towards the two of you. Don't you remember the day I warned you against her, having noted certain suspicious things about her? Couldn't you find any go-between, apart from this woman. (*Mish. does not reply.*) What a lack of prudence. Did you not tell me that, shortly before the ill-fated letter, you had handed Prisca a small gold cross which you had had made especially for her? Then what was to stop you handing her the letter also yourself? (*Mish. does not reply.*) But you claim that you couldn't, as shortly afterwards you wrote to her urgently . . . Yes, indeed! . . . to tell her that you were going with Marnush to say the Easter prayer in secret, and that you would remember her in your prayers! (*Mish. does not reply.*) With Marnush . . . those were your very words!

MISH.: Yes, words I wish I had never written.

MARN.: And then I would have escaped scot-free.

MISH.: Yes, you would have escaped scot-free.

MARN.: And I would not have lost my position with the King. And I would not have come to break my bones on the rough ground of this rough place tonight! And I would not have left my wife and child on their own, a prey to worry amidst the violent slaughter.

YAM. (*after a moment's silence*): Master! Have you, then, left your family in danger?

MARN.: I thank God nobody knows they are Christians or that they are in any way connected with me. The fact that I am married is a secret known only to the three of us so far. Moreover, I have been hiding my wife and child in a remote spot for several years. No! I have no fear for them. Slaughters and massacres have raged before, without any harm touching them.

YAM.: That is through Christ's favour!

MARN.: It would be truer to say that it is an ill fate that our secret became known to the King, not two days after he had ordered the slaughter of Christians.

YAM.: Yes, I can imagine how angry he must have been!

MARN.: It is said that he began to roar with the letter still in his hand. . . . He read it, laughing horribly, then called his daughter, and told her of it, shouting to those around him to prepare the savage lions' cages, and saying that he would give them the feast of their lives!

YAM.: How horrible!

MARN.: If Princess Prisca had not slipped through the palace gate to await our coming, and tell us to flee . . .

YAM.: It was Christ who willed you to escape.

MARN.: Yes! But what sort of an escape is this which separates me from my wife and child? Oh, even as I remember my son, a new day dawns and I do not see him!

YAM.: How you love your family!

MARN.: I live only through them and for them.

YAM.: Be patient . . . God's mercy is at hand.

MARN.: Indeed, just as the sky is at hand near the earth. That mercy which helps only those who can wait.

YAM.: Don't scoff. God is real!

MARN.: God has no part with us here. We cast ourselves into perdition. Except that . . . I did not actually cast myself!

YAM.: Everything on this earth is ordained by God.

MARN.: Except our predicament – that happened through a man's doing!

YAM. (*in disapproval*): God forgive you! This is the sort of talk which should not come from a believer.

MISH. (*trying to rise, but his muscles ache*): Oh! . . .

MARN.: Where are you going?

MISH.: I am going to right the wrong I did.

MARN.: Have a care! What do you think you can do?

MISH.: I will go to the King at once and say to him: I did an injustice to Marnush. His name in the letter is meaningless . . . and here I am, offering my own life instead!

MARN.: Sit down and stop babbling! You might just as well admit that you are going to see your sweetheart!

MISH.: What a dreadul thing to say!

MARN.: What is so dreadful to you?

MISH.: I never realized you were so malicious.

MARN.: That's enough. Sit down, and don't be the cause of another misfortune. Whatever you told the King, he wouldn't believe you. And he might make you reveal where I am by threats and torture.

MISH. (*sitting down again, in despair*): God! Then what can I do for you?

MARN.: Leave all to Christ.

MISH.: If only Christ knew the load I have on my conscience!

YAM.: Do you doubt that he knows? God forgive you! I believe that He knows and that He will give you relief.

MISH.: When?

YAM.: When? God have mercy on you! We don't have the right to ask such questions. We must just believe.

MISH.: I do admire your faith, Yamlikha.

YAM.: I believe in Christ because he is real! All those human beings cannot have thrown away their lives and shed their blood for something that is not real!

MISH.: Were you born a Christian, or converted as an adult?

YAM.: No! I was born a Christian.

MISH.: Just like me then?

YAM.: Yes! But true faith, the faith of certainty and conviction, only lit up the whole of my soul from the day I heard that monk speaking beneath the walls of Tarsus.

MISH.: What monk?

YAM.: It all happened five years ago when I was thirty. Previously all

I had thought about was my sheep. I was a Christian in name only, through birth, not from feeling and conviction. Then one day I went to the City of Tarsus on business. Outside the walls I came across a monk talking to a small crowd. He was hidden from sight by old ruins and stones. I approached and began to listen. In a flash it was as if I had become a different man, as if my eyes noticed things they had not noticed before.

MISH.: What was the monk saying?

YAM.: I don't remember one word of what he said. But I shall never forget what I felt at the time. It was a feeling that had taken hold of me only once before in my whole life – when I was coming down the mountain at sunset. Then I had witnessed a scene of nature more beautiful than I had ever seen before. I spent the night thinking, trying to remember where I had seen that picture before. Was it in childhood, or in dreams, or before I was born? For that beauty, despite its strangeness, was not unfamiliar to me. I rose at dawn, and remembered the previous day's picture. Then a thought suddenly flashed through my mind. This beauty had been there since the beginning of time – since the creation. This was the very same feeling I had when I listened to that monk. The words I was hearing from him for the first time were, none the less, not new to me. Where and when had I heard them before? In my childhood? Or in a dream? Or before I was born? And there was born in my mind the conviction that these words were the truth, since I could not imagine the beginning of time – or the end of time – without them.

MISH. (*somewhat astonished*): Marnush! Are you listening?

MARN.: Yes.

MISH.: What do you say about that?

MARN.: I say that this shepherd is garrulous, and I don't understand a word he says.

MISH.: You understand nothing except that you have spent a night away from your wife and child.

MARN. (*almost scornfully*): Then what did *you* understand from it?

MISH.: I understood that we are far from God, and that our thoughts are preoccupied with other things!

MARN.: What's wrong with that?

YAM. (*shocked*): God forgive you! (*He rises.*)

MARN.: Where are you off to, pious shepherd?

YAM. (*hesitantly*): . . . I . . . er . . . to . . . er . . . I feel hungry. Shouldn't I go to the city under cover of darkness and bring food for you two and myself?

MARN. (*suspiciously*): And will you return to us?

YAM.: I'll leave Qitmir here.

MARN. (*pointing to the dog in astonishment*): Look! Look! He's getting up! Remarkable! Do you see how his form twists and stretches in the darkness? It seems to me as if everyone who has been sleeping in this cave is waking up, as if his limbs are broken! (*A moment's pause.*) You are right, Yamlikha. You must buy us food. I feel as if my stomach is a vacuum, empty even of air. And you, Mishliniyya, aren't you hungry? (*Mish. does not reply.*) Can't you answer? Perhaps you are so preoccupied that you are oblivious even to hunger! (*A moment's pause.*) Yet I don't feel as hungry as I ought to. I feel as though the muscles of my stomach have rusted up, or that they have slept the sleep of the dead, and need a clarion call to wake them up. Yamlikha, you would be doing a good job of work if you were to bring us something to rouse our appetites. Have you any money?

YAM.: I have . . .

MARN. (*feeling in his pocket*): Wait a minute! If I rightly remember, I had some silver dirhems with me yesterday. They are still in my pocket. Take them! (*Yamlikha takes the money and exit.*)

MISH.: Marnush, do you know what was turning over in this shepherd's mind just now?

MARN.: What?

MISH.: Don't you realize that he was in a hurry to leave this place, because he couldn't stand listening to what you said?

MARN.: I don't blame him.

MISH.: Yes, perhaps he was right in his opinion. I also suspect . . .

MARN.: What do you suspect?

MISH.: That our self-love is greater than our love of God. In fact I am inclined to think that we haven't much trust in God.

MARN.: Didn't we pray to Him?

MISH.: Yes. You prayed to ask favours for your wife and child.

MARN.: And you for Prisca.

MISH.: Well at least we did pray to Him. But since we came to the cave, we have thought of no-one but . . . (*correcting himself*) you think of no-one but the one you love. And now you are reproaching me,

God and Christ, and all who brought about your separation. By all means reproach me, Marnush, if you will. But God and Christ . . .

MARN.: I am not reproaching you Mishliniyya – nor God and Christ . . . because I am not thinking of any of you now.

MISH.: Don't you see? You've taken the words right out of my mouth. We don't spare a thought for God now.

MARN.: Mishliniyya, are you listening to me?

MISH.: Yes.

MARN.: God, who gave us hearts, has forfeited some of his rights over us.

MISH. (*after a little thought, shouting gleefully*): You may be right, Marnush . . . (*in doubt*), but . . .

MARN.: Yes?

MISH.: What of the shepherd, this shepherd who has just reminded us of God? Don't you see how he is constantly mentioning God and Christ?

MARN.: Your friend the shepherd is a bachelor. So what's the harm whether he makes a present of his entire soul to God or the Devil?

MISH. (*reflecting, as if trying to convince himself*): You are right . . .

(*Silence.*)

MARN. (*suddenly*): Has the shepherd Yamlikha gone?

MISH.: What do you want of him?

MARN.: Why didn't I tell him to call at my house on the way, to see my wife and child, and give them news of me, and of my impending return?

MISH.: He doesn't know your house. What would you say if I were to go? The very sight of me would completely reassure them!

MARN.: I am afraid lest you make a mistake and get us into trouble.

MISH.: Have no fear!

MARN.: Oh! And of course you will go where you can see *her*, you scoundrel!

MISH.: What harm is there in that? She is waiting for me. She also is waiting – waiting for news of me. Do you remember the day she stood behind the door, urging us to flee? Do you know what she told me when she said goodbye to me, while you were pulling my arm to hurry me up? She said she would look out for me at her window, three days later, at sunrise.

MARN.: And have three days elapsed already?

MISH.: That makes no difference. I will go in any case to spy out the land, and then come back here.

MARN.: And suppose someone spotted you and recognized you?

MISH.: Never fear! I will slip away in the darkness without letting a soul see my face.

MARN. (*firmly and strongly*): No! It would be dangerous for you to go out.

MISH. (*choking with anger*): Are you trying to forbid me?

MARN.: Yes.

MISH.: How utterly selfish you are!

MARN.: I?

MISH.: Yes, you!

MARN.: Woe betide you! Have you so soon forgotten what I have always been to you, and in particular, what I have been to you in this love affair of yours?

MISH.: Today you have erased it all from my memory.

MARN.: Because I showed some misgivings at the impetuosity of one in love like you?

MISH.: Not that: but because ever since we came here, you have thought of nothing but yourself, and what might endanger you.

MARN.: And all you can think of is going to your beloved, even if it brought danger to those who are with you. So which of us is the more selfish?

MISH.: You!

MARN.: I, do you say? How blind and ungrateful lovers are!

MISH.: Speak for yourself – this applies equally to you.

MARN.: I can see my own faults, and am not oblivious of other men's virtues.

MISH. (*scornfully*): If only the shepherd were here, he would tell you that you denied God and Christ, to say the least.

MARN.: To say the least?

MISH.: Yes! I don't want to remind you of anyone else.

MARN.: You are an evil-minded youth!

MISH.: I?

MARN.: Yes! Unlike you, I cannot obliterate everything good from my memory. I can't forget, Mishliniyya, that you were the only one to help me in my secret marriage, and to stand by me in my tricky position when this secret family of mine was started. I can't forget that, with me, you furnished the house. With your hands, you brought us vegetables and fruit by night, because we had not confided our secret to any servant or slave. I don't forget the day my son was born, either – how you had set about weaving his tiny clothes and hats with your own hands, shortly before he came into the world. Yes! But for you, I could not have . . .

MISH.: I don't want you to remember all that! All I want you to remember is that today you have added to my present difficulties by causing me pain and pangs of conscience, by your constant repetition and suggestions that I am the cause of your predicament.

MARN. (*in blame and reproach*): Is this the first time I have exposed myself to danger in your interests? (*Mish. does not reply.*) Won't you, for once, admit to the lover's defect from which you suffer? Blindness, ingratitude, forgetfulness? That's how you are, to put it mildly, aren't you? Admit it!

MISH. (*becoming calm*): I admit that you did indeed expose yourself to danger on my account.

MARN.: All right then! Won't you allow me a little innocent irritation when I am in distress?

MISH.: And I? When did I let you down?

MARN.: Love certainly swallows up everything – even friendship – yes, even faith!

MISH.: Even faith?

MARN.: Yes, because it is itself a faith, stronger than any other faith.

MISH.: I see what you are getting at . . .

MARN.: What am I getting at?

MISH.: Were it not for your Christian wife, you would not have become a Christian . . . you, the convinced pagan, Decianus' right-hand man in the previous massacre!

MARN.: And were it not for you, Princess Prisca would not have become a Christian either, as she followed the faith of her father Decianus.

MISH. (*concealing his joy*): Marnush, do you think she really gave up her religion for this reason?

MARN.: Can there be any doubt about that?

MISH.: You always give me to understand that.

MARN.: Because you yourself are reluctant to understand it, you silly man!

MISH. (*in happy reminiscence*): Yes! I will never forget that night, about which I have long been telling you; the night she was dressed in white, venturing into the Hall of Pillars, where our trysting-place was when all was quiet in the palace. Throwing caution to the wind, I said to her: 'You are an angel from heaven.' She looked at me in astonishment, and asked what angels were. I said to her, in confusion: 'It is a name Christians give to beings higher and kinder than human beings.' Then I remained silent for a moment, then said to her, in pretence: 'I wish you were a Christian.' She said: 'Why?' I said: 'So that I could become your betrothed before God; so that there would be between us a sacred bond that neither of us could break.' She paused a moment, then said, simply and modestly: 'Then I, too, wish I were a Christian.'

MARN.: And shortly afterwards, you were at my door like one mad with joy!

MISH.: Yes! Then you at once began to think for me, and make plans . . .

MARN.: And the plan was that the two of you should go in secret to the monk, so that he could admit her into the religion.

MISH.: Yes! Thanks to your idea and your help. Marnush, I truly do not forget how serious our situation was then. After we had gone, you stayed watching for our return. When Decianus asked about his daughter, you told him she was with her maids at the baths. And you told her worried maids that she was with her father. Yes indeed! But there is nothing terrifies me so much as the memory of Decianus, when he once surprised me in the Hall of Pillars, waiting for Prisca with the Bible in my hand. I can still hear the voice of the King saying to me – and I was past worrying any more – 'What is this book you have?' At that point you came up, Marnush, and snatched it out of my hand, and said, in reply: 'This is my book, your majesty. I left it in this hall.' That was when I realized that you might some time be prepared to risk your life for me.

MARN.: Not for you, but for the sake of a lover and fiancé that I wanted to save for his fiancée.

MISH.: Thank you, Marnush, but . . .

MARN.: But what?

MISH.: But I still can't say thank you for what you have said today.

MARN.: Must we go over all that again?

MISH. (*reflecting*): Yes! . . . (*after a moment*) I don't know . . . How strange is man's make-up! Sometimes we have strength to the point of greatness and martyrdom: sometimes we are weak to the point of degradation and egotism.

MARN.: All this to-do because I am forbidding you to go and see her today?

(*A shout echoes through the depths of the cave.*)

MISH. (*pricking up his ears*): Sh . . .

MARN.: What's that?

THE VOICE (*coming nearer and shouting*): Ho there, you two ministers!

MARN.: Who's there?

THE VOICE: Yamlikha.

MARN.: The shepherd? Why are you shouting like that?

YAM.: Because you are in the darkness awaiting the dawn, when the sun is high in the sky!

MARN.: Where's that?

YAM.: Outside the cave. I came across the entrance, and there it was, open all the time, and we didn't know it. But the remarkable thing is that the light and heat don't penetrate through it to us, as if the sun avoided us in its course.

MARN.: Is that all you have done? Where is the food?

YAM.: If you only knew what I have seen and heard!

MARN.: Tell us!

YAM.: Scarcely had I gone two steps, when I saw ahead of me a rider wearing strange clothes. He looked like a hunter. So I showed him some of the silver I had with me and offered to buy some of his game. He didn't understand me, but seemed terrified, and spurred his horse to gallop away. I seized his horse's reins and stopped him. In the end he took a coin from me cautiously, and began to examine it, while I was watching him, in a mixture of thoughtfulness, fear, and astonishment as he turned it over with his fingers. 'Decianus!' he exclaimed, 'minted in the reign of Decianus.' Then he raised his head, and plucking up courage said to me: 'Have you a lot of these?' I took out all I had, and he said: 'Where did you find them?' 'What do you mean?' I said. 'These old coins', he said, 'this treasure!' I thought the man was mad, so I snatched the coin from him, and left him. He watched me go with a surprised, quizzical and apprehensive look. Then he spurred his horse, and was soon out of sight.

MARN.: You are right. Your friend *was* mad.

MISH.: No, Marnush: don't jump to conclusions.

MARN.: What do you mean?

MISH.: I feel some doubt.

MARN.: What about?

MISH.: About the length of time we have been in this cave. Don't you remember I came here clean-shaven? And now I have a long beard and hair hanging down. I have only just noticed it when I scratched my head.

YAM.: Yes, yes! I too noticed, while taking out a silver coin for that man, that my finger-nails were of unprecedented length. Who knows? Perhaps the man was scared by my untidy dishevelled hair. Here in the dark we don't notice anything, and can't even see each other.

MISH.: Do you think we have been here a week without realizing it?

MARN. (*touching his head*): You are both right! I also don't think I came to this cave with all this hair and beard. This is astounding! Mishliniyya, if only you could see in the dark! With this beard, I must look rather like the saints, as I imagine them . . .

YAM.: Perhaps we have been here a month!

MARN.: Don't be silly! What have we been doing all that time?

YAM.: Sleeping.

MARN.: Does that make sense?

YAM.: Why not? When I was young, I heard from my grandmother and mother that a certain shepherd once took refuge from a deluge in a cave . . . He had faith in God and Christ . . . He slept a month till the flood subsided. Then he woke up, and emerged safe and sound, as when he had entered the cave, without being aware of the passage of time.

MARN.: Old wives' tales!

YAM.: I believe this tale, and can't see anything odd in it. It is said that corpses don't decompose fast in caves, because of the damp. So why shouldn't the story be true, since it happened in a rainy month. And why not, when the will of God and Christ wanted that believer to survive!

MARN. (*half scoffing*): And what about our situation? What do you say to that? Is it rain and flood, or the will of God and Christ?

YAM.: Our case is similar . . . Did I not say that I saw the sun avoiding the cave in miraculous fashion? Wasn't that so that its heat would not harm our bodies? It was the will of God and Christ that willed this miracle, to save believers.

MARN. (*in mild mockery*): Believers, did you say? Thank you, Yamlikha! I think that, but for your presence with us, God and Christ would not have willed this miracle for us.

MISH. (*rising suddenly*): Marnush.

MARN.: Where are you going, Mishliniyya?

MISH.: Whichever way we look at it, the three days must certainly have elapsed.

MARN.: You mean you are going to . . .?

MISH.: And no power on earth shall prevent me.

MARN. (*mocking mildly*): Nor in heaven, either?

(*An uproar is heard from outside the cave.*)

YAM.: Sh . . . Do you hear?

MARN.: What's that?

YAM. (*pricking up his ears*): That's the sound of a great number of people!

MARN. (*leaping up*): Heaven help us! This is the end of us!

MISH.: The end!

MARN.: Yes, without a doubt they will be Decianus' men come to take us. Don't you see, Yamlikha? That distressed man went and revealed where we are. Didn't I tell you that no-one should go out without making sure it was safe? And you, Mishliniyya, are the one who was just about to go out!

(*The sound of the people outside grows nearer.*)

THE CROWD (*shouting, off-stage*): You man with the treasure! Show yourself to us, you man with the treasure! Don't be afraid! Come out to us, and don't be afraid!

MARN.: What treasure? Who is the man with the treasure?

YAM. (*whispering to the others to keep silent*): Sh . . . Sh . . . !

MISH. (*whispering*): I am afraid they will come in and get us!

THE CROWD (*approaching the cave entrance*): There's a cave here! This is the entrance to a cave!

ANOTHER GROUP: Bring torches!

MARN. (*whispering*): What can we do?

MISH. (*whispering*): We are trapped!

YAM. (*whispering*): Then let us commit ourselves to God and Christ.

(*Almost immediately, a light shines into the cave. Then the clamour increases. The people burst in, carrying torches. But . . . scarcely does the first intruder see the three in the torchlight, than he is stricken with fear, and reels back. Behind him, the rest become worried and disordered, uttering repressed cries.*)

THE CROWD (*drawing back in terror*): Ghosts . . . dead men . . . ghosts!

(*Exeunt the crowd in disorder, leaving some of their torches behind. The place is left to the three and their dog, and is lit up. They are thunder-struck, and as stiff as statues, as if these words 'ghosts' and 'dead men' have scared even them; or as if nothing they have seen and heard has penetrated.*)

(CURTAIN)

EXTRACT VII

The Fare, by Maḥmūd Taimūr

(a short story, from 'Shaikh Jumʿa and other stories' – *al-Shaikh Jumʿa wa aqāṣīṣ ukhrā*, 2nd edition, Cairo, 1927, pp. 26 ff.)

Among the facts of life which go on behind the veil of secrecy are disgraceful and painful things. The story-writer whose motto is ever to describe things as they are, considers it his duty to reveal these disgraceful and painful deeds, however grim they may be.

Umm Labība went in to see her mistress, Madam Iqbāl, and told her that the cabman was at the door, demanding his fare. Madam Iqbal frowned, and told Umm Labiba to go and tell the cabman to come back that afternoon. Umm Labiba went off, worried, hoping she would be successful in her attempt to persuade the cabman to defer collection of his bill till the afternoon. No sooner was she face to face with him, than he spoke first, using coarse language indicative of his contempt. She informed him, in accordance with her mistress's command. But being put off like this aroused his wrath, and he began to curse and swear.

The cabman was angry, and he had every right to be. On six occasions he had taken the Lady out for a drive to visit her 'companions in arms'.* His total fare had now reached 300 piastres, of which he had received so far not one piastre. Now this cabman had a wife and children, who had difficulty in getting adequate food and clothing. It was only natural that he should shout angrily when demanding the dues of which he was being deprived, this bad debt. He had come for the sixth time, to be greeted only with procrastination and delay.

The cabman returned to his rank shrieking with anger, despairing of getting anywhere with his shouts and insults. He was determined to get what he was owed that afternoon, cost what it may. But Madam

* The Arabic here means 'Female friends or companions', but the word is used in the diminutive form, for contempt.

Iqbal thought no more of the incident, as if she was long accustomed to it. She went to the mirror, tidied her hair, took out a tin of rouge, and began to paint her wrinkled face, heaving a sigh from time to time.

She was thirty-eight, and had been a model of beauty and decorum in her youth. At eighteen she had married a young reprobate, a gambler and drunkard. He stayed with her eight years, then left her tarred with his own brush. Madam Iqbal was left a widow in her twenties. Her husband, by the time he died, had led her astray, obsessed her with wickedness and vice, poisoning her mind with obscenity and immorality. While she was still young, her husband had driven her on the 'primrose path', and deliberately led her to immorality. For it was he who had incited her, nay commanded her, to drink and take drugs. He it was who offered her to any of his friends who wanted her for a trifling 'quid pro quo'. He it was who induced her to make a bit on the side by prostitution.

The young husband died, leaving his young wife to bear in her heart the ulcers of sorrow and shame, and on her body the pains of disease. At thirty-eight, she was more like fifty-eight. Her frame was thin, her face pallid, her skin yellow, and suffering had given her bags under the eyes.* The modest, beautiful and chaste girl of yesterday, Madam Iqbal, had today become a disgraceful gambler, riddled with disease, fond of all drugs and stimulants, particularly alcohol and cocaine. She had a son of seven, by an unknown father, who had grown up amidst unhappiness and misfortune, and spent his youth in an atmosphere of prostitution and vice. Madam Iqbal had now reached a state of desperation and despair. Her beauty had faded, and men, young and old, generally shunned her. She took up the profession of 'go-between', bringing together young men and profligate women, when she realized that her original business was on the decline. And in so doing, she returned to her former condition, menaced by impending poverty and overwhelming want, which were always on the point of overpowering her. Today she lived in a house whose tattered trappings of prostitution were insufficient to lure even the mean-spirited and impoverished. So she lived from day to day – no, from hour to hour, closing her eyes to what the future would bring.

The cabman returned at the prearranged time in the afternoon, and

* The Arabic refers to a dark frame round her eyes.

began to rant, demanding his fare. But no-one answered. He left his cab in charge of some boy or other, and dashed across the small garden, till he reached the door. He began to knock on it, shouting loudly and angrily. Madam Iqbal was, as usual, in her bedroom, titivating herself up, wearing her transparent night-dress, a relic of the days of her affluence. Her hair was hanging down, she was bare-footed, and her shrivelled breasts were showing from her exposed chest. She heard the cabman ranting, but merely smiled and ignored it. Umm Labiba came in, and told her that the cabman was on the point of storming the 'harem', and was hurling embarrassing abuse without ceasing. Madam Iqbal replied quietly:

'What do you want me to do about it? I've no money.'

At that point, the cabman succeeded in opening the door, and rushed into the holy harem! He entered the hall, shouting, demanding settlement of his account. Umm Labiba ran to him, telling him off for his cheek and nerve, restraining him from his evil intention, telling him to be gone! The two of them kept abusing each other in stinging language for a quarter of an hour, until the maid despaired of getting the better of him, and realized that he was about to get the better of her. So she shouted for help to her mistress. At that moment, the bedroom door opened, and Madam Iqbal appeared in the doorway, wearing the transparent night-dress, done up to the nines, her legs and wrists bare. She spoke as if she had not quite realized as yet what was happening in her own house:

'What's the matter, Umm Labiba?'

The cabman did not allow Umm Labiba to reply, but forestalled her, by shouting and asking to be paid as usual. But Madam Iqbal spoke in a tone of assumed innocence and gentleness.

'Why all this aggressiveness, cabman? Come and take your fare.'

The cabman was astonished at the changed situation, and looked hard at her, trying to size her up, not knowing whether she was lying or telling the truth. When she saw his hesitation, she came out of the room, took him by the hand, and led him in. He, meanwhile, was amazed, not knowing what to say. She said to him:

'Come and take your fare. Why do you not want to enter the room with me? Are you a stranger?'

The cabman, whose name was Shaḥḥāta, went into the room, Madam Iqbal holding his hand, leading him like a condemned prisoner.

Now this cabman Shahhata was a tough, brawny man of fifty-eight, who had learned nothing in his life but how to drive a cab. He had begun as a stable-lad, living in the stables, sweeping up the droppings, cleaning the harness, and washing down the coaches and horses. Then he was promoted to cabman, sitting on the high seat, wearing the coat and jacket obtained at the uniform-seller's. The profit he made from his horses and cab was not sufficient to feed and clothe his five children, and his wife whom sickness confined to the home. He was swarthy, with an ashen beard which he only shaved when in the money. His appearance was dirty, his clothes torn, his toes peeping out of his worn-out shoes. His trousers were tied up with a dirty red scarf. On his head he wore a tarbush which had a black band, with no button. Yet despite the indications of poverty which pervaded his mind and were written all over his clothes and face, he knew of nothing but 'luck', which was the one subject of his conversation, and the one aim of his endeavours. When he was aloft on the fine driving seat, you might hear him singing popular love songs or comic ditties. When a pretty girl of his own class passed in front of him, he would tilt his black-banded tarbush, and start wiggling his tattered shoes, smiling, giving the 'glad-eye', and saying:

'Sweetheart! Sweetheart! Slow down a bit! My heart's on fire!'

He often saw upper-class girls wearing the black transparent veil, or the light barqaʿ* which reveals the features of the face, even endowing it with radiant beauty, swinging in their alluring gait! He would stare at them flirtatiously, murmuring to himself:

'What wouldn't I give for . . .†'

If by chance his fares should be a pair of lovers or sweethearts, and he heard the sound of loving laughter, the moving music of kisses, and the movements of love-making, the heat of passion would be awakened in him. He would shout from the very depths of his heart, talking to himself, cursing his wife with a sigh, and saying:

'Oh how I pity you, Mother Ahmad!'

Then he would feel the eagerness of love, but find no means of quietening his nerves except on the thin, tired horses. So he rained lashes and curses on them!

* The *barqaʿ* is a type of veil worn over the head.

† In the Arabic, 'Oh pain of my heart!'

Cabman Shahhat entered the room, not knowing whether she was serious or joking in what she was doing. He smelled the powder and perfume which permeated the atmosphere, and his frayed nerves were appeased, and his eyes lost their flashing evil look. He began to inspect, with his eyes, the body of Madam Iqbal, while she paced the room, looking for the key of her money-box. Then she opened the box, and emptied the money from it to give him his fare. He looked at her avidly, then his mouth broadened into a smile which clearly conveyed his animal urge.

The cabman Shahhata had never before met a white woman of this class – the bogus aristocracy – in the same room. He had never met one of these girls in these circumstances and in this attire. For had he ever seen any other woman but his crippled wife, brown-skinned, bad-tempered, wearing a dirty blue dress, and a torn black veil? And before today, had he ever seen in front of him such a slender figure unclothed, hidden only by a diaphanous nightdress, through which could be descried those soft, slender legs, that white skin tinted with deep red, that painted face, those alluring eyes? Indeed . . . Cabman Shahhata had never in his life seen such bare feet, such hair in a fringe over the forehead, such prominent white breasts!

At that moment, Cabman Shahhata did not see Madam Iqbal as she really was, with her thin body, pasty face, and hollow eyes, disguised by powder and paint and the trappings of seduction. What he saw was a girl such as he had dreamed about; a white girl who conceals her fine face under a transparent black veil or a light white barqaʿ . . . the same sort of girl whose charming laughter he had heard in his cab, whose body had swayed before him in the street, whose beautiful sweet voice, with its alluring tone, had saddened him.

Madam Iqbal approached him gracefully, affecting coyness, and said to him meekly and humbly:

'I haven't any money today, cabman. Will you come back tomorrow?'

She gave him an imploring look, which contained something of the coquettish and the 'come hither'. Shahhata's eyes caught a glimpse of a strange gleam. Then he said to her wantonly:

'I can't leave here, Lady. As the saying goes, "the pigeon doesn't enter the same way as it leaves".'

Madam Iqbal smiled, guessing what was in his mind. She rushed at him, forgetting his dirtiness and foul smell, giving him a kiss on the mouth which intoxicated him, and almost made him faint.

Madam Iqbal's son, Jamāl, who was seven years old, returned home, looked through the bedroom keyhole, then burst out laughing. As he went away, he met Umm Labiba, pulled her head to his, and began to tell her, in his childish language, the secret he had seen in the room . . . the secret of Cabman Shahhata's remission of the debt due to him by these easy and marvellous means.

EXTRACT VIII

Innocents in Cairo, by Ḥusain Mu'nis

(from the novel *Ahlan wa Sahlan*, Cairo 1958, pp. 138–148 and 161–2)

The convoy reached the Hotel Splendide, and ʿAbd al-Jalīl* found it as Sharrāra had said, nice-looking. At the door stood a man wearing a long blue pullover down to his thighs, and a small turban wound around his head. He took their luggage, and followed the two of them, till they reached a long counter, behind which sat Madam Ṭannāsh. In front of her were some papers, and near her was the safe. She was just as Sharrara had described her: she had a face as round as a full moon, beautiful black eyes, and arms like poles of crystal, which resembled blancmange with strawberries or strawberries with blancmange. The Omdah's† glance strayed between these arms, looking at her till she finished what she was writing. Then she looked up at him, waiting for him to speak. He said not a word, so Abd al-Jalil took over:

'A room for His Honour the Omdah, please, and a bed for me.'

'A room facing north or south?' she asked. 'A bed in a two- or three-bed room?'

The Omdah looked at Abd al-Jalil and said:

'What's all this? Tell them to put a bed or a small settee in my room, and you can sleep . . .'

'I think it best that you sleep alone, sir, and I will sleep with the rank and file . . .'

The woman interrupted:

'A room with or without running water? . . .'

Abd al-Jalil said:

'One with water, facing north, for the Omdah.'

'Thirty piastres a night!'

This shook Abd al-Jalil, and he was about to argue and barter, when the Omdah butted in and said:

* 'Abd al-Jalil, the Omdah's 'factotum' on his visit to Cairo, is a local schoolmaster.

† Omdah is the title of a local tribal leader, who acts as a minor government official.

'All right . . . it's not much . . . We could pay more if necessary . . . out of deference for the Lady.'

The 'Lady' looked at Abd al-Jalil and said:

'And will you sleep with two or three?'

The Omdah said:

'Try and find him a small room adjoining mine. I want him near me.'

'I have a small attic . . . almost over your room, at twelve piastres.'

'Why twelve? Won't you take ten?'

'How many days will you be staying?'

'A week . . . '

'Good! And your name, sir? . . .'

'al-Ḥājj Ṣādiq Mandūr Abū al-Shawārib . . . Omdah of Kufr Suhail, Qaus District, in the Province of Qanā . . .'

'And yours?'

'Abd al-Jalil, at your service', he said, as if he considered himself a torch of knowledge . . . Then the 'Lady' said:

'Abd al-Jalil what? What's your job?'

'Abd al-Jalil Abu Qatab . . . and I'm a . . .'

The Omdah said:

'Staff . . . the Omdah's staff . . . he lives with us on the estate.'

Abd al-Jalil kept silent with painful reluctance. He wanted to say that he was a schoolmaster. He wanted to enhance his status. But the Omdah had anticipated him, and put him in his place. With one word, he had cancelled his rightful designation and his qualifications.

The 'Lady' took two keys, summoned a servant, ʿAbduh by name, and when he came running, she said:

'Number twenty-one for His Honour the Omdah . . . change the sheets and towels, and put a piece of soap for him . . . '

Then she pointed at Abd al-Jalil:

'And take this gentleman to the vacant room on the third floor . . .'

And Abd al-Jalil protested:

'Tell him to change the sheets and towels for me too.'

'The sheets are clean, the towel is clean . . . If you want any soap, you can go and buy it . . .'

He saw that the Omdah had gone, preceded by the servant with the bags, but had left the basket behind. So he took it and followed them, till they reached the Omdah's room. It turned out to be a pleasant one, with a fine bed, settee, wardrobe, and a wash-basin with a tap. The servant prepared the room quickly and efficiently, then stood in front of the Omdah saying:

'Sleep well, Your Honour the Omdah.'

The Omdah made no movement, so the man continued:

'God preserve Your Honour the Omdah.'

The Omdah did not understand, so the servant said:

'I need a drink of tea and cigarettes, sir, and it's up to you!'

Understanding now dawned on the Omdah. He eyed the man contemptuously, took out a piastre, and handed it to him. The man looked at it as if he considered it too little, then shook his head and turned to go. The Omdah said:

'Do you really have to drink tea and smoke cigarettes? Isn't food enough?'

The man said:

'Your Honour, I'm human too!'

'And isn't a man human without his tea and cigarettes?'

The servant went off, accompanied by Abd al-Jalil, up to the third floor. He opened a small room for him, containing a bed, chair and small wardrobe . . . Abd al-Jalil took out two piastres and gave them to the servant. The latter grinned broadly and said:

'God preserve you . . . Now that is humanity and understanding. Who would have guessed that that ox was the Omdah, and you his staff? By heavens, you understand a thousand times better than he . . .'

Abd al-Jalil said:

'I'm not on his staff: but as you see, he doesn't understand . . . I am a teacher and a B.A. I came to Cairo with him as his guide . . . What time is it now?'

'Half past ten.'

'Ah! . . . Time for sleep!'

'Sleep? What sleep? The town is only waking up now . . . Go down into the streets, you will find them full of people. This is Cairo, the finest city in the world.* It doesn't sleep day and night.'

'How do I get to al-ʿAtaba al-k͟haḍrā?'

'Take any tram in front of the hotel.'

'Thank you . . .'

The servant left him, and went off. Abd al-Jalil left the room, and

* Literally, 'the mother of the world'.

went on to the roof. He felt relaxed when he found before him a wide paved area, with the sky above. His memory went back to the distant past . . . the days when he invariably lived in roof-top rooms. Such a man, when he is on the roof-top, feels he is in his natural environment; just as birds feel secure on high branches under the blue arch of heaven. For such men, roofs are their world in which they live at peace. On the roofs they spread straw on which to sleep, under the sun's rays on winter days, and in the night breeze in summer. On the roofs they pray, so that people will see they are pious. In the corners of roofs will be found the water jar. So when they feel thirsty they go to the water jar, and look at their neighbours of both sexes . . . For on the other roofs are ladies and servant-women . . . Women, and, by all that is holy, women coming and going without an outergarment or a veil . . . So from the vantage-point by the water jar, or through the narrow open window, the repressed roof-dweller feasts his eyes and nerves. He raises his window, confident that only the sky and the stars can see him.

Abd al-Jalil had a feeling of well-being. So he returned to his room, poured a little water from the pitcher into the basin, and washed his face. He disliked the fact that the water had gone dirty. So he took the basin and poured its contents on to the roof; then he poured fresh water into it, washed his face and head, and dried them with a towel. Then he put on his turban, and sat on the chair thinking. He suddenly recalled what the servant Abduh had said about Cairo never sleeping at night. He rose, locked his room, and went downstairs, stopping by the Omdah's door. He heard heavy snoring, and realized that the Omdah had fallen asleep. He hurried downstairs, and soon found himself in the street.

Most business houses were closed; but the street was bustling with traffic. He decided to go to the Azhar district, in the hopes that, in a café he knew, he might meet up with some old friend who would help him in the heavy task which weighed him down. He could not wait till the morning: for tomorrow, the Omdah would put him to a severe test, and he did not want to fail.

He hurried along, without deviating, till he reached al-ʿAtaba al-Khadra'. Then he hastened forward till he arrived in the small Azhar Square. Here he passed one of those great houses which stand there. Then there flashed across his mind the name of an old friend – ʿAbd al-Ḥamīd Ẓahrān. He had been searching his memory for this name, but only remembered it when he was in front of the man's house. He looked at the door of the house, but was seized with apprehension. It was more like the entrance to a terrible tomb. He stood where he was, not daring to enter; till one of those living there appeared. He greeted the man, and asked to see Zahran.

'Shaikh Abd al-Hamid Zahran, the calligrapher?'

'Is he a calligrapher, then?'

'Don't you know who you want?'

'Yes, I know him all right; but I haven't seen him for some years . . . He used to live on the second floor, by the stairs. He's tall and very swarthy.'

'Yes, that's the man! He has gone up in the world, and moved from here a year ago . . . He lives now in the Sayyida Zainab District . . . He works as a calligrapher by day, and a proof-reader by night for the newspaper *Egyptian People*. He's one of the best . . .'

'How can I find him?'

'Good Lord, I don't know. Ask for him tomorrow at the *Egyptian People* office.'

'Didn't you tell me he only works there at night?'

'Correct! I remember he told me that they burn the midnight oil there. He once complained to me . . . You do know he's a nice chap?'

'Very! What was he complaining about to you? . . .'

'Lack of sleep . . . He said they stayed in the newspaper office until one or two in the morning.'

'Then I shall find him if I go now?'

'Perhaps.'

'And what's the name of this paper?'

'The *Egyptian People*.'

'Where is it?'

'I remember he told me it was in Muntadayān Street, near Sanniya School . . . Do you know where that is?'

'I think so . . . Good-bye . . . and thank you, sir.'

'Listen . . . when you reach the street, ask for the newspaper office . . . people know of it here . . . it's the paper of the King's Party.'

'The paper of the King's Party!' . . . His heart danced for joy! . . . He walked along briskly, feeling like jumping for joy . . . Every few steps, his tongue would stammer: 'Lord, how generous you are! . . .

You know what others don't know, that I am poor and distressed, and deserve kindness . . . I swear by God that if I do well, I will make things all right for my darling wife . . . It's up to God, wife! . . . and Husain.* It's up to God, Husain . . . and my master ʿAbd al-Raḥīm . . . It's up to God, ʿAbd al-Raḥīm, sir!'

He went on, picking his way in the dark night, till he reached Gulf Street. He went along it in the terrifying darkness, as if he were walking among graves. From time to time, he heard the clatter of a distant tram. He heard also the sound of the warning bell which the driver rings by pressing a foot-pedal, to clear the way by day, and keep himself company by night. He welcomed a tram as a friend when it passed him, hoping it would not go by in a flash, leaving him alone once again.

After a long walk, he reached Khalq Gate, feeling tired. Then he realized that he had ten piastres in his pocket. So he boarded a tram, and in no time reached Muntadayan Street. He went in search of the newspaper office, but did not have to search long. In the distance he caught sight of a building with two policemen at the door. He walked slowly towards it, and was stopped by one of the policemen, who said:

'They've all gone . . . There's no-one here except the printers.'

'I'm looking for the proof-reader Abd al-Hamid Zahran.'

'I think I saw him leave.'

The other policeman said:

'He's gone, Shaikh . . . I saw him go.'

A workman passed, and he asked him about him. The workman told him that Zahran was still there. The policeman who had been positive that he had left said:

'Oh! So he's still in? I thought he'd gone.'

The workman led Abd al-Jalil to where the proof-reader was. They went to the printing works on the ground floor. In a corner sat an *effendi*,† with some papers, and a tarbush in front of him. The workman said:

* The martyred son of the fourth Caliph, ʿAlī, revered by Shiʿites.

† An educated man who wore European clothes used to be called *effendi*, a Turkish term, in the Arab world; more especially in Egypt and the Sudan. It is both a generic term, and the equivalent of 'Mr.' The use of the word disappeared in Egypt after the Neguib/Nasser Revolution, and in the Sudan on independence. It was considered a condescending mode of address, especially when used by Europeans.

'Shaikh Zahran . . . here's someone asking for you.'

The man turned round in some confusion, and said:

'Asking for me? . . . Nothing wrong, I hope? . . . Who wants me at this time of night?'

Abd al-Jalil approached and greeted him. The other returned the greetings, and looked hard at him for some time through his thick spectacles. It was apparent that he did not recognize his visitor, so Abd al-Jalil said:

'I'm your old friend, Abd al-Jalil Abu Qatab . . . Don't you remember? . . . We were together at the Azhar . . .'

The proof-reader said, as if searching his memory:

'Let me see . . . Abd al-Jalil Abu Qatab . . . let me see . . . I remember . . . You are the one who used to live in Maghrabi Lane . . .'

'That's right.'

'Welcome!'

The two men embraced each other as if they were in love. They went on patting each other's backs for several minutes, saying: 'How are you, Shaikh Abd al-Hamid? . . . How nice to see you, Shaikh Abd al-Jalil . . .'

Then they sat down, and Zahran shouted for tea . . .

Abd al-Jalil said:

'I see you've given up wearing the *jubba*,* and become an *effendi*.'

The former shaikh looked at his jacket, and shook some of the dust from it. Then he lit a cigarette and offered the packet to Abd al-Jalil, who declined with thanks. Then he proceeded to say:

'That was some time ago . . . my life with it was a constant embarrassment. It was like a contrary wife who never obeys you. When the weather was cold, it would fly away from you and leave you exposed. When it was hot, it would cling to your body like sticky paper . . . *You* don't wear *it* at all – *it* wears *you*. Only your shoulders feel it – the rest of your body feels the air . . . If you hurry in it, it flutters around you like the wings of a bird. If you go slowly, it hangs at your sides like two sleeves of an old revolving door. It will never stay around you properly unless you hold both ends of it – like an old door that won't stay put unless you wedge shoes in it . . . It suffers from tiresome coyness. I was once boarding a tram, and looked, and there was the *jubba* still in the road . . . I had to stretch out an arm to pull it in . . . Never once

* An outer open robe, here typifying Arab traditional dress.

have I started to wash my hands without it beating me to it, and washing before me . . . Then again, it will insist on sweeping the street behind me . . . It has to be ironed at a men's laundry, and such laundries are a nuisance . . . I've become sick and tired of *jubbas* . . .'

(After further talk about Arab clothes, the two men reminisce, and compare notes on their careers. It transpires that Zahran's job is not as good or glamorous as appeared at first sight. He rarely even receives his full salary.

Abd al-Jalil tells him the reason for his visit. The Omdah and he want more details of the King's impending tour, and hints on how to entertain him. Zahran takes him to his chief, the editor; he, if anyone, will have his ear to the ground, and be able to help.

They meet the editor, and after some discussion which does not get them very far, Zahran is sent on an errand into the machine room. When he is gone, the editor turns to Abd al-Jalil, and says of Zahran:)

'That man's a donkey! I tell you, if he hadn't children dependent on him, I'd sack him! . . . He doesn't understand anything! He makes mistakes in his Arabic, and then says he's a graduate of the Azhar!'

Then he lit a cigarette, took pen and paper, and said to Abd al-Jalil:

'What's the name of your town?'

'Kufr Suhail, Qaus District . . .'

'And the Omdah? . . . Who's he?'

'Shaikh Sadiq Mandur Abu al-Shawarib.'

'It's an important family . . . the House of Abu Shawarib . . . The whole country knows of him . . . He's a very rich man.'

'Not very rich. But he's well-off.'

'Well-off, eh? Then he'll have, let us say, five-hundred acres?'

He said this, looking at Abd al-Jalil in a manner the latter did not understand: but it filled him with misgivings. He waited a moment, then said:

'Much less than that! Very few people in Upper Egypt own as much as that . . . Our Omdah is a man who minds his own business. He has no connexion with the British. So how could he lay his hands on these hundreds of acres?'

'I mean two or three hundred.'

'Something of the sort. I don't know exactly how many he has, but that would be about right . . . I think . . .'

The great writer shook his big, bald head, and said, as if talking to himself:

'Then why should the King visit him?'

Abd al-Jalil said nothing, for this last sentence scared him. So he kept quiet, looking at the fearful physiognomy in front of him. Then the editor smiled, and said:

'All right . . . I think that first of all you should see Rifqi Pasha, secretary-general of the party . . . He'll read the news of the King's tour tomorrow in the paper,* and I will contact him tomorrow to tell him . . . Is the Omdah here?'

'Yes, in the hotel!'

'Good! . . . I will tell the secretary-general that the Omdah will go and see him tomorrow afternoon . . . Tell the Omdah that, and be at the secretary-general's house at five p.m. . . . Shaikh Zahran knows the house . . . Tell him to take you there . . . I am delighted at the news, and shall be pleased to see the Omdah. I have long felt nostalgia for rural delights and for omdahs . . . and chicken, duck, and geese – not to mention *faṭīr*† . . .'

Then he gave a great guffaw, and rose to shake hands with Abd al-Jalil. The latter shook hands with him, pressing his hands, bowing low . . . Then he made for the door . . .

* *i.e.*, in the Royal Party's newspaper.

† Unleavened bread.

EXTRACT IX

Arab Woman in the National Life, by Qusṭanṭīn Zuraiq

(from 'National Awareness' – *al-Wa'y al-qaumī*, Beirut, 1940, new edition, pp. 63 ff.)

In this stage of the national revival, in which every individual among the people is eager to understand the obligations it places upon him, and the task it imposes on him, and to demand those means which will enable him to perform this task and accept those obligations . . . in this critical stage, the stage of alertness and watchfulness, it behoves Arab woman to consider and ponder her special and distinctive share of the national effort; what is demanded of her and hoped from her by way of her part and share in it. Similarly, it behoves all concerned with the realization of national aims to co-operate with woman in this consideration, and to take part in defining the aim and clarifying the means; so that Arab woman may proceed to do her duty with enlightenment and foresight, calmness and conviction.

No duty undertaken by human beings will be correct and complete, unless it combines two complementary elements – knowledge and activity. For knowledge which does not lead the knower to worthy and profitable activity is merely false and transitory knowledge. And activity not based on true knowledge and fine understanding soon suffers the storms of fortune which scatter it to dust. The major misfortune of present times is that, apart from a minority, people act without knowledge, or have knowledge but are inhibited from acting. Thus an Arab girl's national duty begins with true knowledge, and will end in fruitful activity.

Her national duty begins with her knowledge of her country's position, and her understanding of her fatherland's and nation's problems. She will not be a true daughter of her fatherland, nor a living part of it, unless she is firmly linked to it in spirit, and has a deep-seated feeling for its past history, present difficulties and future role. Is it not a matter for sorrow and shame that most of our female graduates from various educational institutions do not have this knowledge or feeling? They live in this land as strangers, linked to it physically, but not spiritually. They walk the ground and breathe the air of their country; but they do not appreciate its spirit or participate in its blessings and misfortunes. They are too preoccupied with the external trappings of transient material things, and the petty adornments of life. Thus, in their dreams they are carried away to foreign lands and strange skies. The only admiration and pride they feel is for the historical remains and heroes of other lands.

There is no doubt that the main blame for this shortcoming lies first and foremost in the home, and then in the school. Nor can we correct this unless parents make a start, and sow in the hearts of their daughters, from childhood, the seeds of true national education. Then educational institutions must nurture this plant, tending and strengthening it, until it blossoms into fragrant flowers and produces copious fruit. Parents who neglect this task are neglecting their prime duty to their nation; and schools which neglect it are failing to perform their function – indeed, they become harmful elements in our set-up. Every Arabic girl who spends her schooldays without being given this national training is incomplete in her education and unsound in her culture, whatever subjects she has mastered, whatever certificates she has obtained. So she must hasten to close the gap and cure the ill, by studying her country's situation, delving deeply into its past and present, until she is linked to it spiritually, and becomes an inseparable part of it. She must also work with her government, to arouse public opinion around her, so that parents on the one hand, and schools on the other, adopt a really national standpoint, so that her 'sisters' do not miss what she herself has missed, but, on the contrary, grow up with a profound knowledge of their country and a precise understanding of the life of the people. In this way they will be at its very heart and will not live – as many of them live today – on the edge of the nation's life, remote from its main currents.

If an Arab girl had this knowledge in its true form, it would naturally lead her to active participation in the service of her country. The national work which would then be open to her would be wide in its scope, and far-ranging. For if she is sincere, there is scope for genuine national service in every one of her activities. Every beat of her heart, every smile on her lips, may lead to the revitalization of some facet –

however insignificant – of our national life. In this brief study, which aims at drawing attention to the subject rather than dealing deeply with it, we cannot define this national work in its various aspects. So let us limit ourselves to its major manifestations.

Let us begin with woman as a friend, then as a wife. The forces of the present age have torn aside the veil differentiating the child from the girl. So that, whereas in the past the girl was veiled from the young man, she now meets him in various circumstances, and exchanges affection and friendship with him. Now the young Arab of today is beset by tremendous difficulties, political problems, economic crises, and social questions. And over and above all this is the inner spiritual perplexity which penetrates every part of his being, and shakes his mental and moral stability. Only too often the world seems dark to him. Desperate dejection hovers over his spirit, making him ineffective, and an impotent – even corrupt – member of the body of the nation. So often, also, the vipers of materialism gather around him, strangling him, and casting him into the abyss, prostrate, his spirit gone, his hope extinguished. Here there opens up a sphere for his partner, woman – be she friend or wife – to perform her real function and play her true part. For woman was created to be man's help-mate in tribulation, his support in weakness, his light in darkness. The heart bleeds today when one looks around and sees so many of our women falling short in their high function. Indeed, they are mostly drawn to the vanity of impermanent things, such as luxurious food, clothing and housing, the desire for externals, the coveting of what is fashionable. Thus they plunge man into the abyss of materialism, instead of rescuing him from it. They make his depression and perplexity blacker, instead of lighting his way with their spiritual torches, thus dispelling his darkness.

No one should doubt what effective national service lies in this quiet humble work. For how many a leader has become a lion in his struggle by virtue of the spirit breathed into him by his wife! How many a man has gathered his broken and scattered self together again under the effect of the influence and fascination over him of some friend or beloved! The Arabs of old said: 'Women are the mothers of men'. From this saying I understand simply that women are men's mothers in spirit, and with their tender fingers they grasp men's stricken spirits, and either raise them to the pinnacle of glory and liberty, or drag them down to the abyss of degradation and servitude.

Now as to Arab woman's duty as a mother, there is no need to expatiate on it here. We know without the slightest doubt that a nation, at the beginning of its revival and the start of its new life, needs men and women strong in mind, body, and spirit. We know also that the first factor in forming and developing such men and women is the mother, who tends them in their early years, and sows the seeds of their personalities. So all we can now say is that motherhood is an important function with vast responsibilities. We – women and men alike – rarely realize how vital it is and seldom put it in its proper perspective in the lives of individuals and of nations. Thus Arab woman must make due preparation and ample provision for it. She must approach it only when she is aware of its importance, greatness, and influence on the nation's future. And we must all aid her in creating this atmosphere, and awakening this awareness, so that the mother may perform her major national function, that of producing for the nation sound members who will preserve its strength and stimulate its vitality.

There remains, finally, Arab woman's duty as a worker in the public service. Our public activities are beset by clamour and confusion. We hear, as it were, the sound of the mill, but it grinds no corn. There is no advantage in women increasing this rising clamour and sinking to the level of most men in office-seeking, intrigue, deluding others, and destructive party squabbles. For in national activity there are several aspects to which politics and materialism have blinded men's eyes. There are also other aspects in which, however aware men may be of them, they cannot work as well as women. Nature has especially equipped women for them, by creating in them affection and sincerity, pouring into them compassion and sympathy. In these aspects – all of them vital – woman's duty arises, and her particular genius stands out.

The nation is full of teeming classes of people over whom hover degradation and distress. They are dragged down by weakness, ignorance and oppression. In the streets are children cast into the world by poverty and ignorance, dispersed there barefoot and ill-clothed.* There they are plunged into the thick of vice, and develop as cancerous

* Literally, 'naked'.

growths in the body of the nation. In workshops and factories, in fields and farms, are men weakened by the spectre of destitution, corruption, and social injustice. In prisons, remand homes, and orphanages, are to be found crippling misfortune, misery and unhappiness. In all of these – and in many other places too – are ills and diseases where it lies in woman's power to pour the balm of love and sympathy, and thus cure them, or at least moderate their impact. Many a sweet smile has revived a despairing heart, and raised it from its depression. Many a tear of sympathy has, by its purity, scattered the shadows of deep misery. Many a life-giving glance has spread hope where there was despair, joy where there was sorrow. So if such fine sympathy could be harnessed, and the sources of this spiritual wealth channelled into welfare and reform societies organized by women, goodness and kindness would gush out, bringing to the people widespread benefit and ample advantage.

Nor is there any doubt that, in this, there is abundant service to the nation, no less important than political activity or material endeavour. One of the best and most militant manifestations of our present revival is the fact that our women's societies have begun to turn to these national objectives, and to undertake the beneficial reform schemes which they entail. But the ultimate objective is still far away, and the road to it is long, with many steep hills to be climbed. Let us hope that Arab woman will advance, until she reaches the point her Western sister has reached, in performing fine feats in these fertile facets of national life.

This, then, is the duty of Arab women in this stage of their national life. Essentially, they must show true knowledge and fruitful effort both inside and outside the home. For it has become clear that the task of Arab woman is essentially spiritual. Her task, in her various aspects – as friend, wife, or mother, or in public service – is the task of reviving and unifying the nation's weakened powers and inner sources of strength. There is nothing unusual in this, for such was woman's task in past ages. And so it still is: light to dispel darkness, and charm to remove burdens and revive resolution and spirit.

This elevated task will become great in our eyes, and its true meaning will become clear, when we remember that the basic problem in our present life is an inner and spiritual one. Political difficulties and economic crises are only symptoms of this spiritual problem.

Neither would be complex and obstinate, were it not for this inner crisis, which weakens the body of the nations and saps its strength; were it not for envy which scatters the ranks and disunites hearts; were it not for materialism and its bonds, vice and its vipers; were it not for servile minds, fettered spirits and degraded souls; in a word, were it not for this spiritual weakness which woman is equipped to overcome and end, by her nature and her temperament. How great, then, is our need for this healing breeze which woman blows on our world, reviving it; for this spiritual dawn with which she envelops us, lighting our way, and guiding us on our course. And how well fitted is Arab woman to undertake this sublime duty, and perform her high function.

EXTRACT X

Abū Nuwās in America, by Ṣafā' Khulūṣī

(from the novel of that title – *Abū Nuwās fī Amrīkā*, Baghdad, 1955, pp. 33–41, the section entitled 'To California')

When Ibn Hāni' [Abu Nuwas] had had enough of Chicago, he suggested going on to California, which Americans regard as the 'Land of Promise' . . . to the green gardens on the Pacific coast, where palm-trees grow, though the temperature never exceeds seventy, summer and winter. Abu Nuwas got his way, as usual. But instead of going by air or rail, we hired a self-drive car. Sometimes the Shaikh drove, sometimes I, across the desert of Texas and the wastes of Nevada. As soon as we reached Las Vegas, the Shaikh threw discretion to the wind and visited the 'hot spots',* murmuring the famous words of the poet Ahmad Shauqi:

Yellow or red, such as are the élite,
Like tender saplings, all of them taste sweet.

I reproached him roundly, and told him not to speak lasciviously in his old age about his youth! 'Did you not say', I said:

'I took the bucket to the well with the seducers,
And pastured the flocks of pleasure where *they* pastured.
I went as far as other men in youthful ways,
But found the pressed juice of it all anathema?'

He said: 'My son, the child is father of the man. In any case, I was deprived of this type of beauty in my youth. Had there been young women like these in my days, I would not have gone after boys. And, anyway, perhaps what attracts me in the American girl is that she looks like a boy:

A boy – if not, a boy resembles her,
Worldly her odour, wondrous her embrace.
Features and fashion are as one in her†
No words with her description can keep pace.

* Literally, 'places of amusement'.

† 'Features and fashion' = her looks and her dress.

The American girl, my son, is a girl in boy's form . . . Look at her pelvis – it's narrow like a boy's. Then her chest has hardly any breasts – again, like a boy. And her hair is cut short like a boy's too:

> Boyish, in her appearance Barmecide,*
>   Temples embellished, and her hair cut short.
> I loved the beauty in her face espied
>   Awhile – but love of stars is not my sort.'

I said: 'Yes, Abu Nuwas: you spoke correctly and said the truth. The American girl is indeed a Barmecide boy, as you say – only more so!'

He stroked his beard a moment, then turned to me and said: 'Your own poet Rusafi hit the mark when he said:

> And when I find a new infatuation,
> What care I for religion's condemnation?

Come along to California with me then, and hang the consequences!'†

I had no alternative but to obey the Shaikh in going to California. We drove the Chevrolet to Reno, on whose gate was written: 'The greatest little city in the world'. The Shaikh said: 'Then this city only suits the smallest great man like me!' We came to a place where a man goes in one door with divorce papers in his hand, and emerges from another with a marriage licence. The sight of people there was astonishing. For the wife would go in the first door with her husband, and they would get a divorce. Then they would go through the second door, where the woman would await her lover, and the man his girl-friend! The marriages would then be concluded on the spot. Then all four would emerge happy, each having changed one spouse for another in less than the twinkling of an eye. 'Have you ever seen anything more remarkable than that?' The Shaikh clapped his hands as he said this. 'But we won't marry in Reno, for the Reno women are divorcees.' The Shaikh gave full rein to his desires, and plunged into the pleasure-houses of Reno, with their shining glass fronts, where the gold-diggers sit, knitting coloured woollens, or reading the colour magazines, waiting for customers. Abu Nuwas stepped gingerly, but was stopped by an official at the door, who said: 'Show me your permit.' 'Why?' the Shaikh said. The official said: 'Because this sort

* Deceptive in appearance, from the Barmecides, viziers of the early 'Abbasid caliphs who would, so it is said, feast a beggar to give him the illusion of riches. (See the *One Thousand and One Nights* for examples.)

† Literally, 'let the storm be after us' = *après moi le déluge.*

of place is out of bounds to the army.' The Shaikh said: 'Do you think I am an officer in the American army? Me, with these oriental clothes and foreign features?' The official laughed, and let him in without a permit. No sooner was he in, than a red-head took hold of his arm, and led him into a private room, luxuriously furnished. The Shaikh was lucky, for a red-head is considered very desirable in America . . . and only the extremely fortunate catch one! . . .

When the Shaikh returned to the motel where we were staying the night, I asked him about his new experiences, and he said: 'My son, what a shame it is for these girls. How can they take on such work? They don't seem at all like *filles de plaisir*. If you saw one of them outside that house, you would think her a respectable girl and wouldn't hesitate to marry her . . .' I said: 'This presents a problem. How, then, can a man distinguish between the respectable and the unrespectable woman?' The Shaikh laughed, and looked as if he were on the top of his form. He said: 'What you say reminds me of an Iraqi who met an attractive girl in some city in the West. He took her to dinners and parties, showing her off to his colleagues as a girl of the highest breeding and purity. He insisted to his friends that she was *virgo intacta*. However, by chance, some of his friends happened to be staying in a Chicago hotel. They hinted to the manager that they would like a "call-girl" – the name given to women who can be hired for casual pleasure. And imagine their astonishment, when they found that the girl brought them was none other than the *virgo intacta* – their friend's girl-friend! The journalist Lee Mortimer, in his book *The Secrets of Washington* tells a similar story – how a certain man gave a dinner for a friend. To make him feel more at home and welcome, he ordered a call-girl. When she came, our friend was utterly flabbergasted. For the girl who came was, in fact, his private secretary, about whose chastity he had never entertained any doubts!'

'Then how can a man distinguish the chaste from the rest?'

'By long experience, questioning and enquiry . . . and the science of physiognomy and palmistry. I mean, by studying the lines on a girl's face, and examining the position of moles on the face and hands, if there are any. The theory of moles seldom goes wrong. They were studied in the sixteenth century by an English expert on palmistry. I have a book on it, if you'd like to have a look at it.'

'I would like to see it, if I may.'

Abu Nuwas' way of 'getting off' with American girls at will astonished me. So I asked him about it, and he said: 'Let me tell you, my son, that the blitzkrieg invented by the late Hitler is the most successful way with Western women. When you meet a Western woman, you must fascinate her at once, using every means of attracting her, employing all your talents. When you have made her fall for you she is mesmerized, and you have no difficulty in getting what you want. Do you remember that girl we met in New York at a private party? Her boy friend, who had been going with her for three months couldn't lay a hand on her, whereas this broken-down old Shaikh was able to dance with her, and give her a long kiss on the mouth. She melted in my embrace, and closed her eyes, surrendering as if in a daze, in full view of everyone! Yet at the very start, she had spoken to me roughly, because I took no notice of her good looks, and because I had used some harsh words to her. She insulted me, and I began to repeat to myself what I had written twelve centuries ago:

Your curses reached me: curse me, if you will! Did not
Your wayward words include my name? Then I'm content!
For sure, in all of it your love for me is meant!
So say the things you want to say, no matter what!

And that girl from the Bronx, who, as soon as any man kissed her, would slap his face: the Iraqis bet your friend the Shaikh, and he kissed her three times, while she laughed for joy, asking for more!'

I stopped him, saying: 'But they let you kiss them in a fatherly way, no more!' He said angrily: 'No, my son. Love is a deep secret. Only he does well at it who has been given an instinctive knowledge of it, and has a talent for ringing the changes in it, according to the situations and circumstances. I agree with the man who said that there are many girls who want you to think that they are the ones to chase and captivate you. So you must give them time enough for that. As for me, I don't need that sort, as my remaining years are few, and my days numbered. I don't know when I shall become, once more, a lifeless picture in your hands. That is the advantage of a sense of the brevity of a man's life: it gives him courage and carelessness, and a kind of brilliant boldness . . .'

'Ah! I remember that party given by an Iraqi in his crowded flat overlooking the lake in Central Park. What a place New York is! My pleasant days there have passed beyond recall.

'I was like an outcast crow in that party. Despite the abundance of pretty girls, only a hoary old woman would sit by me. So I said to myself: I will wreak the vilest vengeance on the lot of them! I took out of my pocket a small tin. When I opened it, there was a chess-board. I said to the old hag: "Are you good at this game?" She said: "Yes . . . but I haven't had a go on such a small board . . . Never mind, I'll try it!" We began to play. The girls around us turned to look, fascinated by the smallness and beauty of the board. When we had finished playing, I brought out some other games which I had acquired for the purpose, such as one which involved covering the fingers with some colourless, sticky substance, then closing and opening them quickly till something like smoke came from between them. Or washing the hands with soap after sprinkling them with a white powder . . . they drip as if with blood . . . or that's what people think. Before that party ended, I was master of the situation, surrounded by a crowd of girls. Some of them sat at my feet, while their husbands were ingratiating themselves with me by various means, such as bringing me alcoholic drinks, handing me cigarettes, smiling at me, and praising my quick wit and sharp mind. All this was "toadying" and "putting on an act", out of fear that I might deprive them of a wife or steal a sweetheart! Yet they didn't escape me. I chose two of their women, one a brunette, the other a blonde. Someone offered me a lift in his car to International House. I sat in the rear between the brunette and the blonde, with my arms round both at once. By heavens! I don't know which of them was the best to kiss and to satisfy the thirst for love! I tasted the lips of the brunette – an Italian – for a while: then those of the blonde – a Saxon – for a while, toying with Italian pomegranates and Californian apples! . . . All this while we were sitting in the back seat in the dark. I glanced at the blonde, and remembered the words of Marwān ibn Abī Ḥafṣa:*

A visitor knocked at your door, a vision vivified,
Light was her hue, beauty and dalliance in her unified.
She led your willing heart, as others in like fashion
Have led men's hearts away, inclining them to passion.

Then I turned to the brunette, and remembered the ode of your modern poet, Bishara al-Khuri, known as the Lesser Akhtal:†

*A.D. 721–97.

† See p. 178, *supra*.

Brown girl, pour your brown breast
  In the world of my mouth;
Your breasts should be caressed,
  Not by dress, but by mouth.'

I said, as if talking to myself: 'God preserve us from impiety, you evil old man!' I think he failed to hear me, for he went on to say: 'Poor Margaret! She wanted me to meet her the following day! But alas! Dates with the Shaikh are hard to get . . . and precious. I enjoyed that intense pleasure, when a woman makes advances to a man, of kicking her without mercy or pity . . . while she beseeches and begs! In the end, I agreed to spend the remainder of that evening with her in her blonde friend's flat on 54th Street:

I greeted her; meanwhile our cups were filled full
  Of fresh wine like saffron, or embers aglow.
She said: Like 'tis wine, and it is not my way
  To mix men and wine – God will not have it so!
Said I: Drink, e'en though it may not be lawful,
  For in your throat, Rīm,* will your sin go with mine.
I pressed her; she said, with a weep pitiful;
  "I'll die of it, then!", and her tears burst aflow.
I treated her kindly, but said secretly:
  "A virgin compelled! May she fret grievously."

I wish you had been there to see your old Shaikh wearing pyjamas on which were pictures of birds and beasts, lying on a feather bed. I won't deny that the two of them were drunk – and so was I. So we indulged ourselves in loving cups of various sorts and kinds . . . such as the mind cannot think of nor the imagination picture!' I said: 'Come now, Shaikh . . . the beauty of desire is for it to remain thirsty, and not be fully quenched.' He said: 'I don't believe in Mutanabbi's blather when he says:

Despite my love for what her wine may hold,
I must not touch that which her drawers enfold.

He lies in this . . . for, my son, it is not in our power to separate the flesh from the spirit, nor love from sex . . . They are both intertwined, interconnected. One leads to the other, unless there is some physical deficiency . . . from which God preserve us! Platonic love is possible

* An Arabic girl's name

between a man and an ugly woman. As for between a man and a beautiful woman, some may think so. But if a man makes a show of it, he must, without doubt, be indulging in some sort of philosophical hypocrisy!'

I exclaimed to him: 'What are you saying? You are always trying to demolish my vaunted theories and cherished principles . . .'

He burst out laughing and said: 'You take your philosophy, and I will keep mine! . . . Haven't you heard the traditional saying of Chosroes?* "I have learned courtesy from the discourteous." You can learn piety and chastity from my profligacy and permissiveness . . . It is not hearing dirty stories and observing rakes that inevitably leads to moral decline. On the contrary, it sometimes leads noble spirits to the greatest levels of virtue. You were created with your conscience. And have I, at any time during our association, told you to copy me in anything?' 'No!' I said. 'I do admit that this is to your credit . . . I do admit that you have shown me a tremendous truth. For I recollect that I have loved virtue since I first read your poetry and that of Ibn al-Ḥajjāj† . . .' He patted my shoulders and said: 'But of course . . . because we depicted vice in its vilest colours, so it repelled you . . . And all you have to do now is to inform your contemporaries of these stories of mine, to make them more attached to virtue.'

* Name borne by kings of Persia at the time of the Arab conquest (early seventh century).

† Died A.D. 1000.

EXTRACT XI

Pot-Smoking, by Muḥammad al-ʿArūsī al-Maṭwī

(a chapter from 'The Bitter Mulberry' – *al-Tūt al murr*, Tunis, 1967, pp. 21 ff.)

Mabrūka took a cup of tea and carried it to her father. The Shaikh had finished the afternoon prayer, but was still sitting cross-legged on the ground with his legs tucked under him, reading the usual passage of the Koran which it was his habit to read after each prayer. Before reaching him, Mabruka caught sight of her sister ʿA'isha, coming into the garden, so she breathed a sigh of relief . . . This time her father would not worry her when he asked whether ʿA'isha had returned.

When she was two yards from him she saw his little finger and his ring-finger locked together, and realized that he had not yet finished reading. So she hastily put the cup down by his right knee, and went away to his rear. The Shaikh merely gave her a disapproving glance, and continued his reading without making any other sign to her.

She rushed to the cottage, and found her sister sitting waiting for her, laughing hopefully. She looked the very reverse of her own scowling and dispirited look. ʿA'isha was surprised when she shouted at her:

– Why are you late?

– Fāṭima insisted that I stay.

– Your father's angry.

– What have I done wrong? This isn't the first time I've gone to see Fatima.

– You shan't go again!

– Have I committed a crime?

– How should I know?

– Very well, then. Let me off this time. But . . .

– Shut up!

– I will mention the matter to father. If he insists on that, it's up to him . . .

– . . .

– Fatima's mother gave me a chicken wing. The meal consisted of macaroni with gravy and chicken. What a lovely meal it was!

– So that's why you are smiling?

– Good heavens, no, sister!

– Then why?

– At an amusing story I heard from Fatima . . . As you seem annoyed, I'll tell it later . . . I will tell it when Papa is relaxing after work and having dinner . . . Must he always be the one to divert us at night? I will divert you this time.

Mabruka was furious at ʿA'isha's attitude, which she thought was mocking her. She wondered what story ʿA'isha would tell that evening? Anxiety and perplexity beset her. Her inquisitiveness drove her to ask ʿA'isha for the story, in the hopes that it would be amusing. Or it might be unseemly, and might increase the Shaikh's suspicions and doubts. So her inquisitiveness got the better of her, and she began to make a fuss of ʿA'isha, and show friendliness to her, so that she would tell her what she had heard from Fatima. She said:

– Father will be preoccupied with the guest this evening. And it simply isn't done to speak in front of a stranger.

ʿA'isha could not fathom her sister's insistence, so she said naïvely:

– Mabruka, what is *takrūrī*?

Mabruka was thunderstruck by ʿA'isha's question.

Takruri! What did ʿA'isha know about takruri? . . . Where had she learned about it? . . . Was this the subject of the story? Then she must hear it. She restrained her anger, pulled herself together, and put her arms round her sister's shoulders, saying:

– Takruri is a sort of hashish which some people smoke – like *naffa** and cigarettes . . . Do you know some story about takruri?

– Yes, I do.

– Then . . . let's hear it!

– Fatima told me that her brother Abdalla smoked takruri with some of his friends. When he got back home, he felt famished. So he went to the kitchen in the dark, and found a saucepan containing meat. The surprising thing is that that meat was raw, yet he gobbled it up without realizing this. Next morning, when his mother went for the saucepan and found it empty, she was wild, thinking some cat or dog had got into the kitchen and eaten the meat. She came out of the

* Hashish which is sniffed.

kitchen wailing and shouting, accusing Fatima of leaving the kitchen door open the previous night. The shouting and uproar between Fatima and her mother became loud. And Abdalla was with them in this uproar . . . with them in his disturbed dreams. He said in his sleep: 'Mother! Mother! Why was the meat raw? Oh! Oh! What a job it was eating it . . . My teeth nearly came out!' His distracted mother shouted:

– Abdalla! Abdalla! Was it you ate the meat? Oh my poor boy! It was raw! What has it done to you?

The mother waited for Abdalla's reply, but he kept silent, saying nothing.

He was asleep, snoring. So she went up to him and shook him, waking him up roughly and violently. After some little effort, Abdalla woke up in trepidation, and pulled the cover over his face, which was yellow and puffy. His eyes were conscious of the light, but would not open.

His sister told me that he was for all the world like a drunkard who had missed his sleep, and was still tipsy. But his poor mother was distraught at his condition, thinking he was ill, raving in a violent fever. She ran to her neighbour's house, hoping she had an aspirin or quinine tablet to relieve his suffering.

Abdalla gradually began to come to, and the sunlight dazzled him. So he realized that he was late for work, and was worried, trembling all over. What excuse could he give his mother? What reply should he make, if she insisted on learning how he had come to eat the raw meat? With a nervous movement, he flung the sheet from him, and got up. He rubbed his eyes and stretched himself, and heard a cracking sound from his back. Then he said to Fatima:

– Why didn't you wake me up, sister?

– I woke you early in the morning, but you pretended you were ill, and I commiserated with you.

– Where is she now?

– She's gone for an aspirin.

– And Papa? What did he say?

– He doesn't know yet.

– Listen . . . give me the soap quickly.

– The soap and towel are in the bathroom.

– If your mother comes before I've gone, tell her I've recovered, and don't need any aspirin. I don't have a head-ache any more . . . Do you hear, Fatima? You're always a good friend!

– But how can you go to work now? Will he accept your excuse?

– I'll try . . . he's a nice chap. You shall have the sweets and the doll tomorrow.

– And the comb?

– The comb as well . . . my darling Fatima! It's agreed then?

– On condition you tell me the story of the meat.

– What meat? You dissatisfied creature!

– The meat you ate from the saucepan . . . when it was raw.

– Damn them all! . . . all rogues . . . Khamīs, Ṣāliḥ and Mukhtār! All of them are rotters who tempted me to smoke takruri!

Fatima's eyes nearly popped out of her head, and she shrieked:

– Takruri!!! Whatever made you? Oh, if only your mother knew! You will die a terrible death! Have you forgotten that my uncle died from takruri . . . died of consumption?

He realized he had made a serious slip in being so frank. So he tried to confuse his sister. Then he decided to be forthright, at the same time threatening her; so he said to her:

– You are wrong, Fatima! But remember, I've warned you! You know how strong I am . . . I swear by God that if mother learns the truth, I'll break every bone in your body!

Fatima was scared stiff, and shuddered, when she heard her brother threatening her. She knew his physical strength and his cruelty when he was angry with her. So she promised to keep quiet and hide the truth.

No sooner had Abdalla closed the door behind him than his mother came hurrying back, holding an aspirin between her forefinger and thumb, muttering inaudibly. When Fatima told her that Abdalla had gone to work, she was relieved and pleased for him . . .

ʿAʾisha kept silent a moment, then continued:

– Fatima told me all this when I was with her today. She knows several anecdotes and stories about takruri. It makes those who take it float in a wide world of fantasy, and in wonderfully attractive visions. Fatima said: It takes one out of reality, and makes one soar in glorious and unusual skies. Fatima stresses this. Who knows? She may be right in what she says, for her uncle used to take it.

When ʿAʾisha had finished speaking, Mabruka said to her:

– Listen, sister, don't tell this tale to your father. He will be extremely angry, and will forbid you to go to Fatima's house any more. Fatima is constantly coming to this garden, so confine yourself to playing with her here.

– But I don't understand why?

– Didn't you say that Abdalla smoked takruri? What will that boy do next? What a waste of his tender youth! I used to be very fond of him . . . but now I'm not!

– And what have I done wrong?

– That family has gone to the bad!

– Are they not respectable, like us?

– Yes . . . But that boy Abdalla!

– Is there anything wrong with him?

– Do you doubt that? A young man like him sliding down into this abyss? I don't want to hear about this again.

Mabruka went off in a flaming rage, to the small hut which the family used as a kitchen. 'A'isha remained, confused and perplexed at her sister's anger. Her little mind could only put it all down to her sister's jealousy of her: so she regretted having told her about eating chicken's wing with macaroni and gravy. She knew that *their* food today would be merely carrots and onions boiled in water, with a few grains of ground barley.

'. . . I was wrong: I had no right to tell her what I had eaten at Fatima's house . . . Greediness . . . Meanness . . . Why didn't I save her part of that wing? It would have pleased her . . . How nice it would have been! I forgot my sister when I was sitting in the circle round the trencher of macaroni with Fatima and her mother . . . It was macaroni flavoured with spices and seasoning . . . I drooled at the very sight of the odiferous vapour rising from the trencher, and gradually disappearing into the atmosphere of the room . . .'

She began to speculate about takruri, and what had been said about it, and this environment which leads to it.

'. . . They say of it that it makes people forget reality . . . reality . . . my reality! . . . Can I ever forget it? . . . Can I live in any other reality? . . . walk as other people walk*. . . stand tall and erect like Fatima? . . . loved . . . like the other girls of the village? . . .

She wished this could be so, if only in the world of fantasy and

* 'A'isha is a cripple.

imagination. If she was able to take takruri, would she live, just for a little moment, in this world of fantasy?

The idea of trying it out took hold of her. Why shouldn't she try takruri? . . . But her whole body shuddered . . . She remembered what her sister Mabruka had said. She respected her, and valued the affection and sacrifice she gave so generously on her behalf. So she rejected these temptations, lest this mood should take hold of her.

She thought it best to go to the kitchen, to help her mother to prepare food for the guest. At least she would cut the vegetables and stoke the fire, as was her lot.

EXTRACT XII

A Stranger, by ʿAbd al-Majīd Ben Jallūn

(the short story, *Gharīb*, from 'The Vale of Blood' – *Wādī al-dimāʾ*, Cairo 1947, pp. 27 ff.)

One intensely dark winter's night, a stranger knocked at the door, having been buffeted the whole night by a violent storm. When the door was opened, the man collapsed on the ground, and they carried him into the house.

The people living in the house looked at each other. This was a strange man, the like of whom they had not seen before in these settlements. But their perplexity did not last long. They hastened to warm the stranger, feed him, and change his muddy, soaking clothes for others, ample and pure-white. A book dropped from the stranger's clothes, without any one noticing.

The humble room was warm and calm, like a haven of rest, a refuge from the howling wind which could be heard outside, violent and continual . . . as if it were the shouts of heaven, as it looked down from on high on the impending future. The wind was shouting: 'Read that book! Read that book!' But nobody heard.

The stranger went out into the settlements. The sun was up, and the sky was clear. The earth breathed, the herbage could be smelled, and beauty was burgeoning all around. The man said to himself: 'This is the land we Frenchmen have promised ourselves.' His eyes shone, as he looked with delight at the vegetation, herbage and cultivation.

The landowner was a kind man, so he said to him: 'I am out of work.' And he was clever at simulating humility and misery.

Henceforward, then, the stranger would live on this farm, his Arabic improving day by day, taking in all around him, examining, learning, mastering all he saw. In time he was to attract attention by his energy and intelligence. He ingratiated himself with the landowner by his zeal for work. He would advise him, and explain to him various modern agricultural methods. In the end, the landowner became very fond of him, and began to treat him as a friend and relation.

So he took his place among the sons of Uncle ʿAbd al-Salām in his household and in his heart. And the latter was an old man, who had spent his life on this farm, feeding the people on it: for they lived under a sort of socialism which was common among Moroccan tribes. He had two sons and a daughter: Muhammad was twenty, Ahmad ten, and Fatima fourteen. Uncle Abd al-Salam was having a good look at his men, 'feeling their pulses', to choose a strong and reliable man from among them to succeed him when he died.

The stranger, whose name was André, realized this, so he used all his skill and intelligence to gain the ascendancy over the hearts of this man and his children, and the farm workers. He prayed with them in the mosque, and dressed and ate like them. So he was able to obliterate the signs of his former life, and became a different person.

He was like them in everything. But he was cleverer and more perspicacious than they. So he stood out among them, and the people praised his intelligence. In course of time, Uncle Abd al-Salam's life began to ebb away little by little. The inevitable day came, and all the farm people wept, following the funeral-procession of the man who had lived for them with heart, mind and body; the man who had brought them a life of sunshine and laughter; under whose kind protection had lived orphans, waifs and strays. They followed his bier, weeping for him as their grandfather, father, brother or friend, as if they felt that they were following the bier of the past.

The people of the farm were filled with anxiety when news reached them from the towns of the war and the occupation. But they were less upset than they might have been at this news because of their belief in their new chief.

André – let us not mention his assumed name, since we know his real one – succeeded Uncle Abd al-Salam in the farm and the house, and the people did not notice any change. They thanked God for having sent them this stranger to preserve their living standards.

At the same time, they noticed a minor and absolutely unimportant matter: which was that he used to be absent from the farm from time to time, only for a few days at a time – never more than four. They would ask themselves about the reason for his absence, and where he had gone. And why not, as their former chief had never once left the farm?

At first they just wondered. But then they began to notice a series of things which were new to them. The people's shares began to change. He would favour some, without actually wronging the rest. Then he began to wear strange shoes. Again, his indoor clothes changed, and he sometimes missed going to the mosque.

The cultivators realized what was at the bottom of it, when a group of Frenchmen visited their fields, and they grumbled audibly. That evening, André talked with Muhammad, Fatima and Ahmad, and told them that from these men he was learning how to improve the state of the farm.

When this had sunk in with the people, one of them came up to him one morning, when he was outside the house, and said to him: 'The farm people do not want to see the likes of these men on the farm again. These are the ones who have brought destruction to the cities, and they must not be allowed to get at the farms as well.'

The blood rushed to André's head, and he determined to nip ideas like this in the bud, before they got out of hand. Had he not boasted to his masters in Rabat that he could prevent such ideas from gaining ground on his farm? So he shouted at the man:

'Go back and tell the men that this is the wish of their chief, Uncle Abd al-Salam's successor and heir.'

'But Uncle Abd al-Salam would have had no dealings with such scum!'

At this point, André lost his temper, and his hot French blood rushed to his head. He attacked the man, seized him by the chest, shaking him, saying: 'Don't you ever talk like that again, or I'll break your head in, you filthy fellow! Do you understand?' Then he let him go.

The news spread everywhere, and people reproached him during working hours as one friend to another. For they could not conceive of chiefdom without friendship. The children of Uncle Abd al-Salam chided him at home, too, and André began to feel that this chiding was alienating him everywhere. He became tired of the act he had been putting on for over five years. So he resolved to exercise his authority in fact, seeing that he must inevitably lose their esteem.

There was a detachment of fully-armed mounted soldiers approaching the farm, with André at their head. When they reached it, the cultivators gathered round them, their eyes nearly popping out of their heads. André dismounted and walked among them, saying: 'Get back to your work! From now onwards, I'll teach you how to do your work, and to obey me as you obeyed Uncle Abd al-Salam. What has happened, fellows, is that you have gone to the bad, so you need to be treated differently. Now off you go to your work!'

It was not long before an imposing building stood on the farm – the office of the dictator André – the trickster André, who, with the aid of his superiors, had become the possessor of this wide territory: it belonged to him, with everything and everybody on it.

Each family had a small herd of cattle and sheep, and André determined that these, too, should be his property alone.

The beauty of life was gone from the farm – that life which had been full of kindness, mercy and love. That beautiful fertile land also was no more, that land which used to feed their bodies and souls at one and the same time. And those cattle and sheep, too, were lost, which had been members of the households. Alas! The days revealed the terrible truth that they had become slaves . . .

Now Muhammad had a beautiful cow he wanted to keep, but André would not let him; and when he defied him, he had him arrested. He did the same to his brother, when he tried to retain some attractive personal possession. And if this was how the sons of Uncle Abd al-Salam were treated, you can imagine what happened to the others!

André had left his poor village in the south of France, poor and destitute. He had left it to secure a worthwhile life for himself. And now he had secured a life of wealth, position and authority. But this was not everything. He had satisfied all his natural urges but one: and when Fatima, daughter of Uncle Abd al-Salam, hurried to the 'palace' to beg for her two brothers' release, there was aroused in him that most hungry and covetous of urges.

The innocent girl fell at his feet, entreating him to forgive her brothers, apologizing to him for their rashness. For she had always defended André to them, considering his defence the defence of her father, who had trusted him. She felt him embracing her, 'making a pass at her', exciting her desire, though his speech was confused. Then he lost control, and pressed her to him with mad strength. She pulled herself free, and stood at a distance from him. Then, in a sudden nervous movement, he pulled out a pistol, and shot at the lamp, shattering it and scattering it in the air. He then threw the pistol on the desk, and rushed at her.

'Get this straight! I will just as surely kill you and your brothers, if you go on behaving like this, you bitch!'

Her eyes flashed: 'Send for them to come here, for I have no alternative but to be a bitch while my two brothers are imprisoned.'

He looked at her for a moment, as if trying to read her thoughts. Then he scoffingly shrugged his shoulders, and made for the door, leaving the girl behind him, foaming with wrath and rage.

Her brothers came in, followed by André, who said: 'Take your brothers, and teach them how to obey the law!'

Boiling with anger, Fatima glanced carelessly around the room. Suddenly her flashing eyes fell on the pistol on the desk. As quick as lightning in mind and movement, she leapt at it, and aimed it straight at André's chest, saying:

'Stay where you are, villain! Close the door, Ahmad; and you, Muhammad, tie him up! . . . Vengeance for the cultivators and the shepherds! Do you remember how you first came to us, a mere nobody, shabbily clothed, covered in mud, trembling in the storm from weakness and exhaustion? Today, we see you in your true light, a dastardly devil! You hold power over this farm and others around it, near and far. But you can never have power over our hearts. And so long as you are powerless to take away the contempt I feel, you are still as you were when you arrived, weak and exhausted! You are now in my hands – I, the simple farm-girl. And you are trembling with terror and fear, despite your knowledge and your authority – because it is I who hold the weapon today. I have snatched it from you, you coward, to reveal you as a weak man cringing before a weak girl. Because the weak girl has a piece of steel in her hand. Stand back, or I'll mangle you!'

He thought better of the step forward he was going to take, saying between his teeth: 'Steady on, you wretch!'

One of the brothers, seized with fear, shouted: 'Don't kill him! Don't kill him!'

She turned to him, without turning the muzzle of the pistol from its aim at André's chest: 'What? Not kill him? He snatched from us our land and liberty, our cattle and contentment. He seized this land which our forefathers owned for thousands of years. And only a moment ago, he came at me, with the intention of raping me!'

These last words were inaudible, as they were accompanied by a pistol shot. It was followed by a cry from André, the stranger, writhing in his blood . . .

NOTES

NOTES

CHAPTER 1

[1] *Dārijī*, an extension of *darīj* (= current, common) is itself a colloquialism.
[2] Traditional assignment of some of this poetry to the fifth century is now considered highly unlikely.
[3] See A. J. Arberry, *The Seven Odes*, London, 1957, 145.
[4] For example, words like *ya'ālīl*, to describe a certain sort of cloud. Much of the rare vocabulary is concerned with natural phenomena.
[5] Maḥmūd Sāmī al-Bārūdī (Egyptian), 1838–1904.
[6] *Dīwān al-Bārūdī*, Cairo 1948, I, 48 ff.
[7] *Ibid.*, I, 135.
[8] Egyptian, 1881–1949. The translation of his poem *Baghdad* will be found on pp. 158 ff.
[9] *Op. cit.*, II, 161 ff.
[10] *Dīwān Ḥāfiẓ*, 2nd edn., Cairo 1952, II, 104 f.
[11] See Arberry, *Poems of al-Mutanabbi*, Cambridge, 1967.
[12] See below.
[13] Abu Firas's poems written in captivity are strangely sad and sentimental.
[14] *al-Shauqiyyāt* [the poet's collected verse], 2nd edn., Cairo, 1951, IV, 195 ff.
[15] S. Moreh, 'Blank Verse in Modern Arabic Literature', *Bulletin of the School of Oriental and African Studies*, London, Vol. XXIX (1966), Part 3, 483 ff., especially 485–92.
[16] *Ibid.*, 488.
[17] S. Moreh, 'Free Verse in Modern Arabic Literature', *Bulletin of the School of Oriental and African Studies*, London, Vol. XXXI (1968), pt. 1, 28 ff.
[18] See below.
[19] These are found in several collections, such as Ibn Qutaiba's *'Uyūn al-Akhbār* (ninth century).
[20] *al-Balāgha al-Wāḍiḥa* [written with Musṭafā Amīn], Cairo, 1946, 4th edn.
[21] For a brief explanation of some rhetorical devices, see A. J. Arberry, *Arabic Poetry*, Cambridge, 1965, 21 ff.
[22] See especially, Extracts III and IV, by Manfaluti.
[23] For English translations of these works, see *The Máqámat of Badi' al Zaman al Hamadhani*, tr. J. Prendergast, London 1915; and *The Assemblies of al Harírí*, tr. T. Chenery, 1867 (Vol. I), and P. Steingass (Vol. II), 1898 (Oriental Translation Fund, London).
[24] *The Epistle of Forgiveness*, ed. Kamil Kilany, tr. into English by G. Brackenbury, Cairo, 1947.
[25] For an abridged translation, see P. Brönle, *The Awakening of the Soul*, Wisdom of the East Series, London, 1904.
[26] French translation, Gustave Rouger, *Le roman d'Antar*, Paris, 1923.
[27] English translation, MacGuckin de Slane, 4 vv., London and Paris, 1843–71: reprinted photometrically 1967.
[28] French translation, C. Pellat, *Le livre des avares*, Paris, 1951.
[29] Ibn al-Muqaffa' was put to death by the Caliph al-Mansur in 774. *Kalīla wa Dimna* has been much translated.
[30] For a summarized account of the *Thousand and One Nights*, see the present author's article on the subject in the Encyclopaedia Britannica.
[31] Taha Husain was born in 1891.
[32] Arabic text, 25. *Al-Ayyām* was translated into English by E. H. Paxton as *An Egyptian Childhood*, London 1932 – Part I; also Part II by Hilary Wayment as *The Stream of Days*, London, 1948.

33 *'Adhrā' al-Hind* (the Maiden of India) (1898) and *Dil wa Tīmān* were set in Egypt of the Pharoahs. *Waraqa al-Ās* had rather less rhyme than the other two.
34 M. Kurd 'Alī, *Rasā'il al-Bulaghā'*, 4th edn., Cairo, 1954, 222 ff.
35 *Ibid.*, 211 ff.
36 See extracts III and IV in the present book.
37 English translation by G. R. Potter, *The Autobiography of Ousama*, Broadway Medieval Literatures, London, 1929.
38 Translated in part in the Broadway Travellers Series, by H. A. R. Gibb, *Ibn Batuta, Travels in Asia and Africa.* The same author commenced translating the full work: two volumes have so far appeared.
39 *'Abqariyya al-Imām*, Cairo, 1947; *'Abqariyya 'Umar*, 1948.
40 *Ḥāyāt ibn al-Rūmī*, Cairo, 1931.
41 *Ma' al-Mutanabbī*, Cairo, 1937; *Tajdīd Dhikr Abī al-'Alā' fī Sijnihi*, 1939.
42 Cairo, 1944. Published by the American Council of Learned Societies in Charles Wendell's English translation, Washington 1953, as *Osman Amin, Muhammad 'Abduh.*
43 First published Cairo, 1937, frequently reprinted.
44 The Arabic for 'history', *ta'rīkh*, also means 'date', 'chronology', and 'chronicle'.
45 See F. Rosenthal's translation, *The Muqaddimah, an Introduction to History*, 3 vv., London, 1958.
46 *History of the Arabs*, 5th edn., London, 1953.
47 All published Cairo. *Fajr al-Islām* (The Dawn of Islam), 1927; *Ḍuḥā al-Islām* (The Forenoon of Islam), 3 vv., 1933–36; *Ẓuhr al-Islām* (The Noontide of Islam), 2 vv., 1945.
48 The introductory section was translated by Gaudefrey Demombynes, in *Le livre de la poésie et des poètes*, Paris, 1947.
49 Published Cairo, 4 vv., 1929–30.
50 Many editions have appeared, the latest being that of *Karam al-Bustānī*, Beirut, 15 vv., 1950.
51 See Rückert's fine German translation, *Hamasa, oder die älteste arabischen Volkslieder*, Stuttgart, 1846.
52 Cairo, 1949.
53 Carlo Alfonso Nallina was a highly respected orientalist. Among his works is *La littérature arabe*, Paris, 1950.
54 1858–1940. He held the Laudian Chair of Arabic at the University of Oxford.
55 In an essay in *al-Naẓarāt* entitled *al-Zaujatān* (The Two Wives). He was referring specifically to Egyptians.

CHAPTER 2

1 'Umar al-Dasūqī, *Fī al-adab al-ḥadīth*, 2nd edn., Cairo, 1950, Ch. I, Sect. 1.
2 See M. K. al-Muradi, *Silk al-Durar fi a'yān al-qarn al-thānī 'ashar*, Bulaq n.d., Vol. II, 310 ff. This work is a biographical dictionary of men of the twelfth century A.H. (= A.D. 1688–1785).
3 *Merveilles biographiques et historiques ou chroniques du Cheikh Abd-el-Rahman al-Djabarti, traduites de l'arabe par Chefik Masour Bey, Abdulaziz Kalil Bey, Gabriel Nicolas Kalil Bey et Iskander Mamoun Effendi*, 9 vv., Cairo, 1888.
4 *al-Adab al-'arabiyya fī al-qarn al tāsi' 'ashara*, Beirut, 1923, 2nd edn., p. 6.
5 See Jabarti, *op. cit.*, II, 124 ff.
6 Finished in 1767; used by William Lane as the basis for his Arabic Lexicon (8 vv., London, 1863–93).
7 See Salahiddine Boustany, 'The Press during the French expedition in

Egypt, 1798–1801', Cairo, 1954 (abstract from *Cahiers d'histoire égyptienne*, Series VI, No. 1, March 1954).

8 Boustany, *op. cit.*, 14, and picture opposite p. 16.

9 *Ibid.*, 30.

10 *Op. cit.*, VI, 5.

11 Koran, XI, 119.

12 Conquest of Crete, 1822–4. His son Ibrahim defeated the revolting Greeks, and subjugated Morea for the Sultan, 1825–6. In 1832 Ibrahim conquered Syria from the Sultan, whose forces, however, defeated him in 1839. In the latter year a Turkish fleet, sent to Alexandria, voluntarily surrendered to Muhammad Ali. For a time Egypt had also control of the Hedjaz. It is difficult to assess how history might have been changed had the Great Powers not intervened. Muhammad Ali lost all his conquests, but was somewhat compensated by the Sultan's recognizing him as *hereditary* ruler of Egypt in 1841.

13 For an account of this writer's achievements, see Albert Hourani, *Arab Thought in the Liberal Age (1789–1939)*, Oxford, 1962, repr. 1967, pp. 69 ff. Hourani's book provides an excellent background for the study of modern Arabic literature, and should be read by all pursuing such a study.

14 1758–1838. See Henri Dehérain, *Silvestre de Sacy – ses contemporains et ses disciples*, Paris, 1938.

15 See Adīb Maruwwa, *al-Ṣaḥāfa al-ʿArabiyya* (The Arabic Press), Beirut, 1961, 145 f., 149 f., 159 f.

16 Muhammad Ali's son Husain had conquered the Northern and Western parts of the Sudan, 1820–2, and founded Khartoum in 1823.

17 *Op. cit.*, 72 ff.

18 As Extract I.

18a Sir Hamilton Gibb, 'Studies in Contemporary Arabic Literature', *Bulletin of the School of Oriental and African Studies*, IV, 745–760; reproduced in Shaw and Polk, *Studies in the Civilization of Islam by Hamilton A. R. Gibb.*

19 He was illiterate until his 40's. See Hourani, 52.

20 The title S͟haik͟h has many varied uses in the Arab world. It means an old man, but is also a courtesy title for teachers and tribal leaders. It was given to professors at the Azhar.

21 The translation is free.

22 The title *Sayyid* is a courtesy title given to prophets, saints, descendants of Muhammad, and men of religion.

23 See previous references to this historian.

24 The Arabic edition dates from 1873–9, printed at Bulaq in 4 vv.

25 *An introduction to the history of education in modern Egypt*, London, 1938, 75 f.

26 *Op. cit.*, 57.

26a For further information about Lebanese history see: W. R. Polk, *The Opening of South Lebanon, 1788–1840*, Harvard, 1963; Fuʿad Afram al-Bustani, *Taʾrīkh Lubnān al-Mūjiz*, Beirut, 1957, pp. 89–147; John B. Christopher, *Lebanon Yesterday and Today*, New York, 1966.

27 C. Huart, *A History of Arabic Literature*, London, 1903, 389; J. M. Abd-el-Jalil, *Brève histoire de la littérature arabe*, Paris, 1946, 224; Francesco Gabrieli, *Storia della letteratura araba*, 2nd edn., Rome, 1956, 272.

28 Huart, *op. cit.*, 390.

29 *Op. cit.*, 272.

30 See Dagher (Yūsuf Asʿad Dāg͟hir), *Masādir al-Dirāsāt al-adabiyya*, Vol. II, Beirut, 1955, 173 ff. Also Cheikho, *op. cit.*, 25 ff.

31 p. 29, *supra*.

32 Catholic Press, Beirut, ed. F. A. Bustani.

33 'Chroniques d'Égypte, 1798–1804', tr. G. Wiet. Cairo, 1950.
34 *Op. cit.*, 58 ff.
35 *Op. cit.*, 635.
36 *E.g.* maternal uncle, good token, army colours, owner, black camel-stallion, etc.
37 It must be borne in mind that the Arabic for hunting, *ṣaid*, does not mean only blood sports, but includes fishing, shooting, and trapping various animals. Otherwise the virtues attributed to it might seem even more far-fetched.
38 Thos. Chenery, *The assemblies of al-Harîrî*, London, 1867, 257. Chenery's translation, as befitted a Victorian readership, is less anatomically exact and without the alliteration which is the main point of the *hikma* (aphorism).
39 The famous Lebanese literary and scientific journal, Vol. II (1899), 1113 ff.
40 Cheikho, *op. cit.*, Vol. II, 54 ff.
41 Poem in stanzas of 5 lines. It is in Cheikho, *op. cit.*, 55. The poet makes the flowers male, but I make them female, as in European tradition.
42 *Op. cit.*, II, 27.
43 *Ibid.*
44 Dagher, 753: 'Īsā Sābā; p. 5 of the Introduction to the 1958 Beirut edition of Yaziji's *Majma' al-Bahrain.*
45 Durham. The first of many Beirut editions appeared in 1854.
46 1074–1143.
47 Gabrieli, *op. cit.*, 312; Abd-el-Jalil, 229.
48 Completed by his son Ibrahim.
49 In *al-Zajal*, Ḥuraiṣa, Lebanon, 1842, 91 ff.
49a Yaziji, *Nafḥa al-Raiḥan*, Beirut, 1964, 2.
49b Yaziji, *T͟hālit͟h al-qamrain*, Beirut, 1883, 32 ff.
49c *Ibid.*, 45.
50 Cheikho, II, 30.
51 *Ibid.*, 31. It should be noted that the name *Ḥabīb* means 'beloved'.
52 First printed Beirut, 1856, repeatedly reprinted. The most recent edition is that of 1958, by the publishing house Dar Sader Dar Beirut, in Beirut.
53 1958 edn., 9–10.
54 These lines are a paraphrase only of the text.
55 A reference to an old Arabic proverb, *li-kulli jadīdin ṭulwa.*
56 1958 edn., 59.
57 *Op. cit.*, 312.
58 *Op. cit.*, 272.
59 *Op. cit.*, 220.
60 For biographical details, see Muḥammad Aḥmad K͟halafullah, *Aḥmad Fāris al-S͟hidyāq*, Cairo 1955. See also, Dagher, 471 ff.; Cheikho, II, 86.
61 *Op. cit.*, 98.
62 Cheikho, II, 86.
63 *Ibid.*, II, 87.
64 See J. A. Haywood, *Arabic Lexicography*, Leiden, 1960. 2nd edn., 1965, 90 f.
65 Istanboul, 1882.
66 Istanboul, 1882, 1st part only. The 2nd part, as yet unpublished, is said to contain most of his philological ideas.
67 Malta, 1834. Reprinted in Istanboul together with the work in note 68 below.
68 Tunis, 1866: Istanboul, together with the above, 1881.
69 Paris, 1885. Cairo, 1919 and 1920.
70 *Op. cit.*, 98.
71 Text used is Khalafullah, *op. cit.*, 36.
71a Quoted by Wiet, 273.
72 Istanboul edn., 273.

[73] *Ibid.*, 128.

[74] Khalafullah, 34–5.

[75] *Op. cit.*, 415.

[76] 231 ff. and 464 ff., Paris edn.

[77] Text used is that in R. Khūrī, *'Aṣr al-Iḥyā' wa al-Nahḍa*, Beirut, 1957, 317 ff.

[78] The Arabic for heifer is a weak pun on the Koranic word for the clot, or sperm, from which God has created man. The similarity would demand the pronunciation of the Arabic 'j' as a hard 'g', as in Egyptian and some Levantine Arabic.

[78a] There is jinas here between kharīf (= autumn) and the verb *takharraftu* (= I have gone out of my mind), the root letters being *kh – r – f* in both words.

[79] The point of successions of near-synonyms is lost in translation, as they are mostly rare Arabic words which the wife is unlikely to understand. The precise meanings are sometimes hard to give, and elude even Arab commentators. There is not consistent jinas or saj' in the Arabic. Shidyaq is really laughing at himself, presenting himself as a pedantic windbag!

[80] The point of the Arabic is that the words tāghī and ṭāghī differ only in the different 't's' of their initials. The former really means 'constantly laughing', but is here translated as 'tittering' to give a tenuous resemblance with the second, which means tyrannical, among other things.

[81] The Arabic word is *jāriyya*, because of its similarity to *jāra*, the female neighbour. The jariyya of classical times was a sort of slave girl, a kind of Geisha girl. She could be bought and sold, and helped to entertain men of means such as caliphs. She could usually sing well, and had at least a veneer of education and culture.

[82] *jār*, neighbour, fem. *jāra*.

[83] The best account of Naqqash's plays is to be found in a London Ph.D. thesis on *Modern Arabic Drama* submitted by the late Ahmed al Tayeb, a brilliant Sudanese scholar and former Principal of the Institute of Education, Bakhter Ruda on the White Nile. See also J. Landau, *Studies in the Arab Theater and Cinema*, Philadelphia, 1958.

[84] Naqqash's plays were first published in *Arza Lubnān*, Beirut, 1869, 496 ff. In 1961 a series of volumes was initiated containing the works of early Arabic dramatists. Vol. I is devoted to Naqqash, ed. Dr. Muḥammad Yūsuf Najm.

[85] The author is indebted for these phrases to Hourani, 99 f. See also Cheikho, II, 126.

[86] = *the bugle(call) of Syria*. See Adib Maruwwa, *op. cit.*, 153.

[87] 11 vv., 1876–1900.

[88] A new Lebanese–Arabic encyclopaedia is at present being produced. Ed. F. A. al-Bustani, 1956 onwards.

[89] Cheikho, II, 48 ff.; Dagher, 315 ff.

[90] *English-Arabic Lexicon*, 1881.

[91] See Adib Maruwwa, 161; 230, 232.

[92] See Chapter I of the present work for mention of some of these classical authors.

[93] Based on the text in R. Khuri, *op. cit.*, 62–3.

[94] Dagher, 693; Cheikho, II, 45 ff.

[95] Aleppo, 1865, Beirut, 1881.

[96] Beirut, 1870.

[97] Cheikho, II, 47.

[98] The following short account of Iraqi authors owes much to Dr. Yūsuf 'Izz al-Dīn's *al-Shi'r al-'Irāqī, ahdāfuhu wa khaṣā'isuhu fī al-qarn al-tāsi'i*

'as̲h̲ara, Baghdad, 1965; and 'Abbās al-'Azzāwī's (Arabic) *History of Arabic Literature in Iraq*, Vol. II, Baghdad, 1962. There is an English as well as an Arabic title-page.
[99] The term *ma'had* designates educational institutions specifically aimed at giving an education in Islamic religious knowledge and the Arabic language. The level may go as high as quasi-university degree level, and in a large city may be like a comprehensive school with a post-secondary/university level added on top. The most famous of all ma'hads is the Azhar in Cairo, now recognized as a university. There – and in many other ma'hads – the curriculum is being widened to include science and other subjects which form part of a general education.
[100] 'Azzawi, *op. cit.*, index, p. 403. Unfortunately this author deals separately with the various literary genres. Consequently, one author may have to be mentioned several times. For this reason, the index ref. is given.
[101] *Ibid.*, 397.
[102] *Maqāmāt al-Hanafī wa ibn Nāqiya wa-g̲h̲airahum*. Abū al Maḥāmid's maqama is on pp. 286 ff.
[103] Cheikho, I, 90 f.; Dagher, 48 ff.
[104] *Op. cit.*, 225.
[105] *Op. cit.*, 319.
[106] Dagher, 610 ff.
[107] Cheikho, I, 100.
[108] *Ibid.*, 99.
[109] *Ibid.*, 101.
[110] Dagher, 88 ff.
[111] 'Izz al-Din, *op. cit.*, 34.
[112] Dagher, 557 ff.
[113] *Op. cit.*, 51.
[114] Cheikho, II, 109; Dagher, 318 ff.

CHAPTER 3

[1] Ibrahim Pasha survived his father by a few weeks only. Abbas' father was Ibrahim's brother, Ṭūsūn. Sa'id was another of Muhammad Ali's sons.
[2] Persian k̲h̲edīv = lord, master. Predecessors had merely been called *wālī* (Arabic governor), and the honorific title of Pasha.
[3] See Afaf Lutfi al-Sayyid, *Egypt and Cromer, a study in Anglo-Egyptian relations*, London, 1968, 6 ff. The whole book is an indispensable guide to the political background of the period 1882–1907.
[4] al-Sayyid, *op. cit.*, 169 ff.
[5] Two men were sentenced to penal servitude for life, six to 7 years' imprisonment, 3 to one year's and 30 lashes, five to 50 lashes. See al-Sayyid, 171f.
[6] *Sultan* was a common name for Muslim rulers and was the highest below that of Caliph (k̲h̲alīfa), which could only be held by the senior Islamic ruler who claimed some sort of hegemony over the whole Islamic world. The Ottoman Sultans did, in fact, consider themselves to have such hegemony in the nineteenth century: those who supported them belonged to the k̲h̲ilāfa (Caliphate) Movement, which became strong in many Muslim lands, even India, during the First World War.
[7] For some examples of his poetry, see Cheikho, II, 15 ff.
[8] *Ibid.*, 17.
[9] *al-dunyā* (fem. = the world) is a shortened form of *al-dār al-dunya* (= the lower world, as opposed to the next world, *al-dār al-uk̲h̲rā*). The word may be used meaning 'inferior'. Note the term *Dār al-K̲h̲ilāfa*, the house of the Caliphate, that is, Istanbul, in the first hemistich.

10 Cheikho, II, 98 f.

11 *Ibid.*, 17 f.

12 *Ibid.*, II, 95 f.

13 Dagher, *op. cit.*, 159 ff.

14 Muslim charitable bequests.

15 The best of many editions is that of Dār al-Kutub al-Miṣriyya, Cairo, 1940, ed. Dr. Muḥammad Haikal.

16 *Ibid.*, 43 ff.

17 Dagher, 238 ff.

18 *Ibid.*, 534 ff., Cheikho, *Ta'rīkh al-ādāb al-'arabiyya fī al-rub' al awwal min al qarn al-'ishrīn*, Beirut, 1926, 100. This will be referred to as Cheikho (20), as it is about Arabic literature in the first quarter of the twentieth century, to distinguish it from the other Cheikho work, about the nineteenth century, to which reference has been made so frequently.

19 *Op. cit.*, 100.

20 See also *Dīwān Ismā'īl Ṣabrī Bāshā*, Cairo, 1938, ed. Ḥasan Rif'at Bey, 144.

21 The translation is rather free.

22 Matran's name is also found vowelled Mitran and Mutran.

23 Dagher lists many of these books and articles: see pp. 287 ff. for Hafiz and 506 ff. for Shauqi. A good comparison of the two is Ḥasan Kāmil al-Ṣairāfī, *Ḥāfiẓ wa Shauqī*, Cairo, 1948.

24 See Chapter I, *supra*.

25 Published in Cairo after his death, ed. Dr. Ḥusain Haikal, and often reprinted. The present author has used the reprint of 1953.

26 The Mulid is a religious festival to celebrate the birthday of the Prophet Muhammad. In large cities, it is celebrated with great public show.

27 *Shauqiyyāt*, IV, 150.

28 *al-'Ilm wa al-ta'līm wa wājib al-mu'allim*, *ibid.*, I, 218 ff.

29 A short account with extracts will be found in Ra'īf Khūrī, *op. cit.*, 131 ff.

30 See pp. 121–124 of the present work.

31 The standard edition of the diwan was edited by Aḥmad Amīn and others in Cairo, 1937, in two volumes. It has been several times reprinted.

32 Diwan, II, 21 f. Needless to say, the pedestrian translation does scant justice to the original.

33 The original says only 'them', but the reference is to the British.

34 Diwan, II, 145–7.

35 The definitive edn. of Matran's diwan is in 4 vv., Cairo, 1948–9. A leading biographical study is Jamāl al-Dīn al-Ramādī, *Khalīl Maṭrān, shā'ir al-aqṭār al-'arabiyya*, Cairo, 1958. A short biography and critical appreciation will be found in the 'Golden Book' mentioned in note 37 below.

36 1911.

37 *al-Kitāb al-dhahabiyya fī mihrajān Khalīl Maṭrān*, Cairo, 1948.

38 London, 1950, reprinted 1967, 15 f. Both the Arabic text and an English translation are given. The quotation above is from Arberry's translation.

39 Diwan, 398 ff.

40 The rich rhymes of the original have been hard to imitate. For example, in the first stanza, the rhyme is the whole word *biṭāqa*. In the first instance it means 'within power/capability' (*i.e. bi-ṭāqa*); in the second, a 'bouquet'; in the third, a 'card'.

41 Golden Book, 109.

42 Dagher, 375 ff.

43 *Ibid.*, 764 ff.

44 *Dīwān Walī al-Dīn Yakan*, Cairo, 1924.

45 *Ibid.*, 55 ff.

46 Dagher, 247 ff.

47 The *Mujmal* of Ibn Fāris (tenth century).
48 The *Mufaṣṣal* of al-Zamakhsharī (1074–1143).
49 Published Cairo, 1939, 3 vv.
50 Diwan, II, 139 ff.
51 See Dr. Yousif Izzedien (Yūsuf 'Izz al-Dīn), *Poetry and Iraqi Society, 1900–1945*. This 60-page work is in English. The author is particularly indebted to Dr. Izzedien for kindnesses during a stay in Baghdad in 1967, when he introduced him to a number of literary figures, and discussed Iraqi poetry with him. Izzedien is himself a poet.
52 Dagher, 292 ff.
53 Published Beirut, 1913.
54 Dagher, 292.
55 See Ch. I of the present work.
56 Dagher, 429 ff.
57 Published Baghdad, 1928.
58 Diwan, Cairo, 1955 edn., I, 183.
59 *Ibid.*, 197.
60 *Ibid.*, 183.
61 *Op. cit.*, 28.
62 *Ibid.*, 27.
63 Dagher, 676 ff.
64 *Ibid.*, *388* ff., and S. A. Khulusi, 'Ma'rūf al-Ruṣāfī 1875–1945', in *Bulletin of the School of Oriental and African Studies*, London, Vol. XIII, pt. 3, 1950, pp. 616 ff.
65 It is described on the title-page as the 3rd edition, and has useful annotations and an introduction by 'Abd al-Qādir al-Maghrabī.
66 Diwan, 187 ff.
67 *Arā' Abī al-'Alā'*, Baghdad, 1955.
68 An Arab saying.
69 An allusion to the Koranic picture of Paradise.
70 Diwan, 220 f.
71 Dagher, 529 f.
72 *Ibid.*, 96 ff.
73 Published Cairo, 1939.
74 Dagher, 613 ff.
75 London, 1962; repr. 1967.
76 Arabic *isti'mār* = imperialism, colonization.
77 See Hourani, *op. cit.*, 103 ff., for a short account.
78 *Ibid.*, 130 ff.
79 *Ibid.*, 164 ff.
80 Dagher, 132, Hourani, 330 ff.
81 Hourani, 84 ff., Dagher, 226 ff.
82 See Hourani, 87 ff., Dagher, 227.
83 Dagher, 127 f.
84 *Ibid.*, 597 ff.
85 See Hourani, 112, who also refers to an impression 'not wholly pleasant'.
86 See, in English, Hourani, 103 ff.; in Arabic, 'Abd al-Qādir al-Maghrabī, *Jamāl al-Dīn al-Afghānī*, Cairo, 1948; in Persian, M. M. Chahārdihi, *Arā' wa mu'taqadāt-i-Sayyid Jamāl-ud-Dīn-i-Afghānī*, Teheran, 1958, and I. Afshar and A. Mahdawī, *Documents inédits concernant Seyyed Jamāl-al-Dīn Afghānī*, Teheran, 1963; in French, Homa Pakdaman, *Djamal-ed-Din Assad Abadi dit Afghani*, Paris, 1969. The present author regards the last named as the best account so far, and has leaned heavily on it for biographical details.
87 Osman Amin, *Muhammad 'Abduh*, translated from the Arabic by Charles

Wendell, Washington, 1953. See also Hourani, 130 ff.; P. Vatikiottis, 'Muhammad 'Abduh and the quest for a Muslim Humanism', in *Arabica*, IV, 1, Jan. 1957, 55 ff.

88 In the Introduction to the collected *Naẓarāt*.

89 See footnote 87, *supra*.

90 *Op. cit.*, 167 ff.

91 *Ibid.*, 170.

92 Undergraduates in Durham reading honours Arabic used to study, at one time or another, both these books. They found them intolerable owing to their language – *Tahrir al-Mar'a* even more than *al-Mar'a al-Jadida*.

93 Dagher, 637 ff.

94 The pseudonym of an Egyptian writer. See pp.205 f.

95 See Chapter I for classical antecedents. The main reference for the modern short story is Abdel-Aziz Abdel-Meguid, *The Modern Short Story, its emergence, development, and form*, Cairo?, 1950. The text is double, in English and Arabic, and a number of short stories are included in Arabic text only.

96 The text is in Abdel-Meguid, Arabic section, 5 ff. The title – literally 'A shot from no shooter' – might be translated as 'A Bolt from the Blue', or even 'Involuntary Generosity'.

97 *Ibid.*, 85 ff.

97a Printed in Cairo 1915. Ref. here is to the 4th edn. of 1922.

97b I, 116 ff.

97c I, 187 ff.

98 In his *al-Qiṣṣa fī Sūrīyā ḥattā al-Ḥarb al-'Alamiyya al-thāniyya* (The Novel in Syria to the Second World War), 54.

99 For a biography in English, see Mikhail Naimy, *Kahlil Gibran, His Life and Work*, Beirut, 1964. The original was in Arabic, published Beirut, 1936.

100 Dates of originals and translations: (a) 1908/1947; (b) 1906/1948.

101 *'Arā'is . . .* , 4th edn., Cairo, 1944, 23 ff.

102 *Op. cit.*, 94 f.

103 From *al-Arwāḥ al-mutamarrida*, 5th edn., Cairo, 1948, 36 ff.

104 Shakir Mustafa, *op. cit.*

105 *Ibid.*, 76.

106 Dagher, 693 ff.; Mustafa, 87 ff.

107 Mustafa, 96 ff.

108 *Ibid.*, 130 ff.

108a Dagher, 442 ff.

108b *Op. cit.*, 257.

108c As G. Zaidan, *al Abbassa ou la sœur du Calife*, ed. C. Farrière, tr. M. Y. Bitar and Ch. Moulié, Paris n.d. (?1920). This translation has run to at least three editions.

108d Dagher, 147 ff.

108e Alexandria, 1904. Antun lived in Alexandria during his first stay in Egypt, then in Cairo during his second stay until his death.

109 Available now in Gibb, *Studies in the Civilization of Islam*, ed. Shaw and Polk, London, 1962, 286 ff.

110 See Dagher, 731.

111 Gibb, 291; Khemiri and Kampffmeyer, *Leaders in Contemporary Arabic Literature*, Berlin, 1930, 20 ff.

112 Khemiri & K., *op. cit.*, 27 ff.; Dagher, 682 ff.; Gibb, 301 ff.

113 *Op. cit.*, p. 301.

113a So in *Concise Oxford Dictionary*, Oxford, 1951.

114 Anouar Abdel-Malek, *Anthologie de la littérature arabe contemporaine, II, les essais*, Paris, 1965.

115 Dagher, 540.
116 *Ibid.*, 404 ff.
117 Vols. I and II, Beirut, 1910–11; III and IV, 1923–4.
118 See Dagher, 830 ff.; Gibb, *op. cit.*, II, *Manfaluti and the 'New Style'*, 258 ff.; Zaki al-Dīn Muḥammad, *al-Manfaluti*, Cairo, 1942.
119 3 vv., Cairo, 1925–6. In the present work, reference is made to the 14th edn. [*sic.*!] of 1955. Note the popularity of the work reflected in numerous reprints.
120 I, 61.
121 I, 75.
122 (*al-Iḥsān fī al-Zawāj*), I, 192.
123 I, 68 f.
124 I, 47 ff.
125 I, 45, in the Essay 'The First Cup'.
126 *Op. cit.*, 264.

CHAPTER 4

1 *Anthologie bilingue de la littérature arabe*, Beirut, 1961, Intr. xii ff.
2 *Modern Arabic Poetry: an anthology with English verse translations*, London, 1950: repr. Cambridge, 1967.
3 Māhir Ḥasan Fahmī, *Taṭawwur al-shi'r al-'arabī al-ḥadīth fī miṣr*, Cairo, 1958, 177.
4 *Ibid.*, 178.
5 I. A. Edham, *Abushâdy the poet*, Leipzig, 1936: see also, Dagher, 55 ff.; Arberry, *op. cit.*, 19–21.
6 *Op. cit.*, 9.
7 *Ibid.*, 21.
8 Edham, *op. cit.*, 32 ff.
9 *Ibid.*, 31 f.
10 *Ibid.*, 26.
11 *Ibid.*, 28 f.
12 From the essay, 'Organised religion and human progress', in *At random*, written in English, published Alexandria, 1937.
13 *Thaura al-Islām*, ed. with intro. by T. A. Surūr and M. Khaffājī.
14 Arberry, 42.
15 Cairo, 1942.
16 Published in *al-Muqtaṭaf*, May, 1944, 426.
17 Fahmi, *op. cit.*, 207.
18 *Ibid.*, 208.
19 *al-shi'r al-'arabī fī al mahjar – Amrīkā al-Shimāliyya* (Arabic Emigrant Poetry–North America), Beirut, 1957.
20 From *al-Jadāwil*, ed. New York, 1927, 89 ff.
21 *Op. cit.*, 12.
22 I hardly think the Egyptian would claim a monopoly of pure Arabic style.
23 See 'Abbas and Najma, *op. cit.*, 177 ff.; Khemiri and Kampffmeyer, 30.
24 'Abbas and Najma, 189.
25 *Ibid.*, 186: the translation is free.
26 See Dagher, 603; 'Abbas and Najma, 193 ff. Selections of his poems have been published, with an introduction, in the *Manāhil al-'Arab* series, Beirut, 1950.
27 Selections (see note 26 above), 123.
28 Dagher, 196 ff.
29 *Mukhtārāt al-udabā'*, Ḥamad Publications, Beirut, n.d.
30 For a reference to the original (Greater) Akhtal, see Chapter I, p.7.
31 Diwan, 76 f.

32 *Ibid.*, 190 f.
33 See examples in the magazine *Shi'r*, XI, Summer 1959, 18 ff., X, Spring 1959, 40 ff.
34 *Ibid.*
35 Summer 1959.
36 *What are the young Lebanese Poets Doing?*, Lebanese Embassy Central Office of Information's Bulletin No. 53, 6. The author acknowledges with gratitude the help of the Lebanese Embassy in London in supplying this and other bulletins.
37 Shi'r, X, 24 ff.
38 Jabre, *op. cit.*, 5.
39 Of his poetry, the collection *Anti lī* (You are mine) was published Beirut, 1950: *Qaṣā'id* (Odes) in 1956.
40 *Qaṣā'id*, 103 ff.
41 *Shu'arā' al-gharī wa al-najafiyyāt*, ed. al-Khāqānī, Najaf.
42 *al-Shi'r wa al-shu'arā' fi al-'Irāq, 1900–1957*, by Aḥmad Abū Sa'd, Beirut, 1959.
43 See 'Inād Ghazwān's article on this poet in the magazine *al-Balāgh* (Baghdad), issue 4, 1966, 50 ff.
44 Ahmad Abu Sa'd, *op. cit.*, 176 ff.
45 *Ibid.*, 191 ff., and Monteil, 99 f. Monteil gives the text and French translation of five poems.
46 Abu Sa'd, 82.
47 *Op. cit.*
48 Abu Sa'd, 221 ff.
49 *Ibid.*, 239.
50 *Ibid.*, 243.
51 In *al-Shi'r wa al-shu'arā' fī al-Sudān, 1900–1958*, Beirut, 1958.
52 *al-Murshid ilā al-shi'r al-'arabī* (The Guide to Arabic Poetry).
53 Published in Khartoum.
54 *Aṣdā' al-Nīl*, 49. The present author worked at the Institute of Education at Bakhter Ruda, which is the subject of the poem under discussion.
55 Tutti Island lies at the junction of the Blue and White Niles at Khartoum. These poems can be found in Abu Saīd, 72 ff.
56 Published in Cairo, 1957.
57 'Afīfī, 252.
58 *Ibid.*, 227.
59 *Op. cit.*, 54.
60 *Ibid.*, 52 f.
61 Tunis, entitled *Farḥa al-sha'b* (the People's Joy).
62 *Ibid.*, 17.
63 The author is indebted to the Jordanian Embassy in London, which generously supplied copious material in Arabic, plus an article by Issa I. Nouri, *The contemporary Arabic literature in the Hashemite Kingdom of Jordan.*
64 Dagher, 744 ff.
65 *Ibid.*, 578 ff.
66 Nouri, *op. cit.*, 4.
67 *Ibid.*, 5.
68 Entitled *Shi'r al-muqāwama.*
69 *Ibid.*, 83.
70 The author gratefully acknowledges a copy of this index sent by the author. It is an offprint, but the journal from which it is taken is not stated. Moreh's article on the 'Arab Literary Revival in Israel', from *Ariel*, Spring 1962, 14 ff., is also acknowledged, with thanks.
71 See further examples on p.204 when discussing this author.

72 *Modern Arabic Short Stories.* Selected and translated by Denys Johnson-Davies, London, 1967.
73 Pierre Cachia, *Taha Husayn*, London, 1956; see also Hourani, 324 ff.; Khemiri and Kampffmeyer, 34 ff.; Monteil, 129, with an extract from *al-Ayyam* in French.
74 *Dhikrā Abī al-'Alā'*, Cairo 1915, repr. 1922.
75 Translated by 'Abdallah 'Inān, 'The social philosophy of Ibn Khaldun', 1925.
76 Part I, 1925: Part II, 1926.
77 1949.
78 1938.
79 *Fī al-shi'r al-jāhilī* and *Fī al-adab al-jāhilī.*
80 *Journal of the Royal Asiatic Society*, 1925, 440 ff.
81 Khemiri and Kampffmeyer, 35.
82 Jean Lecerf and G. Wiet, *Le livre des jours*, Paris, 1947, with a preface by André Gide. See also note 32, Ch. I, *supra.*
83 As *Amāma shubbāk al-tadhākir.* Reproduced in Rabin, *Arabic Reader*, London, 1947.
84 In the 'Use of the colloquial in modern Arabic literature', *Journal of the American Oriental Society*, Vol. 87, No. 1, Jan.–Mar. 1967, 12 ff.
85 Date of original pub. unknown. Repr. 1936.
86 *La caverne des songes*, tr. Khédry, Paris, 1939; *Quei della caverna*, tr. R. Rubinacci, Naples, 1965.
87 Sura 18.
88 See Jacob Landau, *Studies in the Arab Theater and Cinema*, Philadelphia, 1958, for notes on some of the other plays.
89 *Op. cit.*, 201 ff.
90 *Op. cit.*, 114.
91 *The maze of justice*, London, 1947.
92 Oxford University Press, tr. Denys Johnson-Davies.
93 Dagher, 231 ff.
94 *Ibid.*, 236 ff.
95 In *al-Shaikh Jum'a.*
96 *Op. cit.*, 169. A collection of translations by the same author was published in Cairo in 1946 under the title *Tales from Egyptian Life.*
97 Nouvelles éditions latines, Paris: *Le courtier de la mort; La belle aux lèvres charnues; La fleur du cabaret; Bonne fête*, etc.
98 p. 57.
99 Monteil, 205.
100 'Zaabalawi', p. 137.
101 See extract in Monteil, 206 ff.
102 *Op. cit.*, 192.
103 See Monteil, 154 ff., for an extract.
104 See Chapter I of the present work, p.22 and note 47. Also Hourani, 330, and Dagher, 132 ff.
105 *al-Nathr al-fannī fī al-qarn al-rābi'.*
106 Khemiri and Kampffmeyer, 31 ff.
107 *Ibid.*, 27 ff.; Dagher, 682 ff.
108 Hourani, 309–11, 354 ff.
109 Adapted from Hourani, 354.
110 *Op. cit.*, 3 ff.
111 Dagher, 453.
112 2nd edn., Beirut, 1955.
113 Lebanese transliterate their names in French fashion.
114 Extract in Monteil, 50 ff.

115 *Ibid.*, 225 ff.

116 Dagher, 107 ff., Mustafa, 486 ff.

117 *Op. cit.*, 491 ff.

118 *Ibid.*, 503 ff.

119 See Johnson-Davies 192 and the short story included, *The South Wind*, 120; Monteil, 76 ff., with an extract from the *Song of the Earth*.

120 Monteil, 98 ff.

121 See the short story, *The Dying Lamp*, in Johnson-Davies, 51 ff.

122 'The open window' (*al-Nāfidha al-maftūḥa*), Baghdad, 1958.

123 See Johnson-Davies, 191, and the story *The Doum Tree of Wadi Hamid* which he reproduces, 51 ff.

124 Issue 6, 1968, 103 ff.

125 *Op. cit.*, 241 ff.

126 See Monteil 259 ff., where one story, *The Fisherman*, from 'The Vale of Blood', is translated.

GLOSSARY OF ARABIC TERMS

NOTE: This glossary consists of Arabic terms, chiefly literary, which occur frequently in this book. While almost all of them are defined, either in the text of the book or in the notes, it is hoped that this list of them may be useful for easy reference.

Abbasid, anglicised form of Arabic ʿAbbāsī, is an adjective designating the dynasty who ruled the Islamic Empire as caliphs from 749/750 to 1258 A.D. It is used in such expressions as 'Abbasid literature', 'Abbasid poetry', and 'an early Abbasid poet'.

Adab, plural Ādāb, literature.

ʿAtb, see ʿItāb.

Bait, a verse in poetry, usually consisting of two *maṣra*ʿs (see below). The word also means 'house', and 'tent'.

Balāgha, rhetoric; particularly those recognised devices of writing, such as metaphor, simile and *jinās* (see below) which characterised art prose and poetry from the late Ummayad era onwards, and were codified in several books concerning them.

Dīwān, plural, dawāwīn, a Persian word taken into Arabic. In the present work, it occurs only as a shortened form of dīwan shiʿr meaning a collection of poems. Among its other meanings are office, administration, register, and sofa (divan). A poetical diwan usually contains poems by a single poet only, though sometimes it may be a collection of poems by a number of poets which are homogeneous in style or subject, such as 'dīwān al-hamāsa', a collection of chivalry poems (see *hamāsa* below). After a poet's death, his diwan usually contains his whole poetical output. (Here, diwan is equivalent to *kulliyyāt* in Persian, Urdu, and other languages of Pakistan.) But during a poet's lifetime, two or more diwans may be published under his name.

Fakhr, pride, boasting (though not in a derogatory sense). This was admitted as a type of Arabic poetry from pre-Islamic times. Such fakhr could be pride in one's tribe, family, nation or sect, and even in oneself. Verses of fakhr could occur incidentally during the course of a poem on almost any subject: or a whole poem might be fakhr.

Faṣīḥ means 'pure, unadulterated'. It is used in the feminine form, faṣīḥa (or the feminine of the superlative, fuṣḥā) with the noun *lugha* (language) preceding it or understood, to denote correct literary language as used in the medieval literature. Consequently, it is often translated as 'classical'.

Fiqh, Islamic jurisprudence.

Fuṣḥā, see *faṣīḥ*.

Ḥamāsa, chivalry, used of poetry, especially pre-Islamic, about tribal rivalries and wars, illustrating characteristic bedouin virtues such as bravery, loyalty and courtesy. The ideas of bravery, energy and enthusiasm are implicit in the word.

Hijā', satire.

Ḥikma, plural ḥikam, literally 'wisdom'. The term is used of an epigram, aphorism, piece of simple philosophising or gnomic truth which is considered an enhancement of a poem. An example from Mutanabbi is

> We esteem swords and spears,
> But death kills us without a fight.

i.e., however great a man may be in battle, he cannot fight death when his appointed hour comes.

An example from Shakespeare would be:

> Cowards die many times before their ends;
> The brave man only tastes of death but once.

ʿItāb/ʿAtb, chiding, remonstrating, is a recognised type of Arabic poetry, which might be the subject of a whole poem, or part of one. When poets were dependent on patronage, a poet might write an ʿitāb poem to his patron complaining of his ill-treatment of him – such as inadequate financial reward for his verse.

Jāhiliyya, the period in Arabia immediately preceding Islam, more particularly from about 500 to 622 A.D. The latter date is that of Muhammad's flight (hegira, properly *hijra*) from Mecca to Medina, when Islam is considered to have begun, and from which the Muslim calendar commences. The adjective is *jāhilī*, pre-Islamic. Thus one can speak of *al-adab al-jāhilī*, pre-Islamic literature.

Jinās, a device of rhetoric, is the use, in such close proximity as easily to strike the ear, of two or more words derived from the same root, or from similar roots – differing, for example, by one consonant only. Thus, from the root kataba (to write), *kitāb*, a book or letter, forms jinas with *kataba*, he wrote. In perfect jinas, a single word is repeated, with either identical or different meanings. Thus *kitāb* could mean 'book' in both places, or 'book' in one, and 'letter' in the other. *Kitāb* and *kilāb* form imperfect jinas, as there is one consonant different (t and l).

Khamriyyāt, poems about *khamr*, wine.

Madḥ/madīḥ, praise, eulogy, a type of poetry.

Mahjar, emigration. The term used of Arabic writers who emigrated to America to designate the special features of their works, especially their poetry. Thus we read about *shiʿr al-mahjar* (Arab-American poetry).

Mamlūk (anglicised *mameluke*), plural mamālīk, literally possessed, slave. The word is used of non-Arabs, particularly from Central Asia, south Russia and the Balkans, who were taken as slaves, and subsequently enfranchised. They served as army officers and government officials. They usurped power in Egypt, which they ruled from 1250 till the Ottoman conquest of the country in 1517. Subsequently, until Napoleon's expedition of 1798, they formed the ruling class and the landowners under the Ottoman régime.

Maqāla, plural maqālāt, essay, (newspaper or magazine) article. Maqāla iftitāḥiyya, a newspaper 'leader'.

Maqāma, plural maqāmāt, sometimes translated in French as séance, a medieval literary form which survived until the end of the nineteenth century. It is characterised by ornate language, with extensive use of rhetorical devices and rich vocabulary. Normally only a few pages long, individual maqāmāt differ considerably, at times resembling an essay, at times a learned article, at times a short story – or an essay with an anecdotal element.

Poetry is often included, usually to display some skill in manipulating the language or prosody. Whatever the detailed characteristics of a maqāma, it is essentially a linguistic tour de force, a display of virtuosity. Several authors wrote series of maqāmat, within a 'frame story'. (See references to al-Hamadhānī, al-Ḥarīrī, and al-Yāzijī in the Index.)

Marthiyya, see rithā'.

Maṣraʿ, hemistich, half of a bait or verse of poetry.

Masraḥ, theatre.

Masraḥiyya, a play, the noun *riwāya* (story) being understood (*riwāya masraḥiyya*).

Mathnawī (in Persian, mathnavi), poetry in which the two hemistiches of each verse rhyme together, the rhyme changing every verse.

Muʿallaqāt, the pre-Islamic odes said to have been suspended at the Kaʿba in Mecca because of their excellence. While usually there are said to be seven of them, some writers included three additional odes. The Muʿallaqāt are ranked among the finest classical Arabic poetry. Indeed they were long considered second to none, and are still so regarded by many Arabs today.

Muwashshah, plural muwashshahāt, stanza poetry (see Chapter I, p. 9).

Nahḍa, awakening, revival, renaissance, the term used of the Arab revival of the 19th/20th centuries, especially the literary revival.

Nathr, adjective nathrī, prose.

Ommeyad, sometimes spelled Umayyad, Arabic Umawī, is an adjective designating the dynasty who ruled the Islamic Empire as caliphs from 661 to 749/750. The term is also used of the literature of the period.

Orthodox Caliphs, the first four caliphs who ruled from Muhammad's death in 632 to 661. In Arabic they are called the 'rightly directed' caliphs (*al-khulafā' al-rāshidūn*), and the adjective is *rāshidī*.

Qaṣīda, plural qaṣā'id/qaṣīd, ode (see Chapter I, p. 4).

Qiṣṣa, plural qiṣaṣ, story: also used of the short story and novel during the last hundred years or so.

Qiṭʿa, plural qiṭaʿ, a very short poem (literally, 'piece'), generally of no more than four verses.

Rāshidī, see Orthodox Caliphs.

Risāla, plural risā'il/risālāt, essay, letter. See Chapter I, pp. 11 and 18.

Rithā', elegy, a type of poetry. Also called *marthiyya*, plural marāthī.

Riwāya, plural riwāyāt, story, novel. See also masraḥ.

Rubāʿiyyāt, quatrains of poetry, each consisting of two verses, that is, four hemistiches. The adjective is rubāʿī.

Sajʿ, rhymed prose. A work or passage in sajʿ is sometimes said to be masjūʿ.

Sharīʿa, Islamic law.

Shāʿir, plural shuʿara', poet.

Shiʿr, poetry, verse.

Ṣūfī, a mystic in Islam.

Ṣufism, a Western term for Islamic mysticism (in Arabic, taṣawwuf).

Ṣufistic, a Western description of Islamic mystical poetry. Such poetry often uses the terminology of human love and/or wine-drinking, as a metaphorical representation of the mystic's relationship with God.

Uqṣūṣa, plural aqāṣīṣ, a short story.

Umayyad, see Omeyyad.

Wālī, governor (of an administrative province), especially under the Ottoman Turks. It is sometimes spelt Vali, and the province was called a 'vilayet' (Arabic, *wilāya*).

BIBLIOGRAPHY

Note: This bibliography is largely confined to books and articles actually consulted during the writing of the book. Thus it makes no claims to be comprehensive: nor is there any attempt to list editions of the works of all the authors discussed. For further bibliographical information, readers should consult the works by Brockelmann and Dagher mentioned below and marked with an asterisk.

A. WORKS IN ENGLISH

Abdel Aziz Abdel Meduid, *The Modern Arabic Short Story, its emergence, development, and form*, Cairo, 1950.

Abushady, *At random*, Cairo, 1937.

A. J. Arberry, *The Seven Odes*, London, 1957.

———, *Arabic Poetry*, Cambridge, 1965.

———, *Poems of al-Mutanabbi*, Cambridge, 1967.

———, *Modern Arabic Poetry*, London, 1950, repr. 1957.

Salahiddine Boustany, *The Press during the French expedition in Egypt, 1798–1801*, Cairo, 1954.

P. Cachia, 'The use of the colloquial in modern Arabic literature', *Journal of the American Oriental Society*, Vol. 87, No. 1, 1967, pp. 12 ff.

———, *Taha Husayn*, London, 1956.

T. Chenery (v. 1) and P. Steingass (v. 2), *The Assemblies of al Harîrî*, London, 1867 and 1898.

John B. Christopher, *Lebanon Yesterday and Today*, New York, 1966.

I. A. Edham, *Abushâdy the poet*, Leipzig, 1936.

H. A. R. Gibb, *Arabic Literature*, 2nd edn., Oxford, 1963.

———(trans.), *Ibn Batuta, Travels in Asia and Africa*, Broadway Travellers Series, London.

———, *Studies in the Civilization of Islam*, ed. Shaw and Polk, London, 1962.

Taufīq al-Ḥakīm, trans. A. Eban, *The maze of justice*, London, 1947.

———, trans. Denys Johnson-Davies, *The tree-climber*, London, 1966.

J. A. Haywood, *Thousand and One Nights*, Encyclopaedia Britannica.

J. Heyworth-Dunne, *An Introduction to the history of education in Modern Egypt*, London, 1938.

P. Hitti, *History of the Arabs*, 5th edn., London, 1953.

Albert Hourani, *Arab Thought in the Liberal Age (1789–1838)*, Oxford, 1962, repr. 1967.

Ṭaha Ḥusain, (trans. E. H. Paxton), *An Egyptian Childhood*, London, 1932.

———, (trans. Hilary Wayment), *The Stream of Days*, London, 1948.

C. Huart, *A History of Arabic Literature*, London, 1903.

Ibn Khallikān, *Biographical Dictionary*, trans. MacGuckin de Slane, 4 vv., London and Paris, 1843–71, repr. 1967.

(Ibn Ṭufail), *The Awakening of the Soul*, trans. P. Brönle (Wisdom of the East Series), London, 1904.

Yousuf Izzedien, *Poetry and Iraqi Society, 1900–1945*, Baghdad, 1962.

Jibrān Khalīl Jibrān, (short stories in English translation), *Rebellious spirits*, London, 1947. *Nymphs of the valley*, London, 1948.

Denys Johnson-Davies (trans.), *Modern Arabic Short Stories*, London, 1967.

———, *Tales from Egyptian life*, Cairo, 1946.

T. Khemiri and G. Kampffmeyer, *Leaders in Contemporary Arabic Literature*, Berlin, 1930.

S. A. Khulūṣī, 'Ma'rūf al-Ruṣāfī, 1875–1945', *Bulletin of the School of Oriental and African Studies*, Vol. XIII, pt. 3, pp. 616 ff., London, 1950.

J. Landau, *Studies in the Arab Theater and Cinema*, Philadelphia, 1958.
(al-Ma'arrī) *The Epistle of Forgiveness*, ed. Kamil Kilany, trans. G. Brackenbury, Cairo, 1947.
S. Moreh, 'Blank verse in modern Arabic literature', *Bulletin of the School of Oriental and African Studies*, London, Vol. XXIX (1966), Pt. 3, pp. 483 ff.
———, 'Free verse in modern Arabic literature', *ibid.*, Vol. XXXI (1968), Pt. 1, pp. 28 ff.
———, 'The Arab literary revival in Israel', *Ariel*, Spring, 1962, pp. 14 ff.
Mikhail Naimy, *Kahlil Gibran, his Life and Work*, Beirut, 1964.
R. A. Nicholson, *A Literary History of the Arabs*, London, 1907, repr. Cambridge, 1966.
W. R. Polk, *The Opening of South Lebanon, 1788–1840*, Harvard, 1963.
G. R. Potter, *The Autobiography of Ousama*, Broadway Medieval Literatures, London, 1929.
J. Prendergast, *The Maqámát of Badi' al-Zaman al-Hamadhani*, London, 1915.
F. Rosenthal, *The Muqaddimah, an Introduction to History*, 3 vv., London, 1958.
Afāf Luṭfī al-Sayyid, *Egypt and Cromer, a study in Anglo-Egyptian relations*, London, 1968.
P. Vatikiottis, 'Muhammad 'Abduh and the quest for a Muslim Humanism,' in *Arabica*, IV, 1 Jan., 1957, pp. 55 ff.
Charles Wendell (trans.) *Osman Amin, Muhammad 'Abduh*, Washington, 1953.

B. WORKS IN FRENCH

J. M. Abd-el-Jalil, *Brève histoire de la littérature arabe*, Paris, 1946.
Anouar Abdel-Malek, *Anthologie de la littérature arabe contemporaine, II: les essais*, Paris, 1965.
Henri Dehéran, *Silvestre de Sacy – ses contemporains et ses disciples*, Paris, 1938.
Gaudefroy Demombynes, *Le livre de la poésie et des poètes*, Paris, 1947.
Taufīq al-Ḥakīm, trans. Khédri, *La caverne des songes*, Paris, 1939.
(Jabartī) *Merveilles biographiques et historiques, ou chroniques du Cheikh Abd-el-Rahman al-Djabarti, traduites de l'arabe par Chefik Masour Bey, Abdulaziz Khalil Bey, Gabriel Kalil Bey et Iskander Mamoun Effendi*, 9 vv., Cairo, 1888.
al-Jāḥiẓ, trans., C. Pellat, *Le livre des avares*, Paris, 1951.
J. Lecerf and G. Wiet (trans.), *Le livre des jours*, Paris, 1947.
R. and L. Makarius, *Anthologie de la littérature arabe contemporaine*, I: *le roman et la nouvelle*, Paris, 1964.
V. Monteil, *Anthologie bilingue de la littérature arabe*, Beirut, 1961.
C. A. Nallino, *La littérature arabe*, Paris, 1950.
Homa Pakdaman, *Djamal-ed-Din Assad Abadi dit Afghani*, Paris, 1969.
Gustave Rouger (trans.), *Le roman d'Antar*, Paris, 1923.
Maḥmūd Taimūr, French translations of his works; all pub. Paris:
Le courtier de la mort, 1950.
La belle aux lèvres charnues, 1952.
La fleur au cabaret, 1953.
Bonne fête, 1954.
Yusuf al-Turk, *Chroniques d'Égypte, 1789–1804*, trans. G. Wiet, Cairo, 1950.
G. Zaidan, *al Abbassa ou la sœur du Calife*, trans. M. Y. Bitar and Ch. Moulié, ed. C. Farrière, Paris, n.d.

C. WORKS IN ITALIAN

Francesco Gabrieli, *Storia della letteratura araba*, 2nd edn., Rome, 1956.
Taufīq al-Ḥakīm, trans. R. Rubinacci, *Quei della caverna*, Naples, 1965.

D. WORKS IN GERMAN

* Carl Brockelmann, *Geschichte der arabischen Litteratur*, 2 vv., and 3 supp. vv., Leiden, 1937–49.

F. Rückert, *Hamasa, oder die älteste arabischen Volkslieder*, Stuttgart, 1846.

———, (trans. of al-Ḥarīrī's *Maqāmāt*) *Die Vewandlungen des Abu Seid von Serug*, 2 vv., Stuttgart and Tübingen, 1844.

E. WORKS IN PERSIAN

M. M. Chahārdihi, *Ārā' wa Mu'taqadāt-i-Sayyid Jamāl-ud-Dīn-i-Afghānī*, Teheran, 1958.

I. Afshar and A. Mahdawī, *Documents inédits concernant Seyyed Jamal-al-Dīn Afghānī*, Teheran, 1963.

F. WORKS IN ARABIC

I. 'Abbās and N. Y. Najma, *al-Shi'r al-'Arabī fī l-mahjar – Amrīkā al-shimāliyya*, Beirut, 1957.

Muḥammad 'Abduh and Jamāl al-Dīn al-Afghānī, *al-'Urwa al-wuthqā*, Beirut, 1909.

Aḥmad Abū Sa'd, *al-Shi'r wa l-shu'arā' fī l-'Irāq, 1900–1957*, Beirut, 1959.

———, *al-Shi'r wa l-shu'arā' fī l-Sūdān, 1900–1958*, Beirut, 1958.

Abū Shādī, *Thaura al-Islām*, Beirut, 1961.

Taufīq Abū Sharīf and 'Ādil Zawwātī, *Shi'r al-muqāwama*, Amman, n.d.

Muḥammad Ṣādiq 'Afīfī, *al-ittijāhāt al-waṭaniyya fī l-shi'r al-lībī al-ḥadīth*, Cairo, 1957.

Aḥmad Amīn, *Fajr al-Islām*, Cairo, 1927.

———, *Ḍuḥā al-Islām*, 3 vv., Cairo, 1933–6.

———, *Ẓuhr al-Islām*, 2 vv., Cairo, 1945.

Qāsim Amīn, *Taḥrīr al-mar'a*, Cairo, 1899.

———, *al-Mar'a al-jadīda*, Cairo, 1901.

Maḥmūd al-'Aqqād, *'Abqariyya 'Umar*, Cairo, 1947.

———, *'Abqariyya al-Imām*, Cairo, 1948.

———, *Ḥayāt ibn al-Rūmī*, Cairo, 1931.

Nasīb 'Arīḍa, *Muntakhabāt*, in *Manāhil al-'Arab* series, Beirut, 1950.

Muḥammad al'Arūsī al-Maṭwī, *Farḥa al-sha'b*, Tunis, 1963.

———, *al-Tūt al-murr*, Tunis, 1967.

'Abbās al-'Azzāwī, *History of Arabic literature in Iraq* (Arabic text), 2 vv., Baghdad, 1962.

Maḥmūd Sāmī al-Bārūdī, *Dīwān*, ed. Dr. Muhammad Haikal, 2 vv., Cairo, 1940.

'Abd al-Majīd ben Jallūn, *Wādī al-dimā'*, Cairo, 1947.

al-Buḥturī, *Ḥamāsa*, Cairo, 1949.

Fu'ād Afrām al-Bustānī, *Ta'rīkh Lubnān al-mūjaz*, Beirut, 1957.

Louis Cheikho, *al-Adab al-'Arabiyya fī l-qarn al-tāsi' 'ashara*, 2 vv., 2nd edn., Beirut, 1923.

———, *Ta'rīkh al-adab al-'arabiyya fī l-rub' al-awwal min al-qarn al-'ishrīn*, Beirut, 1926.

* Dagher (Yūsuf As'ad Dāghir), *Masādir al-dirāsāt al-adabiyya*, 2vv., Beirut, 1955.

'Umar al-Dasūkī, *Fīl-adab al-ḥadīth*, 2nd edn., Cairo, 1950.

Māhir Ḥasan Fahmī, *Taṭawwur al-shi'r al-'arabī al-hadīth fī Miṣr*, Cairo, 1958.

Ḥāfiẓ Ibrāhīm, *Dīwān*, 2 vv., ed. Aḥmad Amīn and others, Cairo, 1937.

Taufīq al-Ḥakīm, *Ahl al-kahf*, Cairo, 1933.

———, *Yaumiyyāt na'ib fī l-aryāf*, Cairo, 1937.

Ṭaha Ḥusain, *Ma'a al-Mutanabbī*, Cairo, 1937.
———, *Tajdīd dhikr Abī al-'Alā' fī sijnihi*, Cairo, 1939.
———, *Dhikrā' Abī al-'Alā'*, Cairo, 1915.
———, *Mustaqbal al-thaqāfa fī Miṣr*, Cairo, 1938.
———, *Fī l-shi'r al-Jāhilī*, Cairo, 1926.
———, *Fī l-adab al-Jāhilī*, Cairo, 1927.
———, *al-Ayyām*, Cairo, Pt. I, 1927, Pt. II, 1939.
Ibn Qutaiba, *'Uyūn al-Akhbār*, 4 vv., Cairo, 1929–30.
Abū al-Faraj al-Iṣfahānī, *Kitāb al-Afghānī*, 15 vv., Beirut, 1950.
Yūsuf 'Izz al-Dīn, *al-Shi'r al-'Irāqī, ahdāfuhu wa-khaṣā'iṣuhu fī l-qarn al-tāsi'i 'ashara*, Baghdad, 1965.
'Alī al-Jārim, *Dīwān*, 3 vv., Cairo, 1939.
——— and Muṣṭafā Amīn, *al-Balāgha al-wāḍiḥa*, 4th edn., Cairo, 1946.
Jibrān Khalīl Jibrān, *al-Arwāḥ al-mutamarrida*, 5th edn., Cairo 1948.
———, *'Arā'is al-murūj*, 4th edn., Cairo, 1944.
Aḥmad Khalafullāh, *Aḥmad Fāris al-shidyāq*, Cairo, 1955.
Ṣafī al-Khulūṣī, *al-Nāfidha al-maftūḥa*, Baghdad, 1958.
——— *Abū Nuwās fī Amrīkā*, Baghdad, 1955.
Bishāra 'Abdullāh al-Khūrī (al-Akhṭal al-Ṣaghīr), *Dīwān*, Beirut, 1961.
R. Khuri. *'Aṣr al-iḥyā' wa l-Nahḍa*, Beirut, 1957.
al-Kitāb al-dhahabī fī mihrajān Khalīl Maṭrān, Cairo, 1948.
M. Kurd 'Alī, *Rasā'il al-Bulaghā'*, 4th edn., Cairo, 1954.
'Abd al-Qādir al-Maghribī, *Jamāl al-Dīn al-Afghānī*, Cairo, 1948.
Muṣṭafā Luṭfī al-Manfalūṭī, *al-'Abarāt*, 2 vv., Cairo, 1915.
———, *al-Naẓarāt*, 3 vv., Cairo, 1926.
Maqāmāt al-Ḥanafī wa Ibn Nāqiya wa-ghairihim, Istanboul, 1913.
Adīb Maruwwa, *al-Ṣahāfa al-'Arabiyya*, Beirut, 1961.
Khalīl Maṭrān (Miṭrān/Muṭrān), *Dīwān*, 4 vv., Cairo, 1948–9.
Zakī Mubārak, *al-Nathr al-fannī fī l-qarn al-rābi'*, Cairo, 1934.
Zakī al-Dīn Muḥammad, *al-Manfalūṭī*, Cairo, 1965.
Mukhtārāt al-udabā', Hamad Publications, Beirut n.d.
Ḥusain Mu'nis, *Ahlan wa sahlan*, Cairo, 1958.
Shākir Muṣṭafā, *al-Qiṣṣa fī Sūrīya ḥattā al-Ḥarb al-'ālamiyya al-thāniya*, Cairo, 1957.
Nazzār Qabbānī, *Anti lī*, Beirut, 1950.
———, *Qaṣā'id*, Beirut, 1956.
Ma'rūf al-Ruṣāfī, *Dīwān*, 3 vv., 3rd edn., ed. 'Abd al-Qādir al-Maghrabī, Baghdad, 1949.
Ismā'īl Ṣabrī, *Dīwān*, ed. Ḥasan Rif'at Bey, Cairo, 1938.
Ḥasan Kāmil al-Ṣairāfī, *Ḥāfiẓ wa Shauqī*, Cairo, 1948.
Aḥmad Shauqī, *al-shauqiyyāt*, 4 vv., ed. Dr. Ḥusain Haikal, Cairo, 1953.
Rifā'at al-Ṭahṭāwī, *Takhlīṣ al-ibrīz fī talkhīṣ Parīz*, Cairo, 1905.
Maḥmūd Taimūr, *al-shaikh Jum'a wa aqāṣīṣ ukhrā*, 2nd edn., Cairo, 1927.
'Abdullāh al-Ṭayyib, *al-Murshid ilā al-shi'r al-'Arabī*, Cairo, 1955.
———, *Aṣdā' al-Nīl*, Khartoum, 1957.
Munīr Alyās Wahība, *al-Zajal*, Ḥuraisa, Lebanon, 1942.
Walī al-Dīn Yakan, *Dīwān*, Cairo, 1924.
Nāṣīf al-Yāzijī, *Majma' al-baḥrain*, ed. 'Īsā Sābā, Beirut, 1958.
———, *Nafḥa al-raihān*, Beirut, 1864.
———, *Thālith al-qamrain*, Beirut, 1883.
Qusṭanṭīn Zuraiq, *al-Wa'y al-qaumī*, new edn., Beirut, 1940.

INDEX

Abāẓa, ʿAzīz, 134, 205
ʿAbbās I (Khedive), 33, 78
ʿAbbās II (Khedive), 80, 86, 97
ʿAbbās, I., 173
ʿAbd al-ʿAzīz (Turkish Sultan), 46, 69, 81
ʿAbd al-Ḥamīd (Turkish Sultan), 60, 85, 103, 120, 133
ʿAbd al-Ḥamīd al-Kātib, 11, 18
ʿAbd al-Muṭṭalib, 102
ʿAbd al-Wāḥid, ʿAbd al-Rāziq, 185
Abd el-Jalil, 52
ʿAbdel-Meguid, ʿAbdel-Aziz, 127, 130
ʿAbduh, Muḥammad, 7, 21, 24, 92, 93, 110, 116, 120, 121 ff., 125, 134, 143 ff., 164, 191, 193, 207
Abdullah, King of Jordan, 189
ʿAbdullah Fikrī, 82
Abī Shaqrā, Shauqī, 181
Abū al-ʿAtāhiyya, 29, 46, 134
Abū al-Naṣr, ʿAlī, 80 f.
Abū Firās, 9, 102
Abū Ḥadīd, Muḥammad Farīd, 133
Abū Hānī, Ṣāliḥ, 180
Abū Māḍī, Īlīyā, 10, 173 ff., 218
Abū Nuwās, 5, 6, 69, 134, 214, 256 ff.
Abū Saʿd, Aḥmad, 186
Abū Shabaka, Ilyās 173
Abū Shādī, Aḥmad Zakī, 10, 161 ff., 173, 175–6
Abū Sharīf, Taufīq, 190
Abū Tammām, 8, 22, 69
Abū Zaid, the Tales of, 17
Académie Française, 44
Addison, Joseph, 137
ʿAdonis' (pseudonym), 182
Afghānī, Jamāl al-Dīn al-, 24, 116, 118 ff., 122, 123, 143 ff.
ʿAfīfī, Muḥammad Ṣādiq, 187
Age of Depression, 2, 13, 26 ff.
Aḥdab, Ibrāhīm al-, 14, 61
Aḥfād Schools, Omdurman, 215
Ahlwardt, W., 194
Aḥmad Khān, Sir Sayyid, 24, 121
Aḥmad Pasha, Bey of Tunis, 116
Aḥmar, Khalaf al-, 194
Ahrām, al- (newspaper), 192
Akhras, ʿAbd al-Ghaffār al-, 68 ff
Akhṭal, al-, 7, 64
—, the Lesser, *see* Khūrī, Bishāra ʿAbdallāh al-
Aleppo, 9, 21, 36, 38, 63, 132
Alexandria, 30, 36, 79, 85, 168, 196
ʿAlī, the third caliph, 118
Ālūsī family, 110
—, Shihāb al-Dīn Maḥmūd al-, 14, 68, 70
American Arabic literature, 10, 21, 128 ff., 173 ff.
American Missionaries in the Lebanon, 44, 53, 61
American University of Beirut (A.U.B.), 44, 133, 186, 213
Amiens, Treaty of, 30
Amīn, Aḥmad, 22, 24, 116, 121, 207
—, Qāsim, 24, 116, 121, 124 ff.
—, ʿUthmān, 21, 121
Amīr al-Kabīr, Sayyid Muḥammad al-, 29
Andaisha, al-Hādī Maḥmūd, 187
Anecdotal literature, 17
ʿAnḥūrī, Salīm Rūfāʿīl, 115
Anṭakī, ʿAbd al-Masīḥ, 133
ʿAntar, the Romance of, 16, 17, 205
ʿAntīl, Fauzī al-, 172
Anṭūn, Faraḥ, 135
Apollo (magazine), the Apollo Poets, 168, 171
ʿAqqād, Maḥmūd al-, 21, 167, 171
Arabian Nights, see *Thousand and One Nights*
ʿArabī Pasha, 55, 79, 83, 123
Arab-Israeli conflict, 7, 188
Arab Literary Renaissance, 1 and *passim*
— Pen Club (in Israel), 191
— Writers' Union, New York, 174, 175
Arabic, Classical, 1
—, Colloquial, 1, 131, 137, 198
—, Modern Literary, 1
— Literature, ʿAbbasid, 1, 5, 6, 8, 9, 194
— —, Classical, 1, 25
— —, Modern, 1 and *passim*
— —, Ommeyad, 2, 7, 11, 12, 87, 194
— —, Pre-Islamic (Jāhilī), 1, 2, 4, 87, 194 f.
Arberry, A. J., 98, 166, 168, 187
ʿArīḍa, Nasīb, 173, 177 f.
Armenian Church, 37, 55
Arnāʾūṭ, Maʿrūf Aḥmad al-, 212 f.
Arsalān, Prince Shakīb, 115
Art prose, 11, 13, 14
Asadabad, 119
ʿAsalī, Shukrī ibn ʿAlī al-, 132 f., 136

Asia Minor, 9, 26
Assiyut Province, 138
Atlantic Press, New York, 177
'Aṭṭār, Shaikh Ḥasan al-, 34 f.
Aurel, Pierre, 30
Autobiography, 19, 20, 58 ff., 196 f., 215
Avicenna, 24, 44
Awqāf, 83, 282 n.14
'Awwād, Émile Yūsuf, 211 f.
—, Taufīq Yūsuf, 211 f.
Ayyūb, Dhū al-Nūn, 214
—, Rashīd, 173
'Āzār, Iskandar al-, 115
Azhar, al-, 31–2, 34, 102, 120–3, 193, 195
'Azzāwī, 'Abbās al-, 67

Baalbak, 97
Bacon, Francis, 137
Badger, G. P., 63
Badrī, Shaikh Bābikar, 215
Baghdad, 35, 66 ff., 105–6, 110–11, 184, 213–14
Baghdādī, al- Khaṭīb al-, 35
Bahlūl, 'Abd al-Raḥmān, 27
Baidās, Khalīl, 215
Bait, *see* Verse
Bait al-Dīn, 37
Baker, Sir Samuel, 78
—, Valentine, 78
Bakhter Ruda, 186, 192
Balāgha, *see* Rhetoric
Balīṭ, Jurjī Jabrā'īl, 128
Banī Hilāl, the Tales of, 17
Barbīr, Aḥmad al-, 38
Barcelona, 86
Baring, Sir Evelyn, *see* Cromer, Lord
Bārūdī, Maḥmūd Sāmī al-, 6 f., 79 f., 83 f., 167
Bashīr II, Lebanese amir, 37, 39, 40, 44–5
Bashīr, al-Tījānī Yūsuf, 186 f.
Baṣra, 50
Beggars' Opera, 60
Ben Jallūn, 197, 217, 269 ff.
Bengali literature, 9
Bennett, Arnold, 168
Berque, Jacques, 57
Bible, the, 53–4, 61, 63
Bint al-Shāti' (pseudonym), 125, 205 f.
Biography, 17, 19 ff., 166, 194 f.
Biskenta, 175
Blank verse, Arabic, 10, 25, 107 ff., 189
Boito, Arrigo, 85
Bombay, 70
Boston, Mass., 128
Boustany, Salahiddine, 31
Brazil, 173
Brockelmann, Carl, 26
Browne, Sir Thomas, 197
Buḥturī, al-, 22, 111
Būlāq Press, 33
Bureau of Translation, Cairo, 32
Burton, Sir Richard, 17
Bustānī, Amīn Buṭrus al-, 62
—, Buṭrus al-, 43, 61 ff., 71, 124, 133
—, Najīb al-, 62
—, Salīm al-, 62, 126 f., 133
—, Sulaimān al-, 62
—, Wadī' al-, 178
Buthaina, 6
Byron, Lord, 52
Byzantine Empire, 9

Cachia, Pierre, 198
Cambridge, 54, 57
Carlyle, Thomas, 171
Carmen, 135
Ceylon, 73, 83
Charles Martel, Carolingian King of France, 134
Chateaubriand, 135, 163
Cheikho, Louis, 27, 39, 41, 44, 85
Chekhov, Russian writer, 214
Chevallier, Gabriel, 210
Christian-Arab Literature, 36
Christians and Christianity, 24, 27, 36–7, 44, 48, 59, 63, 91, 117, 133, 169, 188, 194, 198, 210, 212, 219 ff.
Chronograms (poetical), 27, 46
Churchill, Sir Winston, 11
Cincinatti, 174
Code Napoléon, 33
Colombo, Ceylon, 83
Commentary, 22, 68, 118, 123
Communism, 164
Copia, Isis (pesudonym), *see* Ziyāda, May
Coppée, François, 135
Copts, 29, 135, 208
Corneille, 60, 98, 163
Courier de l'Égypte, 30
Courteline, Georges, 205
Crete, 83

Crimea, 83
Cromer, Lord, 79, 93

Dagher (Dāghir), Yūsuf As'ad, 39, 168
Daḥdaḥ family, 43
Daḥlān, Aḥmad Zainī, 65
Damascus, 27, 35, 38, 44, 53, 63 f., 212
Damietta, 38
Danānīr, al-Ānisa, 189
Dante's *Inferno*, 16
Darwīsh, Maḥmūd, 190
—, Shaikh, great-uncle of Muḥammad 'Abduh, 121
—, Sayyid 'Alī al-, 35
Dā'ūd Pasha, 66, 70
Décade égyptienne, la, 30
De Quincey, Thomas, 137
Dewey, John, 171
Dhū al-Rumma, 64
Dickens, Charles, 168
Didactic poetry, 9
Dinshawai Affair, the, 79 ff., 88
Ḍiyā', al- (magazine), 19, 126
Don Quixote, 50
Dostoievsky, 208, 214
Drama, Arabic, 15, 44, 59 ff., 91–2, 98, 115, 125, 135, 168, 194, 197 ff., 204–5, 212, 216 f., 219 ff.
Druzes, the, 37, 61, 165
Dryden, John, 9, 91
Dumas, Alexandre, Père, 135, 213
— —, Fils, 212
Dunlop, Douglas, 90

Eban, A., 204
Edinburgh, 57
Egyptian Academy, 104
— National Library, 92
— University, Cairo, 193–4
Elegy, 4, 35, 46 f., 48, 87, 88 f., 94 ff., 98, 105
Eliot, T. S., 164, 180–1
Encyclopaedias, Arabic, 19, 20, 62
Ephesus, the Seven Sleepers of, 199
Epistolary style, *see* Art prose
Erotic poetry, *see* Love poetry
Essay, 18 f., 137 ff., 143 ff., 202 f.
Eulogy, 4, 27–8, 41, 46–7, 70, 81 f., 93, 105
Existentialism, 184
Expressionism, 163

Fahmī, M. H., 167
Fakhr, 4
Fakhr al-Dīn II, Lebanese amir, 37
Falstaff, 50
Farazdak, 7, 64
Fāris, Bishr, 171
Farouk (Fārūq), King of Egypt, 105
Fascism, 203
Fatimids, the, 30
Fawwāz, Zainab, 125
Fayyāḍ, Ilyās, 115
Fénélon, 33
Franco-Prussian War, 1870, 55
Franz-Josef, Austrian Emperor, 78
Free verse, see *vers libres*
Freemasonry, Egyptian, 122 f., 134, 167–8
Freud, 166
Freyha, Anis, 211
Fry, Christopher, 13
Fu'ād I, King of Egypt, 80
Funūn, al- (magazine)
Furaiḥa, *see* Freyha

Gabrieli, Francesco, 52
Galsworthy, John, 136, 197, 202, 207
Gautier, Théophile, 212
Geneva, 86
Germanos, 38
Ghassān, Kingdom of, 4
Ghazzālī, al-, 24
Gibb, Sir Hamilton, 34, 134–6
Gibbon, *Decline and Fall*, 22
Gibraltar, 212
Gide, André, 196
Girls' education, 33, 62, 124 f., 215, 251 ff.
Glasgow, 57
Goraieb, Laure, 180
Gordon, General, 78 f.
Gorst, Sir Eldon, 80
Graham, Billy, 171
Grand Orient freemasonry, 123
Greek Orthodox Church, 37
Griffiths, V. L., 192
Guidi, I., 213

Ḥabbūbī, Muḥammad Sa'īd al, 106
Ḥaddād, Naḍra, 173
Ḥadīth, 118
Ḥāfiẓ (Persian poet), 9
— Ibrāhīm, 7, 8, 80, 86, 87 f., 92 ff., 98, 103, 105, 111, 114, 135, 172

Haifa, 189
Haikal, Muḥammad Ḥusain, 18, 136
Ḥaidarī, Baland, 184
Ḥājirī, al-, 10
Ḥakīm, Taufīq al-, 18, 21, 166, 192–3, 197 ff., 208, 218, 219 ff.
Ḥālī, Alṭāf Ḥusain, 24, 121, 178
Hamadhānī, Badī' al-Zamān al-, 13, 49, 52, 118
Ḥamāsa poetry, 4, 5, 22
Handel, G. F., 115
Hardy, Thomas, 199
Ḥarīrī, al-, 13, 14, 35, 40, 49, 52
Hārūn al-Rashīd (caliph), 134, 159, 205
Ḥasan, Tāj al-Sirr, 187
Ḥassūn, Rizqallāh, 10, 63 f.
Ḥayāt, al- (newspaper), 192
Haykal, *see* Haikal
Hazlitt, William, 137
Hebrew University, Jerusalem, 191
Hedjaz, 6, 65, 105
Hemistich, 5
Heyworth-Dunne, J., 35
Hilāl, al (magazine), 19, 134
Ḥilla, al-, 70
Ḥillī, Ḥaidar al-, 68, 70, 106
Hīra, Kingdom of, 4, 91
Historical literature, Arabic, 21–2, 35 f., 65, 215
— novels, 133 ff., 206, 211, 212 f.
Hitler, 165
Hitti, Philip, 21
Homs, 177
Hourani, Albert, 33, 53, 56, 116, 125, 194
Huart, Clément, 57
Hugo, Victor, 86, 98
Hulagu, 2
Ḥusain, son of Muḥammad 'Alī, 278 n.16
Ḥusain Kāmil, Khedive/Sultan of Egypt, 80
Ḥusain, Rāshid, 191
—, Ṭaha, 14, 17, 18, 20, 22–3, 166, 186, 193 ff., 218

Ibn al-Fāriḍ, 9
— — Muqaffa', 13
— — Rūmī, 21
— 'Aqīl, 35
— 'Asākir, 35
— Baṭūṭa, 13, 20
— Hishām, 20
— Isḥāq, 20
— Jinnī, 56
— Jubair, 13
— Khaldūn, 2, 17, 19, 21, 118, 193
— Mālik, 9, 35
— Qutaiba, 22
— Rashīd, 3
— Sīnā, *see* Avicenna.
— Ṭufail, 16
Ibrāhīm, Katkhudā, 28
—, son of Muḥammad 'Alī, 37, 78, 278 n.12
Ibsen, Henry, 216
Imperialism, 4, 116, 187
Imprimerie nationale, 30
Institut d'Égypte, 30
Iṣfahānī, Abū al-Faraj al-, 22
Isḥāq, Adīb, 60, 120
Ismā'īl, Khedive, 32–4, 55, 78 f., 120, 198
Israel, Arabic literature in, 188 ff.
Istifānūs, Patriarch, 36
'Izz al-Dīn, Yūsuf 70, 109–10
Izzedien, *see* 'Izz al-Dīn

Jabartī, 'Abd al-Raḥmān al-, 27, 31, 35
Jabr, Jamīl, 181, 211
Jabrā, Jabrā Ibrāhīm, 215
Jabre, Jamil, *see* Jabr, Jamil
Jabrīl ibn Farḥāt, *see* Germanos
Ja'far the Barmecide, 134, 205
Jāhilī, Jāhiliyya, *see* Arabic Literature, Pre-Islamic
Jāḥiẓ, al-, 13, 17, 18
Jalāl, 'Uthmān al-, 135
Jalfī, Raḍwān al-, 28
Jamāl al-Dīn, Muṣṭafā, 184
James, Henry, 215
Jamīl ibn 'Abdallāh, 6
Janān, al- (magazine), 62, 71, 126, 128, 132–3
Jarīda, al- (newspaper), 192
Jārim, 'Alī al-, 6, 10, 11, 45, 104 f., 158 ff.
Jarīr, 7, 64
Jawāhirī, Mahdī al-, 184
Jawā'ib, al- (newspaper), 54, 70
Jawwād, Kāẓim, 185
Jayūsī, Salmā, 189
Jerusalem, 50, 110, 191
Jews, 36, 165, 190–1
Jibālī, Taufīq al-, 215 f.

Jibrān, Jibrān Khalīl, 128 ff., 173–5
Johnson-Davies, Denys, 193, 203, 205–7
Journal al-Khedive (newspaper), 33
Joyce, James, 163, 171, 196, 214
Jumhūriyya, al- (newspaper), 192
Jundī, Amīn al- 38, 42 f.
Jung, 166

Ka'ba, the, 3
Ka'b ibn Zuhair, 54
Kalīla wa Dimna, 17
Kampffmeyer, G., 175
Karam, Karam Mulḥim, 211
Karāma, Buṭrus, 38 ff., 44
Kararī, *see* Omdurman
Karr, A. (French author), 135
Kāẓimī, 'Abd al-Muḥsin al-, 110, 184
Keats, John, 167
Kemal, Mustafa (Ataturk), 7
Kerbala, 14, 68
Khāl, Yūsuf al-, 182
Khalīfa, the, Sudanese ruler, 215
Khalīl ibn Aḥmad, al-, 56
Khansā', al-, 206
Kharijites, 12
Khartoum, 33, 79, 186–7, 215
Khedive, 79, 281 n.2
Khemiri, T., 175
Khilāfa Movement, the, 281 n.6
Khulūṣī, Ṣafā', 214 f., 256 ff.
Khūrī family, 43
—, Bishāra 'Abdallāh al- (the Lesser Akhṭal), 178 ff.
—, Émile al-, 182
—, Rashīd al-, 178
Kīlānī, Kāmil, 192
Kirkuk, 66
Kitchener, Lord, 80, 215
Klat, Hector, 180
Kléber, General, 30
Koran, 3, 11, 44, 68, 110, 118, 121, 193, 195, 197, 199
Krylov, 64
Kufa, 50
Kurds, 107, 110

Labīd's *Mu'allaqa*, 4
Laith, Shaikh 'Alī al-, 81
Lamartine, Alphonse, 59, 173
Lamb, Charles, 137
Lane-Poole, Stanley, 104
Lautréamont, Comte de 180
League of Nations, 105, 115
Lee, Samuel, 54
Lesseps, Baron Ferdinand de, 78
Lexicography, Arabic, 29, 56, 62, 63
Literary criticism, 22 f., 194 ff., 207
Littmann, 193
Livorno, 36
London, 54, 63–4, 214
Longfellow, Henry Wadsworth, 173, 176
Love poetry, 4, 6, 7, 67–8, 84, 87, 100 f., 106, 168 f., 176, 178, 181, 182 ff., 185

Ma'ani amirs (Lebanon), 37
Ma'ārif Press, Cairo, 192
Ma'arrī, Abū al-'Alā' al-, 15, 16, 21, 106, 111–12, 193, 195
Macedonia, 188
Māghūṭ, Muḥammad, 181 f.
Ma'had, 281 n.99
Mahdawī, A., 119
Mahdi, the (Sudanese), 215
Maḥfūẓ, Najīb, 14, 206 f., 218
Mahjar literature, 173 ff., 187
Maḥmūd II, Turkish Sultan, 70
Maḥmūd, 'Abd al-Raḥīm, 189
Malā'ika, Nāzik al-, 184 f., 187
Mallarmé, Stéphane, 180
Malta, 37, 45, 54, 56, 132
Mamelukes, 29 ff., 32, 83
Mandeville, Sir John, 20
Manfalūṭī, Muṣṭafā Luṭfī al-, 10, 19, 23, 25, 121, 123, 127, 135, 138 ff., 151 ff., 166
Maqāma, plural *maqāmāt*, 11, 13, 14, 18, 35, 38, 40, 48, 50, 52, 67–8, 135 f., 137
Marcel, Jean-Joseph, 30
Margoliouth, D. S., 22, 194
Maronites, 29, 36, 59, 61, 97, 129
Marrāsh, Francis Fatḥullāh, 64, 132
Marseilles, 36
Marwān II, Caliph, 11
Marx, Karl and Marxism, 135, 203
Mas'adī, Maḥmūd al-, 216 f.
Mashriq, al- (magazine), 19, 126
Maṣra', *see* hemistich.
Massawa, 78
Mas'ūdī, al-, 13
Mathnawī, 9

Maṭrān, Khalīl, 80, 86, 97 ff., 104–5, 115, 133, 167, 170, 172–3
Maṭwī, Muḥammad al-'Arūsī al-, 187 f., 217, 263 ff.
Maudūdī (Pakistani thinker), 118
Maupassant, Guy de, 205
Māzinī, 'Abd al-Qādir al-, 18, 23, 136 f., 171, 208
Mecca, 3, 26–7, 119
Medical School, Cairo, 32
Medina, 26
Menou, Baron Jacques F. de, 30
Messina, 93
Metres (Arabic poetry), 5
Midḥat Pasha, 60, 66, 106
Mill, John Stuart, 118
Milton, John, 24
Miṭrān, *see* Maṭrān
Molière, 60, 173
Mones, *see* Mu'nis
Monorhyme, 5, 8, 9
Monteil, V., 185, 216
Montesquieu, 32
Montpelier, 86
Moreh, S., 10, 191
Mu'allaqāt, 3, 4
Mubārak, Zakī, 207
Muḥammad (the Prophet), 11, 110, 195, 199, 206, 212
Muḥammad 'Alī, ruler of Egypt, 31 ff., 36, 66 f., 78
Mu'nis, Ḥusain, 208 ff., 241 ff.
Muqtabas, al- (magazine), 132
Muqtaṭaf, al- (magazine), 19
Murād II, Turkish Sultan, 65
Mūsā, Salāma, 207 f.
Musical plays, (Arabic) 60, 135, 168
Muslim Benevolent Society, 123
Musset, Alfred de, 203, 212
Muṣṭafā, Shākir, 128, 213
Muṣṭafā Kāmil, Egyptian politician, 85, 93, 94 ff., 98
Mutanabbī, al-, 8, 21, 23–4, 35, 44–5, 52, 83, 208
Muṭrān, *see* Maṭrān.
Muwaiḥilī, al-, 120
Muwashshaḥāt, 9, 42, 107
Mysticism, Islamic, *see* Sūfism.

Nabahānī, Yūsuf al-, 188
Nahas Pasha, 196
Nahḍa, see Arab Literary Renaissance
Na'īma, Mīkhā'īl, 173, 175 ff.
Najaf, 69, 106, 119, 184
Najafī, Aḥmad al-Ṣāfī al-, 184
Najma, N.Y., 173
Nallino, C., 193
Napoleon Bonaparte, 1, 19 ff., 37, 39, 62
Naqqāsh, Mārūn [al-], 43–4, 59 ff.
—, Nicola (Nikūlā), 60
—, Salīm, 60, 120
Nashāshībī, Is'āf al-, 188
Nāṣir al-Dīn, Shah of Persia, 120
National Grand Lodge of Egypt, 123
Nationalist Party (Egyptian), 79, 80, 97, 123
Nazareth, 175, 177, 189, 211
Nazism, 164
New York, 124, 135, 168, 174, 214
Newspapers and journals, Arabic, 14, 18, 33–4, 54, 123, 127 f., 138, 173, 187
Nietzsche, 128
Nöldeke, T., 194, 213
Novel, the Arabic, 15–17, 131 ff., 241 ff., 256 ff., 263 ff.
Nu'mān, King of Hīra, 91
Nūrī, 'Abd al-Malik, 213

Ode, Arabic, 3–5, 8, 46, 158 ff.
Omar Khayyam, *see* 'Umar-i-Khayyām
Omdurman, 186
—, Battle of, 215
Opera, *see* Musical play
Opera House, Cairo, 60–1, 97, 198, 200, 204
Orwell, George, 201
Oxford, 15, 194

Pakdaman, H., 119
Palestine, 4, 165, 185, 188 ff.
Panjabi literature, 9
Paris, 32, 64, 72 ff., 117, 120, 123, 128, 136, 193 ff., 198, 203, 208, 216
Pashto literature, 9
Patriarchal School, Beirut, 44
Penguin and Pelican Books, 192
Persian literature, 9, 35, 44, 65, 83, 86, 107
Poe, Edgar Alan, 173
Poetry, Arabic, 3 ff., 25, 27 ff., *see* Table of Contents for major sections of chapters dealing with poetry

Polemical literature, Arabic, 23–4, 115 ff., 124 ff., 143 ff., 207, 210 ff., 250 ff.
Poltava, 175
Pope, Alexander, 9, 91
Priestley, J. B., 198
Printing Presses, early Arabic, 27, 30, 33
Prose, Arabic, 11 ff. *See also* Table of Contents
Provençal poetry, 10
Prussia, 132

Qabbānī, Aḥmad Abū Khalīl al-, 60 f.
—, Nizār, 182 ff.
Qais, Imrū' al-, 46
Qaṣaṣ (magazine), 128
Qaṣīda, *see* Ode
Qāsim, Samīḥ al-, 190
Quatrains, *see* Rubā'ī
Qusāṭalī, Nu'mān ibn 'Abduh al-, 132, 136
Quwaidir, Shaikh Ḥasan, 35

Racine, 32, 60, 163
Raḍī, al-Sharīf al-, 106
Rāfi'ī, Muṣṭafā Ṣādiq al-, 102
Raqī'ī, 'Alī Muḥammad al-, 187
Rauz Yūsuf (magazine), 208
Rāwiya, Ḥammād al-, 194
Realism, 163, 185
Renan, 135
'Resistance' poetry, Arabic, 187 ff.
Rhetoric, Arabic, 11 ff., 15, 26 ff., 45, 47, 55, 62, 67, 68, 81, 118, 191
Rhyme, Arabic, 5, 11
Rhymed couplets, 9
— prose, 3, 11, 27, 48 ff., 57
Rīḥānī, Amīn al-, 10, 23, 138, 211
Rimbaud, Arthur, 164, 180
Risāla, 11, 18, 137
Riẓā (Riḍā) 'Ali, Governor of Iraq, 66
Robinson, John, formerly Bishop of Woolwich, 171
Robinson Crusoe, 16, 62
Roman Catholicism, 36, 44, 129
Romanticism, 129, 167, 170, 173, 185, 187, 215
Rostand, Edmond, 135, 163
Rousseau, J. J., 32, 135
Royston, Herts, 54
Rubā'ī, rubā'iyyāt, 9, 106 f., 178
Ruṣāfī, Ma'rūf al-, 105, 110 ff., 184, 218
Russia, 107, 120, 132, 165, 175, 177

Sa'ātī, Maḥmūd Ṣafwat al-, 82
Ṣabrī, Ismā'īl, 85 f.
Sacy, Sylvestre de, 32, 48
Sa'īd, 'Alī Aḥmad, *see* Adonis
—, son of Sulaimān Pasha, Governor of Iraq, 66
— Pasha, Khedive (Muḥammad Sa'īd), 33, 78
Saif al-Daula, 9
Saint-Pierre, Bernadin de, 135, 163
Saint-Simon, 135
Ṣairāfī, Ḥasan Kāmil al-, 93
Saj', *see* Rhymed prose
Ṣāliḥ, Ilyās, 115
—, Ṭayyib, 215
Sanskrit literature, 35, 178
Ṣaqqāl, Anṭūn al-, 132
Sardou, 135
Sarkīs, Khalīl Rāmiz, 212
Ṣarūf, Ya'qūb, 19, 87, 138
Satire, poetical, 4
Sayyāb, Badr Shākir al-, 185
Sayyid Aḥmad Khān, Sir, 121–2
Schiller, 57
School of Languages, Cairo, 32 f.
Sermons, 11
Sevastopol, 103
Seven Odes, see *Mu'allaqāt*
Shābbī, Abū al-Qāsim al-, 187
Shā'ib, Fu'ād, 212
Shakespeare, William, 24, 91, 98, 163, 168, 202, 208, 214
Shamshū', Salīm, 191
Sharqāwī, 'Abdallāh al-, 35
—, 'Abd al-Raḥmān, 172, 207
Sharqī, 'Alī al-, 184
Shauqī, Aḥmad, 7, 10, 18, 80, 86 ff., 93, 103, 105, 111, 114, 135, 166–7, 172–3
Shaw, George Bernard, 135, 168, 198, 202, 208
Shelley, 52, 167
Shidyāq, Aḥmad Fāris al-, 19, 20, 43, 53 ff., 61, 63, 71, 126
—, As'ad al-, 20, 53
Shihābī amirs, 37
Shi'ites, 37, 106, 118–19
Shi'r (magazine), 181 f.
Short story, Arabic, 17, 126 ff., 235 ff., 269 ff.

Shubrāwī, 'Abdallāh al-, 35
Shukrī, 'Abd al-Raḥmān, 167
Ṣiddīq Ḥasan Khān, 54
Sidon, 59
Silsila Iqra', 192
Sindhi literature, 9
Solomon the Magnificent, Turkish sultan, 26
Sophocles, 135
South America, 173
Stanza poetry in Arabic, 9, 10, 42 f., 100 f.. 174 f
Star of the East Lodge, 122
Steinbeck, John, 210
Suakin, 78
Suez Canal, 78 f., 198
Sufism, 9, 121, 176–7, 217
Sulaimān Pasha, Governor of Iraq, 66
Sulṭān, 281 n.6
Sunnites, 37, 118
Surrealism, 184
Suwaidī, Shaikh 'Abdallāh al-, 67
—, 'Abd al-Raḥmān al-, 68
—, Abū al-Maḥāmid ibn 'Abdallāh al-, 68
—, Sa'īd al-Fatḥ Ibrāhīm al-, 68
Symbolism, 129–30, 163, 185, 215
Syrian Academy, 44
— Church, 37
— English College, 44
— Rebellion, 1860, 61

Ṭabṭabā'ī, Ibrāhīm al-, 68, 70
Tagore, 211
Ṭaha, Nājī 'Alī Maḥmūd, 171
Ṭahṭāwī, Rifā'at al-, 20–1, 32 ff., 54, 65, 72 ff.
Taimūr, Aḥmad, 204
—, Maḥmūd, 18, 128, 193, 204 f., 208, 235 ff.
—, Muḥammad, 204
Taimūriyya, 'Ā'isha al-, 84
Tāj al-'Arūs (dictionary), 19
Takarlī, Fu'ād, 214
Tamīmī, Ṣāliḥ al-, 68–9
Tarsus, 200
Taufīq, Khedive, 55, 79, 83
Ṭayyib, 'Abdallāh al-, 186
—, Aḥmad al-, 215, 280 n.83
Tel-el-Kebir, 79
Textual criticism, 22, 194 f.
Thiers, Adolphe, 118
Thomas, Dylan, 164, 180
Thousand and One Nights, 15, 17, 60, 116, 132
Tigris, River, 69, 213
Till, Muṣṭafā Wahabī al-, 188 f.
Till Eulenspiegel, 49
Tokyo, 93
Tolstoy, 135
Tours, Battle of, 134
Toynbee, Arnold, 21
Travel literature, 13, 34, 55 f., 72 ff.
Trieste, 36
Tripoli (Libya), 97
Truman, President Harry, 172
Tunis, 54, 116–17, 128, 216 f.
Tūnisī, Khair al-Dīn al-, 116 ff.
—, Qāsim al-, 78
Ṭūqān, Fadwā, 189
—, Ibrāhīm, 188
Turk, Nikūlā al-, 38 f., 44
Turkish literature, 13, 33, 44, 63, 65, 83, 86
Tuscany, Grand Duke of, 37

'Ujailī, 'Abd al-Salām al-, 212
Ukraine, 175
'Umar ibn Abī Rabī'a, 6
'Umarī, 'Abd al-Bāqī al-, 68–9
'Umar-i-Khayyām, 9, 106, 168, 178, 208
Umayyad, *see* Arabic literature, Ommeyad
United Grand Lodge of England, 122
— Nations, 210
Urdu literature, 9, 35, 44, 65, 86, 121, 178
'Urwa al-Wuthqā, al- (newspaper), 118 ff., 123 ff., 137
Usāma ibn Munqidh, 20
U.S.S.R., *see* Russia

Valéry, Paul, 180
Van Dyck, Cornelius, 61
Verdi, *Aida*, 200
Vers libres, 10, 25, 172, 179 ff., 186–7
Victoria, Queen, 7, 47, 97
Voltaire, 32

Wahība, Munīr Alyās, 45
Waqā'i' al-Miṣriyya, al- (newspaper), 33, 54, 123
Washington, D.C., 175

White Nile, 186
Whitman, Walt, 10, 173
Wiet, G., 38, 52
Wine poetry, 9, 84
Women's emancipation, 33, 62, 124 f., 250 ff.
Wordsworth, William, 52, 98, 167, 170

Yakan, Walī al-Dīn, 102
Yale, 214
Ya'qūbī, Salīm ibn al-Shaikh Ḥasan al-, 188
Yāzijī, Ḥabīb al-, 47 f.
—, Khalīl al-, 91
—, Nāṣīf al-, 10, 14, 38–9, 43 ff., 59, 65, 68, 71, 91, 126, 166
Yeats, W. B., 164
'Young Turks', 103, 110

Zabīdī, Murtaḍā al-, 29, 38
Zaghlūl, Sa'd, 93, 120
Zahāwī, 'Abd al-Ḥamīd al-, 133
—, Jamīl Ṣidqī al-, 10, 106 ff., 111, 184
Zaidān, Jurjī, 133 ff., 205, 212
Zajal, 9, 44–5
Zamakhsharī, al-, 45
Zaurā', al- (newspaper), 106
Zawwātī, 'Ādil, 190
Zionism, 4, 116, 167, 187
Ziyād, Taufīq, 190
Ziyāda, May, 211
Zuhair ibn Abī Salmā, 4
Zuraiq, Qusṭanṭīn, 24, 210 f., 250 ff.